RABIN
of Israel

RABIN
of Israel

ROBERT SLATER

St. Martin's Press
New York

Grateful acknowledgement is made to American Broadcasting Companies, Inc. for permission to reprint certain excerpts of interviews with Yitzhak Rabin from the transcript of the ABC News documentary, 'Rabin: Action Biography', © 1975 American Broadcasting Companies, Inc. Reprinted by permission. All Rights Reserved.

Grateful acknowledgement is made to Carta (Jerusalem) for the maps.

Library of Congress Cataloging-in-Publication Data

Slater, Robert.
    Rabin of Israel / Robert Slater.
       p.   cm.
    ISBN 0-312-09368-3
    1. Rabin, Yitzhak, 1922-   . 2. Prime ministers—Israel—Biography. 3. Generals—Israel—Biography. 4. Israel—Armed Forces—Biography. I. Title.
DS126.6.R32S57   1993
956.94'05'092—dc20
[B]   93-20403
                                  CIP

First published in Great Britain by Robson Books Ltd. in 1977. Revised edition first published in Great Britain by Robson Books Ltd. in 1993.

First U.S. Edition: August 1993
10 9 8 7 6 5 4 3 2 1

Contents

RABIN
of Israel

Foreword

The idea of writing a biography of Yitzhak Rabin, Israel's prime minister, took shape in my mind a few months after he was chosen prime minister the first time, back in 1974. *Rabin of Israel* appeared in October 1977. Today, now that Yitzhak Rabin has returned to the prime ministership after a fifteen-year gap, interest in him has never been so great. For that reason we present a new version of *Rabin of Israel*, one that provides a comprehensive look at his life. Included in this version are a new introduction and new chapters on his career from 1977 until the present, which cover the period he served as a defence minister in the 1980s, his triumph as Labour Party leader and candidate for prime minister in February 1992, the spring 1992 election, Rabin's taking power in July 1992, and the crucial, dramatic first six months of his new government.

In researching this biography I was granted a number of lengthy interviews by Rabin. We met four times during his first prime ministership, meetings that were crucial in my understanding of his career and his personality. He took a great deal of time from his busy schedule to talk about the past. I was pleasantly surprised at how much time he allotted me. Because he was prime minister, I never knew whether he would call a halt to our series of interviews, claiming the press of urgent business. Yet, he never did. Still, getting to see him each time was often nerve-racking. Postponements seemed inevitable. Happily, they came only rarely. Once, Rabin postponed one of our scheduled interviews and I only found out the reason later: he had to undertake a secret mission to Morocco to meet with King Hassan. In the fifteen years since *Rabin of Israel* was published, I have met with Rabin periodically, in my capacity as a member of the reporting staff of the *Time* magazine

Jerusalem bureau, conducting interviews once or twice a year, and attending his news conferences and speeches in the Knesset and elsewhere. Indeed, closely monitoring his political career was part of my 'political beat' at *Time* magazine. When it became clear that Rabin had a chance to return to the prime ministership in 1992, I made an intensive effort to stay in close touch with him and his campaign associates, attending numerous briefings, conducting interviews, and spending time on the campaign trail. My final chance to see Rabin privately came on 15 November, 1992 when I joined two other *Time* magazine reporters in interviewing the prime minister.

I also wish to acknowledge several key figures who contributed much to my research: Leah Rabin, the prime minister's wife, who met with me twice during the original research and twice in the summer of 1992 while I was updating the book. She also contributed some photographs and was kind enough to let me peruse an English translation of her memoirs, *All the Time His Wife*. I was fortunate also to meet a number of times with Rabin's sister, Rahel, at her home at kibbutz Manara in northern Israel. She shed much light on her and her brother's childhood.

In addition, I talked to two hundred people who have known Rabin at various stages of his life. The list of those who provided help in my research is far too long to mention here — indeed, a small number asked not to be identified — but I would like to acknowledge a special debt of gratitude to several of Rabin's aides from his days as prime minister in the 1970s: Dan Pattir, his press adviser; Amos Eran, director-general and Yehuda Avner, his adviser on Jewish Affairs. I also want to thank members of Rabin's current prime minister staff: Eitan Haber, the director of Rabin's bureau; Shimon Sheves, director-general of the prime minister's office; and Gad Ben-Ari, the prime minister's press adviser.

I also wish to thank those who gave freely of their time to read the original manuscript prior to its 1977 publication: the late Yigal Allon, Rabin's foreign minister in the 1970s; the late Haim Laskov, a former chief of staff of the Israel Defence Forces and Donald Neff, then the Bureau Chief in Jerusalem for *Time-Life*.

Deborah Baker eased matters considerably for me by helping to translate scores of Hebrew-language newspaper articles as well as transcribing numerous taped interviews for the original manuscript. I would like to thank the following people for making photographs available for use in this book: Rahel Rabin Jacoby, Leah Rabin, Hannah Rivlin, Ada Tamir, Professor Moshe Brawer and Lester Millman — also the Government Press Office's Photographic Department in Jerusalem.

Jean Max, who has been office manager at the *Time-Life* Jerusalem Bureau for many years, rendered important editorial assistance during crucial phases of the updating process. I am deeply appreciative of her efforts. I thank also Jamil Hamad and Ron Ben-Yishai, my colleagues at *Time* magazine, who offered me important insights during the latest round of research. I wish to especially thank Israeli journalist Haim Baram for his advice.

I would like to thank the editor of the original manuscript, Elizabeth Rose. I also thank Louise Dixon, the editor of this updated version, who has laboured hard both in editing and organizing this new manuscript.

I owe special thanks to Jeremy Robson, the head of Robson Books, for the wonderful support he has given me both at the time *Rabin of Israel* was first published fifteen years ago and at the present, while the updating has proceeded.

I have been fortunate, during my fifteen years of writing books, to have had at my side someone who not only cared deeply for me but who was prepared to put so much of her exceptional editing skills into my manuscripts. For that, I thank my wife Elinor. She was my literary partner when *Rabin of Israel* first appeared and she helped enormously with this new version as well. Our children, Miriam, Shimi, Adam, and Rachel, are great enthusiasts of my book career. I owe them much as well.

I dedicate this new version of *Rabin of Israel* to the memory of my parents, Joseph and Gertrude Slater.

Robert Slater
Jerusalem

Preface

It was a few minutes after 10 pm, Tuesday, 23 June, 1992. Election day in the state of Israel. The two Yitzhaks — Shamir and Rabin — had battled for the coveted prize of the prime ministership for the past four months. The public opinion polls had consistently favoured Rabin and his Labour Party. But who could be sure?

Haim Yavin, Israel Television's veteran announcer, was the first to carry the good tidings for Yitzhak Rabin. It was 10 pm, the polls had just closed, and the country's state-run television station was ready to announce the results of its exit poll, in which 20,200 voters at 54 polling stations, had been asked how they voted.

In the past, the TV exit poll had been reasonably accurate. What Yavin would say in the next few seconds would most likely reveal who would be Israel's next prime minister.

'We have the exit-poll results and they tell of an upheaval,' Yavin said, his voice trembling, knowing full well that the nation was hearing of Rabin's dramatic triumph from him for the first time.

Upheaval. 'Ma'apach'. That had been the word Yavin had used, and it told the whole story. 'Ma'apach' means upheaval in Hebrew and it been introduced into the Israeli political lexicon after the Likud's trouncing of Labour in the 1977 election when Menachem Begin took power. Israelis immediately understood what Yavin meant.

Again, an upheaval had occurred in Israeli politics. This time, however, it was Labour that was about to take power. Not the Likud.

As soon as Yavin spoke — and a computer graph showed Labour getting 47 Knesset seats (out of a total 120) to only 33 for

Likud — the ballroom at the Dan Hotel in Tel Aviv, the Labour Party's election night headquarters, exploded into huge cheers, amid cries of 'Rabin, Rabin, Rabin'. Labour Party politicians hugged and kissed one another, whether strangers or friends. Bottles of champagne appeared and suddenly the ballroom took on the appearance of the Chicago Bulls' locker room after it had won the Championship.

'This is the moment I dreamt of,' said an elated Haim Ramon, Knesset member and head of Labour's information drive during the campaign. Behind Ramon a blue and white banner on the wall proclaimed 'Labour under Rabin'.

Almost buried in the dramatic news that Labour would replace Likud as the ruling government, was the startling fact that Yitzhak Rabin had finally come out of the political cold. Sent into the political wilderness in the spring of 1977, when a financial scandal forced him to give up most of his authority as prime minister and not seek re-election, Rabin had almost no hope of ever returning to leadership in an Israeli government. Or so it had seemed then.

Gradually, he had worked his way back into leadership positions. By 1984, when he was appointed Defence Minister in the Likud-led National Unity government, Rabin had come part way towards rehabilitation. The prime ministership still eluded him.

Until this evening. Now, after ruling for 13 of the past 15 years, the Likud had fallen from power. Labour, in opposition for most of the time since 1977, was back in charge.

Another cheer went up at the Dan Hotel when Haim Yavin announced that Meretz, the new amalgam of three left-wing parties, had mustered 13 Knesset seats in the television exit poll. That meant Labour and Meretz together commanded 60 seats, an incredibly high figure, more than pollsters had given the two parties in the weeks leading up to the election.

Yitzhak Rabin would need only one more Knesset seat to form a government.

If the actual balloting confirmed the exit polls, the small religious parties, particularly Shas and the United Torah Judaism Front, would inevitably come running to join Rabin's new government.

Rabin was at home in Neve Avivim with his wife Leah, his

two children Dahlia and Yuval, and his three grandchildren, savouring the victory.

Before the election date, he had thought he had a good chance of winning. His aides had been confident. The polls had spoken of a Labour victory. Rabin was sceptical, however, and deep down, found it hard to believe that the voters would turn the Likud out. Still, he strode around the country in the week before balloting with a look of quiet satisfaction, as if he sensed that he might be heading for a good result.

When Haim Yavin cried out 'ma'apach', Yitzhak Rabin sat quietly, and he remained so as his wife Leah broke into tears. She recalled that moment: 'I felt that a circle had closed. Fifteen years after Rabin resigned as prime minister he is returning to the job. It doesn't happen often that a man returned after 15 years to a job that he leaves.'

Soon after 10 pm, close friends began arriving at Rabin's apartment. Eitan Haber, his spokesman from the defence ministry days. Aliza Wallach, a reporter for the newspaper *Davar*. Gad Ya'acobi, a cabinet minister in Rabin's first government. Ezer Weizman was one of the first to phone. Many others followed.

Leah Rabin recalled that evening: 'I was so excited. I had the feeling that we were returning home to the style that we were familiar with, to our element. I felt a need to go down to the apartment of my parents (who are dead) and speak to them. I wanted to tell them that something marvellous had happened, that we have come home, that Yitzhak, the son of Rosa and Nehemiah, stands at the head of the leadership.'

Rabin left his apartment on his way to the Dan Hotel. Photographers snapped photos. A reporter asked the prime minister-designate: 'How do you feel?'

'What do you think?' was Rabin's terse reply. He offered a small smile. He still did not seem to believe that Labour would outpoll Likud by 12 Knesset seats, a huge margin.

Meanwhile, at the Dan Hotel, all was happy bedlam. Suddenly, the Labour jingle blared out, loud enough so that it seemed everyone in Tel Aviv would hear it. 'Israel is waiting for Rabin', the song said over and over again.

When Rabin walked in, the place grew wilder. It seemed that everyone was singing the Labour jingle. Leah Rabin said later she had seen nothing like that moment. 'It was above and beyond. It was emotional. It was spontaneous.'

Meanwhile, over at the Tel Aviv Hilton, the sullen look on Yitzhak Shamir's face told it all. He appeared in pain, his hands clenching the sides of his chair. He seemed shocked beyond words. Only a day before he had expressed optimism that the Likud would win. A Shamir loyalist had passed the word to the prime minister shortly before the exit poll was announced that the poll would tell of a disaster for the Likud. Shamir did not want to believe it. But there was Haim Yavin speaking of a 'ma'apach'. Journalists who had been escorted into Shamir's suite to listen to the exit poll results announced at 10 pm, sought a quick response from him. The prime minister was tight-lipped. 'I don't have to confess in front of anyone,' he barked. His aides removed the journalists at once. Later that evening, Shamir would tell Israel TV that he planned to retire soon. Over at Metzudat Ze'ev, Likud headquarters in Tel Aviv, Likud cabinet ministers and Knesset members offered frozen stares of depression and anger before the TV cameras. None of them dared pick up the phone to Shamir to offer a kind word. No one knew what to say.

The Labour Party election jingle — 'Israel is waiting for Rabin' — a parody of a Six-Day War song — had come true.

It seemed almost preposterous. Who would have imagined back in 1977 that events fifteen years later would catapult Yitzhak Rabin back into the prime ministership?

On one level, it was not so strange at all that the country wanted Rabin as prime minister in 1992, for he was one of Israel's most formidable political and military figures. He had none of the flamboyance of a Moshe Dayan, none of the intellectual brilliance of an Abba Eban, none of Golda Meir or Menachem Begin's charisma. Yet, at the age of seventy, he enjoyed a record in public life that surpassed every other living Israeli politician.

He was, first, one of his country's most impressive military heroes. During the 1948 War of Independence, he fought on the Jerusalem and Egyptian fronts, and as a senior officer on the Egyptian front, he participated in the post-war 1949 Rhodes peace talks.

Then as the chief of staff during Israel's triumphant Six-Day War of June 1967, Rabin had his country's eternal gratitude for steering Israel through one of its most difficult days. Even when the Israel Defence Forces lost some of their glamour, even when military heroes seemed less fashionable in Israel, Rabin remained the hero of the Six-Day War, a mark of distinction that would never abandon him, a credential that would serve him well down through the years.

He was more than a military hero. A general turned diplomat, Rabin had become a highly successful ambassador in Washington in the years after the Six-Day War. His tenure in Washington had allowed him to rub shoulders with American leaders, to work with Richard Nixon and Henry Kissinger closely, to help Israel navigate through some difficult days, and to develop an appreciation and respect for the United States of America that would endure.

In a quirk of fate, Rabin the diplomat evolved into Rabin the prime minister. He was only 52 years when he replaced Golda Meir in June 1974. He was also his country's first sabra (native-born) prime minister. His rise to political leadership was extraordinary and arose mostly because he was one of the few Labour Party figures who had not been 'tainted' by playing a senior role in the discredited 1973 Yom Kippur War. The country may not have wanted Rabin. It had little choice, however. And so Rabin had served as Prime Minister for nearly three years between 1974 and 1977 before he himself was forced to step down in the cloud of scandal.

Rabin, along with the rest of the country, had little expectation that he would ever return to a leadership role. The scandal focused on an illegal bank account his wife Leah had kept in Washington, DC. Rabin took personal responsibility for the violation and announced immediately (in April 1977) that he was giving up the prime ministership and would not be a candidate for prime minister in the forthcoming national election. Rabin appeared destined to play out the rest of his career as a Labour Party backbencher in the Knesset. At 55, however, he was young by Israeli political standards.

He was not, however, cast aside for good. Almost at once, Israelis seemed forgiving. Yet, for seven years — from 1977 to 1984 — Rabin remained a mere back bencher. In 1984, he moved back into a senior governmental position, becoming Defence Minister in the National Unity government headed by Shimon Peres. He served in that post until March 1990. As defence minister, he presided over the Israel Defence Forces' departure from Lebanon in 1985, ending its three-year occupation of that country, and formally bringing to a close Israel's participation in the war in Lebanon. And Rabin was in charge of Israel's handling of the Palestinian uprising known as the Intifada, which broke out in December 1987 and carries on to this day. The Intifada, though wounding Rabin's reputation abroad, in fact enhanced his image within Israel: while deploring the tactics the IDF employed toward Palestinian Arabs in the occupied lands, the Israeli public appreciated Rabin's resoluteness and firmness in responding to Palestinian attacks against Israeli soldiers and civilians. It also appreciated Rabin's new-found conviction that a political settlement between Israel and the Palestinian Arabs was the only way to resolve the conflict once and for all.

Rabin, the soldier, and Rabin, the peacemaker. Both were part of his political identity in the early 1990s. Both played an important role in making him his country's most popular political figure. Finally, in early 1992, Rabin had a chance to try for the prime ministership. The Labour Party had grown tired of Shimon Peres. Israelis had become weary of the Likud government. They wanted a change. They wanted new leadership. Though Israelis had grown distraught over the right-wing government of Yitzhak Shamir, they did not want a government run by the political left.

As the Labour Party jingle during that 1992 election campaign said accurately, hard as it had seemed fifteen years earlier when he fell from power, the country in the spring of 1992 was waiting for Yitzhak Rabin.

Chapter 1

Encounter in the Old City

Yitzhak Rabin's parents were born in Russia and grew up under the uncertain and frequently violent tsarist rule of the late nineteenth century. Life for the Jewish population of Russia during that time was particularly harsh, punctuated by officially sanctioned pogroms. Confined to one region called the Pale of Settlement, the Jews preserved their way of life, but had to endure both persecution and extreme poverty. Many of them decided to seek refuge in other countries, America being the most popular destination, Palestine one of the least. Of the nearly five million Jews who were living in the Pale of Settlement at the close of the nineteenth century, about one and a half million chose to emigrate to the United States; only a few thousand had ventured to Palestine by the outbreak of World War One.

Nehemiah Robichov was born in 1886 in Sidrovitch, a poor hamlet near Kiev, which contained only a handful of Jews. Already impoverished, the family's plight was immeasurably worsened by the death of Nehemiah's father when the boy was quite small, leaving his mother to bring up the children alone and try to make ends meet. By the time he was ten years old, Nehemiah had found work in a local flour mill. Some time later, he left his home, job, and family, and settled in a larger town, also near Kiev, and again found work in a flour mill. His family heard from him occasionally, but the connection was tenuous. When he left for the United States at the age of eighteen, he severed all ties with his family in Russia, and though in later years he often spoke about them to his children, he recalled relatively few details about his early life.

However, during those teen-age years Nehemiah acquired enough of a taste for socialism to make the Kiev police aware of his presence. Although he was not politically active, he somehow aroused the suspicions of the authorities, who were on the point of arresting him when he left Russia. He arrived in New York in 1904 completely alone, knowing no one, without a word of English. He found employment in a New York City bakery, but New York was to be little more than a transit stop; after moving on to St Louis, where he again worked for a short time in a bakery, he travelled to Chicago, where he spent most of the thirteen years he lived in the United States. Now in his early twenties, he became part of a circle of Jewish intellectuals, bachelors like himself, who propounded socialist and Zionist ideas and lived for the day when they could translate their dreams into reality in the Yishuv, the tiny Jewish community in Palestine. Most of them were poor and struggling to make a living, working by day, studying by night. They all belonged to the 'Poalei Zion' ('Workers of Zion'), an organization which preached socialism in Eretz Yisrael — the Land of Israel.

The young men formed a close-knit group, holding heated political debates, practising their English on one another, wondering all the time if they would survive through the week on their meagre incomes. When one of the group married, his home would become a kind of clubhouse for the rest, and the close relationships would continue as before.

Young Robichov found work in a factory as a tailor, a profession many Russian immigrants had taken up when they reached American shores. At one point, when his studies intensified, he stopped working full-time and confined himself to distributing newspapers and to other small jobs, earning just enough to live on. Although his life was hard, Nehemiah was greatly impressed with America and its values, and in later years he never tired of talking about the qualities he had found there. It is hardly a coincidence that his son Yitzhak also fell under the spell of America. 'I was brought up on my father's stories about the United States,' says Rabin.[1] 'He always used to say it was the country in which he had learned the meaning of freedom and where he had seen the taste for education, and where organizations existed to fight for workers' rights.'

By the outbreak of World War One, Nehemiah Robichov had become a confirmed Zionist, and was a keen candidate for the Jewish Legion then being recruited by two leaders of Palestine

Jewry — David Ben-Gurion and Yitzhak Ben-Zvi — to assist
the Allied efforts to oust Turkey from Palestine. But when the
young tailor went to the recruiting centre, he was disqualified
from service because of an ailment in his legs. Longing to get to
Palestine, he determined to try again, under a different name.
Calling himself Nehemiah Rabin, he walked into another
recruiting centre, offered to serve in the Jewish Legion, and was
accepted.

The new recruit left Chicago for Palestine in 1917. The
journey lasted months, prolonged by stopovers in Canada,
England and Egypt. For the first time Nehemiah met soldiers
from all over the British Commonwealth; he was particularly
struck by the contrast between the British and Australian
soldiers, and was later to become fond of relating how, in 1918,
he had seen an English officer angrily rebuke an obviously
battle-seasoned young Australian soldier for not saluting him as
the two passed each other in the street. Without batting an
eyelid, the Australian told the Englishman: 'Run home and tell
your mother you've just seen a *real* soldier.' No doubt the
Australian, with his casual disregard for protocol, might easily
have passed for a young Jewish fighter from the Yishuv.

Rabin's mother, Rosa Cohen, was born in the town of Mohilov
in 1890, the daughter of Rabbi Yitzhak Cohen, a devoutly
religious man who was totally opposed to Zionism, believing
that Jews should not try to force the fulfilment of their destiny,
but await the Messiah's coming. Rosa's family moved to
Bialystok, then, in 1896 when her mother died, to Homel, in
order to be near Rabbi Cohen's brother, Mordechai Ben Hillel
Hacohen, who, in contrast to Rosa's father, was a staunch
Zionist, and not at all religious. Both brothers had large families,
Rabbi Cohen with eight children, Mordechai with seven. A
year after the move, Mordechai took his entire family to
Palestine. The pogroms of the 1870s and 1880s had made a
terrifying impression on the Russian Jews. Those who did not
emigrate in search of peace and security were finding that their
children were turning into revolutionaries, rebelling against the
oppressive regime under which they lived. It was partly fear that
his sons would be jailed by the authorities that led Mordechai
Ben Hillel Hacohen to leave for Palestine.

In spite of this regime, Yitzhak Cohen would let nothing stand in the way of his religion. Once, while serving as an informal adviser to the Tsar's sister, Princess Ktsenia Alexandrovna, he refused to take a telephone call from her on the Jewish sabbath. Eventually the princess grew accustomed to her adviser's religious sensibilities, and when he came to her palace she made sure that all the Christian icons were covered up, or, in some cases, removed altogether. Again, though it was strictly against the orders of the Russian authorities, Rabbi Cohen built a traditional succah in full public view on his balcony to mark the Jewish festival of Succoth.

He showed the same determination when it came to the education of his children, sending his sons to a Yeshiva. Rosa was quite content to go to the local Christian Gymnasium, but Rabbi Cohen balked at the idea of his daughter violating the sabbath by attending Saturday classes. Already showing some determination of her own at this young age, Rosa would sleep at friends' houses on Friday nights to prevent her father's discovering the truth, and on Saturdays attended the Christian school as usual. In order to pay the school fees, she gave private lessons. Like her uncle, she had no interest in the religious rituals of Judaism, but like her father, she disapproved of Zionism.

Photographs of Rabbi Cohen, with his round, balding head and his neatly groomed black beard and moustache, show him to be a man of authority. He certainly dominated his wife, Sheine Rahel, of whom practically nothing is known. More than anyone else in the family it was he who symbolized the old order. At home he often sang haunting and gay Hasidic melodies, reminders of the past to which he clung with such tenacity. But the old order was changing and the change was taking place all around him. When he was away from home, the children would debate their country's ills, and the troubles of the Jews in particular. Rosa would sit and listen, but rarely participate in these ideological discussions. She heard about the anti-Zionist Jewish Bund, and also about a man named Theodor Herzl, an Austrian journalist and playwright who was advocating the establishment of a national home for Jews in Palestine.

Rosa avoided joining any kind of organization in her childhood, finding that it was quicker and easier to get things done by operating outside a fixed framework rather than from

within. Thus she remained aloof from the various Zionist groups
which were springing up in Russia. She followed a vegetarian
diet, read voraciously, and involved herself in work on behalf of
the ordinary man, the common labourer, who to her mind was
being exploited. She did not seem especially worried about her
own lack of financial means. One winter she could not afford an
overcoat, but instead of staying at home as much as possible, she
made do with a summer one and went about her work as usual.
Once she even journeyed from Homel to Bialystok to visit her
mother's family, but when her relatives opened the door they
didn't recognize the rather oddly clad figure and, mistaking her
for an anarchist, shut the door on the startled girl.

From an early age, Rosa had felt a deep compassion for her
fellow Jews. When in 1905 there was a pogrom in Homel, she
became a medical aide, rushing to the streets each night to help
the victims. She was proud of being Jewish, refusing to hide her
Jewishness even when it might have been safer to do so. Once,
fellow students in Homel chose her to represent them at the
Federation of Student Youth convention in St Petersburg, but
because Jews were not allowed to stay overnight in the city, it
was suggested that she pose as a non-Jew, carrying false identity
papers. Rosa turned the idea down flat, and proceeded to the
Russian capital undisguised, although she placed herself in some
danger by doing so. Fortunately the trip proved uneventful.

Although the Homel pogrom had prompted many of her
friends to think about leaving Russia, and some had already
gone to America or Palestine, Rosa preferred to stay. At that
time her father managed some of the forest estates belonging to
the Tsar's brother-in-law outside St Petersburg. She would seek
out the labourers on the estates — the 'wild people' as her father
called them — and tell them about the coming revolution.

At the outbreak of the Bolshevik revolution she had a job in a
military enterprise — a brick factory in the suburbs of St
Petersburg — but her only reason for working there was to bring
in some money which she would then share out among her
fellow workers so that they would not go hungry. In September
1917 she enrolled in the Polytechnic Institute for Women, where
she took up chemistry. She did not complete her studies.

Rosa was dismayed to find that the long-awaited revolution
actually made life worse for Russian Jews. She was ordered to

join the Communist Party but refused. Because of her
uncooperative attitude, she was moved to an out-of-the-way
factory in southern Russia, where the workers soon demonstrated
their support for her by going on strike. The government's
response was to cut off the factory's supply of raw materials.
Rosa moved to Kiev, and began to think of leaving her
homeland. Hounded by Bolshevik secret police, and with no
prospect but more misery, she decided sometime in 1919 to
emigrate.

She found a job as a medical aide on the Red Cross train from
Kiev to Odessa. She had no desire to go to Palestine, although
she had relatives in Jerusalem; instead, she planned to join some
friends in Sweden, but on arriving in Odessa found that the only
ship sailing from that port in the near future was the *Russland*,
which was bound for Palestine. Desperate to leave Russia, Rosa
decided to take it. She believed her stay in Palestine would be
only temporary, just a brief visit to her family there.

On the *Russland*, she met some Jewish pioneers — mostly men
— who were bound for the Lake Kinneret (Galilee) region to
build a settlement and farm the land, and whose idealism and
energy appealed to her. After a two-day visit to her Uncle
Mordechai and his family in Jerusalem (whom she liked to refer
to as the 'extreme Zionists'), she rejoined the pioneers she had
met on the boat.

Although only twenty-eight, Rosa looked much older. Her
face was lined and her hair had begun to turn grey. She was tall,
and had a long neck, and some of the settlers thought she had an
aristocratic air to her. But with characteristic toughness, she
plunged into the gruelling work during that first winter on the
shores of Lake Galilee. One of the main jobs of the Kinneret
pioneers was to plant cedar trees in the swamps, a task that gave
her a taste of the harshness of pioneering life, as well as an attack
of malaria. The doctor advised her to go at once to a more
healthy part of the country. It was nearly Passover, and she
decided the time had come to pay her uncle a longer visit.

Rosa had spent only a few months with the Kinneret settlers
but her stay had made a deep impression on her. As she joined
her relatives in April 1920, she began to examine her
preconceived attitude and rigid prejudice against settling in
Palestine. She had been disappointed to find that the country

was not as developed or populated as she had imagined, but she was impressed with the Jews she met. One of these was Rahel Yanait, who was particularly active in women's agricultural training. Watching her at work, Rosa began to identify with the aims and aspirations of the Yishuv. She did not have to wait very long before her questions and doubts about Zionism were resolved.

The Palestine that Nehemiah Rabin and Rosa Cohen came to was entering a period of extraordinary political ambiguity and confusion. Until the 1920s Jews and Arabs had lived and worked side by side for years in the Holy Land, both Semitic peoples, neither interested in forcing the other out of the area. The Jewish community in Palestine had been up till then quite small. Even in 1881, when pogroms became rife in Russia, the Yishuv numbered only 25,000; the Holy Land seemed to offer little more than a refuge from persecution. Living conditions were tough; the country had few good roads, and although there was a railway connecting the principal port of Jaffa with Jerusalem, where half of the Yishuv lived, people were too poor to travel on it very often. However, by the turn of the century the Jewish community in Palestine had begun to establish itself. By 1914 nearly 100,000 Jews were living in the Yishuv and after the Balfour Declaration in 1917 Jews began to settle in much larger numbers. The swelling Jewish population found itself confronted by a rapidly developing Arab nationalism, creating for the first time in the region a genuine Jewish–Arab political conflict. A further complication during the post-war years was the presence of the British, who in 1920 were given responsibility for Palestine by the League of Nations.

If the Jews of the Yishuv did not expect the British to embrace their cause wholly, at least the Balfour Declaration — with its sweeping talk of favouring 'the establishment in Palestine of a national home for the Jewish people' — seemed to be an encouragement to them to stay on in the region and to increase their numbers through immigration. But in the following years, the Yishuv found that British policy steadily veered away from the goals of the Balfour Declaration and instead sought to hinder further Jewish immigration into Palestine.

Nehemiah Rabin had volunteered for the Jewish Legion as

part of a plan to settle in Palestine but had, by his own admission, some misgivings about staying. In later years he often joked to his children that the night on which he gave the most serious consideration to his future, his hair turned white. In the end, he chose to stay in Palestine because he could not imagine himself, an ardent Zionist, returning to live in the Diaspora after actually setting foot in Eretz Yisrael.

In New York Nehemiah had become friendly with Yitzhak Ben-Zvi, a founder of the Jewish Legion (he was later to become the second President of Israel). Just after the war both men were stationed at Sarafand, a military base near Tel Aviv, and from time to time they would travel together to Jerusalem, where some friends of Ben-Zvi were making arrangements for the protection of the Jews in the Holy City. Among them were Rahel Yanait, whom Ben-Zvi later married, and Zvi Nadav. Ben-Zvi felt that Nehemiah's experience as a gunsmith in the Legion could be valuable and suggested that he should join them. The three began to organize the training of others in the use of arms, and became part of the new defence committee set up by Ze'ev Jabotinsky, another of the Jewish Legion's founders. Nehemiah was chosen to represent the Legion soldiers on Jabotinsky's committee. He was also put in charge of the arms storehouse and given the task of ensuring that weapons were clean. On Saturdays the committee members would go into the fields between the outlying Jerusalem districts of Bet Ha'Kerem and Rehavia to practise throwing hand grenades. Oddly, Arabs and British looked on while they trained.

As the Jewish holiday of Passover neared in April 1920, tensions between Jews and Arabs intensified and disputes arose among the defence committee members over whether Jerusalem would become the focus for Arab-led disturbances. Jabotinsky, confident that the Arabs of Jerusalem would not act against Jews with whom they had lived for years in harmony, doubted that riots would occur and felt less need then the others to arrange a proper system of defence for the Old City. Nehemiah and Rahel Yanait, however, pressed the case for tighter security arrangements in the Old City, the likeliest target for Arab violence. Their arguments continued up to the first moments of the disturbances, which began on April 4.

On that cool, sunny day, Jews, Christians and Moslems were

getting ready for the start of their respective religious festivals. The holy sites of all three religions were situated within the confines of the crowded, walled Old City of Jerusalem, with its ancient cobblestones, open-air markets and tiny alleyways. As the Arabs paraded towards the Dome of the Rock, they were preceded by a British military band. From a nearby balcony the British Military Governor and his entourage watched the procession. Also watching — but from rooftops outside the Old City — were members of the Jewish defence committee. Arab activists had already been spreading anti-Jewish rumours calculated to drive the Moslem crowds gathered there for the Nebi Moussa festival into a mad frenzy. At the Dome of the Rock, an Arab nationalist leader harangued the crowd against the Jews, rousing the Arabs to sudden uncontrolled violence. With placards, with daggers drawn, shouting 'We shall drink Jewish blood', they swept towards the Jewish Quarter of the Old City, where two thousand Jews lived and worked.

At the main entrance to the Old City — the Jaffa Gate — Jews confronted Arabs in battle, and when the fighting ended, six Jews, four Arabs and a British soldier lay dead. Two hundred and eleven Jews and twenty-one Arabs were wounded. Inside the Jewish Quarter, elderly Jews were locked in a house which was then set on fire. Some women nearby were raped. Stores were looted and burned. Arab policemen, to whom the British had assigned responsibility for maintaining order in the Old City, fled in fear or openly joined the Arab rioters.

When fears about the possibility of Arab riots in Jerusalem had first arisen, the British, anxious to keep Jewish soldiers away from the area of conflict, had ordered Nehemiah and his Jewish Legion colleagues to Jericho, twenty-five miles north-east of Jerusalem. But, hearing that the Jews of Jerusalem were in danger, they had hurriedly returned to the Holy City. Nehemiah went to Jabotinsky's house to see what the other members of the defence committee were doing. He discovered that some had watched the riots from a distance, powerless to help because the British had sealed off the Old City when the trouble began. Others, gathered at Jabotinsky's house, had been embroiled in organizational disputes which seemed somewhat irrelevant at that moment, with the shouting of the Arab mobs nearby drowning their words. A curfew had been imposed on the Old City. The Passover holiday was barely twenty-four hours old.

The next morning Nehemiah persuaded the committee to let him and some colleagues reconnoitre the Jaffa Gate in order to see how best to help the Jews inside the Old City. When they found that the British had barred Jews from entering the Old City, they broke into the Hadassah Hospital and took clothes used by cleaning men. Disguised in these uniforms, they managed to enter the Old City unchallenged.

The riots resolved all Rosa Cohen's doubts about Zionism. Accustomed as she was to persecution in Russia, this new violence in Palestine appalled her, and roused her sympathies on behalf of the settlers. Dressed as a nurse, she had no difficulty in getting past the guards at the Old City gates. As she crossed a courtyard near Jews Street inside the Jewish Quarter, Nehemiah, who was continuing his efforts to help the Old City Jews, caught sight of her nurse's uniform, and called out to her, demanding to know what she was doing there. Rosa retorted that it was none of his business, and the two began to argue. Then, before he realized what was happening, she seized his gun and began to struggle with him. Locked in combat, the two were still screaming at each other in Yiddish when a group of British soldiers came upon them, separated the pair, and managed to calm them down. Realizing that they were there on the same mission, they decided to work together. Thus began, in this rather strange way, the romance of Nehemiah Rabin and Rosa Cohen.

By the second and third nights of the riots, the defence committee had started moving Jews from the mixed Jewish–Arab districts to the new part of the city. Nehemiah found one family of nine hiding inside a building. He led them out and escorted them to the Nablus Gate, where they were immediately surrounded by Arabs. Taking out some hand grenades, Nehemiah got ready to throw them at the crowd if it became necessary, but some British soldiers standing nearby fired into the air and the Arabs fled. Later, several members of the defence committee including Jabotinsky and Nehemiah made their way back into the Old City but were caught by the British. Jabotinsky was arrested and imprisoned. Nehemiah was held for three days at the Migdal David prison and fined £5 for illegal possession of arms.

His release from prison coincided with his demobilization from the Jewish Legion. He took up the option of working on the special labour force, organized by the British to install new telephone lines in Palestine. Rosa went to Haifa where she found work as an accountant in the Hiram construction firm. She met Nehemiah again in Haifa in 1921 and in that year they were married. The exact date of the wedding is not known because both frowned upon celebrating anniversaries and their own birthdays, though later they did relent as far as their children's birthdays were concerned. Rosa Cohen — as she preferred to be called even after her marriage — became involved in defence and labour, the two interests which would occupy her time almost wholly for the next two decades. She volunteered to make the rounds of the various home-owners in Haifa to subscribe to the Defence Fund, and collected the impressive sum of £750. On the labour front, she fought against the policy which excluded Jewish workers from the Haifa port.

Rosa became pregnant in 1921 but continued working into the ninth month of her pregnancy. In February of the following year, while walking to work, she was bitten on the leg by a dog. With the birth of her first baby imminent, Rosa felt she must have the best possible medical care. A warm relationship had developed between her and Mordechai Ben Hillel Hacohen's family in Jerusalem, and she knew that they would welcome her. When she arrived at their huge, two-storey house on Ethiopia Street, she came under the care of her cousin, 26-year-old Hannah Hacohen, who immediately took her to the nearby Sha'are Zedek Hospital.

A few days later, on 1 March, 1922, Rosa gave birth to a boy whom she and Nehemiah called Yitzhak, after the boy's maternal grandfather.

Rosa was eager to return to Haifa, but Hannah insisted that she stay on with them for another month to recuperate. The Hacohens' house, built by an Arab for his harem in the previous century, had twenty rooms and was always full of overnight guests and lodgers, so the additional presence of a mother and her new-born baby was nothing out of the ordinary. Through his banking connections, Mordechai Ben Hillel Hacohen knew a number of important statesmen, and it was not unusual to find him dining at home with such eminent people as Baron de Rothschild and Winston Churchill.

By the spring of 1922 the Rabins were reunited in Haifa. Nehemiah had begun to work for the Electric Company, and Rosa resumed her work on behalf of Haifa's defence. In early 1923 she became the first commander of the Haifa Hagana, the embryonic underground defence unit established to protect the Jewish community of the city against Arab attacks. Running the city's defences and taking care of an infant hardly seem compatible, but she managed to do both.

In 1923 the Rabin family moved to Tel Aviv and lived at first in an apartment on Chlenov Street, not far from Jaffa. Nehemiah became one of the first workers in Pinhas Rutenberg's Palestine Electric Corporation, one of the main pillars of the Yishuv economy. Quiet and easy-going, Nehemiah remained a simple worker with the company for thirty years, his daily routine predictable and uncomplicated — in sharp contrast to his wife's hectic life. Rosa, with her strong will and boundless energy, was not only the more colourful of the two parents but also the more dominant in her children's lives, despite the fact that she was scarcely ever at home. Forever preoccupied with the welfare of Jewish workers, she inspired her children with a certain awe. Significantly, Rabin remembers her 'against the background of the workers' movement of those years: she had her own position, her own principles, she was ready to fight for anything that seemed to her a worthy cause. She was a very austere, extreme person, who stuck to what she believed in; there were no compromises with her.'[2] Rahel, Rabin's younger sister (born on 1 February, 1925), too, remembers that 'She had an ability to organize, and a very authoritarian personality.'[3]

Others remembered Rosa for that strong personality. In 1923, Rosa Cohen had been an accountant for the Solel Boneh building contractors. In later years, Golda Meir recalled to Yitzhak Rabin that she had once been a cashier at Solel Boneh. Rabin replied that his mother had been a cashier in the same institution. 'No,' Golda corrected Rabin, 'I was the cashier: your mother was the accountant.'[4]

Often Rosa would pin small pieces of paper to her dress, notes

to herself reminding her of tasks that she had to do, whether
taking medicine to someone or attending a meeting. 'When we
were out in the street with Mother, shopping or on our way to
visit people,' Rabin recalls, 'we would never get to our
destination on time. We were always being held up because on
the way she would meet someone who took the opportunity to
ask her something or to talk things over with her.'[5] 'We couldn't
walk ten minutes without someone stopping us and talking with
her. I used to pull at her dress and she would buy me ice cream to
keep me quiet,' Rahel remembers.[6]

Rosa, however, was sickly, an aspect of her life that haunted
the young Yitzhak. She suffered from a heart problem. '. . . I
was dogged by the fear that it would bring her to her grave,'
Rabin wrote in his 1979 *Memoirs*. 'Whenever she had a heart
attack, I would run as fast as I could to call the doctor, terrified
that I would return to find her dead. Rahel and I lived in the
shadow of this dread throughout our childhood, and we were
very careful not to upset her.'[7]

Rosa always had time for other people's problems. She rarely
had time, however, to sit through meals in her own house, and
was always dashing off to some important meeting or to
somebody who needed her personal attention. These commitments kept her away from home for most of the day. In addition
to the work she had been doing in Haifa, she took on a variety of
causes when she moved to Tel Aviv, eventually gaining a seat on
the Tel Aviv City Council which strengthened her position in
the struggle for workers' rights. One of her toughest battles was
waged over the right of Tel Aviv workers to their own schools.
The working-class people of the Yishuv felt the general schools
were not providing the right kind of education for their children,
who needed to know how to settle the land, how to work it and
make a living from it, not simply how to read and write. Since
the general schools were controlled by the same conservative
political elements who ran the Municipality, the workers had no
chance of making changes in the curriculum. The only
alternative was to start their own schools, but even getting
approval for this was difficult. However, in 1924 the workers'
organizations of Tel Aviv established the first workers' school,
known as the Bet Hinuch (House of Education). It was located
in the centre of the city on Tschernichovsky Street, next to Gan

Meir, a good-sized park where students could grow vegetables and flowers. During the first few years, the school was housed in two long, uninsulated huts which, when it rained, would be surrounded by a huge pool of water. 'It was hot in the summer and wet in the winter,' Rabin was later to write, 'but we loved it, we loved the special atmosphere that pervaded it. We loved to study in the hut — that is to say, on those days when it was possible to study' — for if the flooding rose beyond a certain level, the students would have to adjourn to the dining room.[8]

· The aim of the school was to produce workers for the Yishuv, not intellectuals, not merchants, but men and women who, when they finished their education, would go to the new kibbutzim which were being established around the country. As kibbutzniks — farmers who would settle the land and at the same time establish a Jewish presence in as many parts of the country as possible — they would be fulfilling the goals of both the labour movement and of Zionism. The school not only supplied the fundamentals of education, but also furnished the children with an ideology, a direction, a model for future experiences. What the teachers hoped to do was to instil in their pupils an affection for the land that, naturally enough, was lacking in many of the new immigrant families who barely knew their adopted homeland. The whole approach and philosophy of the school thrilled Rosa. She enrolled her son at the age of six in the autumn of 1928, and the boy spent the next seven years there, graduating at the age of thirteen in 1935.

Since many of the parents worked all day, the school provided midday meals for the children and remained open until 4 pm, much later than the regular schools. This fitted in very well with Rosa's and Nehemiah's busy life-style. The longer school hours served the purposes of the Bet Hinuch equally well, for the children were kept there for the better part of each day, six days a week, enabling the teachers to have the maximum influence on them. Indeed, the school became something of a second home to many of the children, some of whom even developed the habit of calling their teachers 'Abba' (Father) and 'Ima' (Mother). With his parents away from home so much of the time, the Bet Hinuch clearly dominated Yitzhak's childhood and he remembers his years at the school with a warmth and enthusiasm that he rarely exhibits when talking of his childhood home-life. The school's influence on the children was impressive: at the end of the long school day, many of the youngsters, though tired, found it hard to go home. They gathered outside the school's entrance, sat down in the sand, and talked. Even on their day off, Saturday, teachers and students frequently met and took long walks together, exploring the countryside. These nature hikes forged a link between the children and the land. They certainly gave Rabin a familiarity with his surroundings that later in life proved invaluable.

The pupils were encouraged to be as independent as possible, even to the extent of deciding for themselves what they would learn about each day. The teachers provided the necessary guidance, but as far as possible the youngsters were encouraged to develop according to their own personal inclinations. The atmosphere of freedom and informality pervaded everything. Such conventional aspects of school life as bells, examinations and grades were absent. Discipline — except in the most serious cases — was administered by a joint teacher–pupil committee. The children addressed teachers by their first names, a rare practice in the Palestinian schools of that day.

In his first few years at the Bet Hinuch, Yitzhak displayed little aptitude for formal studies. However, he was keenly interested in sports, especially football, and enjoyed tending the school garden and looking after the school's donkey, Dionio, which was made his special responsibility. The other students helped Yitzhak build a special wooden stable. 'Every morning when it rained,' recalls Rabin, 'I would rush to the stable to see how the donkey was, if she was well, or if she had drowned in the rain.'[9] This sense of responsibility, developed by the Bet Hinuch so early, was to stay with him and become an ingrained part of his character. 'Today I am certain,' he says, 'that during those childhood years — they weren't the most comfortable, but they were very beautiful — I developed the feeling of responsibility towards a job, and my love of landscape and the earth, and a feeling for comradeship.'[10]

Eliezer Smoli, one of the school's ten teachers, was one of the major influences on the boy, although their first encounter was hardly auspicious. The subject of their meeting was Yitzhak's record at school, which by his own acknowledgement had hardly been impressive. Smoli took up the matter with the boy, only to be told that Yitzhak had no intention of making any more effort; he was quite content to go along at his own speed. However, what Smoli could not accomplish, Rosa Cohen did — with a sudden outburst which affected the child so much that he made a new attempt to learn to read and write, and finally succeeded. With Smoli for his teacher, Yitzhak began to discover that learning could be fun: 'He succeeded in implanting in me a feeling for landscape, for nature, for farm life, and for society. He did this not with words or lectures, but rather by means of excursions, exciting experiences, and stories.'[11]

Not surprisingly, the Bet Hinuch was one of Rosa Cohen's favourite public projects, and she became a kind of unofficial patron of the place, looking after its needs and caring for the welfare of the teachers as much as that of the pupils. In much the same way that she had helped hungry workers in Russia, she gave her wages to make sure the children at the Bet Hinuch had enough food. In addition, she managed to persuade her Uncle Mordechai — no easy matter — to give a £3,000 loan to the school so it could move into more modern buildings. Mordechai Ben Hillel Hacohen was convinced that the school was designed to turn out communists, but he was fond of Yitzhak, and hoped that the boy would think of him as a stand-in for his grandfathers. So, when Rosa invited him to see the school for himself before deciding on the loan, he accepted. His first impressions of the school — children dressed in blue shirts, a flag hanging from each class-room wall — led him to think he had been right in believing it to be a communist institution. However, after testing the children on their knowledge of Jewish subjects, he seemed satisfied that they were being taught properly, and happily agreed to the loan.

During his childhood years, Yitzhak Rabin was something of an enigma to teachers and fellow pupils alike, a mixture of introversion and self-confidence. Because he was so quiet, few people really knew him. Some mistook his shyness for rudeness. Some found it the outward reflection of a genuine modesty. Others felt it was a cloak for a sensitive mind. He rarely spoke in class — or outside it, for that matter. He walked to and from the Bet Hinuch every day with classmate Ada Tamir, but he seldom talked to her. He showed great tenderness and devotion to his sister Rahel, but some of the girls at the Ben Hinuch were afraid of him. 'He was shy,' remembers one of them, 'and his way of trying to conceal it was to hit us. He was not at ease in the company of girls in those days.' Rabin freely admits: 'I am an introverted man from many points of view. Everyone likes a certain amount of privacy. Some people are more expressive and some are less — it seems to me that I belong to the second type. It's hard to say how your image or your character traits come about. Undoubtedly there is a process of development from a very early age. Basically I think I have remained more or less what I was.'[12]

Although shy and introverted, he was also self-confident and there was a streak of stubbornness in him. With his parents away from the house all day, he quickly learned to fend for himself. He could not run home to his parents. Once, when he was about six, he was on his way home with friends when some Arab youngsters began to throw stones at them. Yitzhak and his companions grabbed some stones of their own, and a fight ensued which eventually ended in a draw. When he was seven years old, a new outbreak of Arab riots was directed against the Yishuv, during which some five hundred Jews were wounded. The boy was bewildered and filled with a sense of uncertainty which stuck in his mind, for much later, he wrote: 'I lived through such riots as a small boy alone in an empty house, with his parents seldom there. I didn't know what was going on.'[13]

Every summer until he was fourteen years old, the boy would spend a few weeks visiting the homes of his great-uncle Mordechai and of his cousin Hannah. By the end of the 1920s, the Hacohen family comprised some of the most important figures of the Yishuv, and has remained one of the leading families in the country. Since the founding of the State of Israel, members of the family have been in the forefront of the country's leadership — Yigael Yadin became Israel's second chief of staff, a world famous archaeologist as well as a major force in Israeli politics; David Hacohen served for a while in the 1950s as the chairman of the prestigious Committee for Foreign Affairs and Defence of the Knesset, Israel's parliament; Uzi Narkiss was the commander of the Central Front during the Six-Day War of 1967 and helped to conquer and reunite Jerusalem.

Mordechai Ben Hillel Hacohen's house was near that of

Hannah, who was married to Artur Ruppin, the director of the Settlement Department of the Yishuv for many years. The young boy was especially friendly with their two children, Carmella (who later married Yigael Yadin) and her younger brother Rafi. Even though it was summer and holiday time, Uncle Mordechai tried to improve the drifting minds of the youngsters. Once he asked Yitzhak and Rafi to help him sort out the books in his library — more to give them some appreciation of the written word than because he really needed their assistance. The exercise gave the boys a chance to browse through some of the great works of Jewish and general literature. In addition to the library project, they occasionally encountered Dr Joseph Luria, Uncle Mordechai's scholarly lodger who knew nine languages and was a specialist in world literature. He had been in charge of the Education Department of the Yishuv for years. Dr Luria took an interest in Yitzhak and Rafi, suggesting books for them to read and questioning them on various subjects.

Rabin's childhood gave little indication of his later deep involvement in military life. Unlike the Israeli boy of today, who might be inclined to emulate such military leaders as Moshe Dayan or Rabin himself, the young Yitzhak had no indigenous military heroes to admire. The British were the only soldiers in Palestine in those days, and a youngster of the Yishuv was hardly likely to idolize them. When Yitzhak was six or seven he 'started to read a little bit about what was going on. Therefore, my attitude towards the British was that they were outsiders. I looked at them with suspicion. Later on my feelings towards them grew to dislike.' In any case, he had been brought up to believe that farming was a far more worthy pursuit than soldiering. 'I can't recall being very much impressed by any political leader during my school-days,' he says. 'The hero then was the farmer, the guardian — the kind of person who had achieved something that was considered to be symbolic of pioneering in those days. They were not people who had won political prestige, but people who had conquered and achieved.'[14] He seemed destined for a career in agriculture, and would have thought it 'absurd' if the idea of becoming a military figure had been suggested to him then.

Chapter 2

'Have you ever thrown a hand grenade?'

The Rabins' household was simple. In 1931, the family moved from Shadel Street to a two-roomed apartment on Hamagid Street, closer to the pulse of Tel Aviv life, which was to remain the Rabin home long after Rosa's death in 1937. The apartment contained only the minimum furniture necessary for the simplest existence: beds, a few chairs, a table — nothing decorative; it was highly functional, and at night became a hive of activity as Nehemiah and Rosa took turns holding their defence committee and labour association meetings there. When Nehemiah was host to the Metal Workers' Committee, the shouting could be heard up and down the tiny street and the neighbours would complain; defence committee meetings were much quieter, in the interests of preserving secrecy. To make room for the meetings, and, almost as frequently, for the overnight guests, the children would be moved from bed to bed, sometimes even sleeping at neighbours' or friends' houses.

Aware that the children required more attention than she was able to give, Rosa had persuaded a neighbouring family on Shadel Street to move with them to the same apartment block on Hamagid Street, where the two families shared a large kitchen on the same floor. Most days, when the two Rabin youngsters returned home from school they were looked after by the neighbours, for whom they felt a good deal of affection. Much later Rabin was to say: 'I didn't like it [i.e. the arrangements at home], but I understand it. In a way it created a kind of atmosphere in which each one of us had his own life, had his own circle in which he was alone — even though there was a feeling of family unity.'[1]

That sense of family unity was strongest on Friday evenings when the Rabin family sat down to the sabbath meal, the only one in the week which all four sat down to together. Nehemiah made breakfast for himself and the children — Rosa was usually out of the house early. During the week, the children ate their main meal — in the middle of the day — at the Bet Hinuch. The evening meal was prepared hastily, since time was always short and Rosa was so busy. The hectic pace of their lives obviously made a lasting impression on the boy. Talking about his relationship with his own children, he has alluded, with an implied sense of regret, to those prolonged periods when he was left on his own: 'Whenever I was home, I always tried to the best of my ability — not always with success — not to think about work, and to free myself for the children, so that to some extent they wouldn't have the feeling that I experienced during my childhood.'[2]

The houschold had a definite routine — so much so that Rabin remembers it as being run 'like a military camp'. Everyone had to share the chores. Nehemiah usually did the washing in the afternoons, standing outside the house, tossing clothes about in a wooden washtub. If the children needed money for something, they knew where the purse with change was kept, but as a rule they did not go to it, aware that the funds were meant for more important things than satisfying their whims. They didn't seem to mind. Oddly, although the Rabins lived an extremely simple life, the children grew up believing that they were not poor. 'It was considered shameful to speak about money,' Rabin recalls. Ironically, the Rabins employed a maid for a certain period, a most unsocialist addition to the household. But despite her presence, the children had to continue helping with the chores.

The unmaterialistic Rabins were true socialists in another respect: their home was largely free of religion, though a strong sense of Jewishness filled the household. When the family lived on Shadel Street in the 1920s they were directly opposite the Sephardic Synagogue, which Rabin still vividly recalls, together with its spiritual leader, Rabbi Uziel, who was also a neighbour of the Rabins. A leading figure of the religious community to Tel Aviv, Rabbi Uziel eventually became Chief Rabbi of the Yishuv. Though Yitzhak was not religious, the sight and atmosphere of the synagogue had an effect on him and left him with a profound belief in Judaism as a positive force, all the more remarkable in view of his father's intense dislike of religious ceremony — even, later, to the point of refusing to light the traditional candle on the anniversary of Rosa's death. However, although free of religion, the Rabin household inculcated enduring values in the young boy, the most prominent among them being humility.

Nehemiah, like Rosa, had a well-developed sense of civic duty. After joining the Electric Corporation in 1926 he had quickly become active in bettering the lot of his fellow workers. Early on he joined the Metal Workers' Committee, which at that time also represented the Electric Corporation workers, and he remained active with them until 1938, when the Corporation's employees formed their own labour association. He became a member of the Workers' Committee of the Histadrut (the Federation of Israeli Workers) in 1933 and for years was a member of the Tel Aviv-Jaffa Labour Council. Unemployment was a major problem in Palestine in the 1930s, and only about thirty per cent of the members of the Metal Workers' Committee had jobs. Nehemiah took an active part in trying to help the unemployed find work. He had a flair for organization, and was popular with his colleagues. He was offered promotion into the managerial ranks, and his colleagues on the Metal Workers' Committee were forever urging him to take higher positions in the union. But steadfast to the socialist ideal that exalted the simple labourer, he always refused. Perhaps he was at his most characteristic when, holding the red flag high, he marched at the head of the annual May Day parade.

In physical appearance, Yitzhak took after his father with his strong build, high forehead, wavy black hair and penetrating eyes. From Nehemiah the young boy also took his quiet and serious manner, and his deep voice. Rosa, whom Rahel favoured, left her imprint on the boy in other ways. Because of her long absences from home she had little influence on Yitzhak on a day-to-day basis, but she served as a model of the ideal public servant and he deeply admired her. Both parents had a major influence on the direction of the boy's life; it was from them that he learnt socialism and came to prize socialist ideals. Also, growing up in a household that was forever concerned, however little was actually said, with problems of defence, he absorbed early the vital importance to the Yishuv of its defence, and the absolute necessity for each member of the community to devote a large amount of his time to this. Rosa was a member of the supreme command of the secret Hagana defence organization during the 1930s, and Nehemiah was at times mobilized and away from home for weeks on end. Guns were brought into the house and stored away. Nehemiah and Rosa tried to keep this part of their lives separate, and to insulate the children from the growing Jewish–Arab tension, but it was not always possible. One day, a woman who was looking after Rahel picked up a gun that she had found in the flat. It went off, narrowly missing the little girl.

When Yitzhak finished his studies at the Bet Hinuch at the age of thirteen, his parents faced the same dilemma which had confronted them when he was six: how to avoid the general schools of Tel Aviv? Rosa decided that she herself would found a two-year agriculture-oriented school somewhere in the country so that working-class youngsters like her son could continue their studies in an appropriate environment. It would be a kind of extension of the Bet Hinuch. Rosa wanted her children to carry on what she had started in those first days in Palestine with the Kinneret group, and hoped that Yitzhak and Rahel would decide to settle in the same region. The school, called Givat Hashlosha ('Hill of the Three') was built outside Tel Aviv.

The tiny Yishuv (which had numbered 60,000 in 1919) grew to 600,000 in the 1930s. The British had permitted the community to establish a Va'ad Leumi (National Council); it had also stipulated that an appropriate 'Jewish agency' should work with them in implementing the pledge of the Balfour Declaration of a Jewish national home, and the World Zionist Organization was recognized as such. The Arabs looked askance at the Declaration, believing it to be an infringement of their own rights in Palestine, and that at best it ought merely to entitle the Jews to a limited Jewish minority in the Holy Land. During the 1920s there had been an increase in Jewish–Arab tension in Palestine over the question of the Jewish right to immigration, resulting in a rise in Arab violence. The British tended to put the blame on the Yishuv for encouraging immigration and therefore provoking the Arabs. Arab-sponsored riots in 1929 had led to a tougher British attitude towards Jewish immigration.

The Yishuv responded by encouraging young Jews to establish settlements in the remote and hazardous parts of Palestine, asserting by this act that the country was big enough for Jews and Arabs to live together — no matter how many Jews arrived from abroad. Between 1936 and 1938 thirty-six such 'stockade and tower' settlements were built, so-called from their fortifications and the thirty-six-foot high towers, topped by searchlights, which ringed the settlements.

In April 1936 the Arabs again began to riot, under the direction of the Mufti of Jerusalem, Haj Amin el-Husseini, and the Arab Higher Committee. For three years the violence continued, as Arabs killed Jews on the streets and conducted raids against the outlying Jewish settlements. The British did little to stop them; indeed, the few thousand British soldiers in Palestine were no match for the lightly armed but fast-moving Arab guerrillas. What kept them at bay was the 25,000-strong force of the Hagana, the underground self-defence organization of the Yishuv. It had been formed in the 1920s with few men and fewer arms but by the 1930s it had developed into an organized quasi-army, with a high command, a general staff, regional headquarters, local armouries and even a locally based military industry. Paralleling (but sometimes merged with) its defence work were the Hagana's operations to bring immigrants to the Holy Land in the 1920s, and, during the late 1930s, the building of the 'stockade and tower' settlements in northern Palestine. In theory, the Hagana was under the control of the Va'ad Leumi and the Jewish Agency, but it functioned generally on its own. Aware that they alone could not contain the Arabs, the British reluctantly permitted the Hagana to guard the farm settlements around the country. For a time, they also supplied the Hagana with light weapons.

The heaviest fighting between Jews and Arabs tailed off by 1937, but there were sporadic outbursts of shooting until 1939. During the three years of rioting, an estimated 2,200 Arabs, 450 Jews and 140 British were killed. The Yishuv, ably defended by the Hagana, emerged strengthened, notwithstanding the loss of life. Not only had not a single Jewish settlement been abandoned, but owing to Operation Stockade and Tower strategic settlements had been established near the borders of

Lebanon, Syria, and Transjordan. The Hagana, too, still technically illegal, had grown stronger and more self-confident in these last years, though it continued to be under-trained and poorly equipped.

If the Arabs could not defeat the Jews on the battlefield, they did win political points by once again provoking the British into more severe action against Jewish immigration. In July 1937 the six-member Peel Commission, appointed by the British to improve Jewish–Arab relations in Palestine, issued a 404-page report after spending six months conducting hearings and touring the Holy Land. It concluded that the British Mandate was impractical and should be replaced by separate Jewish and Arab States. The Jews should be given the coastal plain, the Jezreel Valley, and Galilee (altogether 2,000 square miles) and the Arabs, the rest of Palestine; Jerusalem would become an international enclave linked to the coast by a corridor. The Jews grudgingly accepted the plan, dismayed at the small amount of territory conceded to them, but nevertheless recognizing that they would at least have some control over immigration into that area — and following Hitler's rise to power in Germany, and with the position of European Jewry becoming ever more desperate, immigration was a vital issue. The Arabs were contemptuous of the plan and immediately stepped up terrorist activity; whereupon the British outlawed the Arab Higher Command and ordered the arrest of the Mufti, who, however, managed to escape.

In 1938, the British placed Palestine under military administration, but this did little to restore peace. A year later, in May 1939, seeking a compromise, the British announced a White Paper which would allow 15,000 Jews to immigrate annually to Palestine over the next five years, after which further Jewish immigration would be stopped altogether. Jewish land purchase was to be cut back drastically. To the Yishuv leadership, the White Paper was nothing less than the renunciation of the Balfour Declaration.

The turmoil of the late 1930s in Palestine touched Rabin personally. Upon enrolling at Givat Hashlosha in 1935, he had his first encounter with military life: Hagana training sessions began when a youngster was thirteen years old; they took place for several hours every day at the school. Rabin was taught how to use a pistol and how to stand guard.

Like most Jewish youngsters in the Yishuv, the boy joined one of the youth movements after his Bet Hinuch days, choosing one which was labour orientated. It was known as Noar Ha'oved ('Working Youth'), and met in the Bayat Ha'adom ('Red House'), on the Tel Aviv beach. There in the afternoons the children discussed a variety of subjects, including the Bible, literature, music, economics and social problems. Rabin found that talks on literature, music and the Bible boring, but was fascinated by social problems and economics. He spoke very little, preferring to listen.

In the evenings the youth movement was organized as a kind of evening school to give some education to youngsters who had dropped out of school and were already working during the day. Occasionally there was rivalry between the different youth clubs. At the festival of Hanukkah, for instance, Rabin and his fellow members collected candles and paraded through the streets of Tel Aviv, singing holiday songs and carrying their flag, a blue-and-white banner with two red strips attached to it, the symbol of the socialist cause. The right-wing Betar youth movement which had engaged in fistfights with them on previous occasions, attacked them and a battle broke out between the two groups.

The two years at Givat Hashlosha were clearly a period of transition for him, during which he seemed to become more assertive, more interested in his studies. In October 1937 he began his studies at the Kadoorie Agricultural High School for boys, located near Kfar Tabor in the Lower Galilee. By choosing the two-year course the school offered rather than the four-year academic high school education available in Tel Aviv, which enabled a youngster with ambitions to go on to a university, he was setting his face towards a career on a kibbutz. Getting into the school posed quite a challenge for the boy: although only in its fourth year in 1937, there were already some 150 boys competing for the thirty places available, and though the Bet Hinuch had given him a strong foundation in certain fields, it had not given him much of an academic grounding, for instance, in English or mathematics. He had made much progress at Givat Hashlosha — where the principal had commended him as 'A good student in the important subjects, industrious in his work and well-behaved' — but still he failed the entrance examination to Kadoorie. However, the school authorities permitted a second attempt several months later and this time the boy was determined to pass. He worked between ten and twelve hours a day at his studies, and when he took the exam again he passed with flying colours — and found that the preparation had given him a taste for learning.

Conditions in the three-storey, white-stone school building were primitive: all twenty-five boys in Rabin's class lived in one large room on the second floor. The building was rarely heated; even in winter the boys took ice-cold showers at the end of each day.

He had hardly begun there when the sad news came that his mother had died. Rosa's death in November 1937 caused widespread grief within the Yishuv. Some one thousand people attended her burial. At the head of the funeral procession were children from the Bet Hinuch, for which she had done so much in the previous years. Both the Histadrut and the Tel Aviv City Council offered eulogies; two men spoke on behalf of the city's clerks; finally a man from the Tel Aviv Workers' Council offered a few words. In honour of its founder, the Givat Hashlosha school decided to change its name to the Rosa Cohen School. Natan Fiat, the principal of Kadoorie, wrote to Rabin in Tel Aviv on November 16 to express his sorrow at Rosa's death: 'Your mother was one of the great women in Israel whose names are associated with the lofty idealism of the nation . . . May you find comfort in studying for the profession you have chosen, for your own good and for the good of the public which your mother loved so much and to which she gave so much of her time in her short life.'

Although most subjects fell easily within his grasp, Rabin found English particularly difficult. His report card shows that he did best in zoology, chemistry, botany, poultry-breeding, and bee-raising. He had a good record in physics and agronomy as well. Both his teachers and classmates expected him to become an outstanding scientist one day, and perhaps take up research at the prestigious Weizmann Institute in Rehovot, one of the major scientific institutions of the Yishuv. He won the top prize at graduation: the Walker Prize for Scholarship. However, although he had earned the most points for his work, the school directors felt that another boy was equally bright, and that the two of them should share the prize. This the boys agreed to do, but the donors of the prize — the British authorities — insisted that the school should give it to Rabin. In the event, neither boy collected the seven and a half British pounds' worth of farm equipment that went with the prize.

Some of Rabin's happiest moments at Kadoorie were spent on the football pitch as captain of the school team. He adored the game, and would go to matches on Saturdays with his father when they were together in Tel Aviv. He was intolerant of those on his own school team who did not play well, and was not slow to make his disapproval obvious.

When he began at Kadoorie, Rabin had absolutely no ambition to become a full-time soldier. He thought only about farming and moving into a kibbutz: 'My purpose in life was to serve my country and I believed that the best way to do it was to prepare myself to be a farmer.'[3] However, his military training intensified at Kadoorie and it was during this time that he began to feel the likelihood of becoming personally involved in the Arab-Jewish struggle. Kadoorie was in the peculiar position of being run under British auspices but unable to take advantage of the protection of the British army because the school was so isolated. In fact the British took little interest in the defence of the school, and the students realized that it was fundamentally their own responsibility. The nearest Jewish settlement, Kfar Tabor, was too far away to be of assistance if the Arabs attacked. At the same time, to avoid provoking the British, defence arrangements had to be made with as much secrecy as possible.

Yigal Allon, then a sergeant in the Hagana for the Lower Galilee region, was responsible for training the Kadoorie youngsters. He had graduated from the school three years before and was stationed at Kibbutz Ginossar, along the western shore of Lake Kinneret, not far from the school. But even before Allon could begin training the boys in earnest, the school had been organized informally so that the students were prepared in the event of an attack. The top class was responsible for the weapons, which consisted entirely of rifles. Rabin's class dealt with all the other tasks, including message-carrying and supplies. At night the boys took turns doing guard duty.

Tensions ran high, the training and guard duty interfered with the boys' work and the school was more like a fortress than a place of study. Towards the end of 1937 the school came under attack, though the students soon realized that the operation was more in the nature of sabre-rattling than an actual attempt to overrun it, with the Arabs simply firing repeated rounds at the school building.

In the summer of 1938, the riots worsened and in view of the tense atmosphere, the British decided to close the school down — three weeks before the end of Rabin's first year. In the autumn he gladly answered a summons from Allon to join him at Ginossar, where he remained for the next six months. As soon as he arrived, he joined the other youngsters being given a ten-day training course nearby at Migdal where they learnt to use revolvers, rifles and hand grenades. Allon took a liking to Rabin, recognizing that he had qualities which could be put to military use. Allon remembers: 'He had a sort of analytical approach to problems. He would never say he understood something before he really did understand all that it involved. Once he said that he understood, you knew that he did.' As his first commander, Allon justifiably takes credit for discovering Rabin's soldiering abilities.

Following the six months at Ginossar, the boy spent another similar period of Hagana duty at Ramat David in northern Palestine. He returned to Kadoorie during October 1939, and graduated from the school on August 20, 1940. Fiat wrote to Nehemiah Rabin, asking him to attend the graduation so that he could discuss the boy's future, and suggested that instead of becoming a farmer, as most of his students did, the boy should study water engineering at the University of California. Fiat was certain that Yitzhak would be accepted because of his academic record; he would probably not even need to take an entrance examination, though he would have to improve his English. The idea appealed to Rabin, who realized that water would be a major preoccupation of the Yishuv in the coming years. His father made the necessary application to the university, and Rabin awaited the reply at Kibbutz Ramat Yohanan, near Haifa, where he joined a group which planned to establish a settlement somewhere in the region. It was while he was waiting that another offer came up which he felt he had to accept.

*

Sooner or later, the events of World War Two were bound to impinge on the boy. Many of his friends had already enlisted in the British army. By 1942, there were 19,000 Palestinian Jews (ten per cent of them women) serving in British uniform — the number was to reach 32,000 by the end of the war. After the publication of the White Paper in 1939, it had been extremely difficult for the Jews of the Yishuv to swallow their differences with the British and fight side by side with them against a common enemy; but David Ben-Gurion (who had become chairman of the Jewish Agency in 1935 and as such was the Yishuv's leader) issued a directive: 'We shall fight the war as if there were no White Paper, and we shall fight the White Paper as if there were no war.'

In the spring of 1941 members of the Hagana High Command began to feel that the Yishuv's chances of defending itself against a possible Nazi invasion were being lessened because the Zionist leadership was permitting so many Palestinian Jews to serve abroad in the British army. In the event of the Nazis overrunning Palestine, the Jewish settlements would be at the mercy of the Axis Powers and the local Arabs. The Hagana comprised dedicated but relatively untrained men, recruited from the ranks of the workers on a part-time basis; what was needed was an independent, well-equipped, mobile, and permanently mobilized task force — subject, of course, to the Hagana's authority. This special task force was formed in May 1941 by Yitzhak Sadeh, a Russian-born Hagana veteran, and was recruited in total secrecy. The Palmach (as it was called from the acronym of the Hebrew for 'Shock Companies') came into existence at a time when the morale of the Yishuv had plummeted to a new low. An undercurrent of resentment had been building up among those who wished to see more dynamic action and leadership. Poverty was too great a problem to ignore even though it was wartime; immigration needed a boost after the depressing effect of the British White Paper; unemployment was rife. The Hagana itself was coming in for a great deal of criticism from the Yishuv, who tended to see its members as draft-dodgers, and the organization as failing in its primary objectives.

In the face of such great uncertainty about the future it was a formidable task to create a band of dedicated, trained men and women to undertake the defence of the Jews. At first the Palmach attracted young idealists; but they lacked the necessary soldiering talents. The new fighting force required the best possible recruits and it needed them in a hurry. Appeals were made to the pioneering youth movements and to the collective settlements, where idealism already flourished and where the best potential for future soldiers existed. Very quickly the 'Palmachniks' grew into an elitist band which enjoyed an almost legendary reputation; it was, after all, the very first institution of the Yishuv to be controlled and run by a generation actually born in the country. In contrast with the under-trained Hagana recruits, the Palmach force comprised six companies of soldiers who had the benefit of full-time commando-style training. By 1947 the Palmach constituted some 3,100 soldiers, including 1,000 reservists, both men and women, and fully half of its members had spent three years of full-time training as compared with the fifty days which were all many of the Hagana soldiers had been given.

At about the time the Palmach was being formed, the military situation of the Allies worsened and the British began to plan an offensive into Syria and Lebanon in an attempt to stave off a German attempt to take over the entire Middle East. For such an offensive, the British needed a special force which could cross Palestine's northern frontier easily, which knew the terrain and the necessary languages, and which could be relied upon to carry out sabotage missions. The Palmach fitted the bill perfectly. The situation was urgent, and an alliance of sorts was struck: the British agreed to allow the Palmach autonomy outside the framework of the British army, even to the extent of respecting its clandestine nature and not demanding the real names or addresses of those Palmach members participating in action; in return, the Palmach gained experience in playing a direct role in the security of the country. Companies A and B — one hundred men in all, the most experienced of the Palmach — were recruited for the operation.

One day the kibbutz secretary at Ramat Yohanan approached Rabin and asked if he was willing to volunteer for a special unit. He agreed, and was told to await further instructions. Six weeks passed, and then a company commander by the name of Moshe Dayan came to the kibbutz and asked him some questions.

'Do you know how to fire a rifle?'

'Yes,' the boy replied.

'Have you ever thrown a hand grenade?' Dayan asked him.

'Yes,' said Rabin again, wondering where this was leading.

'Do you know how to operate a maching-gun?'

This time, the boy answered somewhat reluctantly, 'No.'

'Can you drive?'

'No.'

'Can you ride a motorcycle?'

'No.'

'All right,' said Dayan briskly. 'You'll do.'[4]

The Allied invasion took place in June 1941; a week before it began Palmach teams went into action, some scouting the northern border, some crossing into Syria and Lebanon. Rabin — recruited into Company B — was told to report to Kibbutz Hanita, which skirts the Lebanese border inside Palestine. By coincidence, on the day that his orders arrived, he had invited his father to Ramat Yohanan. Telling him only that he had to go off, but hoped to be back the next day, Rabin disappeared. Nehemiah waited a day or so for his son to return, and then went back to Tel Aviv to await further news. Three weeks later, looking tired but happy, Yitzhak visited his father in Tel Aviv and explained where he had been.

Allon, in charge of Company A, had taken his force across the north-eastern border of Palestine. Moshe Dayan had led Company B, in which Rabin was serving, across the northern border, near Rosh Hanikra, along the Mediterranean coast. Rabin belonged to one of several groups within the company which were to infiltrate the Lebanon and destroy the telephone communications between the cities of Zur and Sidon along the Mediterranean coast. He and two colleagues crossed the border, twenty-five kilometres from their starting point, at night, and then marched another ten kilometres inside Lebanese territory to the village of Binai el-Jubal. Being the youngest (he was nineteen), Rabin was chosen to climb the telephone poles, pliers in hand, and cut the lines, before all three returned to base, also under cover of darkness. Dressed as civilians, they were in danger not only from the Lebanese but also from the Allied forces, who had not been notified of their arrival.

The assignment was the most dangerous that the young man

had yet been given but he found the experience stimulating. 'No one forced me to do it,' he says. 'It was on a voluntary basis. I enjoyed it. I must admit that my part was very simple in that invasion: a lot of walking, no fighting. Though you had to get up a telephone pole — that wasn't easy.'[5]

The Lebanese raid provided the Palmach with valuable experience. The strike force learned how to set up proper commands, how to acquire much-needed intelligence, and how to use its men properly; perhaps most importantly, the experience gave the Palmach a necessary boost to its self-confidence and enhanced its reputation among those in the Hagana command who openly wondered whether the force was really essential.

After the raid, when Rabin was reunited with his father and sister, he said little about the operation, but when, on his return to the kibbutz, he was invited to address several hundred kibbutz members in the dining-hall, he accepted. Dressed in shorts, an open-necked shirt and sandals, Rabin gave a lengthy description of the operation, demonstrating a genuine ability to analyse military events precisely and lucidly. His audience was fascinated, and convinced that here was someone with a bright military future.

With the success of the Lebanese raids, Yitzhak Sadeh pressed the Hagana to give the Palmach its own training camps, and, reluctantly, the High Command permitted the establishment of two such bases. One was in a eucalyptus grove in Kibbutz Ginossar; the other, to which Rabin went, was in the heart of a forest near Kibbutz Bet Oren, near Haifa. Conditions were austere, the Hagana providing no tents for the men, who slept under trees on straw mats. Eventually, disturbed at the cost of maintaining separate training camps with funds so short, and now that Syria and Lebanon were under Allied control, the Yishuv leadership, never very enthusiastic about the Palmach anyway, ordered them to be disbanded. The Palmachniks reluctantly obeyed orders, but continued to remain partially mobilized.

In the autumn of 1941, Allon commanded the first training course for Palmach section commanders at Kibbutz Alonim in the Western Galilee. The Lebanese raid had boosted Rabin's reputation, and he was one of sixty who had been selected to train there. Almost imperceptibly, the youngster who had aimed to settle on a kibbutz and had been educated for that kind of life, had become a soldier.

Early in 1942 Allied fortunes in the Middle East again worsened, and there seemed a real danger that the Germans would overrun Palestine. Once more the British turned to the Palmach to enlist their aid in harrying action against the enemy if things went badly. This time the British offered to finance and train three hundred members of the Palmach as saboteurs and scouts. The Palmach agreed, and a full-scale course covering sabotage and demolition was organized in a camp in a forest near Kibbutz Mishmar Ha'emek, in northern Palestine. There Rabin and his fellow trainees studied topography, tracking, and map-reading. The battalion was now introduced as a tactical unit, the main principle of the Palmach training being active defence — seizing the initiative and launching pre-emptive attacks at any hour of the day or night. However, when the British sensed victory in the Middle East early in 1943, after El Alamein, they decided to end their shaky alliance with the Palmach, disbanded the camp at Mishmar Ha'emek, and confiscated the Hagana arms which had been used in the joint effort there.

Once again the Palmach, an expensive luxury for the Hagana, seemed destined for dissolution. But Yitzhak Tabenkin, a veteran leader of the kibbutz movement, saved the day by proposing that the 'Palmachniks' become part-time farmers on the kibbutzim, earning their own living, in return for which they would be given bed, board, and cover for their secret military work. For fourteen days a month the Palmach men would work as farmers, and for the other sixteen they would be free to pursue their military activities, using the kibbutzim as bases. In this way both the Palmach and the kibbutzim benefited, since the recruits came largely from the settlements anyway, and the kibbutzim could not afford to be without their workers for long periods of time; in addition, the presence of the young Palmach soldiers meant extra defence. Some 'Palmachniks' were hostile to the idea, embittered by the implication that their services were not considered worth the Yishuv leadership's direct support. A number of them enlisted in the British army rather than join the kibbutzim, but the majority, including Rabin, remained in the Palmach. Like the rest, Rabin spent most of his time on military affairs, but whenever he could he helped out, trying to involve himself as much as possible in the life of the kibbutz, the life for which he had been educated.

In 1943 he became a platoon commander at Kfar Giladi, a kibbutz founded thirty years earlier and located in the Huleh Valley close to the Lebanese border. There he was involved in directing the movement of illegal Jewish immigrants from Syria and Iraq via Kfar Giladi to safer points further south. Anti-Jewish violence and a pro-Nazi putsch in Iraq in 1941 had made the plight of Jews living in Moslem countries desperate. Arab-speaking members of the Palmach infiltrated Syria and Iraq and arranged to transport these Jews secretly to the Palestine border, skirting Arab patrols on one side of the frontier, and British patrols on the other.

Although Rabin and his platoon engaged in no military encounters during this period, he took the opportunity to train his men in the modern tactics he had studied in his command course. The men, until then, had been used to fighting like partisans, moving around on foot with packs on their backs, without the advantage of transport. Rabin taught them how to conduct lightning attacks using a car or a jeep, instituted night journeys over long distances, and toughened up his men by allowing them as few breaks as possible.

Training in the Palmach was all the more challenging because it had to be done without arousing the suspicions of the British, whose attitude towards the strike force was ambiguous at best and more often downright hostile. When the Kfar Giladi platoon went on a spring march near the Dead Sea, it was in the guise of a sporting club. On the way, the food the men had brought with them turned rotten and they had to use their wits to survive in the hot desert. During the manoeuvres they launched a simulated attack on a tiny oasis, using live ammunition. As the men moved towards their target, a young soldier, excited and disoriented, lobbed a hand grenade in his commander's direction. Rabin yelled a warning to the soldier beside him as the grenade fell about a foot away from them. Fortunately the sand absorbed the explosion and they escaped without injury.

The final difficult — and dangerous — mission was the

organization of a secret truck convoy which had to get past the British at the southern tip of the Dead Sea in order to pick up waiting supplies. The manoeuvres had been the first in which full-scale live-ammunition exercises had been carried out at platoon strength, and all those who participated had remarked the calmness under stress and the quick thinking of the 21-year-old platoon commander.

It took a certain amount of personal discipline to remain in the Palmach during the war years. The pressures on members of the strike force to join the British army were heavy. For one thing, some influential members of the Yishuv felt that the Jewish community would be better off bolstering the Jewish Brigade than creating its own independent military machinery; for another, the Palmach men had no uniforms and consequently passed unrecognized and unhonoured for the part they were playing in the war. At first, in the early years of the war, Rabin believed that the Palmach should remain independent of the British army but informally linked to it in case fighting broke out in Palestine and each needed the other's services — as they had in 1941, with the invasion of Syria and Lebanon. But by 1943, with the tide of events in the Middle East turning in favour of the Allies, he became convinced that a truly independent Jewish force was a necessity. Since, after the war, the Yishuv was bound to clash with the British on the question of Jewish immigration, 'the military strength of the Jewish community would be a key factor in the outcome,' he asserted. [6]

Rabin kept up the spirits of his men, sometimes by doing the unexpected, sometimes by demonstrating his own loyalty to the cause. By this time he had gained a reputation as a quiet but forceful and exemplary leader; however on one occasion Rabin uncharacteristically appeared to defy standing Hagana and Palmach orders. Members of both the Hagana and the Palmach were under strict orders not to carry weapons openly for fear of being stopped and questioned by the British and exposing the underground organization. Obtaining enough weapons and ammunition was, however, a constant problem — and at the time of the incident, in the autumn of 1943, Rabin's platoon was impatiently awaiting a three-inch mortar it had requested from the Hagana command. One day, as the platoon was going

through a training exercise, Rabin surprised his men by
suddenly riding off on his motorcycle in the direction of a
Hagana training-ground near Kibbutz Ein Hashofet, apparently
to visit friends there. As he approached he noticed a three-inch
mortar very much like the one his platoon had requested. He
picked it up and returned with it to his men. Impatient for the
platoon to gain experience of certain kinds of weapons, Rabin
perhaps overlooked the fact that he was jeopardizing the whole
organization by being so overt. Members of his platoon recall
that the Hagana was furious, but no one could remember Rabin
being brought to account for his action. His men were amused as
well as impressed at the thought of their young commander
riding a motorcycle through the streets of Afula with a live
mortar inside his satchel bag. But, riding back to the platoon's
base, then at Tel Yosef, twenty-five kilometres from the training
ground, Rabin was most likely thinking grimly to himself how
difficult it was to train under the constraints imposed on the
Palmach.

Despite his handsome appearance, Rabin had no great
reputation as a ladies' man. He led a busy life and found little
time for such amusements. Then, in 1944, he met a young high
school girl from Tel Aviv named Leah Schlossberg, a dark-
haired fifteen-year-old, born in Koenigsberg, Germany on
8 April, 1928, who had immigrated with her parents and sister in
1933. Their first 'meeting' occurred in an ice-cream store on Tel
Aviv's Allenby Street. Eyeing her future husband, Leah thought
of the description of King David: 'Chestnut hair and beautiful
eyes!' No words were exchanged then. They bumped into one
another several more times; eventually they sought out one
another. Leah asked friends who this attractive man was and she
learned his name — Yitzhak Rabin. 'Something about him —
his appearance, his walk — had captured my heart. He seemed
different. Then one day we came face to face and I asked him:
"Your name is Yitzhak?" He answered: "Yes." "And I'm
Leah." '[7] Members of the Palmach were already romantic
figures in the eyes of high school girls, but Leah was also
attracted by certain aspects of Rabin's character. 'He had great
serenity,' she remembers. 'He was terribly shy. He struck me
immediately as being extremely intelligent, seeming to make

very critical and severe judgments of people. There was a tremendous sense of dedication to what he was doing, but he loved it — there was no question about it.'[8] When she graduated from high school in 1945, Leah joined the Palmach and was stationed at Kibbutz Ein Harod, where she went through the usual military training for new recruits.

Although the Palmach was not active in military missions during the war, membership in itself was a dangerous thing. It was, after all, an underground organization whose existence had been tolerated by the British only in the early days of the war. Rabin had to be especially careful since, as a commander in possession of information about the size of various Palmach units, their locations, weapons and members, he would be of great interest to the British, whose clutches he narrowly escaped in the late summer of 1944. He and his platoon had been training at Tel Yosef, living over the kibbutz cowshed. As platoon commander, Rabin had his own room which also doubled as the platoon headquarters. Next door to him, sharing a room, were Yehuda Tajar, Yochai Ben-Nun, and Amos Horev, his three squad commanders. One day a Palmach commander named Yitzhak Tavori visited Rabin from Kibbutz Afikim to talk about a course he was preparing for Rabin's platoon. As he sat on Rabin's bed, Tavori gazed at the young commander's pistol lying on the table. Then, before the stunned Rabin could prevent him, he picked it up, aimed it at his own head, and pulled the trigger. The bullet penetrated his brain, killing him instantly. Rabin called to the other officers to come quickly, and he, Tajar, and Natan Gorali, the kibbutz's liaison man with the British, began to consult about what should be done.

The problem was not just how to explain to the British police the presence of an illegal gun; if the British searched Rabin's room they were bound to find evidence of the Palmach. It was therefore agreed that they should pretend it was Tajar's room, and that Tajar would take whatever punishment the British decided upon for illegal possession of arms. The three also decided that Tajar should make the thirty-minute drive to British police headquarters and report the incident, thus giving the others time to remove all obvious traces of their activity from the room. In the event, the police did not come to the scene of the suicide for several days, and the incident passed off without serious consequences for the Palmach.

Meanwhile, Zionist leaders both in Palestine and in the Diaspora were pressing the case for Jewish statehood in the Holy Land. In May 1942 the American Emergency Committee for Zionist Affairs had called a special conference at the Biltmore Hotel in New York City, where the six hundred assembled Zionists urged 'that Palestine be established as a Jewish commonwealth integrated in the structure of the new democratic world', a statement which was endorsed six months later by the Jewish Agency Executive in Jerusalem. Rabin, a simple platoon commander, was not involved in the struggle — he was in any case cut off from the outside world most of the time. Like most other young men of his day, he thought the idea of a Jewish State a far-off dream, not a practical goal that might be realized in the foreseeable future. 'I don't believe that in the last half of the 1930s or the early part of the 1940s I thought in specific terms how we would become a Jewish independent state,' he recalls. 'I believe I thought in more practical terms of what could be done to advance the cause, by being stronger, by increasing the Jewish population, by founding more settlements. But I was not thinking then in political terms how to bring about a Jewish State.'[9] In the early 1940s when he was attached to settlements belonging to the leftist Kibbutz Hameuchad movement, he had certain reservations about the partition plan proposed by the Peel Commission. But gradually he moved into the political camp of David Ben-Gurion, who felt that a Jewish State should be set up as quickly as possible, and as statehood appeared increasingly imperative, it became more and more crucial for the Palmach to adopt the proper military strategy and tactics in order to function as a national liberation army.

The Palmach prided itself on adjusting to the military situation it faced rather than relying on conventional military wisdom, taught by specialists unfamiliar with the Middle East. Practically all the young Palmach commanders fell under the unorthodox but powerful tutelage of Yitzhak Sadeh, the leading theorist of the Palmach, who advocated the use of surprise tactics and unconventional methods.

The strongest military influence on Rabin in the 1940s was, he feels, his immediate commanders. Indeed, they were bound to be influential if only because the training camps — located on remote kibbutzim — were so isolated. Rabin rarely left the kibbutz at which he was stationed; even the long marches that took him away from the region were infrequent. Thus he, like the others, heard and saw little of the outside world. Information about what was happening outside Palestine arrived slowly, if at all. The only military theorists with whom the Palmach came into contact on a regular basis were the local commanders. Later Rabin devoured books about World War Two, but he was more interested in the various resistance movements than in the conventional armies of the European powers.

In the four years since he had become a member of the Palmach, Rabin had acquired a reputation as one of the leading thinkers of the strike force. Other commanders, even his seniors, often sought his advice or opinion. He was not only a willing and persevering soldier, he had a special understanding of the unique role of the Palmach. If this burgeoning Jewish commando force was going to ignore most established military doctrine, it could only do so by replacing it with new theories and practice, and for that it needed men of special intelligence, men like Rabin who could work out a practical solution for everyday problems, who could take into account the major restraints imposed on the men — the relative paucity of manpower, the lack of weapons — and overcome them by capitalizing on their one advantage: familiarity with the terrain. Rabin won the admiration of more senior commanders not so much for bravery in the field of battle — although he frequently demonstrated cool-headedness under fire — but rather for the painstaking way in which he examined military problems and for the originality of his thinking. When military theory was being fashioned not by some unseen hierarchy, but by the rank-and-file soldiers themselves, everyone had his own ideas about what methods to use. Advice came from many quarters. But Rabin, being by nature quiet, shy, serious and thorough, took the time to look at problems in depth. Before he committed himself to an idea, he examined it for flaws from every possible angle. 'You knew,' says one of his squad commanders at Kfar Giladi in 1943, 'that you were in the presence of a man who took full responsibility for his decisions, and who made decisions in the full consciousness of what he was doing.'

Rabin's self-confidence stemmed from his uncanny foresight and from his own thoroughness. He particularly enjoyed military tactics, in which he excelled. His superiors, both Yitzhak Sadeh and Yigal Allon, whom he greatly respected, had drilled into him that he must avoid slavishly following the military doctrines of others. Copying their tactics meant copying their mistakes too, and this the tiny Palmach force, with the heavy constraints already imposed on it, could not afford. If any models were to be employed, the French and Yugoslav partisans would serve to show how thorough familiarity with native terrain could be exploited. Inventiveness was much more valuable than a knowledge of historical precedent. Rabin understood this completely.

With the end of World War Two, the half million Jews of the Yishuv were determined to help the Jewish refugees from Europe find a secure, permanent home in Palestine. The British, however, remained adamant in their refusal to allow immigration beyond the limited number set down in the 1939 White Paper. As the refugees crowded together in displaced persons camps throughout Europe, desperate to reach Palestine, hopes rose in the summer of 1945 that the seemingly pro-Zionist Labour Government — newly come to power — might open up the gates to them. But by the summer's end it had become painfully clear that the British Government's policy had not changed at all. The British not only refused to let Jews enter Palestine, but wanted to evict so-called 'illegal immigrants' who had successfully got into the country. This, more than any other action of the British, incensed the Yishuv leadership. Accordingly, when the Hagana learned that the British planned to return a group of 203 immigrants who had entered the country on foot from Syria and were being kept in Atlit detention camp, eight miles south of Haifa, it set about rescuing them. It was the first major, open military confrontation between the Yishuv's military forces and the British. All previous anti-British action on the part of the Hagana had been small and carried out under cover of night; this time the attack was undertaken in broad daylight, with a far more daring objective than the hit-and-run raids of the past.

The Hagana selected the Palmach's First Battalion, which

had responsibility for the northern region of Palestine, for the task. Commanding it was Nahum Sarig; his deputy was Rabin. In the weeks before the operation, Rabin helped to collect weapons from Palmach units in a dozen nearby kibbutzim and bring them to the staging area at Kibbutz Bet Oren, near Atlit. The Hagana had been able to infiltrate some men in the guise of teachers into the detention camp. These passed the word to Jewish policemen working there to jam the rifles of the Arab policemen inside the camp ready for the attack on 10 October, 1945.

The 250-man attacking force comprised three units: one, led by Rabin, was to break into the camp, capture the police quarters, and prevent the police from interfering with the rescue; a second, led by Sarig, was to take the refugees to waiting trucks along the main Haifa–Tel Aviv road (from there they would be driven to Kibbutz Yagur); a third, remaining outside the camp, was to set up roadblocks and to take on the British at the nearby army base if they gave any trouble.

Rabin's men met with little resistance from the policemen and managed to disarm them without a shot being fired. After thirty minutes — the time allotted for the refugees to be safely escorted from the camp — Rabin signalled his men to begin the long march to Kibbutz Yagur. Feeling that the operation had gone unusually well, he offered his unit the choice of marching to Yagur or running two kilometres to catch the trucks heading for Yagur with the refugees. The unit elected to race for the trucks, but, as they neared the main road, they came upon a dismal sight: suitcases which the refugees had not been able to bring themselves to leave behind in the camp lay strewn along the wayside, leaving a well-marked trail for any RAF spotter planes overhead to follow. Even worse, the youngsters and the weak among the refugees were slowing up the entire evacuation.

Rabin and Sarig held an urgent consultation, realizing that the present plan would have to be scrapped, for the refugees would never manage to reach the trucks before the British arrived. They decided to split up the refugees between them: Sarig would take the hundred strongest to the trucks and then on to Yagur, while Rabin would accompany the weaker ones on foot to Bet Oren, a nearer kibbutz. With luck Rabin's group would soon be reinforced by the unit which had been keeping the British army base under surveillance.

Since the new plan required Rabin's refugees to make the tough climb up Mount Carmel, he immediately ordered his group to abandon its belongings. The ascent still proved agonizingly slow; to speed the march up, the soldiers carried the younger children. The youngster on Rabin's shoulders, unnerved by the whole experience, urinated on the commander, who, sweating from the gruelling march, barely noticed. At one stage a British patrol came upon the refugees, and when it was confronted by the Palmach force, shooting broke out and one British policeman was killed. It was the only casualty of the entire Atlit operation.

Sarig and his refugees came safely to Yagur just before dawn, but Rabin's group, slowed down, failed to reach Bet Oren before daylight. Spotting British forces near the kibbutz, Rabin told his refugees to hide in the forest. The Palmach force prepared for a battle with the British, but nothing happened.

The refugees' only hope of escaping the attention of the British was to steal into the kibbutz. Rabin placed thirty of his soldiers at the front of the group, and thirty in the rear and, using an entrance unknown to the British, he led his charges into the settlement. The British failed to realize what was happening until it was too late, though they held the kibbutz under siege and there were fears that they might stage an attack. Another deception was necessary: the Hagana organized buses from Haifa bringing no fewer than fifteen thousand Jews to Bet Oren, where they casually walked into the kibbutz and mingled with the refugees, making it impossible for the British to distinguish those who had been rescued from Atlit. Unable to cope with the situation, the British left. The refugees were safe.

Word of the Atlit success and Rabin's role in it filtered back to Kibbutz Ein Harod, where Leah was stationed. 'The next day,' she recalls proudly, 'the man who ran the kibbutz's defence came up to me and shook my hand. I felt so happy, because they recognized that Yitzhak and I belonged together.'[10] Characteristically, Rabin played down his role in the operation. 'The planning and execution weren't bad,' was all he would say.

In 1946 there were a quarter of a million Jewish refugees waiting in displaced persons camps in Europe, hoping to find a way of reaching a safe haven. The path to Palestine continued to be blocked: the British by now were preparing to purge the Yishuv of its activists and to sabotage Jewish efforts abroad to infiltrate refugees into the country. In March 1946, an Anglo–American Committee recommended that 100,000 Jews be admitted to Palestine immediately, but Prime Minister Attlee refused the proposal. Faced with this intransigent attitude, Jewish resistance groups in Palestine stepped up their activities. The main groups were the Irgun Zvai Leumi (National Military Organization), known as the Irgun, and the much smaller Lohamei Herut Yisrael (Fighters for the Freedom of Israel), known as Lehi or, as the British called it, the Stern Gang. The Irgun, which numbered about two thousand, was the military arm of the dissident Revisionist Party, and was comprised mostly of new arrivals from Eastern Europe. Having seen their families killed by the Nazis, their sole aim was to bring survivors to Palestine. The Stern Gang, named after the Hebrew poet Abraham Stern, never numbered more than a few hundred; its membership came largely from the slums of Palestine's major towns. The Stern Gang believed that only political assassination would effect a change in British policy on Jewish immigration.

In 1946–47, as the British sent back every refugee ship which approached Palestinian shores, both dissident groups turned on the 'enemy' with violence — in direct opposition to the wishes of the Yishuv leadership. They set fire to British military installations, shot down British soldiers, engaged in beatings and kidnappings. When the British imposed the death penalty on members of the gangs, they retaliated by executing British personnel and, on 22 July, 1946, blowing up a wing of the King David Hotel in Jerusalem, where the British had administrative offices. Some one hundred British, Arabs, and Jews were killed in the explosion. Although the political authorities of the Yishuv expressed horror and repugnance at the outrage, the British denounced the entire Jewish population.

Between 1945 and 1947 only 71,000 Jewish immigrants reached Palestine; immigrant ships found it increasingly impossible to break the blockade. On 14 May, 1946 the British detained 1,760 men, women and children, including three hundred orphans, who were passengers on the Hagana ship *Max Nordau*, after it was caught nearing the Palestinian shore. The

Hagana ordered the Palmach to respond in massive terms. Railways, bridges and police stations became prime targets. Rabin's First Battalion was again active. When Sarig ordered Rabin to storm the British Police Mobile Forces station at Jenin in June 1946, the young deputy commander felt reconnaissance work inside the station was vital. He disguised himself as an electrician, and went by motorcycle to the station. There he easily gained admittance by pretending to have come to make a routine check; once inside he moved around freely, and left as soon as he had all the information he required.

Elated at his success, Rabin drove his motorcycle at break-neck speed to Haifa, where Allon, the over-all Palmach commander, and Sarig awaited him. In his haste he failed to notice the truck in front of him quickly enough, and crashed. He was thrown some distance and knocked unconscious. His next recollection was of waking up in the Rothschild Hospital in Haifa. His left leg had been broken in two places, and he was wearing a large cast. Still in possession of his soldierly instincts, he made sure that one of the Hagana operatives in the hospital transmitted the information he had obtained at Jenin to his commanders. Command of the Jenin operation was given to someone else, but in the event the mission was abandoned. After a brief time in hospital, Rabin went home to Tel Aviv to convalesce with his father in their flat on Hamagid Street.

On 18 June the Palmach decided to carry out a coordinated series of attacks on eleven bridges around the country in an attempt to deal a major blow to the British. In the attacks ten of the bridges were destroyed or severely damaged. The incident predictably angered the British, and provoked a widespread search for Hagana and Palmach leaders. On 29 June, 100,000 British soldiers and 1,500 police surrounded numerous Jewish settlements and virtually laid siege to them. Curfews were imposed on major cities with Jewish populations. Twenty-seven settlements were searched for arms and three thousand Jews were taken to detention camps at Atlit, Rafiah and Latrun. Most Hagana leaders had been forewarned of the British plan and had gone into hiding; relatively few arms were discovered.

On 'Black Saturday', as that day has since been called, Rabin, his father and a friend were arrested. They were taken to the British unit's headquarters in a school on Balfour Street, where the British informed Rabin that he and his father were on their wanted list. He and Nehemiah were conveyed to Latrun in an armoured car — not the most comfortable means of transport for someone with a broken leg. There they were fingerprinted and kept for several days, before being taken to Rafiah at the southern tip of the Gaza Strip for more permanent detention.

Life was hardly comfortable. The prisoners were crowded together into a few large huts. They were given thin stretchers and blankets, but little else. Things improved when the men were distributed among some twenty huts, where they were allowed newspapers and could listen to the radio, but had few other comforts. Nehemiah's dignified conduct under this regime served as a model for his son: 'Our being together in the same prison camp was a great comfort; in everything he did and in the way he behaved he had only one purpose: to lighten my load, in case things were getting me down.'[11]

Nehemiah was released after three weeks, but Rabin was detained for six months. The thought of escaping rarely crossed his mind. The Hagana and Palmach had already instructed the men that they were to avoid attempts to break out on their own, and instead wait for forces from the outside to free them. Indeed, during his stay at Rafiah, Rabin received word that the Palmach might attempt a rescue. At the same time, rumours began to circulate that the British planned to move Jewish prisoners to East Africa. According to the rescue plan which Rabin subsequently learned about, Palmach men were to attack by sea and evacuate the prisoners. 'We would have had to go a few kilometres on sand,' he recalls. 'I was scared to death that because of my leg they wouldn't risk taking me along. I walked about all day long to make sure that my leg would not fail me.' For two weeks he carried out the most intensive kind of physiotherapy to strengthen his leg. In the event, the rescue mission was abandoned, but Rabin's leg improved dramatically.

When a Jewish Agency representative, Dr Chaim Sheba, tried to obtain Rabin's release, the head of British intelligence replied, 'He'll remain in detention even if he breaks both legs.' The most that Sheba could do for him was to have him sent to the Gaza military hospital for treatment. The period of imprisonment gave Rabin time to think about his future which looked bleak. 'I found my leg misshapen and lifeless . . . I remain depressed, seeing myself as a semi-cripple for life and convinced that my leg would never again function properly.'[12] In view of his injured leg he felt his days as a soldier had come to an end, and used his spare time to study algebra, realizing it would be necessary if he were to resume his formal studies and re-apply to study water engineering at the University of California. However, it was not easy to decide to give up the only life he had known since leaving Kadoorie six years earlier, and he could not make any decision without reference to his commanding officers. He went to see Israel Galili, then the commander of the Hagana forces, and Yigal Allon, the commander of the Palmach. The meeting proved decisive for his future.

'You are free to do whatever you want,' Galili told him and then went on: 'The World War is over, but *our* war has only just started.' It was a subtle but clear-cut command. Rabin weighed his options briefly, and resolved to remain in the Palmach. With the battle for the Yishuv's survival imminent, he had no wish to be ten thousand miles away in California quietly engaged in studies.

Chapter 3

'The hell with it — turn the radio off'

The violent activities of the Jewish resistance movement increased during the winter of 1946-47, leaving the Mandatory Government with only two alternatives: to continue the frustrating struggle against an embittered and increasingly stubborn foe, or to get out and turn the entire problem over to the United Nations. Hoping to salvage the situation at the last minute, Foreign Secretary Ernest Bevin had proposed in that winter that 96,000 Jewish immigrants be permitted to enter Palestine over the next two years; that a new trusteeship under the UN be formed; and that a constituent assembly be called in four years to prepare a constitution for an independent Palestine, to come into force only after Jewish and Arab consent was given. But both Jews and Arabs turned the idea down. Hence, on 18 February, 1947 Bevin announced that Britain would submit the Palestine problem to the UN General Assembly. He did not say whether the British Government would abide by the UN's decision, but the meaning of Bevin's action seemed clear: Britain was paving the way for its departure from Palestine.

A United Nations Special Committee on Palestine (UNSCOP) was formed towards the end of June 1947. It held hearings in Palestine during the summer, went to Germany and Austria to interview displaced persons, and — perhaps most significantly — talked to the dazed refugees on the *Exodus*, a small wooden Hagana ship which had arrived in Palestine from Germany in July, and which had been turned back by the British. The members of UNSCOP heard how British troops had boarded the boat, dressed for combat in helmets and masks, armed with clubs, pistols and grenades. They also met Hagana officers, and realized the depth of their determination and confidence in their ability to defend the Jewish community against the Arab attacks, which would be the inevitable outcome of a recommendation for partition.

On 1 September, 1947 the committee produced its recommendations: the partition of Palestine into two states, and an international enclave consisting of Jerusalem and its surroundings, linked by an economic union. A minority recommendation suggested a federal Arab-Jewish state. Neither alternative satisfied Jews or Arabs. After two months of debate, the General Assembly adopted the majority report of UNSCOP. Britain was called upon to withdraw from Palestine by 1 May, 1948, and the two States were to be established by the following 1 July. A UN commission was to supervise and maintain order during the first two months. However, the Arabs opposed the UN decision, and a military confrontation between Jews and Arabs seemed all but inevitable. For that reason the Yishuv greeted the UN decision with a mixture of elation and apprehension.

Militarily, the odds seemed heavily in favour of the Arabs. Against the poorly armed and only partially trained Jewish forces, numbering when fully mobilized 650,000, the Arabs could draw on one million Palestinians and the regular armies of five Arab states — at least in theory. Hagana weaponry was limited, numbering at the start of the fighting only 10,000 rifles, 1,990 machine guns and 440 light machine guns. The Hagana's artillery was virtually non-existent and its air force lacking any sophisticated aircraft. The Arabs, moreover, had the advantage of tactical superiority. Being the ones who would start the war, they would gain an important advantage simply on the basis of that initiative. And they controlled most of the hilly areas of Palestine, while the Jewish forces were clustered in low-lying towns and settlements. The Arabs in general had superior weaponry and ready access to sources of supply in the Arab world. Significantly, they had the tacit support of the British as well. However, the Jewish forces had desperation on their side; they were fighting for survival. This, plus the fact that only 6,000 of the one million Palestinian Arabs had had any military training, gave them some kind of chance.

After his release from prison in the winter of 1946-47, Rabin was approached to take on a surprising new assignment. Yigal

Allon, the commander of the Palmach, was considering whom to appoint as head of the strike force's Second Battalion, whose main task was to guard the water pipeline which ran through eleven new settlements in the southern part of the country. The logical choice should have been someone experienced and senior; instead, Allon decided on Rabin, now twenty-five years old.

In his new job, Rabin joined in the endless debates about whether to use the traditional British military doctrine or the unconventional, untested home-grown methods of the Palmach. He held no brief for the British way, as he clearly demonstrated in the summer of 1947 when he gave Haim Laskov, British-trained veteran of the Hagana and at that time a security officer for the Palestine Electric Corporation, a tour of the defences of the Negev settlements under his command. Stopping at one of the concrete security towers ringing the settlements, Laskov berated Rabin for relying on these 'death traps', and argued that these watch towers would simply be targets for enemy armour, artillery and aircraft fire. An advocate of the Japanese bunker and slit trenches (foxholes), used regularly in the British army, Laskov noted that they were being employed only sparingly at the settlements. Rabin was convinced that the settlements would have to deal with only lightly armed Arab bands; the towers, with the advantage they offered of long-range observation, seemed preferable to foxholes. When regular Arab forces stormed these settlements during the War of Independence, they turned out to be useless; Laskov argued later that only those settlements which gave greater emphasis to slit trenches were able to defend themselves successfully.

When the United Nations finally issued their decision on 29 November, 1947, Rabin felt the same bitter-sweet emotion that others in the Yishuv were experiencing, knowing that a fierce struggle lay ahead for the Jewish community in Palestine. At that time he was assigned to Palmach staff headquarters in Tel Aviv, where he had the task of ensuring that the needs of the Palmach units around the country were met, often visiting commanders in the field for on-the-spot assessments. On one of these inspection tours, in February 1948, he visited Uzi Narkiss, then the local commander of the Etzion region, south of Jerusalem. Rabin's visit was plagued with trouble from the moment he landed. A young girl approached his plane while its propeller was still turning. Her hair was caught in it and she died instantly. Later, as Rabin and Narkiss talked, they heard a loud explosion. Two soldiers had been preparing land mines nearby when one of the mines exploded accidentally, killing one of them outright. The other died in a Tel Aviv hospital.

After hearing Narkiss describe the urgent problems of his men, especially their lack of ammunition, Rabin felt anguished at the precariousness of the defence situation. The danger was overwhelming, supplies were few, and the Jewish forces were heavily out-numbered. On 1 February, 1948, a general mobilization was called by the Jewish Agency and the Va'ad Leumi, and the Palmach called up men from the reserves. Though the fighting was intensive between December 1947 and the following spring, the war did not become truly conventional until May, when the British left and the regular forces of the neighbouring Arab nations attacked the Yishuv.

In the early part of 1948 the Jews found it increasingly difficult to get supplies through to the 100,000 Jewish residents of Jerusalem (one-sixth of the Yishuv, of whom two thousand lived in the crowded Jewish Quarter of the Old City). Normally, thirty truckloads of supplies a day drove along the Tel Aviv–Jerusalem route, but the Arabs stepped up their attacks during this period. They realized the deep significance Jerusalem held for the Yishuv and believed that an Arab victory over the Jews there would inflict a death blow to the entire Yishuv. Their attacks on the convoys carrying supplies to Jerusalem occurred for the most part in the beautiful, mountainous area between the ancient Roman fort of Castel and Shaar-Hagai. Between these two points the road runs through a narrow, deep, wooded ravine. Arab snipers hidden high above the road were easily able to pick off drivers and vehicles without the risk of being spotted and hit by return fire. On 24 March, hundreds of Arabs attacked one of the convoys. When the shooting was over, seventeen Jews were dead and fourteen armoured cars destroyed. Later that month, two more convoys bound for Jerusalem were ambushed; by the end of March efforts to send supply convoys through to the city had come to a standstill, and it was under virtual siege.

The Jews, however, were determined to open the road

regardless of the cost. At the end of March, David Ben-Gurion ordered the Hagana command to bring up a force of fifteen hundred men to break open the way to Jerusalem. Operation Nachshon, as it was called, was a success: in early April the Hagana captured the Arab strongpoint on Mount Castel, commanding the Tel Aviv–Jerusalem road, and opened up the route again for supplies. Meanwhile Rabin was mopping up Arab resistance in the villages near the road and making sure that no village was left intact enough to be used as a base of operations by the Arabs. Nachson's success brought demands from Hagana units around the country that the men borrowed for that operation should now be returned to help in the battles taking place elsewhere. Responsibility for guaranteeing the safety of the road fell once again to the Palmach, which had had the same task before Nachshon. To do the job, a new brigade was organized, the second to be formed from among the Palmach units. The Harel Brigade, as it was called, comprised two battalions; one was ordered to secure the eastern end of the road, the other, the western end. Its commander was Yitzhak Rabin.

The Hagana command had to make a difficult decision: whether to order Rabin's brigade to attack the Arabs in the villages near the road before letting the convoys through, or whether to try to guard the convoys as closely as possible without undertaking separate operations against the Arabs. Common sense dictated the strategy of the separate attacks, but time was of the essence: the Jews of Jerusalem desperately needed supplies. Rabin would have preferred to attack the Arab villages first, and let the convoys wait until the road was as safe as possible, but his counsel did not prevail.

Between 15 and 20 April, 1948, the five days during which the Harel Brigade was guarding the Jerusalem Corridor, three major convoys got safely through to Jerusalem and Rabin's men captured three Arab villages. Each convoy consisted of between 250 and 300 supply trucks — carrying food and (secretly) arms and ammunition — and extended for ten miles as they travelled the narrow, winding road. Fortunately the gentlemanly British officers were reluctant to search the women soldiers travelling in the vehicles, for whatever arms they found while frisking the men were confiscated. However, though the road was temporarily made safer for the convoys, the operation was carried out at considerable cost in human life, and ended before it could have a decisive effect, much to Rabin's regret.

The fighting during this brief period, as Rabin acknowledged later, was among the toughest he experienced in his whole military career. It was 'the most difficult part of the War of Independence for me, a war fought by those who believed and who were far more confident than could be expected — but a war with really empty hands.'[1] Exhausted from continuous fighting, with little ammunition, the Jewish forces went into battle under the worst possible conditions. As the fighting went on, and more and more of Rabin's men were killed or wounded, the survivors grew angry, despondent, bitter; they turned on each other, and they turned to Rabin for reinforcements, for some sign of hope. He could give them neither.

Oddly, his pleas for more help found some in the Hagana command openly sceptical that things could be as bad as he described them. Seemingly without justification, he acquired something of a reputation: 'He was not the only one to exaggerate the seriousness of a situation in order to get more equipment from the general staff and more reinforcements,' Yigael Yadin, then the Hagana's chief of operations, remembers, 'but he certainly succeeded in painting a situation in bleak terms.'[2] Rabin's frustration was real, and stemmed from his inability to muster more troops and, more importantly, from not being permitted to finish what he and his men had begun. For he had learned — much to his anger — that his brigade was to be diverted from the Corridor to Jerusalem itself. 'Operation Jebussi' was being planned, and the Harel Brigade was to join the Jerusalem-based Etzioni Brigade. He and his men were to go into the city on the next convoy. Rabin wrote much later that the decision to move the brigade was a 'serious mistake', for it meant that the Jerusalem Corridor, left undefended, would fall once again under Arab control.[3]

David Shaltiel, the Hagana commander in Jerusalem, summoned the Harel Brigade to the city after a series of events there had dramatically escalated the situation. On 13 April a convoy of doctors from the Hadassah Hospital and professors from the Hebrew University had been ambushed at Sheikh Jarrah, a section in east Jerusalem. The passengers were massacred and the vehicles captured while the British did nothing. Five days later Arab forces had taken over the Augusta Victoria Hospital on Mount Scopus, a vital strategic point because it overlooked the city. In addition, there were increasing reports of an imminent British evacuation of strategic positions inside Jerusalem, well before the 15 May deadline. Though reinforcements for the Jewish forces fighting in the city had been promised within ten days, Shaltiel felt the situation was urgent and asked the Hagana command for eight more companies at once.

Riding in Rabin's bumper-to-bumper convoy on 20 April were David Ben-Gurion and Yitzhak Sadeh, who was to command the impending Operation Jebussi. The 350-truck convoy, stretching for sixteen miles, was the largest ever to make the journey to Jerusalem. It carried loads of flour, rice, sugar, margarine and matzo, the traditional unleavened bread Jews use to celebrate the Passover festival. The vehicles at the head of the convoy arrived safely in Jerusalem; but thousands of Arabs hidden in the hills at Shaar-Hagai had planned a mile-long ambush. They opened up with a barrage of gunfire which damaged the first few vehicles to enter the ravine, and these blocked the way for those behind. Some of the drivers tried to make their way between the damaged vehicles but this only added to the confusion. The Arabs were well dug in, and efforts to dislodge them failed, but the return fire from the convoy was enough to hold them off.

Rabin realized that reinforcements were vital if the convoy was to be saved, and managed to get through the blockade to Ma'ale Ha'amisha, a kibbutz not far from Jerusalem. There he organized help which set out in the evening in armoured cars and on foot, and freed the convoy. All but six of the vehicles were able to get out of the ambush; but twenty Jewish soldiers were killed. Rabin, Ben-Gurion and Sadeh arrived safely in Jerusalem. However, the Arabs were again in control of the Jerusalem road, and Jerusalem was under siege once more.

Commanders like Yitzhak Sadeh were continually urging more aggressive action on the part of the Jewish forces within Jerusalem before the British left on 15 May, on the assumption that Arab resistance would be weaker before that date. They were eager to do battle with the Arabs, believing that well-managed offensives could turn the tide in the Jews' favour. Sadeh told Rabin that if only they could press home their attack now, 'Jerusalem will be ours forty-eight hours after the British leave.' He envisaged a simple mopping-up operation, failing to take into account the Arabs' own growing determination and eager anticipation of the British departure.

Rabin thought that for the Jewish forces to achieve the maximum impact against the Arabs, it was far better to cut off their supplies than to risk a head-on confrontation. Jewish control of the Ramallah–Jerusalem Road would eliminate Ramallah as a source of supply for the Arabs, an argument he made forcefully to David Shaltiel, but to no avail. In Shaltiel's opinion, the plight of the beleaguered Jews in the Old City demanded that attention be focused on the city itself rather than on its surroundings. Since the British were likely to be in Jerusalem until 15 May at least, Rabin felt it made better sense to concentrate on the suburbs, for the British still held the key strategic points inside the city, and occupation of those was essential to the control of Jerusalem. However, Shaltiel felt that the British presence, although a nuisance, was not so great an obstacle as to warrant further delay.

The Hagana formulated Operation Jebussi in late April. The plan was to cut off the Arabs' sources of supply while Jewish forces swept over the northern and southern fringes of the city, driving out the enemy and blocking their much-needed access routes. It was partly what Rabin had been advocating, though he had wanted Jewish forces to operate outside the city rather than from within. Had Jebussi succeeded, Jewish troops would have gained some of the most strategic points of the city — Nebi Samuel (the highest of the Judean hills) in the north, and the Arab quarter of Sheikh Jarrah and the Mount of Olives (both in the eastern part of the city), while other Hagana forces took control of the Arab quarters of Katamon, the German Colony, Talpiot, and Silwan (all in the south), thus virtually encircling the city.

From the very outset the operation met setbacks. Nebi Samuel was the first reversal, when the Jewish troops lost the vital element of surprise. An earlier raid against nearby Bet Iksa had succeeded, but the Arabs were alerted to the fact that a bigger attack was imminent and wisely dug in at Nebi Samuel, waiting for the Jews to make their move. When the battle was over, forty Jews lay dead, and the vital strategic point they had hoped to conquer was still in Arab hands. Sadeh and Rabin could do nothing but hope for better luck in the battle for Sheikh Jarrah, where a Jewish victory would effectively sever the Arab road link between the Old City and Ramallah. Ironically, though the attack was successful, the British proved to be the most serious problem: since Sheikh Jarrah was on their evacuation route, they insisted the Jewish forces withdraw from the section, promising not to turn it over to the Arabs after the Jews had left. Rabin's men refused, and the British countered with artillery and heavy tank fire. Rabin's troops were forced to depart from Sheikh Jarrah — but only temporarily. The British kept their word and permitted the Jewish soldiers to reoccupy the areas as soon as they themselves had left Jerusalem.

Rabin directed the battle for Katamon, which soon fell, but casualties were high, and conditions were made worse by the shortage of ammunition. At times Rabin's men had to stop fighting altogether and await the arrival of the plane which was flying in shells from Tel Aviv. Ten Hagana men died and another eighty were wounded in this battle, which also left eighty Arabs dead. With the fall of Katamon, Arab resistance in the southern part of Jerusalem began to falter, but it was only a partial victory, since Jewish forces were in control of only one of the three points they needed to conquer in order to turn the tide.

Typical of the frustrations Rabin experienced in the Jerusalem campaign was Operation Maccabi, a series of attacks which he directed in mid-May aimed at reopening the road to Jerusalem, but which failed to achieve the objective because his troops were summoned elsewhere. During the operation Rabin experienced serious difficulties in his personal relations with the men under his command, which made the entire enterprise unpleasant and unhappy for the young brigade commander. One reason for the considerable strain in relations has already been mentioned: the unusually high number of casualties suffered by his Harel Brigade, which had embittered the troops in earlier battles. Harel's two battalions had lost 220 men, with another 617 wounded, and 220 suffering from severe fatigue between April and June, 1948. In other words, roughly half of the 1,500-man brigade could be counted a casualty of one sort or another, a statistic that Rabin as the brigade commander had to take responsibility for. The casualty figures were on the men's minds and Rabin was a prime target for their anger. They were used to commanders who could mix easily with them, who could show their feelings with an affectionate slap on the back or a friendly word, whereas Rabin's apparent aloofness and serious manner placed a constraint on the relationship.

Rabin had many problems with one battalion commander in particular, Joseph Tabenkin, an outspoken, ambitious man whose nature clashed with the subtle, cautious, and introspective Rabin. The two men argued continuously over battle tactics, and because they were in senior positions their antagonism set the tone for relations between Rabin and the other men.

In Operation Macabbi the main target for the Harel Brigade was Bet Mahzir, a large Arab village which had been serving as a base of operations against Jewish convoys. Tabenkin thought the timing of the attack was wrong and made his opposition known to Rabin. He felt that the brigade was not ready to tackle such an important assignment as Bet Mahzir, but Rabin was adamant in his refusal to put off the attack. It began on 12 May and took three days to complete. Rabin had hoped that it would take only one day, and believed Tabenkin had deliberately slowed up the operation to give his men time to rest. In fact, according to Uzi Narkiss, who commanded the force that took the village on the third day, things went much more easily than he had expected; he blamed fog for the delay on the first day and the men's unwillingness to fight in daylight for the delay on the second.[4] Tabenkin replaced Rabin as commander of the Harel Brigade in July 1948 when Yigal Allon made Rabin his operations officer for Operation Dani. Allon has asserted that the change in the Harel Brigade command had nothing to do with Rabin's differences with Tabenkin or with others.[5]

Once Bet Mahzir had been taken, control of the road to Jerusalem was once more in Jewish hands. Because that control extended only to Shaar-Hagai, the Hagana pushed beyond it to the south-east, repairing the road where possible, until it maintained supremacy all the way to Hulda, near Latrun. However, both the Harel and Givati Brigades had to be removed from the Jerusalem Corridor to deal with the full-scale invasion of regular Arab armies that was beginning. Thus

Latrun, situated above the Tel Aviv–Jerusalem road, was left
for the Arabs to take without opposition — and the road to
Jerusalem was again blocked.

David Ben-Gurion stood before the National Council in the
small, shabby Tel Aviv Museum at 4 pm on 14 May, 1948 and
proclaimed the independence of the State of Israel. Under tight
security — and fearful that the British would try to pressurize
Jewish leaders into postponing the announcement — the Yishuv
established the first Jewish State for two thousand years. With
Jerusalem under siege, Tel Aviv was selected as the site of the
proclamation of statehood; but Jerusalem was chosen as the
capital of the new State. That evening came news that the
United States had recognized the new State; three days later,
the Soviet Union followed suit. The Council elected a
Provisional Council of State with Dr Chaim Weizmann as
President and David Ben-Gurion as Prime Minister.

While the Jews of Tel Aviv rejoiced in the streets, waving
flags, dancing and singing, Rabin and his men were battling for
the village of Bet Mahzir, sixty miles to the east. When the
announcement of statehood had come over the radio, an
exhausted soldier trying to sleep had yelled for it to be turned off.
Rabin himself was so tired that he gave no thought to the
significance of the broadcast: 'I was so preoccupied with the
battle problems that it took me hours to realize what a change
had taken place. But I always remember that tired soldier who
said, "The hell with it — turn the radio off." '[6]

At midnight, eight hours after the State was proclaimed, the
British High Commissioner sailed from Haifa, and the Mandate
came to an end. That same evening the regular armies of seven
Arab States (Syria, Iraq, Trans-Jordan, Egypt, Saudi Arabia,
the Yemen, and Lebanon) invaded Palestine, determined to
crush the Jews before they had time to put the new State on a
firm footing. Eleven days later, on 26 May, the Provisional
Government of Israel approved the creation of the Israel
Defence Forces (IDF) which were to be the one and only armed
force of the new country. Ya'acov Dori was the IDF's first chief
of staff, but owing to his poor health, Yadin, chief of operations
and second in command, functioned as the de facto chief of staff
throughout most of the War of Independence.

As independence was declared, the plight of the two thousand Jews in the Old City of Jerusalem became even more desperate. The Arabs, with the full knowledge of the British, had kept practically all Jewish traffic out of the Old City, though during December and January a few Hagana soldiers and some arms were smuggled into the quarter in trucks containing food and medical supplies. The 20,000 well-armed Arabs in the city (there were altogether 65,000 Arabs living in Jerusalem) hoped that the Jews of the Old City, half-starved and cut off from the Jews in the New City, would simply leave; but the Hagana could not surrender such precious territory without a fight. The option of a hasty evacuation was rejected and the decision made to defend the Quarter.

Arab attacks after 14 May against the Jews both inside and outside the walls of the Old City were stepped up. David Shaltiel decided to mount an operation on 18 May to break through the gates of the Old City and reach the besieged Jewish Quarter. He asked Rabin if he was prepared to send his troops in to help in the rescue. The question posed a serious dilemma for Rabin, since he had not been instructed to take part in the Old City attack by the general headquarters of the Hagana. Rabin sent his operations officer, Etiel Amichai, to talk to Shaltiel and after some discussion it was agreed to call Rabin into the deliberations. According to Shaltiel's plan, Harel units under Rabin would try to enter the Zion Gate, the closest to the Jewish Quarter, and provide a diversion to draw the Arabs away from the Jaffa Gate, where units of the Etzioni Brigade would try to break through. Rabin agreed to the plan, but with great reluctance.[7] For one thing, he could not understand why the main attack had to come at the Jaffa Gate, when the Zion Gate was much closer to the Jewish Quarter. For another, he was surprised to find that Shaltiel planned to use troops in the Jaffa Gate attack who were much less experienced than his own. He suggested instead that they combine their forces for one major assault on the Rockefeller Museum, at the north-west corner of the Old City outside the wall. The museum overlooked the only access road to the Old City, and whoever controlled the building could effectively keep enemy reinforcements from reaching the Old City. However Shaltiel was not to be persuaded and the two men exchanged harsh words before

Rabin agreed to participate in the attack.

In the event, an administrative breakdown caused the Etzioni Brigade units to arrive late for their planned attack on the Jaffa Gate, and they alighted from their armoured cars in full view of the Arabs, who successfully held them off. Ironically, the Jaffa Gate attack served to distract the Arabs' attention from Rabin's forces, who, meeting little resistance, captured Mount Zion outside the Zion Gate.

The next night, 19 May, they broke through the Zion Gate, bringing the besieged Jews much-needed supplies and ammunition. But their small force could not possibly hold out against the Arabs in a daylight attack, so they were forced to retreat towards Mount Zion under cover of darkness. Yigael Yadin asserts that the plan failed to secure the approval of the Hagana command 'and that created chaos'.[8] But the Jews of the Old City were by then nearly starving and desperately low on ammunition. About ten days later, plans were laid for another attack through the Zion Gate in the south and the New Gate in the north. However, on the morning of the planned attack — 28 May — representatives of the Jews in the Old City began discussing surrender terms with the Arabs. Among the bewildered soldiers watching from Mount Zion four hundred yards away, as the Jews walked to Arab headquarters carrying a white flag, was Rabin. As part of the surrender terms, 290 Jews between the ages of 14 and 70 were taken prisoner. Another 1200 were allowed to pass through the lines to the New City.

The failure of the Jews to relieve the Old City in May 1948 left a legacy of bitterness, especially among those who felt that the troops under Rabin should have stayed on and fought during the 19 May attack, instead of retreating. Some even criticized Rabin personally, but he has justified the withdrawal on the grounds that 'if the force had remained, it would not have been able to succeed.'[9]

The crucial part of the war occurred between 15 May and 10 June, a period of impressive Arab gains and mounting Jewish anxiety about their very survival. While the Jews searched about desperately for money and arms, the Arabs made the most of their advantage: the Egyptians brought their troops within twelve kilometres of Rehovot; the Jordanians gained control of the Arab towns of Ramla and Lydda (where Israel's only international airport was situated); Syria had put a bridgehead across the Jordan River in the Upper Galilee; the Jewish Quarter in Jerusalem's Old City had fallen; and Israeli attempts to capture the key towns of Latrun and Jenin had been staved off. Heavy casualties, shortages of arms, and a dwindling supply of manpower placed the Jews in a precarious position in those early months of the fighting. However, the Hagana was generally better trained and more highly motivated than the Arabs, factors that eventually proved decisive. Many of the Arab attacks against Jewish settlements were being turned back. Jewish forces were liberating both the Upper and Lower Galilee, including the port of Haifa. By June the war was at a stalemate, paving the way for the one-month cease-fire which took effect on 10 June.

Following Ben-Gurion's ban on separate armed groups within the new state, the right-wing Irgun organization had agreed on 1 June to dissolve itself. In early June, however, the Irgun ship *Altalena* set sail from southern France with a cargo of 5,000 rifles, 250 light machine guns and a number of anti-tank weapons. It carried five hundred men aboard. The Provisional Government of Israel ordered the Irgun to turn the ship over to it, but this demand was met with a staunch refusal. The ship anchored off Kfar Vitkin on 20 June, as Israeli soldiers waited on land, prepared to prevent any attempt to unload the arms. Many former Irgun men now enlisted in the Defence Forces left their units and came to Kfar Vitkin, but the attempted revolt failed, and they surrendered to the Israeli army units. During the night the *Altalena* set sail for Tel Aviv to the south, where it anchored on 22 June opposite the Ritz Hotel, then the headquarters of the Palmach.

Rabin had come to the headquarters for a meeting, but arrived early in order to visit Leah, who was working there. As he approached the building he saw the *Altalena* and two landing craft nearing the shore. The Government had ordered the Irgun to hand over the ship or it would be taken by force; units of the Tel Aviv Brigade had begun to deploy themselves along the beaches. As the ship approached, the soldiers decided to disperse, abandoning their weapons and creating a total breakdown of order. Allon, the Palmach's commander, was summoned by Hagana headquarters to take command of the situation, but was only there for a short time, leaving Rabin, who had known nothing of the background to the *Altalena* affair, effectively in charge.

He had only forty men under him, most of whom had been wounded at the front and were convalescing at headquarters, carrying out the functions of military policemen in the meantime. Rabin began to organize them for battle, unthinkable though it was that they should take up arms against fellow Jews. When the *Altalena* again refused to surrender, the Irgunists and Rabin's men exchanged fire, both sides using machine guns, hand grenades, and rifles. Rabin picked up the phone and spoke to Moshe Kelman, the commander of the third Palmach battalion, telling him to bring his unit to headquarters immediately. The fighting lasted ten hours. Eventually, the ship was set on fire by a field gun from the shore. The passengers and crew were helped to safety by the men of the defence units. Fourteen Irgunists died in the battle; Rabin lost one of his men and several were wounded. The army took control of the boat and the day after Rabin began to prepare a Palmach unit nicknamed the 'Desert Beasts' for a raid on the Irgun headquarters on King George Street in Tel Aviv. On 20 September, 1948 the Government gave the Irgunists twenty-four hours to agree to obey all the laws of the infant state: all its members liable for enlistment were to serve in the Israel Defence Forces, not in separate units. The Irgun surrendered its arms and complied.

The *Altalena* affair had been the most serious test the new state had had to confront, but Rabin never had any doubt about the morality of the Government's action in taking up arms against fellow Jews. To him the principle of statehood was at stake, and the Irgunists were challenging that principle: 'It was a threat to the legal Government and the local forces.'[10]

With the advent of Operation Dani in July, Rabin took on the first of a series of planning posts which would occupy him for the rest of the war. The Arabs were too close to Tel Aviv, necessitating an operation against Ramla and Lydda — successful, as it turned out, but in the process Rabin had a close scrape with death. He and Allon had decided to move their command headquarters to a more advanced position so they would have a better idea of how the fighting was progressing. Allon was behind the wheel of an open Ford convertible, and had decided to take a short-cut through a field as the car approached the front line just south of Ramla. Suddenly the car was jolted by the explosion of a land mine underneath the front wheels and the two men were thrown out. The mine ripped through the car, completely destroying the vehicle, but neither man was badly hurt. Rabin received a minor foot injury. A sapper had to be summoned to lead them safely out of the field without triggering off other mines.

Rabin never actually proposed marriage to Leah, but neither doubted that they would marry each other. The ceremony took place on 23 August, 1948 at the Bet Shalom (House of Peace) in Tel Aviv, and was obviously an ordeal for the 26-year-old officer. He had been shy about his relationship with Leah up to the very day of the wedding; he told Allon and others whom he invited that the wedding was to start thirty minutes later than was actually the case, in the hope that the ceremony would be over by the time they got there. However, the rabbi was thirty minutes late, so Rabin's subterfuge failed to work, and all the guests had arrived by the time the ceremony began.

Yitzhak appeared in uniform as did his comrades in arms. Leah wore a white dress, white sandals and white stockings. She had planned to wear specially bought Greek sandals which had crossover thongs half up her knees, not the stockings. Her aunt, however, feared that the rabbi would refuse to perform the ceremony if Leah wore no stockings; so seconds before the event, Leah strapped the sandals on over the stockings.

After the wedding the newly-weds moved into Leah's parents' flat on Rothschild Boulevard in Tel Aviv, their home for the next two and a half years. It was a choice dictated both by concern for Leah's ageing parents and by the Rabins' lack of finances.

Rabin had no time to get used to his new marital state. The war was far from over, and within a day of the ceremony Yeroham Cohen, then an intelligence officer for the newly created Southern Command, was pounding on his door. Allon was waiting for Rabin to join them at the nearby Workers' Restaurant, where he asked Rabin to serve as deputy commander of the Southern Front in the role of chief operations officer. The second cease-fire, which began on 10 July, 1948, was still in existence. Planning for Southern Front operations was to begin right away, since everyone expected the war to resume in the autumn. During that summer, the IDF created military ranks, and Rabin, upon his appointment to the Southern Front, became a Segan-Aluf (lieutenant-colonel), the third highest rank in the new army.

The cease-fire along the Southern Front remained intact until the autumn, but it slowly gave way to renewed fighting between Israeli and Egyptian forces. On 6 October the Israeli high command ordered an all-out attack on the Negev in an attempt to drive the Egyptians out once and for all. It began nine days later and lasted a week. By 22 October Operation 'Ten Plagues', as it was called, resulted in the Israeli forces opening the main road to the Negev and capturing Beersheba, as well as the coastal strip between Ashdod and Yad Mordechai. But although the Egyptian army had been pushed further south — away from the populated areas of the new Jewish State — they remained in the Negev, inside Israeli territory.

Although 'Ten Plagues' ended in a formal truce between the Israeli and Egyptian troops, fighting persisted as both sides sought to improve their positions. Egyptian soldiers at the Faluja crossroads, south-east of the Mediterranean port of Ashdod, refused to surrender to the Israelis in early November, despite being surrounded and short of food. Only after the Egyptian high command had acknowledged that it could offer no reinforcements did the Faluja commander, Major Said Taha, agree to talk about surrender terms.[11] On 11 November Yeroham Cohen spoke to the Egyptians and arranged for Taha and his fellow officers to meet Israeli commanders at Kibbutz Gat, an Israeli settlement some twenty-five kilometres east of Ashkelon. Cohen escorted the Egyptians there and introduced them to the Israeli officers, though he carefully avoided using the Israelis' names in keeping with the Government's policy of secrecy in military matters. Though the main negotiations were undertaken by Allon and Taha, Rabin had a chance to talk to a young Egyptian liaison officer named Gamel Abdul Nasser. Nasser asked whether the insignia Allon and his men were wearing — a sword between two ears of corn — was that of the

Palmach. When told it was, Nasser smiled ruefully and said, 'That being so, everything is clear to me.' He was intensely interested to know how the Israelis had managed to force the British to leave. Rabin explained what military measures were used, and Nasser smiled appreciatively. 'You know,' he said with a wry grin, 'we are fighting the wrong enemy at the wrong place at the wrong time. Our main enemy is the British, and our main problem is how to gain real independence. We should be fighting the colonial power rather than you.'[12]

In November 1948, after much bitter argument, Palmach headquarters were finally disbanded. The actual decision had been taken by Ben-Gurion, as head of the Provisional Government, on 7 October, but it was postponed when heavy fighting broke out in the south. Oddly enough, a separate Palmach Command under Yigal Allon had existed even after the formation of the Israel Defence Forces in May 1948. The three Palmach brigades had been placed under the control of the IDF's general headquarters in the spring of that year, but they still maintained their distinctive character. The Palmach Command after May had only administrative responsibilities, since the general headquarters directed strategy and tactics were at the discretion of the local brigade and front commanders. Hence, it became increasingly inefficient for this independent Palmach structure to continue.

As the dissolution of the Palmach was being implemented, the Israeli forces in the south prepared themselves for more fighting — the Egyptian army was still not broken, and remained unwilling to negotiate an armistice with the Jewish State. The Israeli goal was to control the entire Negev, but the main Egyptian forces were entrenched in two spots there: along the Mediterranean coast between Rafiah and Gaza and, further inland, between the villages of El Auja and Bir Asluj (south of Beersheba). During December 1948 the IDF tried to drive the Egyptians from these places in Operation Horev.

In early December, the Israeli command decided to concentrate its attack on Auja, since the Egyptians there presented a greater threat to the central Negev than they did along the coastal strip. But getting to Auja appeared nearly impossible, for the Egyptians controlled the main north-south

artery from Bir Asluj. The Israelis, referring to old maps, found
another, by now largely forgotten route from Beersheba to Auja,
an ancient Roman road that connected the two sites in an
almost direct line. Because the road had not been used for many
years its surface had deteriorated, making it difficult if not
impossible to transport heavy trucks and tanks. The chief
engineer of the Southern Front reported gloomily that the road
was impassable. Front commander Allon then sent Rabin's
deputy, Amos Horev, who thought that it was still possible to
move on the road. The chief engineer of the IDF came down
from Tel Aviv to examine it: he concluded that tanks would not
be able to make the journey. Finally, on 17 December, Allon
sent Rabin, who said he believed it would be possible to use the
route if some repairs were made to the road. He was right, and
for that decision he won widespread praise. Ten days later, on 27
December, Israeli forces captured Auja, and were thus
positioned for a further advance into the Sinai and an attack on
the rest of the Egyptian army.

Acting without orders from the high command in Tel Aviv,
Israeli forces under Allon and Rabin thrust further south on
27 December, into the region of Abu Ageila and El Arish, part of
Egyptian territory inside Sinai, increasing the fears of the
outside Powers, particularly the US and Britain, that Israel
intended to remain in the Sinai. But Allon and Rabin felt the
Israelis would be missing a golden opportunity to inflict serious
damage on the Egyptian forces and, in the process, to force them
to talk about making peace with the Jewish State on a serious
basis. On 29 December Abu Ageila fell to the Israelis. That
morning, exhilarated at their success, Rabin, Allon and Cohen
drove into the village, established a headquarters tent, and
began planning an attack on El Arish, further south along the
Mediterranean coast. By midday, they were in a convoy on its
way to El Arish, but three miles outside the Arab town the
Israelis received orders from Yadin, the IDF's chief of operations
in Tel Aviv, to halt the drive.

Allon sent for a Piper Cub in order to fly immediately to Tel
Aviv to protest personally to Ben-Gurion. He ordered Nahum
Sarig, the commander of the Negev Brigade who was about to
lead the drive into El Arish, to march on the town the next
morning unless he had heard to the contrary. Rabin and Cohen

drove to Beersheba to wait in the Southern Front's communications van for word from Allon, who finally phoned at 2 am. He had bad news. The brigade was to go no further. Rabin was furious.[13] He was sure that an Israeli victory was imminent. Gloomily, he and Cohen drove through the night until they reached Abu Ageila, where they passed word to Sarig to make no further approach toward El Arish.

During the next week, Allon struggled to convince Ben-Gurion that Israeli forces should finish the task of defeating the Egyptians at El Arish. The Prime Minister resisted all pleas. He himself had come under strong pressure from Britain and the US to withdraw Israeli troops from Egyptian soil. Furthermore, he feared that Israeli military activity in the Sinai would interfere with international efforts to bring the Arabs and Israelis together at a peace conference. He dismissed Allon's and Rabin's contention that leaving the Egyptians in full strength and unchallenged so close to the centres of population in Israel might trigger another war in the near future.

Armistice negotiations between Israel and Egypt began on 13 January, 1949 at the Hotel of Roses on the Island of Rhodes. Rabin attended the talks as a member of the Israeli delegation, representing the Southern Front. The senior Hagana commanders had wanted Allon to go, but he refused, still angry that the military campaign against Egypt had ended so abruptly. He would have liked Israel to take the Gaza Strip, the southern half of the Negev, and the Hebron Mountains before negotiations got under way. The country would then have been in a better position to keep the Egyptians at bay and to make another assault on Jerusalem — this time from the rear. However Ben-Gurion would not countenance the idea.[14]

Allon could have sent any of three men working under him: Rabin, Amos Horev, or Zarubavel Arbel, chief of intelligence for the Southern Front. He was not eager to send Arbel since he wanted him to work on Operation Fait Accompli (the campaign to capture Eilat, the southern port on the Gulf of Aqaba, and the southern Negev from the Jordanians). Rabin, too, wanted to stay and participate in the Negev campaign and he suggested that Horev go in his place; but Ya'acov Dori, the chief of staff of the IDF, insisted that if Allon wasn't going, then Rabin must: as operations officer he was the most knowledgeable about force deployments and terrain. Allon persuaded Rabin that it was indeed important for him to attend. 'See to it,' he told him, 'that no agreement is reached which is less than peace. And don't agree to anything which gives us less than Gaza.'[15]

Rabin had a personal reason for not wanting to participate in the talks. He was unsure how to tie a necktie — as were many other Israelis, who normally shunned them in the warm climate of the Middle East — and at Rhodes he would have to wear a tie to all the meetings! However, before he left, Yeroham Cohen made up a tie and loosened it sufficiently so it could be slipped over the head. But that was not the end of the story. When the Israelis and Egyptians were about to sit down for a negotiating session one day in the hotel, Rabin was missing. As representative of the Southern Front, they could not begin without him. Yigael Yadin, the leader of the delegation, found him in his room looking most dejected. It transpired that a valet had spotted the made-up tie and decided it needed ironing. Without reference to Rabin, he had taken it away, pressed it, and returned it — unmade. Now Rabin was at a loss, and had decided that to miss the session was the only possible solution. Yadin tied it for him and the two men proceeded downstairs to carry on with the business of making peace.[16]

Rabin's presence at the talks was particularly helpful to Yadin, who felt relieved that an officer from the Southern Front was on hand to give advice and support. The two men developed a good relationship that was cemented partly by the secret planning they were engaged in for the forthcoming Operation Fait Accompli.

Rabin, reflecting the generally gloomy mood in the Southern Command, felt ambivalent about the negotiations. He participated in them, offered advice to the best of his ability, but wondered — like Allon — why the talks were taking place before the Israelis had beaten the Egyptians on the battlefield.

When he was not involved in the talks, he took part in some of the sports provided in the hotel. He learned how to play billiards and mastered the game well enough to beat most of his challengers. He played table tennis too, usually partnered by Yadin. The games room at the hotel could be said to have played a crucial part in the negotiations for it was there that

Israeli and Egyptian officers mingled during the recesses, and though at first both sides were cool, friendlier relations did develop. Rabin learned as much about the real aims and aspirations of the enemy in that room as he did at the negotiating table. What he found out both pleased and disturbed him. He was glad to hear the Egyptians say that peace was inevitable and that the Rhodes talks were an important part of the process of achieving it; but less pleasing was the Egyptian view that it might not be possible to attain true peace as quickly as the Israelis had hoped — that it might even take years. Rabin remembers: 'Their mood was optimistic, even euphoric, but not for the immediate future. They said: "It is impossible *now* to make peace, but once we establish a relationship, etc. etc., *then* we hope that it will be possible." '[17] Rabin deduced that the Egyptians meant they could not make peace until certain military objectives had been achieved, for the Egyptian people would not accept peace on those terms.

Though hopeful about the prospects for peace, Rabin was also a realist. He knew there was still work to be done on the battlefields, and he disliked the direction the Rhodes talks were taking. On 10 February, two weeks before the agreement was finally signed, he wrote to Allon that he felt that the Israelis were giving too much away at the peace table.[18] Except for Yadin and Rabin, the other members of the Israeli delegation were prepared to accept — more or less — Egyptian demands which Rabin thought would erode many of the gains made on the Southern Front. 'In my opinion,' Rabin wrote to his commander, 'any concession now is too early. We have had a long breathing space, and we can endure a war of nerves better than the Egyptians.'

The Egyptians were demanding that Israeli forces vacate the Gaza Strip fringes and make the entire Negev a neutral zone, and that they should withdraw from Beersheba, the key town in the southern Negev. Yadin returned to Israel for consultations, carrying Rabin's letter to Allon with him. Rabin was confident that Yadin would not return to Rhodes unless he got a clear decision on standing firm with the Egyptians. 'Except for the two of us,' Rabin wrote to Allon, referring to Yadin and himself, 'all the members of the delegation are ready for additional compromises . . . simply to achieve an agreement with the

Egyptians. It is possible that, after coming here as a senior member of the military delegation, I will be forced to put my signature to something I cannot agree to.' He asked Allon to consider replacing him with Horev or Arbel: 'I have had enough of diplomacy and politics.'

Arriving in Israel, Yadin bore the news that Rabin could not be a party to the agreement under present circumstances. He asked Allon to persuade him to sign the agreement, believing Israel had little choice. Allon retorted that if he were Rabin, he would not sign the document either. The front commander answered Rabin's letter, sending his reply back with Yadin the next day, 15 February. 'Naturally,' he wrote, 'the talks are not only influenced by the military situation. The political element is the determining factor . . . Our mood here is not optimistic. I'm afraid that the blow we inflicted on the Egyptians has not been exploited sufficiently in the negotiations and it seems to me that the enemy is growing stronger . . . I know that it is not in your power to greatly influence the decision. But my situation is thus . . . The atmosphere is poisoned and they [i.e. Ben-Gurion and Moshe Sharett, the Foreign Minister] can't bear advice contrary to their views, which, of course, are slanted by political connections and quite a bit of outside pressure.' Allon added that he would try to make his feelings known to Ben-Gurion, although he saw no hope of persuading the Prime Minister to share his own and Rabin's view of the negotiations at Rhodes. 'I understand your fear that at the end you will be forced to sign a document of compromise, but Yadin has promised me that it will not be so. Nevertheless, if the decision is taken out of our hands, you will act, of course, according to your conscience. My suggestion about sending Zarubavel [Arbel] or Amos [Horev] in your place has been refused, so carry on trying to influence the talks . . . I hope that we shall see each other soon . . . Shalom from all the friends who are simply longing for your return and are cheered in the meantime by the 'Halutzot' [Pioneering] story that's going the rounds about you and your tie.'

Rabin was furious at what the Israelis were about to sign. 'Why should Egypt get a slice of Palestine?' he asked Walter Eytan, one of the delegation's leaders, a few hours before the signatures were about to be put to the document.[19] Eytan told him: 'An armistice with Egypt is worth the Gaza area. And besides, this is only a temporary military armistice. When we have full-scale peace talks, then we can press for better boundaries.' Rabin was not convinced. He felt that by leaving Egypt in control of the Gaza Strip and Jordan in control of the Hebron Mountain region south of Jerusalem, the likelihood of another round of war was greatly increased. He consulted Allon, who could offer him no comfort: 'We have to obey orders, but since the absence of your signature is not going to reduce the legality of the document, if you have finished your job and have drawn the best possible map, you might as well come home.'[20]

On the night before the signing, the Israelis and Egyptians celebrated with a festive banquet which Rabin attended, though he did not intend to sign the next day. Both sides were in high good humour. At one point Colonel Rahmani, an Egyptian officer, asked why the Israelis had not struck harder in Gaza during Operation Horev. Rabin explained that the Gaza thrust was simply an Israeli feint to distract the Egyptians from the real assault farther inland. 'You should have attacked Gaza,' Rahmani told him. 'It would have caused us quite a setback.'

That same night Rabin flew home on a UN plane. He carried with him an unusual item: a carton of butter. It was a present for Leah's mother, who missed this precious commodity more than anything else during Israel's austerity. Allon congratulated him on his work at Rhodes, and on his integrity in refusing to sign the armistice accord. 'This agreement,' he told Rabin, 'will not bring peace. If Egypt really wanted peace, they would have negotiated for it immediately without this armistice. The cease-fire will eventually bring a new war with Egypt.'[21] Rabin agreed.

The armistice agreement was signed on 24 February and with it came the hope that the Arab–Israeli conflict might be on its way to a peaceful resolution. But, since nobody believed that it would happen quickly, each side had tried to get the most out of the peace talks. Israel, for her part, had fought off Egyptian efforts to force an Israeli withdrawal from the entire southern Negev. Egypt managed to retain its hold over the Gaza Strip. It was agreed that the Jewish State would keep Beersheba, but that everything west of a line running between that city and Eilat would be an area of restricted military movement for the

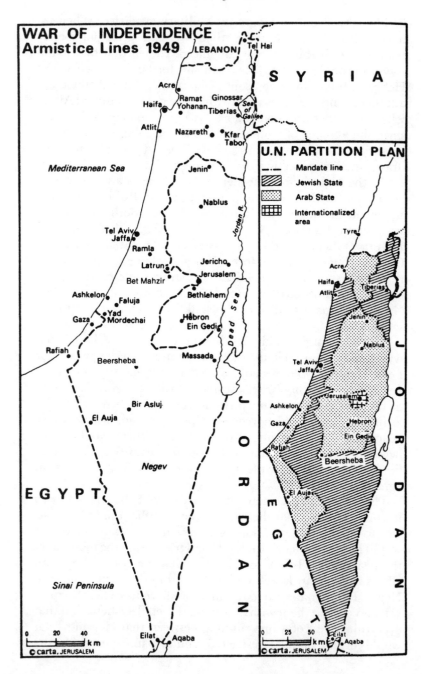

WAR OF INDEPENDENCE
Armistice Lines 1949

LEBANON   Tel Hai

S Y R I A

Acre
Ramat   Ginossar
Yohanan   Sea
Haifa   Tiberias   of
Galilee
Atlit   Nazareth   Kfar
Tabor

Mediterranean Sea

Jenin

Nablus

Tel Aviv
Jaffa
Ramla
Latrun   Jericho
Bet Mahzir   Jerusalem
Ashkelon   Bethlehem
Faluja
Yad   Hebron
Gaza   Mordechai   Ein Gedi
Rafiah

Beersheba   Massada

Bir Asluj

El Auja

Negev

E G Y P T

Sinai Peninsula

0   20   40
km
© carta, JERUSALEM
Eilat   Aqaba

J O R D A N

Jordan R.

Dead Sea

U.N. PARTITION PLAN

-·-·   Mandate line
////   Jewish State
····   Arab State
Internationalized
area

Tyre

Acre
Haifa   Tiberias
Atlit
Jenin

Nablus

Tel Aviv
Jaffa
Jerusalem
Ashkelon
Gaza   Hebron
Ein Gedi
Rafiah   Beersheba

El Auja

J O R D A N

E G Y P T

0   25   50
km
© carta, JERUSALEM
Eilat   Aqaba

Israelis. Everything to the east of the line would be an area of restricted military movement for the Egyptians. In effect, this gave Israel the freedom of operation it desired to act against the Jordanians without violating the armistice accord with Egypt. Plans for Operation Fait Accompli were already under way and the Israelis, in pressing the Egyptians to agree to this territorial division, knew exactly how they intended to deploy their troops in the Negev region. On 6 March the Israelis began the operation against the Jordanians, and six days later raised the Israeli flag over Eilat, 155 miles south of Beersheba, the final phase of the War of Independence. As part of the operation, the southern Negev had been conquered and the western shores of the Dead Sea, Massada, Ein Gedi and the Judean wilderness secured.

Chapter 4

Chief of Staff

The tiny Jewish State had achieved its independence in a bloody, 17-month-long war which had claimed 6,000 Jewish lives, slightly more than one per cent of the entire Yishuv — and more than in all subsequent wars combined. Soldiers, exhausted from the long battle, thankfully donned civilian clothes again, wondering how long it would take to make the new State of Israel truly secure. Most accepted the painful reality that it would be a long time. Israel, after all, was bordered to the north, east, and south by hostile neighbours who, despite defeat, were still not ready to live in peace with the Jews. Even after Egypt (in February 1949), Lebanon (in March 1949), Jordan (in April 1949) and Syria (in July 1949) had signed armistice agreements with Israel, they remained bent on its destruction, using every kind of hostility short of all-out war: an economic blockade was imposed; diplomatic and trade relations were withheld; transit to and from Israel through the Suez Canal and Arab countries was forbidden; a campaign of terrorism began. The one crack in the otherwise impenetrable wall was the Mandelbaum Gate, which separated Jordanian-controlled East Jerusalem (which included the Old City) from Israeli-held West Jerusalem. There, traffic could move both ways; it was the only crossing point between Israel and the Arab world — and its use was confined by the Jordanians to non-Jews.

With the War of Independence over, the Israelis turned to the task of gathering in all those Jews who wanted to immigrate. By virtue of a law passed in the Knesset in July 1950, known as the 'Law of Return', every Jew automatically had the right to immigrate to Israel and become an Israeli citizen. It was Israel's answer to the Peel Commission, the White Paper and Ernest Bevin, a declaration to the world that the gates were open. With that, Jewish immigrants poured into the new country, stateless, homeless, the persecution they had suffered in World War Two still a living nightmare. In 1949 alone nearly 250,000 came; and by the end of 1951, Israel's population had increased to 1.5 million, more than double the figure at the time of the War of Independence.

When the war was over, senior IDF officers realized that the time had come for a thorough review and proper organization of the armed forces: future wars would be far more sophisticated and on a larger scale. However, they found it difficult to persuade the population at large of the necessity for an institutionalized army. The sheer relief of seeing hostilities come to an end left little room for enthusiasm for the project. Some 80,000 Israelis were demobilized during the summer of 1949, and, with that, the standing army virtually disintegrated. But in time the modern Israel armed forces took shape, their basic outlines drawn up in the 1949 Defence Law. Men and Women were conscripted for two years' military service at the age of 18. Men were to serve 31-day periods in the reserves annually until the age of 39, and then two-week periods annually until the age of 55. Through the years, the period of compulsory service has been lengthened to three years. Reserve service fluctuates with the rise and fall of tensions: after the Yom Kippur War of 1973, for example, men served 30–40 days a year. Few women were actually called into the reserves though they have always played a prominent role, sometimes even in combat. During the War of Independence, they took an active part in the fighting, but afterwards the IDF limited them to staff work. They have, however, always received combat training.

The main threat to Israel's security in the early 1950s came from Arab infiltrators whose entry into Israel was facilitated by the refusal of Arab states to police the armistice lines: in 1951, for instance, 137 Israelis were killed or wounded. But the Israeli army was in no position to mount an effective campaign to stop this terrorist acticity, and the Government was too preoccupied with immigration to devote much attention to the problem.

Clashes with the Syrians on Israel's northern border — in particular a well-publicized one at Tel Mutilla, a small rocky hill north of Lake Kinneret, on 2 May, 1951 — showed how undertrained the Jewish forces were. In the Tel Mutilla incident, a small force of Syrian infantry had stormed the demilitarized zone near the border and occupied the hill. Only after four days of bitter fighting did the Israelis finally succeed in forcing them back — with the loss of 27 Israeli soldiers, far too many considering the size of the Syrian unit. The length of the battle also indicated that something was amiss in the army's training methods. Other Arab raids and similar Israeli responses emphasized the point.

The end of the war had marked a major turning point in Rabin's life. Had he wished, he might have entered civilian life and tried to acquire the university degree in water engineering that he had hoped for at the close of his high-school days. But by temperament he was a military man, fired by the need to provide security for the new nation. The wretched fighting conditions he had experienced, particularly during the battles for the Jerusalem road in early 1948, left him determined to do what he could to make sure Jewish soldiers were better equipped to fight the next war, if there should be one. 'I had sworn,' he said, 'that if I lived to see the end of the war and continued in military life, I would do everything in my power to see to it that we should never fight under such conditions again.'[1]

However, continuing in the Israel Defence Forces was no easy matter for a veteran of the Palmach like Rabin. Although the organization had been disbanded in November 1948, its officers retained a strong sense of allegiance to it. Ben-Gurion could not tolerate this seemingly misplaced loyalty and embarked upon a campaign to root them out of senior army positions. Since most Palmach veterans were associated with the Mapam Party (the union of a 1948 merger between the Ahdut Avoda and Hashomer Hazair Parties), the chief rival of Ben-Gurion's Mapai Party, the campaign the premier was waging had the appearance of a political struggle. Yigal Allon, for example, the commander of the Southern Front, discovered while abroad that he had been relieved of his post.

Proud of the Palmach's record, Rabin found his loyalty divided. He agreed with Ben-Gurion that it was right — and necessary — to disband the Palmach, but he was bound by strong ties of friendship and brotherhood to his wartime colleagues in the strike force. It pained him that the Palmach, without which 'a real catastrophe would have befallen the Jews', was being shunted aside when the IDF could benefit from it. 'We won the War of Independence,' he remarked sorrowfully of those days, 'but we lost it within the army.'[2] In June 1949 Rabin was appointed commander of the Negev Brigade. In the autumn of that year he was faced with the most serious test of his loyalty in the clash between the IDF and the Palmach.

The Palmach had called its third national conference for 14 October, 1949 at the north Tel Aviv Exhibition Stadium. IDF officers who were Palmach veterans were placed in an awkward position, since Ben-Gurion had issued orders banning uniformed officers from attending. Rabin, now the most senior-ranking Palmach veteran still in uniform, was in a dilemma. He did not want to disappoint his Palmach colleagues by not appearing; but there had been rumours that the prime minister would dismiss any officer who did attend, and Rabin did not want to jeopardize his career.

Realizing that it was particularly important to keep Rabin, as the most senior officer, away, Ben-Gurion devised a plan that would give him an excuse not to attend the conference. The prime minister asked Rabin to meet him on the evening that the conference began, in order to go over some military matters. Rabin could scarcely refuse — or at least, so Ben-Gurion thought. The two men began talking at 4:30 pm in the prime minister's home in Tel Aviv. The conference was due to start four hours later. Among the subjects they discussed was the conference: Rabin told the prime minister that he was wrong to put the men of the Palmach in such a dilemma. Ben-Gurion replied simply that there was no room in the army for separate organizations. But the question of Rabin's own attendance at the conference did not arise. At 7 pm Ben-Gurion suggested that they break for a meal and continue talking afterwards. Looking at his watch, Rabin replied that he had to go somewhere, quickly made his excuses, and left. The prime minister made no comment, but he must have known where Rabin was going. Dashing home to change out of uniform into a white shirt, Rabin, still out of breath, told Leah about his meeting with the prime minister, then ran off to the reunion, arriving late.

This act of defiance on Rabin's part might be construed as courageous, or foolish; but it certainly demonstrated his integrity and the strength of his convictions. 'I saw in Ben-Gurion's order,' he said later, 'a demand to dissociate myself from my friends, with whom I had fought and passed through the seven circles of hell both before and during the war.'[3] In the event, the premier did not dismiss him for attending the conference, but two days later he was reprimanded for breach of discipline. Though he escaped punishment at the time, Rabin was to pay for it with the retardation of his military career. He did not become chief of staff until 1 January, 1964 — fifteen years after the incident — whereas some believe he might have been given the appointment as early as 1953 — after Mordechai Maklef and before Moshe Dayan — had he not defied Ben-Gurion that evening. For in late 1952 Maklef had wanted to appoint Rabin deputy chief of staff, but Ben-Gurion vetoed the idea, citing the conference incident. Rabin himself acknowledges that his decision to attend the conference 'had certain implications for the way that I moved through the echelons of the upper command'.[4] The incident was still very much in Ben-Gurion's mind in 1960, when, shortly after he appointed Zvi Zur as chief of staff, he summoned Rabin, then deputy chief of staff and chief of operations, and told him that at least part of the reason why he had been passed over for the top post was his disobeying of orders in 1949.

Yet, five years later, in 1965, a more relenting Ben-Gurion brushed the entire episode off as trivial. 'Do you remember objecting that I had put you into a dilemma by asking you not to attend that conference after the war?' the former premier asked Rabin when they met at a social occasion in Tel Aviv. Slightly embarrassed that the subject had been raised, Rabin was silent. 'And then I said, "If that is the way you feel, you must go",' Ben-Gurion added with a twinkle in his eye. Rabin felt constrained to reply: 'I'm glad that's the way you remember it. But if what you say is correct, why was I reprimanded?' Ben-Gurion replied tersely, 'That was all wrong.'[5]

Though he did not lose his job over the affair, Rabin was still not clear about what kind of future he would have in the army. As commander of the Negev Brigade he was kept active, but the post scarcely satisfied his instincts for leadership. In the autumn of 1949, the brigade was demobilized, effectively leaving Rabin with nothing to do.

He learned that Haim Laskov, the veteran British-trained Hagana officer, had begun to organize a battalion commanders' course, and expressed interest in joining it as a course instructor. Laskov had been given the job of retraining and reorganizing the IDF after the war, a task that required great ingenuity and resourcefulness since the army was little more than a mélange of military philosophies and styles. It lacked organization and structure and it was beset by conflicts between those who had been trained by the British, and those who had served in the Palmach. What was needed was a meeting place to sort out the differences and impose some kind of unifying system.

Laskov was delighted to recruit Rabin, but only on condition that the young man was not politically active; he did not want to find that he was subverting the training course by giving undue emphasis to Palmach doctrines. Urging Rabin to improve his understanding of English so that he could read the manuals, Laskov accepted him as an instructor. At about the same time that he began working on the course, Rabin was promoted to colonel, a rank the IDF introduced in early 1950.

Three one-month courses were arranged at the outset, with a gap of about one month in between each to give Laskov and his staff time to review and change the course material. At that time he had recruited, among others, six men from the Palmach (including Rabin), three former British army officers and an air force man. Rabin joined the group as the second course was getting under way in order to learn what he would be teaching later on.

The course was indeed a 'test area' for ideas and opinions on terminology, tactics and strategy, staff procedures, operational planning techniques and standing operational orders for war. Now that the pressure of war was over, officers could formulate the knowledge they had acquired, learn from each other's experience, and perfect or discard techniques. To take one example, the Israeli forces knew little about the concept of a 'fire plan' during the war. This was a British army procedure for coordinating and working out in advance all phases of a battle. Although the Israeli artillery had sometimes worked out its own fire plan, it had never been coordinated with other arms of the fighting force. Now that time had come to systematically work out an Israeli military doctrine.

Rabin, whose reputation as an able military planner was now established, took over as head of the course when Laskov left. In early 1951, he was appointed director of the division of military operations and left the battalion commanders' course. Yigael Yadin, the chief of staff, personally selected him for this new appointment, which was considered important within the general staff framework. The IDF's failure to cope with Arab infiltration, together with the self-evident truth that the army simply could not afford to rest on its laurels, were strong incentives to continue the painstaking job of organizing the army efficiently. Rabin's job was to prepare contingency plans for every possible military situation.

He was still strongly influenced by Palmach thinking, and the tactics it had used so successfully during the war — the indirect approach, rather than the frontal attack, the element of surprise, the outflanking of the enemy. He preached these methods to the men under him, rather than the more formal, traditional British approach.

Rabin liked to be at the centre of things: he wanted to know every detail of every matter, and to involve himself personally as much as possible. This kind of intense involvement sometimes produced difficulties with those under him who relished their independence. On one occasion in the summer of 1952, it was brought home to Rabin that he could not run everything himself. The IDF were carrying out a tactical exercise under the direct command of Laskov, who was now the chief of the air force. As director of the division of military operations, Rabin had overall responsibility for the exercise. When the time came to attack a certain target, Rabin ordered Laskov to use four Spitfires. The air force chief was incensed, naturally thinking that it was his decision what type of plane to use and how many, in an exercise over which he presumably had direct command responsibility. He yielded to Rabin, but after the exercise, brought the matter up at a debriefing session supervised by Yigael Yadin. Both Rabin and Laskov argued their case for making the decision, and the dispute was settled in Laskov's favour.

Those who worked with Rabin in those days shared his sense of mission. Working 18-20 hours a day on plans, charts, and organization schemes, they did not begrudge the time expended: they were planning the future Israeli army, their work was crucial to the survival of the State, and they found fulfilment in that. Still a Palmach officer at heart, a soldier who was more at home with small units, with individuals, than with the large departments which make up a modern, well-run army, 'Rabin really thought that running a brigade was like running a company, just a bit bigger,' recalls an associate of that period. 'He had no concept of the general staff, how you move an army, the intensive organization that's behind an army. But he picked up these things very quickly. He grew with the job, although he was brainwashed by the Palmach's concepts. It was part of his philosophy of life, but he had the capacity to grasp very quickly the difference between a vagabond army and a real army.'[6]

The Rabins' first child had been born on 19 March, 1950, a daughter named Dahlia. In the autumn of 1952, the Rabin family moved out of Leah's father's flat to the Tel Aviv suburb of Zahala, a favourite area for army officers; it was to be their home for the next twenty years, off and on. The home, simply furnished, three and a half rooms in size, marked the first time that Yitzhak and Leah had their own home. All the men in the neighbourhood wore uniforms; in front of each house was a car with military licence plates. Life slowly became more normal: they made friends among other married couples, and Rabin even found time for some jobs around the house and gardening. They would spend evenings playing games of scrabble with neighbours, especially Mordechai Maklef (chief of staff, 1952–53).

In November 1952, Rabin was sent to England to the British Staff College at Camberley, on a nine-month course designed to turn bright young soldiers into competent staff officers and potential generals. The experience was not overly pleasant for Rabin, although he and Leah were thrilled at the idea of living abroad for an extended period, particularly since they had never been able to spend much time together. Having lived through the 'bad days', as he calls them, when Jewish forces were fighting the British, he could never shake off the bitter memories they left. Those British officers who had fought in Palestine in the 1940s tended to avoid him while he was at Camberley, which hardly helped to smooth things over, though there was the odd humorous exchange. By coincidence, the battalion commander who had arrested Rabin on Black Saturday — 29 June, 1946 — in Tel Aviv, was the commandant at Camberley. One day Rabin was told that he wanted to see him. Somewhat surprised, and wondering what he could have done wrong, Rabin arrived at the commandant's office and received a friendly welcome. The two men talked for a while over coffee, Rabin all the time wondering about the reason for the invitation. Finally the commandant asked him whether he had read the report in the newspapers that morning that a bomb had been thrown in Tel Aviv near the Russian Embassy. Rabin said he had read about it. 'It's interesting how times have changed,' said the commandant, 'Now the Russians are your target, not us. It seems to me you must feel the need to blow up something all the time.' It was the first reference he had made to their previous encounter.

On another occasion the commandant called all the foreign students into his office for a friendly get-together, where the Israeli and Jordanian officers found themselves next to each other in the reception line. The commandant, who enjoyed bird-watching and duck-hunting, exchanged a few words with each man. When he spoke to one of the Jordanians he mentioned some places in Jordan where he had been duck-hunting. Then he moved on to the Israeli officers. Looking at Rabin, the commandant murmured, 'Of course, in *your* country, I was the duck that you were hunting.'

The impression of that course at Camberley which remains with Rabin is that it was dull: 'So much time was allotted to technical work that was really boring.'[7] Indeed, he was so bored and miserable he almost decided to return home. However, after five months of frustration, he resolved to take a more positive view of the course, and derive what benefit he could. As a result be began to enjoy it — in a limited way. Throughout the nine months his poor command of English plagued him and prevented him from gaining as much from the course as he might have.[8]

Maklef had sent Rabin to England in the hope that he would come to realize the usefulness of some of the British military methods, but as one of his associates said later, 'Rabin wasn't ready for England.' And one of his superiors at that time says: 'I don't think England ever impressed him. He was so introverted and so convinced of the superiority of the Palmach way of doing things that the British had nothing to offer.'

Yet the Rabins enjoyed life in England enough to contemplate staying on after the course ended in November 1953. They lived in a big country house that had been converted into flats, where they met and made friends with people of all nationalities. Though they could not afford a car, Rabin bought a bicycle. He and Leah would take turns going to shows in London so that someone was always home to look after Dahlia. Once, while at the theatre, Rabin felt everyone was staring at him. Worried that there was something wrong with his appearance, he checked and found all OK; he then discovered that he was seated next to Greer Garson. The military situation was relatively calm in Israel, and there seemed no pressing need to return. Rabin therefore applied for a place at the London School of Economics. The chief of staff granted his request for an extension of his stay abroad, and all seemed set. Then Rabin received word from Moshe Dayan, who was about to replace Maklef as chief of staff, that he wanted him to return to Israel to join his team in general headquarters as director of training for the army. Rabin eagerly packed his bags and put aside all thoughts of continuing his studies.

The Rabins returned home. Yitzhak was in the army's Training Branch; Dahlia entered kindergarten, and Leah was in the early stage of pregnancy. She had been told to stay in bed. At times, Yitzhak would return from the General Staff to warm the food and serve Leah in bed, and then have a meal with Dahlia — all in thirty minutes. Then he returned to work.

He had gone to Camberley as a colonel, then the third-highest rank in the Israeli army. When he had completed the course, his British instructors felt he was qualified to serve in the Quartermasters Corps — and nothing more. Dayan learned of this upon Rabin's return, and penned him a note, saying, 'I hope you won't take what they wrote too seriously' — and promptly promoted him to major-general (though, as was customary in the IDF, it would take a year — until December 1954 — for the promotion to become effective). Rabin's fellow officers, too, had a better opinion of him than the British. One officer who served under him during the early 'fifties remembers that everyone recognized his ability; it was accepted that Rabin was destined for high places.

Rabin was always prepared to take on more responsibility and heavier burdens, but always curiously reluctant to give up the post he already held: having put so much energy and effort into a job, he was not eager to relinquish it. But he was thrilled at the chance to join the Dayan team. As a prelude to the new assignment, the chief of staff sent him to the United States in the summer of 1954 to study instruction methods as well as the overall organization of the US army. Dayan wanted to upgrade the status of the training department, which had been a sub-staff division of the general staff branch; henceforth it was to be autonomous and known as the training branch.

In appointing Rabin, Dayan seemed to be indicating that it was time to reintroduce some of the Palmach spirit into an army that in his view was now top-heavy with British-trained officers. Indeed, after taking up the post, Rabin acted very much like the Palmach veteran he was, insisting that every senior officer undergo paratroop training, and being one of the first to submit to this order. Rabin and Dayan did not agree on everything, but they found common ground in their dislike for the conventional.

Rabin chose to keep his paratroop training a secret from Leah. She was pregnant with their second child and he saw no reason to 'disturb' his wife with this dangerous business. Yitzhak jumped in the mornings and returned to his office in the afternoons. Chatting with his wife on the phone each day, he reminded her to heat the boiler for a bath, labouring hard to make sure she suspected nothing. Even when he complained of a sore finger, Leah thought nothing of it. Yitzhak notified Leah one evening that he was off to check a training site at 4 am when in fact he was about to make his first jump. Again, her suspicions were not aroused. Yet, when the alarm clock went off that morning, she confessed to him that she had just had a strange dream. She dreamt that she had said to him, 'Why don't you tell me where you're going. Are you hiding something from me?' Only after the course was complete did Yitzhak acknowledge to Leah that he had not slept well that night and had been shocked by her question.

Rabin was the proverbial new broom when he took up his appointment. One of his first acts was to revise the system whereby officers of the various wings were trained at separate institutions. Instead, he set up a new staff college, with schools directly connected to the general staff. By unifying this system, he hoped to unify the army, giving the soldiers and officers a common terminology and training. He threw out the old pamphlets and manuals the army was using, finding them a hodge-podge of instructions that hindered rather than helped the formulation of a coherent policy. They were replaced by new comprehensive manuals.

While at Camberley, Rabin had been struck by the British emphasis on the use of tanks, and he advocated greater use of armour in the IDF. Dayan, however, who had found armour to be very slow-moving during the War of Independence, was not persuaded. The two men debated the matter endlessly. On another point Rabin was more successful: Dayan, eager to remove certain officers whom he thought of little value, decided to alter the command structure of the army by reducing it from three commands (North, South and Central) to two. Rabin fought the proposal, and eventually managed to persuade the chief of staff to leave things as they were.

The only event of major significance in Rabin's life during 1955 was the birth of his son, Yuval, on 18 June. In early 1956 Rabin was appointed commander of the Northern Front. So that he could be closer to his work (command headquarters were in Nazareth) the Rabins moved to Haifa, where they lived in rented flats for two years.

The job gave Rabin the opportunity to travel widely, visiting civilian settlements, learning at first hand the problems of farming under the continuous threat of Syrian gunfire. He acquired a reputation as a commander who understood the settlers and their problems, and who could be counted on for maximum support. However, his appointment was viewed by some as an attempt by Dayan to keep officers associated with Yigal Allon out of the top command: Dayan's antagonism towards Allon outweighed his previous sense of confidence in Rabin, and when the opportunity arose in 1956 to pick a new chief of operations in the general staff, Dayan by-passed Rabin and chose Meir Amit.

As Rabin took up his duties in the north, the situation along Israel's southern frontier with Egypt was rapidly deteriorating. When the Israeli planning for the Sinai Campaign of 1956 began, Rabin felt if not resentful, certainly disappointed at being left out in the cold. His troops in the north had to be particularly watchful and alert during the 1956 war, but Rabin's description of himself then as an unemployed general is apt.

The Sinai Campaign had its roots in 1955, when President Nasser of Egypt decided to sponsor guerrilla attacks from the Gaza Strip and Jordan against Israeli civilians and targets. The 12,000 Fedayeen infiltrators ambushed traffic, blew up wells and destroyed homes, killing four hundred Israelis and wounding another thousand. Nasser also closed the Straits of Tiran to Israeli shipping. The Egyptian President's hand had been considerably strengthened in 1955 when he worked out an arms deal with Czechoslovakia; his threat to 'reconquer Palestine', issued in 1956, sounded even more menacing in the light of his new armaments.

The object of the Israelis' campaign was simply to end the guerrilla attacks and reopen the Straits. There would be no attack on Cairo, no destruction of the Egyptian armed forces. The goal of the war, which began on 29 October, 1956, in Dayan's words was 'to confound the organization of the Egyptian forces in Sinai and bring about their collapse'.[9]

The Israeli advance into Sinai was coordinated with Britain and France. Indeed, France had undertaken to protect Israeli airspace over the country's major cities. Within 100 hours, the Israelis had swept through the Sinai and had taken control of the entrance to the Straits of Tiran. On the second day of the campaign, the British and French intervened on the pretext of trying to separate the combatants when in fact they were carrying out a planned invasion of the Canal Zone. (Nasser had nationalized the Suez Canal in retaliation for the American withdrawal of an earlier offer of massive financial aid.) The two European countries issued a joint ultimatum to Israel and Egypt to stop the fighting. Israel agreed, but Egypt did not. Then Britain and France, exploiting the fact that Egypt was distracted by the Israelis, launched an abortive raid on Port Said, ostensibly to protect the Canal for international navigation.

The Russians by this time were threatening to intervene unless Israel relinquished its newly conquered territory and with that the US coerced Israel to withdraw by threatening to withhold financial aid in the future. By March 1957 the Israelis had withdrawn from the Sinai and a United Nations peace-keeping force had taken their place. Israel had attained its objective: the reopening of the Straits of Tiran. It had also curbed the Fedayeen attacks. For the next ten years, Israel's border with Egypt was to remain quiet.

Though he played no direct part in it, the Sinai Campaign was significant for Rabin. For one thing, it vindicated his belief that the withdrawal from Sinai at the close of the War of Independence would only lead to renewed warfare. (As prime minister, negotiating indirectly with the Egyptians in 1975 for a new Sinai withdrawal, Rabin would point out to US Secretary of State Henry Kissinger, the mediator, that Israel had already learned two painful lessons, and would require concrete evidence of Egypt's peaceful intent before retreating once more.)

With border incidents on the northern frontier a constant threat, Rabin was determined that the soldiers under his command should be adequately prepared for battle. In 1957 Aharon Doron was serving under him as commander of the Golani Brigade, and recalls Rabin being 'mainly interested in the operational side of whatever we were doing. It's not that he neglected logistics, but he didn't want to be involved in such matters. For instance, he wouldn't inspect units for dust or untidiness. He loathed having to bother with the question of whether a soldier's rifle was clean or not. He believed that was someone else's job, not his.'[10]

During visits to Doron's brigade and to other units stationed near the frontier, Rabin would constantly be asking all kinds of operational questions, testing the men's readiness for battle, basing his interrogation on his own detailed knowledge of both sides of the border.

In 1957 Rabin paid his second visit to the United States, this time to Fort Bliss, Texas, where he participated in an orientation course for senior officers on new weapons and modern warfare.

Israel and Syria, in 1956 and 1957, were still fighting over the definition and interpretation of the 1949 armistice agreement.

The battles were small and concerned minor pieces of territory; the two countries were testing each other out, each hoping to win the war of nerves without recourse to a larger-scale confrontation. For the Israelis the stakes were disproportionately high, because their failure to combat the Syrians at any point might be misinterpreted as a sign of weakness and acquiescence, which would encourage the enemy to launch bigger attacks. Rabin believed a steadfast policy in this matter to be vital, and demonstrated his zeal on several occasions. For instance, one day in September 1957 his deputy, Oded Messer, had taken a group of fifteen men on a reconnaissance mission along the Syrian frontier. A Syrian force had taken control of a key hill in the area near Tel Azazyiat, high up in the eastern Galilee, and when Messer's party approached the spot, shooting began. It was 9 am. Withdrawal became the wisest course after several of the Israelis had been wounded, but they had difficulty in disengaging because of their advanced position. Against their small arms the Syrians had mortars and other heavier weapons. Fortunately — because of what Messer jokingly called Rabin's 'pedantry' — the force had radio liaison with the command's headquarters in Nazareth. When Rabin heard that several men had been wounded he rushed to the scene within the hour. Though it was clear that the men had to extricate themselves as soon as possible, they also had to impress upon the Syrians that they were not going to yield an inch without putting up a good fight. Rabin promised the men tanks, and instead of an immediate retreat, the men hung on grimly until the armoured vehicles arrived two hours later. While the tanks went into action, the wounded were taken to safety. Although the Syrians held onto the hill, the Israelis made their point: now the enemy understood that they could not attack with impunity. The size of the territory was of no consequence, it was the principle of not yielding that mattered.

On another ocasion, in the region of Tel Katzir, on the south-eastern section of Lake Kinneret, the Israelis and Syrians found themselves fighting over a two-acre plot. The land itself had absolutely no agricultural value, but the Israelis interpreted the armistice agreement of 1949 to mean that it belonged to the Jewish State. When the Syrian resistance proved tougher than expected during the first day of fighting, the Israelis ordered up large numbers of forces, far more than seemed necessary for a fight over two acres. Messer asked Rabin whether it was really worth fighting for such a small piece of land that had no strategic importance. Rabin told him: 'If we give up a part of our rights today, we may one day be forced to concede them all. And we aren't going to give up. If we don't succeed today, we'll try again tomorrow, using some other means.'[11] The Israelis employed armoured tractors for the first time against the Syrian enemy, and eventually forced their withdrawal from the two acres.

As far as Rabin was concerned, the Israelis had to meet aggression with aggression in every instance, and this entailed careful planning and painstaking checking of every detail in every operation. Oded Messer had learned this lesson on his very first day as Rabin's deputy in the autumn of 1957, when the Northern Command had planned a small operation to destroy a building along its northern flank near the border. Rabin asked Messer to check on the planning of the operation. When he reported back that everything had been duly checked, Rabin asked him who from northern headquarters was overseeing the operation when it took place. Messer replied that the operation was a small one, that it was in the charge of a battalion commander, that there would be a brigade commander present; surely there was no need for anyone from headquarters to be there. Rabin told him: 'You never know. Such small operations, in the general atmosphere of our relations with the Syrians, can very easily develop into a big incident. So my principle in the Northern Command — even if the operation is a very small one — is to have someone on the spot who is able to take the fullest responsibility. Even if the operation is so small that it could easily be led by a platoon commander, I insist that either myself, or you, or the chief operations officer be present.'[12]

At the end of 1957, changes were about to be made in the army's high command and Rabin was obviously a candidate for one of the important posts. Dayan called in Rabin, Meir Amit and Zvi Zur, all senior officers, and told them that he was going to relinquish the post of chief of staff, and that he had recommended to Ben-Gurion that Amit take over the position, with Zur as his deputy. In addition, he had proposed to the premier that both he (Dayan) and Rabin should go on study courses on behalf of the army. The strategy was not lost on

Rabin, who bitterly resented being by-passed again. He agreed, however, to the study course, but asked that it be abroad. When Dayan refused the request — he himself was going to study at the Hebrew University in Jerusalem and he thought Rabin should go there, too — Rabin refused to go on a course at all. Zur pointed out that Haim Laskov was absent from the meeting, and surely he was a candidate for the post as well. In the end Ben-Gurion, as Zur rightly suspected, made Laskov Dayan's successor as chief of staff. Zur became Laskov's deputy. Amit became head of the Central Command and Rabin remained commander of the Northern Front.

During the summer of 1958, the Rabins left their home in Haifa and returned to Zahala. Leah started teaching English, a move that did not please her husband who argued that her investment of time and effort was not worth the small compensation. Leah stood her ground, continuing to work for two years before admitting to Yitzhak that he had been right. Remaining at home after that, Leah felt pleased that she could offer their children the kind of home that Yitzhak had missed because of Rosa Cohen's prolonged absences. 'I felt', she wrote, 'though he never said it, that it was important for Yitzhak to know that I was home with the children, and that enabled him to throw himself body and soul into whatever he was doing . . . I sensed that if anything compensated for his own childhood, and for the immense effort invested in what he did, it was the security of knowing that I was at home on "a full time job".'[13]

In early 1959, after three years as commander of the Northern Front, Rabin concluded that he was going no further in the army, that his chances of becoming chief of staff were slender, and that he might as well consider returning to civilian life. Instead of picking up his earlier ambition to become a water engineer, he considered business administration. He had been administering a major organization, the IDF, for years now. The skills he had acquired would surely stand him in good stead in the business world. He approached Laskov with a request to study at the Harvard School of Business in Boston, Massachusetts. Laskov agreed, and Rabin promptly applied for a two-year course. He was to leave for the United States in the summer of 1959, and begin his studies that autumn, but his plans were overtaken by events.

In April 1959 a decoy and mobilization practice of reservists was arranged, and as is usual in exercises of this nature, code names were broadcast over the radio, signalling men to go to their bases immediately. Unfortunately the public had not been warned that the mobilization was only a practice run and a great many thought the call-up was real and that Israel was about to go to war again. There was a shake-up of the top command in the wake of this error. Yehoshophat Harkabi, the director of military intelligence, was replaced by Chaim Herzog, Meir Zorea, director of the general branch, left. Rabin became one of the prime beneficiaries from the changes that occurred, taking over from Zorea. At the age of 37, he had finally joined the inner circle of the top command, and from that moment on was considered a likely candidate for the post of chief of staff. Even Ben-Gurion could do little to stop his progress now. Appointing Zvi Zur chief of staff, the prime minister knew that Rabin would be troubled at being passed over. He summoned the disgruntled Rabin and offered comfort: 'You will be the next chief of staff.'[14] Though Rabin may have thought the promise somewhat empty, Ben-Gurion repeated it to him several times over the next few years.

During the early 1960s Rabin earned a reputation for being the most capable staff officer in the IDF; it was even said that he carried so much information in his head, it would not matter if the army's computer broke down. He travelled extensively during this period, visiting Europe and the United States to learn about the latest kind of equipment and the newest techniques. He wrote some articles, mostly for the army journal, about his own military concepts, and these articles became essential reading for junior officers. On 24 January, 1961 he was appointed deputy chief of staff, retaining the post of chief of operations.

There were continual battles within the IDF about how the modern arms Israel was acquiring should be integrated. One such dispute concerned the air force, which during the early 1950s had been consistently overlooked when funds were being allocated within the IDF — priority was given to the ground forces. But in 1958, the youthful, assertive Ezer Weizman became head of the air force and under him the air wing became more dynamic. In the early 1960s, when Israel acquired its first batch of Hawk missiles, there was much debate about which arm of the IDF should be given responsibility for them; Rabin, aware that the US army kept its Hawks within the ground forces' purview, disagreed with Weizman's argument that as Israel was small and close-knit, the country's air defence should be controlled by one arm — the air force. The debate was finally resolved by Chief of Staff Zur, who decided in favour of Weizman's point-of-view, but as a compromise, adopted Rabin's proposal that some ground forces should be transferred to the air force.

Extreme caution was always Rabin's maxim when it came to the nation's security; there was no room for mistakes or false economy. In 1961, the director-general of the Defence Ministry, Moshe Kashti, proposed developing local production of radio equipment in order to curb Israel's dependence on outside sources which were inevitably more costly and difficult to obtain. Rabin vigorously opposed him: 'I cannot afford to be weak where communication is concerned,' he told Kashti. 'Local production might give us the necessary equipment, but it will take a long time. If we buy it abroad, we can get it immediately.' On security matters, Rabin insisted, 'We cannot take any risks.'[15] As usual, a compromise was reached whereby radio equipment was to be purchased abroad as and when it was needed — until the IDF's needs could be supplied by local production.

Rabin also proved cautious in decisions about the pace of building up the army. The IDF then had only one regular brigade and two reserve brigades, and there was argument about whether a new regular brigade should be added, or whether the battalions within the brigade should be strengthened. Israel was having difficulty in acquiring tanks at that time, and it seemed more prudent, Rabin thought, for the country to defer the decision of creating a new brigade and concentrate instead on increasing the strength of the battalions. The IDF could always add more brigades — and more tanks — when it was able to get the necessary equipment. But Zur overruled him and, much to Rabin's regret, the decision was taken to create a new brigade.

However, one decision which Rabin was able to influence involved the planning of the new Knesset (Parliament) on the

Givat Ram ridge in Jerusalem. The building, located two kilometres from the frontier, was originally designed with its entrance facing towards the Mar Elias Monastery, in the Judean hills to Jerusalem's east. Since the Jordanians had gun emplacements near Mar Elias, Rabin advised that the entrance to the Knesset be situated elsewhere, to ensure that people arriving there could not be cut down by gunfire. In 1956, Jordanian machine-gunners at Mar Elias had fired into a group of archaeologists and students who were viewing excavations at Ramat Rahel on the Israeli side of Jerusalem, killing four and wounding seventeen. It was obviously wise to avoid the possibility of such a recurrence in the vicinity of the Knesset.

Rabin commanded the respect of those around him, even when there were differences of opinion. 'Some say he is unable to make decisions,' says Oded Messer, his senior assistant in those days, 'but I don't believe this is so. If they mean by decision-making ability the ability to make *quick* decisions, they are right. He is perhaps slow to make a decision. But when he decides, the decision is based on sound judgment. He sticks to the decision, and uses every means to carry it out.'[16] Ruhama Hermon, Rabin's long-time secretary, has vivid memories of army officers making sure they had done their homework before meetings with Rabin. 'Generals used to tell me that when you came to a meeting with Rabin, you had to know the subject inside out because he always asked you about it and he always knew better than you did.'[17]

In late 1960, Rabin was again visiting the United States, a country for which he felt a long-standing and deep affection. He was impressed with the American army, its sophisticated weaponry, its size, its obvious preparedness. He was struck by the American atomic deterrent, a weapon, he said, which small countries like Israel should be familiar with 'because every atomic explosion can affect them, even though at first glance these countries seem to be on the fringe of events.'[18] Though he admired the electronic gadgetry and equipment at the US army's disposal, it was the concept of deterrence which intrigued him most. 'Just like us,' he told *Ma'ariv* on 9 December, 1960, 'the Americans base their defence on deterrence, that is to say, the ability to wipe out the other side, if it tries to destroy you; the ability to destroy combined with the reluctance to go to war.' He was also impressed by the general political acceptance of the need to maintain the army's preparedness, and to provide the necessary means for its organization.

The adoption of deterrence might solve some of Israel's military problems, Rabin thought. In a speech in December 1962, he said that it was 'necessary to use the weapon of deterrence to maintain a normal way of life on the border, in addition to its being vital for the security of Israel's existence.' The IDF should try to avoid clashes with the Syrians as much as possible, he advised, and adopt a policy of deterrence which would give the nation the necessary security without the costly involvement of fighting. 'It is preferable to demonstrate a readiness to use strength,' he told his listeners, 'rather than to deal the blow.'[19]

In October and November 1963, Rabin visited France and the US, accompanied by Aharon Yariv, deputy director of military intelligence. In France Rabin inspected the French 'wonder tank', the AMX 30, in which Israeli defence experts had shown much interest. Rabin astounded the French by asking to ride in the tank as it went through its paces. One French general commented that he was so well versed in armour it seemed as though he must have begun his career as a tank commander. Rabin thought the French AMX 30 tank very good, but very expensive. In the United States, he and Yariv put forward the Israeli case for acquiring more tanks. They visited Fort Bliss in Texas, where Israeli units were learning how to use Hawk anti-aircraft missiles, which Rabin found most impressive.

On 5 December, 1963 Rabin was made seventh chief of staff of the Israel Defence Forces. His appointment to this position shortly after Ben-Gurion's resignation the previous June seemed hardly a coincidence. Levi Eshkol, who replaced Ben-Gurion as premier (and defence minister) did not have the same suspicious attitude towards the Palmach which the 'Old Man' had harboured. However, there were suggestions that the ageing prime minister had given his blessing to the appointment before he left office. Another rumour was that Rabin had been selected in order to pay off a political debt to the leftist Ahdut Avoda party, which had split from Mapam in the early 1950s. It was certainly true that Rabin's name had been linked with Ahdut Avoda, as had the names of most Palmach officers. But Rabin had tended to shun political activity while in the army — indeed, when he sought the nomination for prime minister in April 1974, one of his strong points was, significantly, a lack of identification with any of the Labour Party's factions, including Ahdut Avoda — so the idea seems unlikely. (In 1965, Ahdut Avoda aligned itself with the Mapai Party, and in 1968 these two political bodies, plus the Rafi party, formed the Israel Labour Party.)

Rabin's supporters were pleased that someone with 'strength and wisdom' was to replace the retiring chief of staff, Zvi Zur, whom they considered weak and uninspiring. Rabin, now forty-one, radiated confidence, and others responded to this quality in him. He was described in the *Jerusalem Post* on December 16, 1963 as 'soft-spoken . . . with a hint of freckles, a quiet but authoritative voice and unhurried movements, all conveying the impression of a man at peace with himself. He is capable of a most un-general-like grin, especially when non-military subjects like hobbies are discussed.'

The new chief of staff was to share the ntional leadership with such political veterans as Golda Meir, Foreign Minister Abba Eban, Deputy Premier and Education Minister Pinhas Sapir, who held both the Finance and the Commerce and Industry portfolios, and Moshe Dayan, now Minister of Agriculture. The army belonged to Rabin. 'Let us continue to secure the sovereignty of the State in its entirety,' he said in his first Order of the Day on 1 January, 1964, 'to set up the conditions that will enable development to take place, and to build up a fighting force that will deter every enemy.' He cautioned that the army had to be strengthened because 'as in the past, there are conflicts in store with countries opposed to our development'.

Now that he had at last attained the position for which he had been training, in effect, for most of his life, it was clear that he would carry out no revolutionary changes in the structure and style of the IDF. He was too conservative by temperament for that, and he was too much a part of the military establishment to consider upheaving the very system that had brought him to this position. He had few anxieties about the task before him, though naturally there were uncertainties about the Arabs, who had been making some bellicose noises of late, reviving fears that they might be preparing for a third round of war. But everything seemed to point to the contrary: Israel's borders had never been so quiet. Gunfire had not been heard along the Egyptian front since 1956, which was remarkable given the level of violence there before the Sinai Campaign. There were always skirmishes along the northern border, but no one seriously thought Syria would take such a drastic step as war.

Egypt was always potentially the main threat, if only because it was the most powerful of the Arab nations. As Rabin prepared to take up office, however, fifty thousand Egyptian soldiers were involved in a war of several years' standing in the tiny Yemen, thousands of miles away. Nevertheless, the increased flow of arms into Egypt during the early 1960s was an uncomfortable reminder that President Nasser was capable of unleashing a very effective war machine against the Israelis, even though he was already fighting a war in the Yemen. Egypt had spent nearly $300 million on defence in 1960–61, but over the next five years it was to double that figure: the size of its tank force nearly doubled to 1,200 tanks; the number of its jet fighters increased to 350. Relying upon West Germany as a vital source of arms (largely army surplus), the Israelis acquired by the mid-1960s $125 million worth of equipment. In the summer of 1960 Israel and France had signed their first agreement on the sale of French Mirage jets to the Jewish State, a plane that was to prove crucial to the Israeli air effort in the Six-Day War. In the mid-1960s Israel began to turn towards the United States to acquire the additional weaponry it needed, since the US was the only nation which could effectively compete with the Russians — who were supplying the Arabs — in the arms field. By June 1967, Israel, according to unofficial foreign sources, had 800 tanks and 197 warplanes.

While some were optimistically predicting in the mid-1960s that Egypt posed no real threat to Israel, Rabin took a more realistic, cautious view, warning in an interview in *Yediot Aharonot* on 15 April, 1964 that the 'principal danger to Israel lies in Egypt's determination to create and obtain weapons that will enable them to hurt us'. He was worried by the complacent resignation shown by some of his countrymen, who in their darkest moments became convinced that time was inevitably on the side of the Arabs. He railed against such gloomy thoughts, insisting that Israel could prevail, if only the proper measures were taken. 'If I thought time was working against us,' he said in an interview in *Herut* that same day, 'that would mean I didn't think we had a chance to continue our existence. We must put all our efforts into withstanding the modern weapons in which our enemy excels — and this is something we have the ability to do.' Syria had not signed the armistice agreement of 1949 with the intention of coming to peace terms with Israel. But this did not mean they were ready to launch a major war against the Jewish State — at least, not without the support of the Egyptians — though they could make themselves a nuisance to the Israelis. That was precisely what they tried to do during this period. Provoking the Israelis into making major raids into Syrian territory was a dangerous step, but there were advantages: Israel could be labelled the 'aggressor', and lose world sympathy, while Syria, as the aggrieved party, stood to gain enough sympathy to make Israel's case even weaker.

Unsure of their ability to defeat Israel on the battlefield, some Arab states, especially Syria, looked around for other ways to strike. The country's heavy reliance on water resources seemed a weakness worth exploiting. In 1964, the Israelis were completing the National Water Carrier, a nation-wide irrigation network carrying water from the Jordan River in the north to the arid regions of the south. The Arabs gathered in Cairo 13–16 January, 1964 for the first of what became periodic summit conferences. They resolved to allocate £6.25 million sterling to diverting the sources of the Jordan River in Syrian territory, which would thus disrupt the Carrier project. They also decided to establish a unified Arab command. The Israelis made it clear that any attempt by the Arabs to divert the Jordan's sources would be considered an act of war by the Jewish State, thus forcing the Syrians to turn to Egypt for support. But President Nasser would not be a party to the diversion plan, calculating that Egypt was not ready to take Israel on in an all-out war. Syria, nevertheless, went ahead with attempts to sabotage the Carrier, and put additional pressure on Israel by clandestinely supporting terrorist activity on a major scale. The Arabs, meeting at their second summit conference — this time in Alexandria 5–11 September, 1964 — voted £5 million sterling for the establishment of Palestinian terrorist units, which Syria was to organize and train. The IDF were in a quandary over these attacks: opposed on both moral and practical grounds to a policy of reprisal raids that would result in the killing of Arab civilians, they favoured retaliation against the Syrian armed forces. However, such a policy was handicapped by the IDF's need for restraint, to keep their artillery in check for fear of escalating the situation. Rabin had a solution to the dilemma: Israel would strike at the Jordan diversion project initiated by the Syrians, keeping the attack on the level of a local border incident by using tank gunners who would remain on the Israeli side of the frontier. If the tanks could inflict sufficient damage on the Syrian earth-moving equipment at the base of Mount Hermon, there would be no need to use the air force or artillery and risk provoking open warfare. Major-General Israel Tal, the commander of the armoured corps, had often told him that he was sure his tanks could knock out the Syrian earth-moving equipment by firing from Israeli territory.

One evening in the spring of 1965, Tal received a telephone call from Rabin, who was discussing the Syrian problem with the prime minister. 'I've told Eshkol that you can put a stop to them by using tanks. Bar-Lev [Rabin's deputy chief of staff, who was also a tank expert] here says it's impossible.' With his usual exuberance and self-confidence, Tal assured him that it was perfectly possible. After a few seconds' consultation with Eshkol, Rabin told Tal, 'The prime minister wants to know what guarantee you have that you can do it?' Tal answered testily, 'The guarantee is that I will aim and fire the tank *personally*.' The decision was taken: 'All right,' Rabin ordered, 'go ahead tomorrow morning.'

The next day the Syrians opened fire on an Israeli patrol travelling toward the Dan springs near the frontier. General Tal had taken up his position in one tank, with a crack marksman in a second, and upon hearing of the Syrian shooting, they opened fire. Within four minutes, they had shot up the earth-moving equipment on the Syrian side and set it on fire. From Nukheila, where they were engaged in the diversion scheme, two kilometres from the frontier, the Syrians moved back to a position six kilometres from the frontier, above the B'not Ya'acov Bridge. There they enjoyed a major topographical advantage over the Israelis. Perched on the western ridges of the Golan Heights, the Syrians were defended by a thick line of fortifications, 2,000 feet above the Israeli troops in the Hula Valley.

Tal boasted that he could still destroy the Syrians' machinery. Before giving the final approval, Rabin and Eskhol visited the spot personally on 13 May, 1965. There they gave Tal the order to fire and watched as yet again he struck the target. Afterwards, the Syrians moved further and further away, and the tank battles against them became increasingly tougher, but Rabin, in Tal's view, 'conducted a very sophisticated strategy: refusing to let the Syrians deprive us of the water, but managing to avoid a full-scale war.'[20]

Between 1964 and 1966 the strategic problems facing Israel were sufficiently limited to allow Rabin to conduct a methodical campaign to build up the armed forces for a battle that seemed, at best, far off. The Syrians' bark — for the moment — appeared more ferocious that their bite. This was due in part to Rabin's cautious but ultimately successful policy of repulsing Syrian attempts to harm Israel, not only with cross-frontier tank battles, but also with the air force: on 13 November, 1964 Rabin ordered an air strike in retaliation for a Syrian raid on two border kibbutzim, Dan and Dafna. It was the first time that Israel's air force had been ordered into action in peacetime. Rabin's policy was helped by the fact that the Syrians never seemed to have a government in control long enough to consolidate military action against Israel: by February 1966 Syria had had seventeen coups since its independence in 1944, and it therefore scarcely seemed to constitute a major threat.

Rabin was constantly on the watch for signs of Arab unity — the danger signal that would indicate they were contemplating belligerent action against the Jewish State. The two summit conferences in 1964 caused him some concern. On 25 September, just after the Alexandria conference, he noted in an interview in the *Jerusalem Post*: 'The main feature of events in the past year has been the fact that the Arab countries, despite their differences and antagonisms, have found a way of talking to each other.' He was confident that the Israelis could withstand more pressure — renewed guerrilla efforts by the Palestinian units, Syrian shelling, even all-out war — as long as they kept up their military strength, and continued to have access to foreign arms markets.

Throughout 1966 the Syrian problem worsened. Between February and July, there were ninety-three border incidents involving the laying of mines, shootings, and acts of sabotage. Rabin would often visit the Syrian frontier. Not every visit, however, was as eventful — or dangerous — for him as the one in August 1966 near Lake Kinneret, when, following an Israeli reprisal raid against the Syrians, he toured the frontier where the raid had occurred. He was joined by Ezer Weizman, the new chief of operations, and David Elazar, head of Northern Command. The three men donned swimming trunks in order to conceal their rank from the Syrians, who were no doubt watching their movements from the Syrian side of the border. Suddenly they spotted an Israeli naval patrol boat which had run aground on the eastern side of the lake, its 10-man crew still aboard. Though technically the boat was in Israeli territory, the Syrians were within shooting distance. The three senior officers decided to board the boat to try to help refloat it. There were armed Syrians only fifty yards away, but for some inexplicable reason, they held their fire. Eventually, another naval boat came and towed the grounded one to safety — but not before the Syrians had photographed Rabin and the other two generals trying to free the boat. That photograph was discovered in Kuneitra by Israeli forces when they overran the Golan Heights during the Six-Day War in June 1967. The Syrians had kept the picture, though apparently unaware of its subjects' identities.

The Syrians were not always so slow to arms. Indeed, Rabin felt that the Syrian Government posed far more of a threat to Israel than the Palestinian guerrillas whom it sponsored. In his efforts to warn them against further provocations, he got into some minor trouble with his own Government. In an interview published on 11 September, 1966 in *Ba'machane*, the IDF weekly, Rabin said he believed that Israel should react to Syrian acts of aggression by taking steps directly against the perpetrators 'and against the regime which supports those acts.' A week later, Prime Minister Eshkol, slightly embarrassed by Rabin's bluntness, told the Cabinet that while Israel would hold Syria responsible for the sabotage incidents across her borders, Rabin's statement in *Ba'machane* had been misinterpreted. Israel, he explained, pursued a policy of non-interference in the internal affairs of other governments. He was satisfied that

Rabin had not intended to convey any other idea; however, the Cabinet Security Committee decided to reprimand the chief of staff. Rabin took the news calmly: 'I deserved it,' he said tersely.

In March 1966 Rabin made a good-will trip to the Far East, where he visited six countries during three weeks. The trip gave him a glimpse of a part of the world that he did not know. The region was going through the turmoil of the Vietnam war, a war that Rabin discovered was viewed there largely as a conflict between the US and the Chinese. Generally the reception he received was friendly. He visited the Philippines, South Korea, Burma, Thailand, Cambodia, and Japan, where he was fascinated to find a strong sense of tradition despite the technological advance of a highly industrialized nation.

He gave some lectures to military colleges, and in his spare time took photographs. What intrigued him most was the way the small Asian countries he visited were forced to adjust to the might of China, a country that would inevitably, Rabin felt, swallow up the rest of Asia. 'It will take time,' he told those travelling with him, 'but this is China's natural living area.'[21]

Rabin's relationship with Eshkol was subtle and complex. The two men did their best to appear in harmony at all times, but in private they often clashed. Yet Eshkol relied on Rabin to be his chief adviser on military affairs, and Rabin reciprocated with total loyalty. Originally Eshkol had wanted his relationship with Rabin to be on a very formal footing, and had asked him to put every order to his soldiers in writing, against his signature — presumably so that Eshkol could have a record of them and pass judgment on them. Rabin eventually persuaded the prime minister that such formality was highly unpractical. He found Eshkol's ways difficult in other respects, too. For instance, Eshkol insisted on meeting members of the general staff privately, without the chief of staff's presence. At first Rabin objected strongly, but in the end he yielded to the prime minister on this point, though it remained a bone of contention between the two men.

Eshkol and Rabin also quarrelled over the size of the army's public relations unit, a matter of great sensitivity to the prime minister, who found difficulty himself in putting over a public image. Rabin doubled the size of the Army Spokesman's Office, incurring the resentment of Eshkol who felt the move to be extravagant and designed merely to dramatize Rabin, at the expense of the premier. They differed, too, over the way the army ought to be organized. One example was the question of who should have responsibility for mobilizing the reserves. Rabin wanted to keep it within the IDF, while Eshkol preferred it to be in the hands of the Ministry of Defence. Rabin won this particular point.

However, these differences were overshadowed by their unanimity on the vital question of security. Eshkol came to rely totally on Rabin's judgement in the matter of reprisal raids against terrorists. The prime minister made the final decision, but based it on Rabin's recommendations. The longer the two leaders worked together, the more Eshkol trusted Rabin's judgement. He constantly told his aides that Israel was far better off than the US at that moment, for President Johnson, like Eshkol, knew little about military affairs and therefore had to rely on his generals. But, the premier would explain, LBJ's military advisers had misled him on such important matters as the Gulf of Tonkin incident. Rabin, in Eshkol's view, had almost infallible judgement; even the fiasco of the Samoa raid was quickly forgiven and Eshkol defended Rabin publicly.

This incident occurred on 13 November, 1966. Israeli soldiers — in half-tracks and light tanks — carried out a reprisal raid against the village of Samoa inside Jordan, which was sheltering Palestinian guerrillas who had been operating on Jordanian territory. The Israelis did their best to avoid inflicting civilian or Jordanian army casualties in order not to bring down international censure upon themselves. The object was to demolish only those houses used by guerrillas, and nothing else. The buildings were cleared before being destroyed, and the operation would have gone off smoothly but for the unexpected arrival of a Jordanian infantry battalion. The Israelis fired warning shots, but to no avail; some fifteen Jordanians were killed before the battalion retreated. Rabin became the target for strong criticism within the Cabinet. 'I had no way of knowing,' he told the ministers, 'that the Jordanians would be foolish enough to try and shoot at such a strong opposing force.' Rabin was prepared to offer his resignation over the affair, and, as one official who saw him appear before the Cabinet put it, 'he came with tears in his eyes'. But Eshkol stood by him, and he weathered the storm.

Completing his third year in the post at the end of 1966, Rabin had some important achievements to his credit. He had strengthened both the infantry and the armoured corps, improved the managerial systems of the IDF, streamlined the administration, and introduced new techniques, including the use of computers. He had reorganized the support services of Ordnance and Logistics as well, determined to make sure that the errors of the 1956 Sinai Campaign did not recur. In addition, he had established a new Israeli strategy for dealing with the Syrians, and it appeared to be working. Eshkol could have asked Rabin to step down after three years' service as chief of staff. By the early 1960s it had become customary for Israeli chiefs of staff to serve that long, and no more — although the prime minister could, if he chose, ask the army chief to stay on indefinitely. In view of the uncertain situation prevailing along the northern frontier, and pleased with Rabin's record, the premier asked him to continue in the post. On 25 December, 1966 the Cabinet confirmed Eshkol's request to extend Rabin's service for another year. The public response was friendly. Newspaper editorials praised him, with *Ma'ariv* calling him 'a commander of stable thought, much action and many accomplishments'. The *Jerusalem Post*, echoing this, proclaimed Rabin 'a cool and determined leader'. Rabin himself as usual said little about the job. 'Difficult,' he told one newspaper interviewer, 'but interesting.' That was all.

Chapter 5

'They cannot rejoice wholeheartedly'

The public mood in Israel on the eve of the Six-Day War of June 1967 was one of self-confidence, a feeling which Rabin as chief of staff encouraged at every turn. 'In the eventuality of war,' he said simply on 24 March, 1967, 'the Israel Defence Forces will win.' It was a statement he made often, and he firmly believed it. Terrorist incursions, especially from Syria, required the army's constant vigilance, but they did not affect the strategic dominance Israel enjoyed and would continue to enjoy. However, terrorism was escalating and could become an uncontrollable problem if it was not dealt with firmly: there was a danger that the Syrians might mistake Israeli constraint for weakness. In mid-May Rabin warned of this. The one major cause for concern was the growing power of the Arab war machine, built up over the past few years by vast amounts of arms from the Russians. However, there had been no trouble on the United Nations-patrolled Israeli–Egyptian border for the past decade. Because of this, Israel had pared its defences down to a few armoured brigades which were training near the southern frontier, but were not permanently stationed there. 'As long as there is no political cooperation among the Arab countries,' Rabin said in an interview in *Yediot Aharonot* on 14 May, 1967, 'one need not expect any military cooperation against Israel.'

Only on the northern frontier, where Israel and Syria were playing a tit-for-tat war of nerves, were there skirmishes. The most serious incident erupted on 7 April, 1967, when the Israelis shot down six Syrian planes. The Syrians had already been warned about aiding terrorists in their forays across the border, and when Syrian warplanes appeared in the skies on that April day, the Israelis struck, determined to teach them a lesson.

'Today,' Rabin said with typical understatement, 'they discovered they had made a small error.'[1] The destruction of the planes put new pressure on Egypt to join Syria in a renewed all-out war against Israel; the Soviet press was quick to claim that the Israeli air attack heralded the invasion they had been forecasting for months. From February 1966, when another coup had brought to power a new government in Syria, the Syrians had been using terrorism against Israel as much to lure the Egyptians into the contest as to harry the Jewish State. Until May 1967 Nasser had been able to refuse the Syrian bait, insisting that he would not become involved in a war with Israel 'for the sake of one Syrian tractor'.

Syrian inability to challenge Israel alone, together with Egyptian unwillingness for another round of war, made the Israelis over-confident. Reflecting this mood, Rabin travelled to London early in May for a four-day private visit. Though he engaged in fund-raising activities for Israel, for the most part he avoided making arrangements to meet British Government leaders. His personal mood was relaxed enough for him to go to see a play. He had no special worries about the near future. But it was the calm before the storm.

Conventional Israeli opinion places the blame for the Six-Day War squarely on the shoulders of President Nasser. But in darker moments, Israelis have wondered whether they may have contributed to the tensions of that period and thereby helped to bring about the war themselves in some indirect way. Unpleasant and uncomfortable broodings, they must nevertheless be taken into account, especially since, as Rabin himself has pointed out, the Egyptians gained the impression between 10 and 15 May that Israel was planning a major attack against Syria. One event, linked with Rabin — at least in the public's mind — has often been cited as the main Israeli contribution to the deterioration in the Middle East at that time. On 12 May a senior Israeli military officer held a background briefing for newsmen during which he gave the distinct impression that Israel was planning a major military move against Syria, ostensibly to crush the terrorists, but with the ultimate aim of overturning the Syrian regime. It was widely believed at the time that the officer was Rabin himself, a view that has subsequently been discredited.[2] However, the chief of staff himself hinted in an interview in *Lemerhav* on 14 May, 1967 that Israel might take military steps beyond the kind normally used against terrorists. Syria might be the target, he warned, because its government had supported the terrorists. Whether or not Rabin was the briefing officer on 12 May, the briefing itself apparently spurred Nasser into taking action against Israel — indeed, he claimed later that it was the main factor which led to his decision to move troops into Sinai three days afterwards.

Rabin had been invited to spend the evening of 14 May — the eve of Israel's nineteenth Independence Day — quietly with some friends at the home of Venezuelan industrialist Miles Sherover in Jerusalem. Uzi Narkiss — Rabin's old colleague from the Palmach days, now commander of the Central Front, which included Jerusalem — was there. So were Yigael Yadin, Rabin's former commander from the 1948 war, and Rabin's boyhood companion Mordechai 'Moka' Limon, the commander of the navy during 1951–54 and now the Ministry of Defence's representative in Paris.

Rabin was light-heartedly recounting stories of his earlier war-time experiences, when the telephone rang. It was Colonel Rafi Ephrat, his adjutant. The message he relayed to Rabin was from Aharon 'Arele' Yariv, the director of military intelligence: the Egyptian army had been ordered into a state of alert, scheduled for the next afternoon.

Rabin took the news calmly. 'Very interesting,' he told Ephrat in his deep voice, showing no unusual sign of concern. 'We're going to have to keep our eyes open.' The prime minister of course had to be briefed on the news, but there seemed as yet no cause for alarm. Returning to the gathering, Rabin rejoined the conversation without mentioning his telephone call.

A military parade had been planned in Jerusalem for the morning of 15 May, as part of the Independence Day celebrations, but it had been decided to keep it low-key: only infantry units were to take part: there were to be no armoured vehicles or aircraft. The last thing the Israelis wanted was to provoke the Jordanians, who since 1948 had continued to control the eastern half of the city. The 1949 armistice agreement with Jordan had defined the kind of arms that could be kept in Jerusalem, and the Israelis had no intention of breaking the pact. The Israeli leaders began to assemble in the lobby of the King David Hotel at 9 am. Some 18,000 Israelis had gathered at the Hebrew University stadium ten minutes' drive away. Another 200,000 people were crowding the parade route. By 9:30 am Prime Minister Eshkol, Rabin and their party were due to leave for the parade in a convoy of three cars. When Eshkol arrived, Rabin took him aside and gave him the latest news about the Egyptian state of alert. The two agreed to meet after the parade — by which time Rabin knew that the Egyptians had begun moving troops totalling more than two divisions into eastern Sinai. The troops were taking up positions in the centre of Sinai, but, curiously, were not being deployed near the permanent, reinforced Egyptian division stationed along the length of the Israeli border. It was decided to declare a state of alert and send reinforcements to the undermanned southern frontier. The general staff was surprised at the Egyptian move, but no one felt undue alarm. No one believed that Egypt intended to take on the Israelis in a full-scale war when 50,000 Egyptian soldiers were committed to the struggle in the Yemen.

Returning from the parade on that hot May morning, Rabin quickly took off his uniform. Suddenly, his daughter Dahlia screamed: 'Daddy, there are Jordanian soldiers on the wall with binoculars, and they're looking this way. They'll see you in your underpants.' But the Jordanian soldiers were intent on watching the Israeli parade.

At 5:30 pm Rabin was back in his office in Tel Aviv, where he heard a brief report and then telephoned General Israel Tal.

'Talik,' asked the chief of staff, 'do you remember "Rotem"?' 'Rotem' was the code name for an operation undertaken in 1960 when Rabin was chief of operations and Tal, then a colonel, was commander of the 'S' Armoured Brigade. Faced with the sudden massing on the southern frontier of four hundred Egyptian tanks, Rabin had ordered Tal to meet the concentration of enemy forces with his tanks.

Talik took the broad hint instantly, but was eager for more details. Rabin told him to come over to his home right away. Thirty minutes later, Tal arrived at Rabin's home in Zahala. 'The Egyptians,' Rabin informed him, 'have entered Sinai with a force of 500 tanks.' There was no knowing whether the

Egyptians intended war — although this seemed unlikely — or
whether it was simply a ploy to extricate themselves from the
Yemen, or a move to impress the Syrians. Whatever the reason,
the IDF had to be prepared; Tal was to put all regular units of
the armoured corps on alert, but not to mobilize the reserves yet.
Within a few hours over a hundred Israeli tanks were deployed
against the Egyptian forces arrayed on the other side of the
frontier.

Forgoing a special Independence Day reception given by the
Mayor of Jerusalem, Teddy Kollek, Eshkol called together
Rabin, Abba Eban, the foreign minister, and Ya'acov Herzog,
the director-general of the prime minister's office. Rabin
informed them that the army was reinforcing its Negev positions
with an armoured brigade since the Sinai borders were virtually
bare, but that the general staff feeling was that the reserves need
not be called up for the time being, since Egypt was unlikely to
start hostilities.

On 16 May, Rabin went ahead with a tour of army units to
which he had invited all the former chiefs of staff. 'The
Egyptians are continuing to concentrate troops in Sinai,' he told
them. 'Usually, they keep about one division and 250 tanks in
that area, but they've supplemented them with another
hundred. [There were another 150 on the way.] There's no
doubt that it's a show of strength, but what will they do next?'[3]
Dayan predicted that Egypt would demand the withdrawal of
the UN forces from Sinai and, inevitably getting its way, would
then be in a position to seal off the Straits of Tiran, at the foot of
the Red Sea, the easiest place to blockade Israeli shipping.
Rabin, on the other hand, could not accept that the situation
would deteriorate so rapidly or so dangerously.[4]

However, it did. Nasser found the presence of the 3,400-man
UN Emergency Force in Sinai uncomfortable while he was
engaging in a show of strength. He demanded the evacuation of
the force, but only from Sinai — not from either the Gaza Strip
or Sharm El-Sheikh. Even so, the situation was worsening.
Rabin suggested to Eshkol that Nasser had been carried away in
an excess of megalomania, while Arab propaganda had incited
the masses to believe that Israel, in spite of the outcome of the
Sinai Campaign, could be defeated. He assured the prime
minister that all precautions were being taken; a reserve brigade

of tank crews had been mobilized the night before, and others would soon be called up. But he was still reluctant to believe that Egypt meant war. 'It's a war of nerves,' he told the Knesset Security and Foreign Affairs Committee, while acknowledging that his main concern was that Nasser would now try to block the Straits of Tiran. Everything seemed to point that way.

The one small ray of hope lay in the fact that Nasser had not demanded that all the UN troops leave. Perhaps he was merely bluffing after all. Still, no one could be sure what Nasser had in mind. Addressing newspaper editors on 18 May, Eshkol and Rabin asked them to stress the falsity of reports that Israel had concentrated its troops along the Syrian frontier and was preparing for an attack. The least they could hope to do was remove any suspicion in Nasser's mind that Israel was on the brink of launching an attack against Syria.

Rabin expressed forebodings about the UN withdrawal.

'What are you worried about that for?' asked Hannah Zemer, reporting for the morning newspaper *Davar*. 'Let the UN get out of Gaza. It hardly matters.'

Choosing his words carefully, Rabin replied, 'I don't think the UN force will leave Gaza without abandoning Sharm El-Sheikh. Neither do I think that Nasser will take Sharm El-Sheikh without closing the Straits.'[5]

The UN Secretary-General, U Thant, responded — far too hastily, some thought — to Nasser's demand by threatening to withdraw the entire UN force, confident that the Egyptians would back down from this ultimatum in order to avoid war. Since Nasser's original demand did not specify whether all or only part of the UN force should leave, or for how long, U Thant came in for some severe criticism for his quick capitulation. It has even been suggested by some that Nasser was only bluffing, but with U Thant's unexpected compliance, he could not lose face by backing off. He insisted that all UN troops must leave, including those in Gaza and Sharm El-Sheikh, and by 19 May the UN force had been removed entirely.

By then there were 70,000 Egyptian soldiers and 600 tanks in Sinai. Egyptian units had moved into Sharm El-Sheikh. Even more ominously, some of the Egyptian troops fighting in the Yemen had been transferred to the Sinai. The Israeli leaders tried to put on a show of confidence. In order to reassure the nation that things were normal, Rabin went to Lod Airport near Tel Aviv twice within a few hours, first to see off the Liberian chief of staff, and then the Israeli President Zalman Shazar, who was off to Canada. Meanwhile Eshkol, feeling that Israel was not doing enough to prepare for possible battle, ordered Rabin to mobilize the reserves.

By 20 May Rabin and his staff had refined their strategy in case of war. This time, unlike 1956, when the aims of the Sinai Campaign were more limited, the objective would be the destruction of the Egyptian army. This necessitated the prior destruction of the Egyptian air force, Rabin thought, and meant that Israeli tanks had to conquer the forward and central parts of Sinai. Once this was accomplished, Sharm El-Sheikh would fall without any special difficulties. Although the 48 American Skyhawks and 50 French Mirages which had been ordered for the air force had not yet arrived — indeed, the Skyhawks only reached Israel after the war, and the Mirages never came because of the French arms embargo — the air force, under Ezer Weizman's direction, had developed into a dynamic fighting force. Its 197 combat aircraft included 72 Mirages, 20 Super-Mysteres, 40 Ouragons, 40 subsonic Mysteres, and 25 Vautour light bombers.

The next few days were unquestionably among the most difficult in Rabin's life. Like many others, he had been caught off-guard by the swift and dramatic developments since 15 May, unwilling to believe that war would come. He certainly believed that Israel had no reason to attack Egypt unless strongly provoked — and up until 23 May that had not happened. After the war, in an interview on Israel Radio on 24 June, 1968, Rabin said that he could not think of 'a more serious mistake than to take military action before the other side makes an act of war.' The closing of the Straits of Tiran would constitute such a *causus belli*, in his opinion, but until then the consensus was that Israel should keep its powder dry.

To his surprise and dismay, he soon found that virtually everyone in high office had developed the habit of deferring to him — including the prime minister (who was, of course, also the defence minister). He became, in effect, the final authority, the key decision-maker, a position normally held by the premier. It was unfamiliar territory, and he felt that decisions involving peace and war were too important to be made by only one person. He yearned to share the burden, but subtly, irrevocably, he had been chosen by the others to render the final opinion. The experience wore him out and took its inevitable toll. 'For me,' he said later in one of the rare instances when he talked about this period, 'it was hell.'[6]

He was caught in the middle of contradictory pressures. While some were insisting that the nation should take all necessary measures to protect itself against the Egyptian threat, including a daring, pre-emptive strike, others were expressing fears that Israel, by mobilizing, was simply provoking Egypt into a war that no one, including Nasser, really wanted.

Above all, he was beset by doubts and anxieties about letting the nation down, about using his skills too little or too late. If war came, Rabin would take it as a sign that he had personally failed somehow, and so he drove himself to explore every avenue in order to prevent this outcome. 'He was forever haunted by the feeling that he hadn't done enough,' his wife Leah recalls.[7] He was one of only a handful of men who knew the facts: among others, that most of the ground-to-air missiles ordered from the United States had not yet been installed; that of Israel's four submarines only one was actually available for immediate service. He was only too conscious of how sparse Israel's defences were in Sinai, and was preoccupied with the thoughts of the damage the Egyptian army could inflict on the Israelis, should they open fire soon after 15 May.

The burden lay heavily on his shoulders. 'I was put in a position where the Government was saying: "What do you want us to do? You have to tell us." And when I told them what we had to do, they asked what was going to be the price, and I said it was going to be heavy, that it wasn't going to be a picnic, it was going to be a war.'[8] Despite the number of leaders who met, conferred, argued, and gave advice, Rabin realized that the final decision on whether Israel should go to war was his. 'I had the feeling, rightly or wrongly, that I had to carry everything on my own. I felt that I had been chosen to be the one who carried the burden, but that I had no right to make the decision, and I was torn between these two feelings.'[9]

The personal 'hell' Rabin was going through was evident to his close associates. 'Suddenly,' his secretary Ruhama Hermon remembers, 'he felt he didn't know what to do. He had to decide everything by himself . . . What would happen to those young boys who were going to fight? Maybe it was the wrong step, and if something terrible happened, it would be his fault.'[10] The pain and tension showed on Rabin's face. Finding he could share the load with no one else, he turned inward; it was difficult to talk even to those with whom he was close. Eshkol noticed the change in him, too. He found the chief of staff increasingly nervous, and mentioned it to his aides. Rabin naturally set the mood for the men around him, and if he was edgy, others took their cue from him. One senior official who watched as Rabin spoke to newsmen on 21 May remembers his 'stammering, nervous, incoherent replies. It was almost as if he had lost his nerve, was out of control.'[11]

He wanted guidance. He had plenty of advice — all of it contradictory, and from people whose judgment he had little reason to trust; what he needed was to talk to someone whom he respected. He turned to David Ben-Gurion, 'my teacher' as he liked to call him. Rabin's relationship with Ben-Gurion had generally been good except for the unfortunate incident concerning the Palmach conference in 1949. Indeed, Ben-Gurion, as has been noted, in time overcame his grievance, and Rabin looked upon the former premier as a mentor, someone to whom he could turn for advice on military matters. Eshkol was no friend of Ben-Gurion's, but realizing Rabin's agony of mind he gave his approval for the meeting. Rabin phoned the 'Old Man' and they agreed to meet at 7 pm that day — Sunday, 21 May — at Ben-Gurion's home in Tel Aviv.[12]

The meeting shattered Rabin's morale. 'As soon as I opened the door — I didn't even have a chance to say hello — Ben-Gurion launched into the attack: "What's going on? Are you *trying* to endanger Israel? In 1956 I didn't begin the war until I was sure the skies over Tel Aviv and our other cities were protected by the French air force — and here you are, entering into a war in just any old way."' The decision to mobilize the reserves, over which Rabin had a greal deal of influence, particularly annoyed him. Egypt, he thought, had only been bluffing in Sinai, but in view of the Israeli call-up Nasser would now probably be provoked into taking serious military action.

'I thought I would be given some encouragement by Ben-

Gurion,' Rabin says, 'but it was just the opposite. The load of responsibility that I carried on my shoulders grew even heavier.' He came away from the meeting shaken and shocked, with none of his doubts resolved about the correctness of the decisions he had taken. Instead, the doubts were joined by feelings of guilt. He was now even less sure that the preparations he had made were sufficient, or even that they were not in themselves provocative, and, worst of all, he was less confident than ever that Israel could stand up to such a war.

On 22 May, Rabin met the foreign minister, Abba Eban, in Eban's Jerusalem home on Balfour Street. Eban came away from the meeting even more gloomy than before. He had asked Rabin how he could help in the military crisis. The chief of staff replied tersely: 'Give me time, time, time. We *need* time.' Conscious of how thin the Israeli defences were in Sinai at that moment, Rabin was searching for ways to postpone a confrontation with the Egyptians.

If his mind had been overburdened, so too his body had been overtaxed. He had been working between fifteen and twenty hours a day since the crisis began eight days before. He went home each day, but only to snatch a few hours' sleep. He had increased his cigarette smoking to between 60 and 70 per day. He tried to be everywhere at once: as chief of staff, he felt he should be with his troops to make sure that they were adequately prepared for war, if it came; but Eshkol required his presence at high-level meetings, and this proved a physical and psychological drain on his energies.

Nasser's decision to close the Straits of Tiran on 23 May reached Aharon 'Arele' Yariv at 1:30 am. Yariv then phoned Rabin, who in turn placed calls to Eshkol and Eban. At 7:30 am Rabin joined Eshkol and the general staff in the war room in Tel Aviv. Victory was certain, Rabin told them, but the price would be high. (After the war, he acknowledged that he had in mind war losses numbering thousands of dead, with tens of thousands wounded.) The night before, Rabin had told his wife that 'if Nasser closes the Straits of Tiran, it means war'; but now that it had happened, he refrained from advocating the opening of hostilities. Cabinet ministers, continuing to defer to Rabin's judgment, were content not to press for war, as long as the chief of staff did not think it necessary.

At 9:30 am Rabin met the Ministerial Committee on Defence. Those who attended described his briefing as very 'sober'. He gave the impression that war could still be avoided; though the Egyptian closure of the Straits of Tiran — cutting off Israel's southern port of Eilat — was an act of war, the Israelis needed to gain time. He proposed that Israel should take the matter to the United Nations Security Council. Eban, however, argued that turning to the Security Council was a sign that Israel had no intention of acting militarily itself, and would weaken its position.

That morning the Israelis hoped that the Western powers, particularly the US, Britain and France, would make it clear to Egypt that blocking the Straits constituted interference with their own shipping — but such a complaint was not made. The US merely asked Israel for another forty-eight hours in which to come up with some diplomatic action that would persuade Nasser to rescind his decision to close the Straits. The Israelis, with little other choice, agreed. A decision was taken to send Eban to Paris and Washington for further discussions.

What happened to Rabin during that day and its interminable meetings has been shrouded in mystery and controversy, but undoubtedly something dramatic did befall the chief of staff, an illness that has been variously described by various people. Leah Rabin said later that this was the day he 'broke'.[13] The change in him was obvious to everyone who saw him. 'He was on the verge of exhaustion,' remembers Leah. 'I told him if he didn't rest, I didn't see how he was going to make it.'[14] Writing in his 1979 *Memoirs*, Rabin felt unable to explain what had come over him. 'Late that evening, after a day of tension and meeting after meeting in smoke-filled conference rooms, I returned home in a state of mental and physical exhaustion. Ever since then I have repeatedly asked myself, what happened to me that evening? How did I get to such a state? Now, twelve years later, I still lack a definitive answer. There can be no doubt that I was suffering from a combination of tension, exhaustion and the enormous amounts of cigarette smoke I had inhaled in recent days . . . The past few days had seemed endless. Meals were taken on the run and only when the occasion arose. I had hardly slept, and I was smoking like a steam engine. But it was more than nicotine that brought me down. The heavy sense of guilt that had been dogging me of late became unbearably strong on 23 May.' He remembered Ben-Gurion's words that he bore the responsibility. Though he felt that the IDF was properly prepared, '. . . perhaps I had failed in my duty as the prime minister's chief military adviser. Maybe that was why Israel now found itself in such difficult straits. Never before had even I come close to feeling so depressed. . . .'[15]

One of the first to arrive at Rabin's home on the evening of 23 May was Yariv. He sensed that Rabin was tormented by the fear that he had not ordered enough men and arms to the southern frontier to defend the country against the Egyptians massing there during the past week, and told him that he was wrong to be so worried; that everything was proceeding well. But despite his efforts to cheer Rabin up, Yariv could see that he was scarcely listening. He seemed like a man in a dream, hardly speaking.

Discouraged, Yariv went home and had been there only a short while when Leah's sister telephoned. She had just learned of the chief of staff's troubles from Leah, and begged Yariv to go back to Rabin's house. Instead, Yariv went to the airport to meet Haim Bar-Lev (head of the general staff branch 1964–66), whom Rabin had summoned back from a Paris study mission. Yariv later regretted going to the airport rather than to see Rabin again, feeling he might have been able to prevent the events of the next twenty-four hours.

Most of those who saw Rabin during his illness have described it as both physical and psychological. 'He had to rest,' says a close friend, Ya'acov Hefetz, who was then serving as the chief of staff's financial adviser. 'I don't like to use the word collapse, because he didn't collapse. He was physically worn out. He had worked so hard.'[16] Rabin had only rarely spoken in public directly about the illness, and though it became known to many Israelis after the war, the precise details were never publicized. The first detailed version to be made public is the now-famous document by Ezer Weizman which was published in April 1974, at the height of Rabin's campaign for the prime ministership.[17] Weizman gives a similar account in his memoirs. It has been suggested that his version should be viewed with a certain amount of scepticism since he bore a grudge against Rabin for not supporting his candidacy for the position of chief of staff when Rabin retired in December 1967. In addition, Rabin and Weizman had a history of cool relations, although Weizman later acknowledged that he had received everything he wanted from Rabin in the way of equipment for the air force. However, no one — including Rabin — has ever disputed most of the facts which Weizman presents in his account of Rabin's illness.

Weizman contends that Rabin showed signs of stress even before 23 May. 'As the suspense built up, and especially as mobilization went ahead and intelligence reports poured in telling of Egyptian forces entering Sinai, I sensed that the chief of staff was progressively losing his balance.' Rabin had altered previous decisions, could not make up his mind, and, Weizman wrote, such things had the effect of creating 'insecurity all around him — in his talks with the prime minister and at general staff meetings.'[18]

According to Weizman, Rabin phoned him at 8 pm on the evening of 23 May, his voice weak, pleading with him to come round immediately. He found the chief of staff sitting in semi-darkness. Speaking with quiet deliberation, Rabin told him: 'I have involved Israel in its greatest war yet. I have involved Israel through the series of mistakes I've made. Since this battle is going to be fought primarily in the air, and as we cannot afford a leader who makes mistakes, I want to resign. You take over as chief of staff.'[19]

Weizman records that he was shaken by this, and took a few moments to answer Rabin. 'You know that I want to be chief of staff,' Weizman told him, 'but not in this way. I won't accept the post. In the present difficult circumstances, the changeover would be a heavy blow to the army's morale. The Government is already hesitant about going to war, and your resignation won't help them make up their minds. As for you, Yitzhak, if you resign now, you'll be finished for the rest of your life. Summon up all your strength. I promise to do the best I can to help you get through. You'll be the victorious chief of staff. You'll reach the Suez Canal and the Jordan.'

Rabin looked at him uncertainly. 'Are you sure?' he asked. Weizman replied firmly, 'I'm as sure as I'm sitting here.' He advised the chief of staff to get some rest and promised to return in the morning. Meanwhile, he gave instructions that all telephone calls to Rabin be re-routed to him for the time being, and contacted an army doctor. When the doctor, Eliahu Gilon, arrived, he and Weizman agreed to describe Rabin's illness as 'nicotine poisoning', a plausible enough diagnosis in view of his heavy smoking.

Leah Rabin says the doctor decided her husband needed twenty-four hours' rest, and gave him an injection to help him sleep. Under the effect of the sedative, Rabin slept most of the time until 3 pm Wednesday and awoke feeling 'one hundred per cent better'.[20]

In his *Memoirs*, Rabin acknowledged that he asked Weizman, 'Am I to blame? Should I relinquish my post?' but he emphatically denied ever saying that he offered the chief of staff post to Weizman. 'I made him no such offer, nor was I empowered to "bequeath" the job to him or anyone else. That is not a chief of staff's prerogative.'[21] Formally speaking, Rabin is correct that one chief of staff cannot appoint his successor. But these were extraordinary times: it was the eve of war, the Israeli chief of staff had suddenly taken ill and been placed on the sidelines. Weizman, as head of the General Staff branch, was certainly an understandable choice to take over as acting chief of staff on an emergency basis. Rabin admitted that he was considering resigning, and he must have realized that his resignation would perhaps put Weizman in charge of the IDF, at least for the foreseeable future.

Weizman had called a meeting of the general staff for 8:30 am the next morning (24 May). Before going there, he visited Rabin at about 7 am. According to Weizman, Rabin again asked him if he was prepared to take over, but Weizman assured him he had not changed his mind. After calling on Rabin, Weizman stopped at the house of his brother-in-law — and Rabin's neighbour — Moshe Dayan. They had a brief talk, from which Weizman gained the impression that he had been right to refuse to take over from Rabin: Dayan implied that Weizman would not win the support of his army colleagues for seeming to 'grab' the job of chief of staff while Rabin was temporarily incapacitated.

At 8:30 am Weizman met the army's regional commanders and placed the army in battle formation. Rabin later wrote that he felt Weizman had acted 'rashly' in calling the general staff together without his knowledge.[22] The air force was put on alert. Around the room there were some bewildered stares, as commanders wondered where the chief of staff was. Weizman had decided that neither the generals nor the public at large would be told about Rabin's state of mind at that time. Only certain staff officers were let in on the secret, and even they were not told the entire story. Weizman ordered the generals not to communicate with Rabin. Some at the meeting already knew the situation, and needed no explanation. Ya'acov Hefetz, who was at Rabin's house during his illness, says that the chief of staff switched from cigarettes to chocolates once he became sick. But, he adds, nicotine poisoning 'was not the whole truth. He was physically worn out. Never before had such a responsibility rested on the shoulders of an officer, a military leader. It was a mixture of physical and mental fatigue.'[23]

Rabin spoke only in the most general way about that day, without attempting to describe or assess what had happened to him. He cast doubt on Weizman's version, but did not discuss it thoroughly. People close to him suggested that it would be in his best interests to reveal the truth — the public was bound to be sympathetic and understanding. But he has always rejected the idea. 'The truth is,' he said on Israel Radio on 24 June, 1968 a year after the war, 'that I had a certain accident as a result of which I left my work for about twenty-four hours. The accident was mine and mine alone and only I carry the responsibility for it. The descriptions that I read are not correct.' When asked if he had been suffering from anything more than nicotine poisoning, Rabin gave no reply.

During the late morning of 24 May, Weizman visited Eshkol to inform him about the previous hours' events and the orders he had issued in place of Rabin. Eshkol thanked him, telling him that he had done the right thing. Late in the afternoon, Eshkol met Rabin's doctor at military headquarters in Tel Aviv and asked him what Rabin was suffering from. Weizman reports that Dr Gilon (who refuses to talk about the incident) said, in English, 'acute anxiety'. Whatever Rabin had — whether nicotine poisoning or 'acute anxiety' or some combination of the two — he had recovered enough by mid-afternoon of 24 May to see his brother-in-law, Reserve General Avraham Yoffe (who was to command a division in the Six-Day War). He informed his visitor that the doctor had said he was weak from too much smoking. Yoffe tried to boost his spirits by reporting that the soldiers' morale was high, and he urged Rabin to make a pre-emptive strike against Nasser. Rabin closed the brief conversation with the news that he would be back at work the next day.[24]

Weizman went again to Rabin on the evening of 24 May and begged him to return to his post. History would judge him poorly if he didn't, he told the chief of staff. The following day Rabin saw Eshkol at the prime minister's office in Tel Aviv, and told him he was fit to work. 'I had a personal problem,' Rabin told Eshkol, 'and I regret it. But I do consider myself fit for duty now. Yet if you think I should relinquish my post, I shall accept your decision without protest.' Eshkol dismissed Rabin's offer to resign with a 'No problem' and turned to other matters.

The main problem facing Rabin was how to re-establish his authority, having been away from his post at such a crucial juncture. General Tal felt the whole incident could be shrugged off if handled quickly and honestly. To his regret, Rabin did not follow his counsel. He returned to his duties, but refused to talk about the incident. Tal felt that by not talking about it openly and immediately, the episode might not only be misunderstood now, but even exploited by some later on.

The immediate response of many who were told of Rabin's illness was to interpret it as a sign of Israel's weak leadership. Here was Eshkol's chief military adviser giving way under pressure at a time when the entire nation was looking to the army and the Government to take the proper measures against the Egyptian threat. Eshkol's radio address to the nation on 28 May, during which he frequently stammered and lost his place, and seemed generally unsure of himself, added to the growing national self-doubt and dissatisfaction with the leadership.

Nasser's closure of the Straits of Tiran on 23 May was followed by other actions that gave the distinct impression of a country determined to go to war. 'Everything Egypt had was being sent into Sinai,' recalls Rabin. Towards the end of May, Egypt, Syria and Jordan made joint defence arrangements; the combined potential Arab strength — aided also by Iraq, Kuwait, Saudi Arabia and Algeria — amounted to some 547,000 soldiers, 5,404 tanks and over 900 aircraft. The Israelis had a fighting force of 275,000, 800 tanks and nearly 200 aircraft. It was now crucial that Israel determine how much support it could count on from the United States. Unlike 1956, Israel now seemed to be standing alone, without the support of any other country, not even France, which was refusing to supply planes because of the arms embargo which they had imposed on 2 June. Rabin had no doubts about where the United States stood. He felt sure it would withhold support, but he wanted the American position made clear once and for all, so that Israel would know it was on its own. Ya'acov Herzog, the director-general of Eshkol's office, proposed that a cable be sent to the foreign minister, Abba Eban, in Washington, asking him to clarify with US officials the extent to which they were willing to implement past pledges. Rabin persuaded Eshkol that Israel needed this clarification, in effect, to free its hands, and the prime minister reluctantly agreed. In *Ma'ariv* on 2 June, 1972 Rabin explained that the cable had not been designed to secure a military pact with the US, but rather 'to clarify for ourselves exactly how we stood, and how much we could rely on others. The purpose was to point out to Israel that in fact we had no one to rely on but ourselves, that we were on our own, and we alone were responsible for our fate. That helped us to make a decision.'[25]

During those latter days in May, when fears were being expressed that the Egyptians might attack at any moment, the unwillingness of the Cabinet to take decisive action cast a gloom over the nation. The generals begged the Government to march against Egypt, arguing that firm military action was needed, not subtle diplomatic manoeuvring.

Rabin made frequent trips to the fronts during this period and broadcast messages over the radio, boosting the army's morale and calling upon the soldiers to be patient. 'I know the waiting is hard,' he told them on 30 May, 'but I can assure you if war comes it will not be fought on our soil.' The army, Rabin liked to say afterwards, was like a 'coiled spring', with many of its commanders itching for battle.[26] On 31 May, Rabin was telling the nation over the radio that war was imminent, and the army had to be on its guard. 'The transition from peace to a state of war may be precipitous,' he warned, 'and this fact obliges us to maintain our constant preparedness, to be ready for instant action.'

He visited the Jerusalem reconnaissance company on an inspection tour, and discovered that the company commander, Major Yussi, was also a Kadoorie graduate. Rabin noted that he was the major's senior by ten years. 'That's what makes me — to my regret — chief of staff,' he joked, 'instead of commander of a reconnaissance unit.' He told the men: 'It's a question of nerves — who will break first. We don't want to fight, but as long as they are on our borders we can't go home.'[27]

Rabin's long-time friend, Uzi Narkiss, commander of the Central Front, took him on a tour of Jerusalem's front lines. Narkiss was concerned that, if the fighting began, Jordan would make a rush for Government House, the one piece of non-Jordanian territory in Jerusalem which could be captured without difficulty. He asked Rabin to approve the moving of Israeli troops into the demilitarized zone, and the bringing up of a bulldozer to dig trenches, both of which would be blatant violations of the 1949 armistice agreement under the very noses of the UN officers in Government House, which served as UN headquarters. Rabin at first had his doubts about the idea, but he eventually agreed, and Narkiss gave the order.

The prospect of Israeli soldiers fighting again in Jerusalem greatly moved Rabin. Lunching at the Jerusalem Brigade Headquarters that day in early June, he encouraged the hundred officers in the room to think of what they might accomplish in the coming days. 'I fought here in '48,' he said. 'I hope if we have to fight here in this war, that you will complete what we were unable to finish.'

The Government took no decisions as May ended, although the public were demanding action of some kind, blaming the nation's leaders for their indecision, and pressing for the appointment of Moshe Dayan, the popular hero of the Sinai Campaign, as 'Israel's Saviour'. Rabin, painfully aware of Eshkol's indecisive image, accepted the nation's will, and supported Dayan's candidacy for the national leadership. He feared, however, that Eshkol would decide to give Dayan command of the Southern Front, thus ousting Rabin's old Palmach colleague, Yeshayahu Gavish, who had an excellent reputation as a field commander, and so Rabin pressed for Dayan's appointment as minister of defence, which, on 1 June, he was duly made. A day later the Israeli leadership secretly planned to launch hostilities, setting the date of Monday, 5 June.

The Israelis had gained the time they needed to plan the strategy of the coming war. Right up until the last moments, the plan, approved by the Cabinet, was for a limited offensive to capture Gaza and northern Sinai, which would place Israel in a strong bargaining position for the reopening of the Straits of Tiran and the withdrawal of Egyptian forces from the Peninsula. It was known as the 'minimalist' or 'limited' strategy, and was closely identified with Rabin, as was another concept ingrained in the planning of the IDF: the notion of the 'mailed fist'. Rabin had once explained, before the war: 'We use our armour like a mailed fist, thrusting with speed and momentum deep into enemy territory — not to take his positions, but to throw him off balance and make his position untenable.'[28] Even though this was at the risk of advancing along a wide front, and having few lines of communication, Rabin believed that by using the 'mailed fist', the IDF could overwhelm the main force of the Egyptian army, concentrated along Israel's southern borders, and once this was accomplished the Egyptians would soon reopen the Straits.

Israel's perilous military situation called for a bold, dramatic strategy, one that would immediately place the enemy on the defensive. 'Our overriding concern,' said Rabin, 'was that no matter who made the first move, our first act must be to strike a crushing blow at the main body of the enemy force. A major achievement on our part was needed within hours — a day — or the first few days — in order for this to have its effect on the fighting spirit of the other side. A victory in the air was needed both to crush the enemy air force quickly and so that our planes would be free to assist ground and sea forces.'[29]

The basic military plan for combating the Egyptians had been outlined and developed in 1964. It was a plan which Rabin had helped devise and one which had become part of the operational thinking of the IDF; however, the new defence minister had reservations: even if the IDF captured Gaza and northern Sinai, he thought, there was no guarantee that the Egyptians would reopen the Straits. Dayan favoured an Israeli sweep into Sinai with the aim of putting the entire Egyptian army out of action, and occupying the area — which would thus restore the credibility of the IDF. Yeshayahu Gavish's diary states that Rabin told him shortly after Dayan's appointment to give the 'limited plan' to the minister for approval. Gavish had his own, wider plan, but Rabin told him to stick to the 'limited' one. The Southern Front commander urged Rabin to let him mention his personal plan, and Rabin finally agreed. At the initial meeting between Dayan and Rabin at which Gavish was present, the new defence minister told Rabin to present the plan. Rabin ordered Gavish to present it. Unsure of what to do, the Southern Front commander asked Rabin, 'Which of the two?' Rabin, apparently persuaded by now that the 'limited' plan needed alteration, answered, 'The second one' (i.e., Gavish's wider plan, which resembled Dayan's). On the basis of this, orders were then issued that the attack, if and when it came, would be mounted on three axes into Sinai, in the general direction of Bir Gafgafa, and toward the Mitla Pass.

No matter how effective Israeli air strikes might be, the nation would still be faced with the massed enemy armies on three fronts. Jordan seemed to pose the least problem: the general view at military headquarters was that if King Hussein could find a way of keeping his country out of the fighting, he would. Accordingly, the IDF organized the Jordanian front, including Jerusalem, along defensive lines. Even though Rabin had sounded eager to finish the job left incomplete in the Jerusalem fighting in 1948, he was in fact anxious to avoid a clash in the Holy City if possible, because of the heavy price Israel would have to pay in human life. The Syrians were a greater threat, but the Israelis decided to concentrate their attention primarily on the Egyptian front, and only when victory was assured there would they turn to their northern frontier.

The Six-Day War began on the morning of Monday, 5 June. Beginning at 7:45 am, wave after wave of Israeli planes swept over nine Egyptian airfields; every ten minutes two pairs of planes would carry out precision bombing raids: first the runways were put out of action with delayed-action bombs; then aircraft on or near the runways were attacked (supersonic fighters had top priority, then other combat aircraft, and only at the end were transport planes bombed). Aircraft in the open were attacked with cannons and rockets; bombs were reserved for runways and hangars.

Before the pilots went into battle, Rabin told them in a voice
choked with emotion: 'I have so much to say to you; I cannot
find the words. Let me paraphrase Churchill's words: never in
the field of human conflict has the fate of so many depended on
the skill and courage of so few. It is you who will decide the
destiny of our people and our state.'

Three hours after the first planes swept over the Egyptian
fields (left unprotected because the Egyptians thought underground sites too costly), Rabin learned from Air Force
Headquarters that the raids had been an enormous success. He
telephoned Leah with great satisfaction in his voice. 'The
Egyptian Air Force is totally destroyed,' he told her. In the
afternoon Israeli planes attacked two Jordanian and five Syrian
air-bases with much the same success. One Iraqi air base was
struck too, but the Israelis discovered that most of the enemy
aircraft were at other, more remote airfields. By the end of the
first day of the war, Egypt had lost 122 supersonic planes, 75
subsonic fighters, 27 light bombers, 30 TU-16 medium
bombers, and 32 transports. Most of the 452 Arab aircraft
destroyed during the entire war were knocked out on the
ground. Israel lost only 26 aircraft in the initial two days of the
war — 46 throughout the entire six days (all but three to ground
fire).

The war was effectively decided during that first day of battle.
At the outset, the Israeli leaders portrayed the daring air strikes
which opened the war as a defensive reaction to Egyptian
aggression. 'On the morning of 5 June,' Rabin told a news
conference on 7 June, 'the shelling of settlements started on the
border, as did troop movements and the movement of
considerable air groups. We had to defend ourselves. Israel is too
small a country to take only half measures in its defence.'

Once the enemy's air force was out of action, it was time for
the ground forces to go into battle. Later that morning, Rabin's
calm voice giving the order to move came over the tank officers'
receiving sets, and the tanks began rolling in the direction of
Sinai to take on the Egyptian army.

A few hours after Egypt and Israel began fighting, Syria
launched an attack, its Migs strafing a number of villages in the
Haifa region. On the second day of the war, attacks by three

Syrian armoured columns were beaten back. The Syrians, however, kept up their fire against the settlements and built-up areas near the frontier throughout the war.

Although a partner in the defence pact with Egypt, Jordan waited on the sidelines during the first morning of the war. But during the afternoon, apparently basing their decision to join hostilities on reports from Cairo that the Israeli air force had been knocked out of action, the Jordanians launched an air attack and began artillery shelling of Jewish Jerusalem, an Israeli airfield in the north, and the suburbs of Tel Aviv.

During the early evening of 5 June, artillery shells, fired from Kalkilia on Jordanian soil, fell on Zahala and Tel Aviv, eight miles away. Shells passing overhead forced Leah and the children to race for a foxhole. 'I want to be where my father is,' 12-year-old Yuval said quietly. His father, the chief of staff, was at general staff headquarters in the underground war room in Tel Aviv. A nearby house had taken a hit. Leah and the children returned home. Phoning her husband, Leah asked him if he knew that Zahala had come under fire. 'Yes,' he said coolly, then, 'by morning it will be OK.'

At 1 am on the second morning of the war, Rabin broadcast nationally a summary of the day's events. He described the extent of the Israeli ground penetration into Sinai that day, revealing that the IDF had captured Rafiah and El Arish as well as parts of the Gaza Strip. He said little about the Jerusalem fighting, except that Government House, the former UN headquarters, was now in Israeli hands, after falling to the Jordanians earlier in the day — and that Israeli troops had captured certain points around the Holy City. Finally he told the nation of the devastating blow struck to the enemy's air force. (Some senior army men had pressed Dayan and Rabin to announce the Israeli air victory earlier in the day in the hope that this would keep King Hussein from entering the war, but they had decided to delay the communiqué.)

Rabin spent most of the early part of the war in the command room in Tel Aviv. Except for a few brief visits to the fronts, he did not leave the command post. Those who worked with him during those days found him quieter than usual, more evasive, and some attributed this to the fact that he was still recovering from his illness of the previous fortnight. He slept on a folding

camp-bed in his office, a telephone nearby. He went home twice
in the first few days, but only for brief visits. His adjutant, Rafi
Ephrat, urged him to rest more, but he resisted. He was invited
to make a tour of the West Bank of the Jordan, but refused to go,
saying that while the war was still on he had to be where the
decisions were taking place; the West Bank fighting, spasmodic
and brief, scarcely required his personal attention. On another
occasion, he flew by helicopter to a point outside Beersheba,
some 80 kilometres from Jerusalem. When he landed, he was
informed that three seriously wounded soldiers were in danger
of losing their lives if they were not evacuated at once. Rabin
immediately put his helicopter at their disposal, waiting three
hours for it to return and enable him to continue his tour. He
had no patience with those who tried to divert him from the war.
Later, when the Israelis had taken Jerusalem, he was invited to
attend a victory concert there, but with some anger in his voice
he explained why he couldn't bring himself to go: 'Today, when
soldiers are being killed? I have no time for concerts.'[30]

By the third day, Rabin was able to tell his countrymen that
the Egyptian forces had been totally destroyed and that
Jerusalem had been reunited and was in Israeli hands. He
concluded with these words: 'All these actions were achieved by
the Israel Defence Forces, alone and unaided.'

From a strategic point of view, the war could not have gone
more smoothly: 'From the beginning,' Rabin told a newsman
after the fighting, 'to its end, there were no real errors — I mean
errors that might have influenced the result of the entire
campaign. It is true that small mistakes were made along the
way, but it is almost unbelievable that a war of this dimension
and pace could be fought with so few errors. It was all due to the
excellence of the command at every level.'[31]

On the fourth day, Gavish, the Southern Front commander,
cabled Rabin: 'I am happy to inform you that our forces are
sitting on the banks of the Suez Canal. Half of the Suez
Peninsula is in our hands.'[32] Though the Sinai fighting was
tough, it went more smoothly than the Israelis had imagined. 'I
estimated that the campaign against the Egyptian army would
continue from one to three days longer than in fact it did,' Rabin
told *Ma'ariv* on 4 October, 1967.

The battle for Jerusalem was more complex. Uzi Narkiss, the

Central Front commander, was asking for approval to launch an assault on various places around Jerusalem, including Latrun and the Abdul Aziz Hill, but the military leaders wanted to make sure the fighting on the Sinai front was going well first. The battle for Jerusalem began about 11 am on the first day of the war. Narkiss wanted to open an attack just before midnight on 5 June, focusing on the police school and the Sheikh Jarrah district. In view of the Israeli victory in the air, Rabin thought a daylight attack the next day better, since they could then have the advantage of air support, but Narkiss argued that such support was useless, since it was unlikely that the planes could hit their targets with enough precision within the city. Rabin told him: 'Discuss both plans with Motta Gur, and let me know which you consider best. I'll make a decision based on what you decide.' Narkiss and Gur (then commander of the paratroop brigade in Jerusalem), agreed to attack at night, and the assault was set for 2:30 am, 6 June.

The purpose of the attack was to encircle Jerusalem. Gur's paratroopers hoped to reach Mount Scopus and the Mount of Olives in the eastern part of the city, and from there to move out towards the Jericho road, cutting Jerusalem off from the east. The first target, as the paratroopers set out, was the Jordanian police school compound, which had been converted into a fort during the fighting. Beyond it was the major Jordanian fortification on Ammunition Hill — and beyond this lay both Mount Scopus and the Mount of Olives. Battling their way through intense fire from the school, Israeli troops cut through four fences before reaching the Jordanian trenches on the periphery of the compound. The battle for the trenches was achieved only by fierce hand-to-hand combat. At Ammunition Hill, the next Israeli objective, where a system of bunkers and 40 machine-gun emplacements had been built behind heavy stone walls, the fighting was even more difficult, but eventually, with the loss of 21 Israelis, the Jordanian position fell.

A scheduled attack on the Augusta Victoria Hospital — located between Mount Scopus and the Mount of Olives — was called off because of heavy Israeli casualties in battles elsewhere in the city, but it was taken the next day (7 June), as was the Jericho road, thus closing the ring round Jerusalem. With that, Mordechai ('Motta') Gur ordered his troops to storm the Lions'

Gate and begin the conquest of the Old City. Once the Old City
had been breached, Israeli soldiers moved quickly through its
tiny alleyways to take control of the Temple Mount and the
adjacent Western Wall, the holiest site in Judaism. No moment
of the conquest of Jerusalem during the Six-Day War was
sweeter for the Israelis than this. After a 19-year absence the
Jews had returned and regained the Jewish Quarter which had
surrendered to the Arabs in May 1948.

When the Israeli military leadership entered the Old City, it
was naturally a very emotive occasion. Dayan at first wanted to
make a triumphant entry on his own, but he apparently had
second thoughts and asked Rabin and Narkiss to join him. The
experience of entering the Old City as the chief of staff of the
triumphant Israeli forces moved Rabin to the extent that he
later described that day as the 'peak of my life'.[33] As soldiers
raced up to embrace him at the Western Wall, he told them: 'It
is with affection and pride that the whole nation salutes you
today for the decisive victory you have brought us.' Thousands
were listening to his words over the radio, in addition to those at
the Wall. 'It was not handed to us on a silver platter. The
fighting was savage and hard. Many of our comrades in arms
have fallen in action. Their sacrifices shall not have been in
vain . . . The countless generations of Jews murdered, martyred
and massacred for the sake of Jerusalem say to you — "Comfort
yet, our people; console the mothers and the fathers whose
sacrifices have brought about redemption."' He reminded his
listeners that he had been in the city and fought for it during the
War of Independence; his entry into the Old City was therefore
'for me perhaps the most important event that has occurred
during these fifty-five hours'. Years later, speaking on American
television, he talked again about the experience: 'I think, if there
can be something for a human being that can be called the
fulfilment of a dream, that is what I felt when I neared the Wall
then. And to a Jewish boy who was born in Jerusalem, grew up
in Palestine, managed to see the creation of a Jewish state,
commanded a brigade in '48 and failed to liberate the Wall, who
became, nineteen years later, chief of staff, and then as chief of
staff to be able to bring about the liberation of the Wall, who can
achieve more than that?'[34]

Leah Rabin was visiting wounded at a hospital in the Tel

Aviv area when her husband's driver arrived with a note from the chief of staff's financial adviser Ya'acov Hefetz: 'In an hour's time there is to be an international press conference with the chief of staff and the minister of defence, because of the liberation of Jerusalem. It's a historic conference. Try to be there.' Upon arriving at Bet Sokolov for the press conference, Leah saw her husband for the first time since he had left home the previous Monday morning. He looked thin and tired to her. His eyes were red from lack of sleep. He seemed to be fighting to hide his own emotions.

Pressure mounted throughout the first few days of the war for Israeli action against the Syrians. Daily artillery exchanges between the Israelis and Syrians continued 5-9 June. The Israeli settlers who farmed within range of the Syrian artillery situated on the Golan Heights saw the war as an opportunity for settling old scores. The Northern Front command, headed by David Elazar, was in full accord; Rabin himself, a former commander of the Northern Front, openly sympathized with their wishes. Only Dayan objected, haunted by the Soviet threat that, if Israel attacked Syria, the Russians would enter the war directly. 'In the Six-Day War,' Rabin said later, 'we all had our traumas. For Moshe Dayan it was the Russians; for me it was the Arab armies deployed against us.'[35] Dayan also felt that an Israeli attack on the Golan Heights would need air support, and he could not guarantee this until the battles for Sinai and Jerusalem were over.

However, Rabin, supported by Elazar, pressed the matter and by 7 June Dayan was ready to cede a little. He told Rabin that he would approve an Israeli assault against the Syrians, but the IDF were only to occupy Syrian territory up to three kilometres from the international boundary, a limitation that effectively meant taking over the Golan Heights ridges, but nothing more. Rabin found the conditions unacceptable and told the defence minister so: 'To attack just for the sake of three kilometres is to expend effort and to shed blood without gaining anything worthwhile.' Dayan, displaying little interest in the project, said, 'If you abide by my conditions, fine. If you want more, no.' Rabin decided to consult Elazar before making a final decision. He promised himself that he would not budge from his opinion, confident that Elazar would agree with him.

Elazar concurred wholeheartedly: 'I'm not for the plan either. If the limit is three to four kilometres, get back to Dayan and tell him no. I'm not going to take responsibility for the shedding of blood for nothing. It wouldn't change the basic situation and I don't see any purpose in fighting for it.'[36]

The pressure intensified. At a Cabinet meeting on the night of 8 June Rabin presented a plan for attacking the Golan Heights, but told the ministers that whatever the IDF accomplished depended largely upon how much time it had before a new cease-fire was imposed. The Syrians had already agreed to the UN-sponsored cease-fire of 8 June in the hope of preventing an Israeli offensive. It was likely they would seek another one in the event of an Israeli assault on the Golan Heights, especially if the fighting were going against them. In an unprecedented step, settlers from the farm villages under the Golan Heights were permitted to attend the Cabinet session to present their reasons for wanting the attack. The Cabinet favoured Rabin's plan, with the exception of Dayan — so it was put off. It was midnight on the fourth day of the war.

Rabin felt able to sleep at home for the first time since the fighting had started. His wife Leah found him in a 'foul mood' because the war was about to end and Dayan was unwilling to approve an attack on the Golan Heights. When Rabin returned to command headquarters the next morning (Friday), he was greeted by Weizman who said that Dayan had been looking for him half an hour before — he had changed his mind and was now in favour of taking the Golan Heights. Dayan had told Elazar to prepare the attack. Dayan and Eshkol had a written agreement dating from the defence minister's appointment to the office, which stipulated that Dayan could not open a new front without Eshkol's approval. Dayan contended that he had merely ordered preparations for the Golan attack, and could have called them off at any time in the next few hours if Eshkol, when told of the decision, had opposed it. Explaining why he had made no great effort to contact Rabin before ordering the attack, Dayan claimed later that the chief of staff had gone on record as being in favour of the plan, and it was only he (Dayan) who had opposed it. In effect, he was saying that he considered contacting Rabin unnecessary.

Rabin telephoned Elazar immediately and learned that

Dayan had told him to begin the attack at noon and to see to it that it went quickly. 'Nonsense,' Rabin told the Northern Front commander. 'It's going to be a tough fight. Do it carefully. Plan, don't rush; do it as quickly as possible, but don't rush.'[37] Feeling that Dayan had underestimated how long it would take to overcome the Syrians, Rabin rushed to Northern Command headquarters by helicopter to direct the fighting personally. 'Don't forget "Galinka",' Rabin had warned Elazar over the phone before leaving. Both men vividly remembered a friend of theirs from the fifth battalion of the old Harel Brigade who had been killed at Abu Ageila in the 1956 Sinai Campaign. The chief of staff felt that Dayan had ordered the men to rush into battle at Abu Ageila without due preparations. He was determined that it shouldn't happen again.

By 7:30 am Rabin was at the northern command post, helping to redirect the troops who had been pulled back the night before. The air force went into action at 9:40 am and two hours later an armoured brigade led the Israeli ground forces into battle. The Syrians, with five infantry and four armoured brigades atop the rocky slopes of the Golan Heights, were ready. The Israelis used bulldozers to clear the way for their armoured vehicles on the lower slopes, and, aided by the air force, had achieved a firm foothold by the end of the day. At some points during the assault, infantry soldiers climbed the Heights on foot and fought hand-to-hand for the Syrian strongholds. On Saturday morning, 10 June, the IDF continued the attack, and within a few hours the Syrian defence collapsed completely. In many cases, so swift was the Israeli victory that retreating Syrian soldiers had no time to destroy weapons, ammunition or secret documents. Tanks were abandoned with their engines still running, and their radios on. Kuneitra, the Syrian administrative capital on the Golan Heights, fell without a fight at 2 pm. When a cease-fire went into effect at 6 pm that day, the IDF controlled the entire Golan Heights up to a line which extended from the western peaks of Mount Hermon, south through Kuneitra, then descending to the Yarmuk River.

The Syrians had built fortifications on the plateau and slopes of the Golan which, by most standards, should have been impregnable: bunkers and pillboxes were placed deep in the rocky soil; every strongpoint was lined with masonry, with heavy slabs of concrete above. The only part of the defences exposed to the direction of an Israeli attack were narrow firing ports. The subterranean bunkers were stocked with equipment and ammunition, and around all these defences were minefields and barbed wire. The Syrians had not taken into account the courage and perseverance of the Israeli soldiers who braved minefields and formed human bridges to scale the barbed wire in order to reach the Syrian positions, in the face of a heavy barrage of gunfire. In all, they lost 115 men in the fighting for the Golan Heights, with another 306 wounded. The Syrians lost an estimated 2,500 men, with another 5,000 wounded.

Sometime during the fighting on Friday, 9 June, Rabin visited the troops on the Golan Heights. As he was touring, soldiers who had been listening to their radios rushed up to ask him if he had heard the news: Nasser had resigned. Rabin's reaction was cautious; he told the men that this was probably a political manoeuvre and that Nasser would return. He asked them if they knew who Nasser's successor would be and was told that Zakaraya Muhieddin (Nasser's Vice President) had been prominently mentioned. Rabin remembered him from the fighting on the Southern Front in 1948 and rattled off dozens of small details about the man and his career.

The war was over. Israel had won a victory of startling proportions — 'greater', Rabin said, 'than any known in Jewish history'. The IDF stood on cease-fire lines which encompassed 70,000 square kilometres of territory, three and a half times the size of pre-war Israel. One million Arab inhabitants of the land captured by the Israelis had come under Israeli occupation. Israeli troops controlled the western bank of the Suez Canal and the western bank of the Jordan River, a pair of seemingly ideal boundaries. The price — for Israel — had been steep: 803 dead (777 soldiers and 26 civilians); 3,006 wounded (2,811 soldiers and 195 civilians). Estimates for Arab casualties were far higher: Egypt was said to have lost 10–12,000 men, with 20,000 more wounded; Jordan had 1,000 dead, and 2,000 wounded.

Notwithstanding the losses and casualties suffered, a mood of euphoria set in on the Israeli side, reflected in the widely felt conviction that the Arabs now had no choice but to establish a durable peace. The loss of the precious territory conquered in

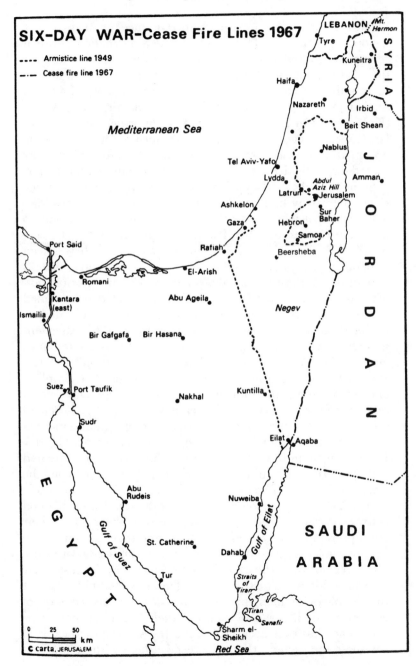

SIX-DAY WAR-Cease Fire Lines 1967

---- Armistice line 1949
-·-· Cease fire line 1967

Mediterranean Sea

LEBANON
Mt. Hermon
Tyre
Kuneitra
SYRIA
Haifa
Nazareth
Irbid
Beit Shean
Nablus
Tel Aviv-Yafo
Lydda
Abdul Aziz Hill
Latrun
Jerusalem
Amman
Ashkelon
Sur Baher
Gaza
Hebron
Samoa
Rafiah
Beersheba
Port Said
El-Arish
Romani
Kantara (east)
Abu Ageila
Ismailia
Negev
Bir Gafgafa
Bir Hasana
Suez
Port Taufik
Nakhal
Kuntilla
Sudr
Eilat
Aqaba
JORDAN
Abu Rudeis
Nuweiba
SAUDI
Gulf of Suez
St. Catherine
Dahab
Gulf of Eilat
ARABIA
EGYPT
Tur
Straits of Tiran
Tiran
Sanafir
0 25 50
km
© Carta, JERUSALEM
Sharm el-Sheikh
Red Sea

the war would, so they were persuaded, induce the Arabs to seek negotiations at once. The Israelis made a distinction between Jerusalem and the other conquered territories: on 15 June, 1967 the Cabinet decided to annex East Jerusalem and the surrounding area — Mount Scopus, the Mount of Olives, Sheikh Jarrah, Sur Baher, Sha'afat and the airport at Atarot (Kalandia). On 27 June the Knesset confirmed the decision. Israel would negotiate with the Arabs for the return of all the occupied territories except Jerusalem; the Holy City, now united under the Israelis' control, was to remain in their hands.

Some thought the Egyptians would be forced to make peace since their army had been so badly defeated. While acknowledging that it would take the Egyptians at least a decade to rebuild their war machine, Rabin thought the chances for real peace no better and no worse than before the war. He was keen to deflate the jubilant mood for fear that it would give Israelis false illusions. For the same reason he disliked any glorification of the war, and the names that had been suggested for it seemed to him ridiculous. 'I do not think this war needs a special name,' he told the army magazine *Ba'machane* on 5 July, 1967. 'Its extent and results speak for themselves. All the names suggested until now — "The War of Daring", "The War of Salvation", or "The War of the Sons of Light", are too pretentious. The simplest, and to my mind, the most apt name is the "Six-Day War", reflecting the six days of creation.' Even that seemed ostentatious, but the name stuck. In a magnificent and moving speech at the Mount Scopus campus of Jerusalem's Hebrew University on 28 June, 1967, where an honorary doctorate had been conferred upon him for his service to the nation during the war, Rabin said: 'The elation of victory has seized the whole nation. Yet among the soldiers themselves a curious phenomenon is to be observed. They cannot rejoice wholeheartedly. Their triumph is marred by grief and shock, and there are some who cannot rejoice at all. The men in the front lines saw with their own eyes not only the glory of victory but also its cost: their comrades fallen beside them, soaked in blood. And I know that the terrible price the enemy paid has also deeply moved many of our men. Is it because neither their teaching nor their experience has ever accustomed the Jewish people to exult in conquest and victory, that they receive them with such mixed feelings?' It was unquestionably one of the most remarkable speeches Rabin has ever made. At a time when the nation was swept up in the army's stunning victory, he chose to reflect on the suffering that had been inflicted on both sides.

The public only infrequently gets a glimpse of the real men behind its leaders' image. Military figures like Rabin are known only through their public appearances, and they are judged by their public image. What the people saw of Rabin in those days — before, during, and immediately after the Six-Day War, they liked and admired. He had expressed the nature of the Israeli victory to the country and to the world, and he was given a good deal of the credit for the victory. Only one other, Moshe Dayan, cast a longer shadow, and the two men were often compared, with the question constantly being asked: which one deserved the most credit for the Israeli victory?

Soon after the war ended, Leah Rabin found her daughter Dahlia on her bed crying, 'Mother, there is no justice. No justice at school, no justice in the scouts, none anywhere.'

Why did she feel this way, her mother asked.

'All the children say that Dayan won the war, not Daddy . . .'

Leah tried to calm her down, 'Dahlia, I know there will be many who say that, and others who say differently. Each of them made a massive contribution to this victory, which is so gigantic that there is glory for both of them and a lot of others. Now, do me a favour, don't cry, there's no cause even if this success has many fathers. Whatever happens, your father has a very respectable place in it.'[38]

The question of whether Rabin or Dayan deserved the most credit for Israel's triumph was, and still is, difficult to answer. Rabin did so much to prepare the army for that major test of 1967 that his role can hardly be understated — as Dayan's enthusiasts would like it to be. On the other hand, Dayan's dramatic re-entry into the Government on 1 June proved so decisive in lifting the sagging morale of the army and the public that his contribution to the victory cannot be discounted. Rabin's admirers argue — with much justice — that the military machine Dayan found when he entered the picture had already been readied for battle, and it only needed to be ordered into operation. The war was carried out so efficiently that the senior general staff, including Rabin, were less crucial to the

day-to-day running of the war than they were, for instance, in
the Yom Kippur War of October, 1973, where hard, risky
decisions had to be made all the time. Rabin's role was thus
reduced during the actual six days of fighting. He made
decisions related to the timing of certain major offensives, but
the key assignments were handed over to subordinates like
Haim Bar-Lev, Ezer Weizman, and local field commanders.
Rabin seemed content with this arrangement. Some thought it
uncharacteristic of him, normally a man who liked to make all
the decisions, big or small. But as Dayan took over most of the
planning, it seemed natural to Rabin to accept it.

Dayan's defenders contend that the defence minister wisely
enlarged the strategic plan against Egypt to include a knock-out
blow to the Egyptian army and the occupation of the Sinai
Peninsula, something the original plans lacked. However, a
decade after the war, Dayan admitted that Rabin had
disobeyed his order to halt the IDF 30 kilometres west of the
Suez Canal. According to the former defence minister, Rabin
believed such a restraint 'would have been bad for Israel.'[39]

Dayan tried to stem the rising tide of Rabin's popularity: he
rebuked Eban for including Rabin's name in a Security Council
speech when the foreign minister was listing the heroes of the
war. A week after the war Dayan made it clear that he felt all
credit was due to him, and to him alone. 'Anyone who says that I
came in and found everything ready is just trying to obscure the
issue.' He did his best to keep Rabin out of the limelight, a fact
which made Rabin's position as chief of staff less and less
attractive after the war. The Israeli public realized little of the
tension between the two men, and, ironically, lavished its praise
on Rabin rather than on Dayan. Dayan became the darling of
the international community, the hero of the foreign media; but
an Israeli public opinion poll nominated Rabin as the Man of
the Year in 1967, with 42.1 per cent, followed by Dayan with
27.4 per cent, and Eshkol, third, with 10 per cent. A second
Israeli poll at the time, which canvassed opinions as to who had
contributed most to the Six-Day War effort, put Rabin on top,
with 45.6 per cent, and Dayan in second place, with 31.5 per
cent. The polls are indicative of a point that needs to be stated:
Rabin and his work before and during the war have been
generally underestimated by the international press, largely

because so much attention was focused on Dayan.

The war brought Rabin much closer to the Israeli people. For the first time they made known their admiration for him and their gratitude for a job well done. One of Rabin's aides had mentioned that the chief of staff had a weakness for chocolate bars with nuts: Israelis began sending in chocolate bars in such quantities that Rabin's staff had to make a special plea to them to stop.

Because he was able to triumph both on the battlefield and in his own personal crisis, Rabin's behaviour during the pre-war 'waiting period' seemed largely irrelevant. The Six-Day War made him a military hero. His reputation soared at home and abroad. Suddenly he was the triumphant leader of the Israel Defence Forces, and no longer just another chief of staff. He came to symbolize the legendary feats of the IDF during those six days in June 1967.

No event shaped the image of Yitzhak Rabin in the public's mind as much as the Six-Day War. For the rest of his public career, he would be identified with that war, with the frightening moments on its eve, with the glory and triumph of the Israeli army during its six days, and with the spectacular changes in Israel's political map. When people asked themselves in later years whether Yitzkah Rabin would make a worthy prime minister or defence minister, his intimate involvement in the 1967 war was all the credentials he required. The Six-Day War, therefore, became Yitzhak Rabin's calling card for political leadership.

Chapter 6

On to Washington

The Six-Day War swept away the nation's self-doubt, and
replaced it with a new spirit of self-assurance. However, peace
was no nearer. Israel was militarily in a strong position, but little
else had changed for the better; the Russians were as great a
threat as ever. Rabin argued that Israel's best strategy was to
ensure its military supremacy, while at the same time making its
peaceful intentions and goodwill clear to the Arabs. To remain
the strongest force in the Middle East, Israel had to strengthen
its ties with the US. To convince the Arabs that it sought peace,
Israel had to show itself flexible on the question of returning
Arab territories occupied in the Six-Day War. Some thought it
might be possible to enter into relations with the Arabs without
having to give up any occupied lands. Rabin believed this view
was unrealistic: 'A genuine agreement can only be achieved at a
price. And the price is territory. To go to the Egyptians and say:
"We want peace, but you must agree to our new border being
the Suez Canal" — is a beautiful dream; in reality it's
impossible.'[1]

The American decision to suspend arms deliveries to the
Middle East after the Six-Day War angered Rabin. He felt that
the United States should capitalize on Israel's victory to try to
draw the two sides into peace negotiations. The way to do this,
he thought, was for the US to increase arms shipments to Israel
in order to make clear to both the Arabs and the Russians that it
was fruitless to pursue the military option. Instead, the Johnson
Administration had simply encouraged the Russians to begin
resupplying the Arabs.

Two weeks after the war the Russians demanded — without
success — the immediate evacuation of Israeli troops from the
occupied lands, using an emergency session of the United

Nations as their forum. Then in August came the Arab Summit Conference at Khartoum, where four principles were laid down: no peace with Israel, no recognition of Israel, no negotiations with Israel, and insistence on the rights of the 'Palestinian people in their own country'. The only apparent step forward came on 22 November 1967 with United Nations Resolution 242, which required Israel to withdraw from occupied territories in exchange for an Arab pledge of non-belligerency. The states of the Middle East were called upon to define permanent and safe boundaries, to demilitarize zones, to permit free shipping and to work out a just solution of the Arab refugee problem. The clause calling for Israeli withdrawal from territories occupied in the recent conflict pleased the Arabs, though its phrasing left open the crucial question of whether all or only some of the territories were to be returned. The Israelis welcomed the Resolution's pledge that each side would respect and acknowledge the political independence of all states in the Middle East 'and their right to live in peace within secure and recognizable boundaries free from threats or acts of force.' Both sides signed the document, though less in the belief that they were mapping out a Middle East peace, than because the language was loose enough to allow for a variety of interpretations. Hence, while committing themselves to virtually nothing of substance, each side succeeded in giving the impression that it was helping the momentum towards peace.

In his capacity as chief of staff, Rabin spent much of that post-war summer explaining the Israeli 'miracle' to an avid public. The nation had a new hero; newsmen pursued him; in Ramat Gan, a street was named after him. However, he was preparing to retire from military life. Despite his sudden fame and the glory of the moment, he had few regrets. He had built up the IDF into a supreme war machine, and seen it perform nearly flawlessly, but the work of the past four years had taken its toll. He found it unbearable to have to make decisions every day that affected the life — and death — of his men. Few people knew this, for he continued to be a very private man. He was eager, too, to take leave of Moshe Dayan, who saw no room for him in the army over which he now presided: their relationship, already cool, had deteriorated still further after the war.

For years he had been mulling over the idea of spending an

extended period in the United States. From his father he had learned to admire the sense of freedom which prevailed in the US and the raw energy this freedom released. As early as November 1963, when they were visiting Washington, he had confided to Leah his ambition to become Israel's next ambassador to the US when Abe Harman, the current envoy, retired. He realized Israel's links with Europe were becoming tenuous after the 1956 Sinai campaign, and it was clear that the US was emerging in the early 1960s as the Jewish State's main ally.

In a conversation with Eshkol just before the Six-Day War, Rabin had proposed himself as the next Washington envoy. The prime minister had seemed surprised. He could not imagine a native-born Israeli like Rabin wanting the job: the two previous ambassadors, Abba Eban and Abe Harman, had been born in South Africa. Rabin had gone as far as seeking the support of Eban, then foreign minister, and Golda Meir, then secretary-general of the ruling Mapai Party, but before a final decision could be made, the May crisis leading up to the Six-Day War had intervened.

With the war over, he renewed his bid. Time was now short: both he and Harman would be retiring within the next few months. He had no strong feelings about being a diplomat. He simply wanted to be at the centre of events, and at that time the place to be was Washington. 'I'm not pretending that I sacrificed myself,' he acknowledged. 'I did something that I believed was good for me and at the same time good for the country.'[2] He thought his credentials were sufficient to gain him the appointment: simply being a sabra would give him a better understanding of his country than those who preceded him, and, as a former chief of staff, he would be in a good position to preside over the growing military relationship between the US and Israel.

Other candidates for the job included Dr Ya'acov Herzog, Eshkol's brilliant political adviser, who was perhaps the most logical choice. But, though the prime minister at first favoured him, he eventually decided that he was too valuable to send away. Walter Eytan, the veteran diplomat who played a leading part in the Rhodes armistice talks in 1949, was another likely candidate; so were Joseph Tekoa, Israel's representative at the

United Nations, and Ephraim Evron, the Deputy Chief of Mission in the Washington Embassy. Faced with such competition, Rabin campaigned aggressively for the post, making known to the key people his strong interest. Initially Eshkol was cool towards the idea, fearing that the presence of a senior military man in Washington during the height of the Vietnam War might damage Israel's image as an unmilitaristic nation, but he eventually came round to supporting Rabin.

The public knew little about these developments because all news concerning changes in military personnel was censored for fear of lowering morale among the soldiers. By the time word did get out, Rabin had secured the enthusiastic backing of Eban, and had even put pressure on the foreign minister to let him begin the Washington assignment earlier than the scheduled date of March 1968. 'I can't stay in the army one day past 31 December,' he told Eban. 'In fact it's going to be hell to stay until then.' But there was little Eban could do to bring the date forward.

Rabin's colleagues were saddened at his departure. There was to be only one sour note. Ezer Weizman had long expected that he would replace the out-going army chief. As the day approached for Rabin to leave, Weizman was eagerly hoping for some words of encouragement and support, but none came. Finally, he decided to take up the matter directly. In a personal confrontation that was marked by Weizman's bitterness, Rabin remained non-committal. Weizman left the meeting, slamming the door. Haim Bar-Lev was chosen to succeed Rabin, leaving Weizman furious.

The new ambassador arrived in Washington on 17 February, determined to consolidate the prestige Israel had won from the Six-Day War. He had come to the United States to help bring peace to the Middle East, he told newsmen upon his arrival. 'If I am not successful in achieving this,' he went on, 'at least I will try to make Israel strong. In my previous job, my primary mission was to prevent war, and when this became impossible, I had to win the war. We failed in the first mission. We succeeded in the second.' (One newsman, greeting Rabin at the airport, asked if it was significant that Israel had sent its top soldier to Washington. 'In Israel,' Rabin replied, 'practically everyone is a soldier, and some of us become generals.'[3]) The Soviet newspaper *Izvestia* greeted Rabin's arrival in the United States with a front-page article which labelled him an 'extremist' and accused him of being 'one of the leaders of Israeli aggression against the Arabs'. The appointment, according to the article, reflected 'the strengthened military–political collaboration between Washington and Tel Aviv'.

After nearly a week of sightseeing and settling in his new job, Rabin wrote to his sister Rahel.[4] He described their stopover in France en route from Israel, where one incident had particularly struck him: 'By coincidence the President of Iraq [Abdel Rahman Aref, who was overthrown the following July] was visiting Paris at the same time as Leah and I. The whole city was covered with Iraqi flags. They were hanging from all the Government buildings. It was really a bit too much for me . . . We're beginning to organize for the long haul. We've stopped being tourists and begun to arrange what in the army is called "ha'maslul ha'shani" [one's second career]. We have begun also to look at the new realities and the problems, but we will overcome them . . .' (a reference to the unrest in the US at that time, and Rabin's confidence that it would not impede his presentation of Israel's case to the US Administration). 'Life in the US is completely different from what I'm used to . . . and so is the job.' The letter was full of references to the Vietnam War, the racial problems, and the drop in gold prices. 'America,' he wrote with characteristic understatement, 'has many sorrows now.' On 6 March, he presented his credentials to President Johnson at the White House.

Eleven days later he again wrote to Rahel, describing his first direct contact with the American political process. Israel was not to introduce television until May 1968, and therefore Rabin had not realized the impact it could have on politics. On 17 March television interviews were conducted with Senator Robert F. Kennedy of New York, who only the day before had announced his candidacy for the Presidency, and Senator Eugene McCarthy of Minnesota, who five days before had defeated President Johnson in the New Hampshire primary. 'Today,' wrote the Ambassador, 'we saw McCarthy and Kennedy on television. Seeing them live in an interview that can't be planned in advance gives the public the chance to see each tiny reaction. You really get closer to public figures through television . . . In the meantime, I'm speaking to people, giving lectures, etc., and apparently that is to be my way of earning a living here. My English needs improvement but I'm polishing it up.'

On 31 March, Rabin was invited to the home of Washington journalist Eli Abel to watch the President speak to the nation on television. A number of other officials and newsmen had gathered. At the end of his speech, Johnson announced — to everyone's suprise — that he would not seek re-election. The crowd watching the television tended to take the announcement with a pinch of salt, assuming it to be another of Johnson's platform tactics. For Rabin, however, the implication was more serious: if Johnson were telling the truth the ambassador would soon be dealing with a new, unknown Administration.

Before that would happen, though, the US was to go through much more painful turmoil. Rabin's most immediate experience of this came in April when Washington erupted in a series of racial disturbances which turned the streets of the capital into a veritable battlefield. The rioting focused on the city's business district. Rabin was shocked, but curious. What he saw on one occasion was 'really unbelievable. I watched people looting and policemen just standing by. No one dared do anything.' Another time, race riots delayed his arrival at a dinner at the home of the Federal Income Tax Commissioner. Despite the diplomatic identification his car carried, the police held him up at a blockade while they consulted their superiors about what to do. While he waited, Rabin reflected on the irony of his predicament: it was the first curfew he had encountered since the British left Palestine in 1948. 'Suddenly I saw Haifa and Jerusalem in the days of the curfew and I thought to myself: Great — twenty years on and several thousand kilometres away, and you're back living under a curfew again.'[5]

Although foreigners, the Rabins found it difficult to insulate themselves from what was happening around them. On 8 April, four days after the assassination of civil rights leader Dr Martin Luther King, Leah wrote anxiously to Rahel: 'No one knows where it will end. Since we arrived, so much has happened. Last week, Johnson resigned and then, at the end of the week, the riots occurred. We are really going through a seminar on the problems of the United States. Even though we are not involved, and we feel no fear or pain, it's still very depressing to be a witness to such a sad show. The riots, I think, are a symptom of a problem whose solution is very, very far away.'

Other events during those first six months touched Rabin personally, too. A meeting had been arranged between the ambassador and Robert F. Kennedy while Rabin was in New York City on 4 June, the day before the California primary for the Presidential nomination. In view of the senator's full schedule, Kennedy's aides had suggested just a picture-taking session with no talks beforehand. Rabin, however, insisted that the two men talk before the photographers were allowed in, and Kennedy's staff gave way — but it was all academic. After winning the primary the next day, Kennedy was slain by an assassin's bullet.

Events in the United States during much of 1968 depressed and worried Rabin. His image of the mighty giant was shattered and in its place he found 'bitterness — the endless struggle, the lack of guidance, the lack of clarity of purpose, the question mark over everything.'[6] He began to feel that the US was fast becoming a second-rate power, whose deterioration could have far-reaching consequences for the entire world. Rushing to fill the power vacuum created by America's new weakness would come the Soviet Union, and its first target, he predicted gloomily, would be the Middle East; the first sacrifice, Israel. The leading democracy of the free world, he felt, was falling apart.[7]

The most stunning proof for Rabin of the decline of American power was the Johnson Administration's failure to discover the Soviet plan to invade Czechoslovakia in August 1968. By an odd chance, Rabin gained first-hand knowledge of Washington's late awakening to the Russian move. He had been talking to Johnson's National Security Adviser, Walt Rostow, in the White House one day when the subject turned to Jerusalem. 'In my opinion,' Rostow told the ambassador, 'the greatest problem standing in the way of peace will be Jerusalem. You won't be able to compromise there.' He asked Rabin to devote an evening to telling him all about Jerusalem, its geographic and historical aspects as well as its political situation. Rabin agreed, and at the appointed time they met in Rostow's office in the White House basement, where for 45 minutes Rabin talked with the aid of maps and photographs about Jerusalem. At 6:15 pm, the telephone rang: Dean Rusk, the secretary of state, was on the line. Rabin suggested that he wait outside the office, but Rostow indicated that it wasn't necessary. Suddenly, Rostow turned white. He put the telephone down. Rabin continued to talk about Jerusalem, but the White House official's mind was obviously on other things. Fifteen minutes passed. Again the phone rang. Rostow's first words were, 'Yes, Mr President.' Again, Rabin suggested that he wait in another room, and this time, Rostow nodded his head in agreement. The lecture on Jerusalem was over for the evening. The date was 20 August 1968. The Soviet Union had invaded Czechoslovakia: there was nothing the United States could do. The Russian ambassador in Washington, Anatoly Dobrynin, was requesting a meeting with the President immediately. Rabin was a sad witness to the weakness of a crippled giant.

He also felt grave concern about America's difficulties arising out of the Vietnam War, which was absorbing the country's resources and diverting its attention not only from its domestic crises but also, it seemed to Rabin, from the problems of the Middle East. As a military man, he was appalled at the way the United States was pursuing the war. 'The first thing that shocked me was the lack of direction — I couldn't make out a goal, let alone any clear-cut idea of how to achieve it.'[8] He revealed his feelings about the war to Joseph Alsop, the writer of a nationally syndicated newspaper column, who cited the heavy casualties suffered by the enemy as proof of the effectiveness of the American war effort. Rabin argued that this was nonsense, that a war of attrition was futile: 'Headcounting won't lead anywhere — that is not the way to wage a war.' Alsop was furious at this attack on American policy.[9]

Rabin was an unusual ambassador, very different from the type of diplomat whose flawless command of the language is matched by an unerring sense of protocol. Rabin knew virtually nothing of the world of diplomacy, and what he came to know of it he disliked. As the architect of Israel's stunning victory in the Six-Day War, he had arrived in Washington with an impressive reputation. He was, in the view of his close friend US Senator Henry Jackson, 'the George Marshal of the Six-Day War, a brilliant strategist and tactician.'[10] Few men could talk about their country's military situation as well as Rabin could about Israel's: his expertise was not lost on either the Administration or Congress. However, there was some nervousness on the part of a few American officials about his being a military man, based on the assumption that a diplomat ought to be a diplomat, and not a general. His inability to speak English fluently was also a handicap when it came to establishing personal contact. He set about correcting this almost immediately, taping his speeches and replaying them in order to be word-perfect. Before facing a panel of newsmen on the CBS 'Face the Nation' programme for the first time in 1969, he asked aides to fire questions at him for practice. He issued instructions to his speechwriters to keep the language plain so that he would sound the same in private conversation as when making a public speech.

To his dismay, a great deal of his time was taken up with an institution he found alien and irrelevant: the Washington cocktail party. He disliked the ritual reception lines, the polite formality, and above all, the formal wear. Maurice Amitai, an aide to US Senator Abraham Ribicoff and later head of the American–Israel Public Affairs Committee in Washington, once teased him about the discomfort he was obviously feeling that evening in his tuxedo. 'I guess you came early,' he joked, 'in order to make the most of the evening.'[11] The remark brought a grimace from Rabin. One traditional trait of the diplomat — verbal self-restraint — Rabin never could master. It made for lively conversation, but it soon gave him a reputation for being less than the model diplomat. Once, during a luncheon with a British editor, he patiently explained why he thought Britain didn't matter any more in geo-political terms, and why only the US was important. 'And he's supposed to be a diplomat?' the editor remarked later.

Rabin was proud of the difference between himself and the traditional type of envoy, and encouraged people to think of him as only a temporary member of the diplomatic corps. A career diplomat would never look bored at banquet tables, like Rabin. A career diplomat would remain politely non-committal, but not Rabin. His manner was for many a refreshing change and appealed to a wide variety of acquaintances. Senator Jacob Javits, one of the handful of American Jews in the Senate, found his 'sense of mission' admirable. A ranking member of the Nixon Administration praised him as 'well-organized, orderly, and systematic'.

Despite initial problems, Rabin found the job liberating. Gone were the awesome responsibilities of military life and the barriers which his rank interposed between him and others. Even his natural shyness proved no great handicap, since he intended to become acquainted with official Washington slowly and carefully. He was always accessible to aides, but he believed in the concept of the chain of command, with the ambassador holding the final authority.

He was passionately interested in the way the American Government functioned, particularly in the field of foreign affairs: 'For me it was the best school in which to learn world politics. I wouldn't have learned what I did in ten years at university.'[12] He was most impressed with the intricate mechanism known as 'checks and balances' which prevented any of the three branches of Government from becoming too powerful. It provided a stability which, particularly in 1968, seemed crucial to the American political system.

Rabin's first aim upon arriving in Washington was to capitalize on the military triumph of the Six-Day War and convert it into diplomatic gains for Israel, whose relationship with the United States was far from perfect. Unfortunately it was a time when America was experiencing a popular movement towards retrenchment. Traditionally, the Israeli ambassador looked to the six-million-strong American Jewish community as the key source of support for the Jewish State; for that reason Eban and Harman had spent far more time talking to Jewish rather than non-Jewish groups. They had found these audiences friendly, often effusive. Rabin, too, reached out to the American Jewish community but the initial contact was cool and formal. Language was still a problem; he was a sabra, and that was strange to some American Jews. 'Some people,' said his close friend Norman Bernstein, a leader of the Washington Jewish community, 'would have liked him to be more of a personality, a man who would come and embrace them, put his arm around them and be close and friendly. Basically, that is not in his nature.'[13]

There was another difficulty underlying Rabin's relationship with American Jewry. The problem stemmed from his harsh view of what was happening to the American people in general as the true cost of the Vietnam War began to emerge. America in the late 1960s, he felt, was displaying far too little of the sense of mission which had brought about victory in World War Two; in addition, the country was failing to recognize how dependent on it the rest of the free world had become. The most glaring manifestation of this was the upsurge of popular feeling in favour of withdrawing the American presence from around the world. The consequences of such an isolationist policy for countries like Israel were all too obvious. Rabin was appalled to find some leading members of the American Jewish community supporting this view. He lectured them privately about the dangers it posed to Israel, and thus fell foul of some people who considered themselves friends of Israel. 'Yitzhak Rabin has one code of morality,' according to Marvin Kalb, the ex-CBS diplomatic correspondent and a close friend of Rabin, 'and that is the security of the State of Israel.' That code of morality drove him to approach groups whom no Israeli ambassador had previously considered worth approaching: church bodies, military think tanks, members of the American right-wing who, regardless of their political views, held opinions on defence that accorded with his own. He found considerable support for the Jewish State among Baptists during his trips to the South. He continued to speak to Jewish groups, but less often than his predecessors had, preferring to concentrate on reaching a section of America which he felt had gone untapped for too long.

Although the United States had been the first country to recognize the State of Israel, the relationship between the two nations had been under constant strain in the following years. This was reflected in the way American Presidents treated Israelis, both those who came on occasional visits and those who took up temporary residence in the US. As late as the Presidency of John F. Kennedy, Prime Minister David Ben-Gurion was accorded the privilege of meeting the President only in a New York hotel. The United States reserved White House invitations for its closer friends. Israeli ambassadors were consequently quite often left out in the cold. They were able to maintain a wide-ranging network of official contacts, but never came close to the senior men in the Administration. Talks with the President were rare. Frequently, American Jewish leaders, such as the Republican Max Fisher of Detroit or the Democrat Abraham Feinberg of New York, were asked to press Israel's case with the President. With the growing warmth of the Kennedy and Johnson Administrations towards Israel, matters improved, but only slightly. Rabin, a diplomat who had no time for conventions that kept him from doing his job effectively, was determined to change the system: 'I wanted to be in a position where the Administration and the Congress would turn to me rather than to a middleman.'[14] American Jewry — particularly the leaders — rebelled quietly. They didn't mind Rabin's decision to enter into a direct relationship with the Government that much, but they did object to being used in emergencies to pressurize key officials in the Administration without having had some say in discussions.

Rabin's first task was to obtain economic and military assistance from the US; his second, to convince the US that Russian penetration in the Middle East must be deterred; his third, to persuade the Administration to let those involved in the Middle East dispute resolve their problems without Superpower dictation. His policy was to suggest that Israel's goals converged with American interests in the Middle East, and this simple fact, he thought, would be enough to keep American arms flowing into Israel.

Rabin had troubles with the Johnson Administration from the start. The State Department official responsible for the Middle East was Lucius Battle, a man Rabin described once as 'pleasant, cultured, and positive', but very reserved and formal. The ambassador might have made some progress with him, but in October 1968, Battle resigned, and Rabin's relations with the Department took a decided turn for the worse. The problem was Battle's replacement, Parker Hart, a former Ambassador to Turkey, who had spent most of his diplomatic career in the Arab world. Rabin's first encounter with Hart in October 1968 was memorable: 'I entered his office — and thought I must be having a heart attack. I thought the ceiling would collapse on me. On every wall, on every side, covering every centimetre, they were staring at me — Arab rulers, with and without keffiahs, with and without moustaches, sheikhs, princes, rulers, presidents. The only agreeable picture in the whole gallery was that of the Turkish President.'[15] Rabin was, not unnaturally, shocked at such insensitivity on the part of the man with whom he would have to deal so closely on vital matters affecting the Jewish State. Realizing that his main contact in the State Department was an Arabist 'in mind and blood' (Rabin's own words), the ambassador was distressed that he now had no one with whom to discuss the delivery of Phantoms, and for the remainder of the Johnson period, he worked through the Pentagon almost exclusively — a precarious undertaking for a foreign envoy, but under the circumstances the only practical solution. Understandably, Rabin looked forward to the inauguration of the Republican Administration of Richard M. Nixon in January 1969.

Nixon had campaigned on the pledge that he would turn the previous era of confrontation into one of negotiation. He saw the necessity for fulfilling his promise in the Middle East, where the Russians, having become a Mediterranean power for the first time after 1967, posed a direct threat to American interests. The local Arab–Israeli conflict, in which the antagonists were the client-states of these two Superpowers, provided ominous possibilities for future confrontation.

The ambassador's acquaintance with Nixon dated from August 1966. Defeated for the Presidency in 1960, Nixon was hoping for another opportunity in the 1968 elections. In search of it, he travelled abroad extensively, gaining experience and meeting foreign heads of state. In Israel, where he seemed something of a political has-been, he was accorded a rather less than royal welcome. During the early part of the visit, Nixon and Rabin were guests at dinner in the Tel Aviv home of the American chargé d'affaires, where the conversation centred on Nixon's recent visit to South-east Asia. Rabin was the only other guest who had any firsthand knowledge of the region, having been there only a few months before. With this in common, the two men got on well, and Rabin offered Nixon a military helicopter for a day of touring round the country. It was an experience which Nixon did not forget: he was the first American in public life to visit the country after the Six-Day War and it was during that trip that he said, 'If I were an Israeli, I would never give up the Golan Heights'. At a Tel Aviv news conference, Nixon declared that Israel should not withdraw from occupied territories 'until there is a peace settlement'.

The two men met again for ninety minutes in the Mayflower Hotel in New York in August 1968, shortly before Nixon was named the Republican Party's choice for President at its convention. Rabin had sought the meeting, depressed by what he saw happening in the US, and sensing that Nixon, with his professed belief in a strong America and desire to honour American commitments abroad, would signal a change in the country's direction. Nixon assured Rabin that he was confident he could pull America out of its doldrums. Both he and his likely Democratic opponent, Senator Hubert H. Humphrey of Minnesota, wanted some kind of understanding with the Russians, he said — but Nixon did not think it possible to conduct negotiations without being strong. It was an opinion that accorded perfectly with Rabin's own.

Many Israelis wondered what effect Nixon's Presidency would have on American–Israeli relations. He had sent a special envoy, William Scranton, to the Middle East after winning the election in November, and the message that Scranton returned with had given rise to grave concern. He had spoken of the need for the US to be more 'even-handed' in its approach to the problems of the Middle East, a phrase that suggested a new American inclination towards the Arabs. Yet Rabin was cautiously optimistic about the new Administration; the Democrats had shown little favour towards Israel, in his view, and when it came to the crunch, had provided little political support. There was a slight chance that Nixon would be more sympathetic to Israel than his predecessor.

The first few months of the Nixon Administration gave glimmerings of hope in this direction. Nixon seemed more orderly than Johnson. He had convened the National Security Council a number of times in the early days of his administration — a good sign, Rabin thought, and one that indicated that perhaps Israel might be given more careful consideration. In March 1968, Eban came to Washington for talks with the new President. The foreign minister was fretful, suspecting the Nixon would move away from the generalities of the Johnson Administration, and begin to talk about the specifics of a final Middle East settlement, something Israel strenuously resisted.

Specific proposals from outside powers would, the Israelis were convinced, lead to unacceptable territorial concessions on the part of the Jewish State. The results of the Eban–Nixon talks pleased Rabin and persuaded him that Israel could look forward to enjoying strong support from the President. However, in the coming months, Nixon's manoeuvring with the Russians made him less sure, though this did not prevent the two men from continuing their good relationship.

Rabin found that he could adopt a relaxed tone with Nixon. In 1969, the President had invited a number of foreign ambassadors in Washington to a formal dinner at which they were expected to wear, in addition to white ties, any military decorations they had received. Rabin was slightly taken aback. The Israeli army, shunning formality, had made it a practice not to award military decorations, and hence he had none to wear. During the dinner, Nixon noticed Rabin's apparent modesty, and asked him about his medals. 'I would have thought a general such as yourself would have plenty of them,' he said with a laugh. Rabin replied, 'Mr President, the only award I received after the Six-Day War was an honorary doctorate from the Hebrew University, and it's a little difficult to pin a certificate on my suit.'[16]

Diplomatic activity in the Middle East was proceeding on several levels in 1969. There was the mission of UN emissary Dr Gunnar Jarring, and also the far more secret behind-the-scenes efforts of America and Russia to work out the terms of a Middle East settlement. Jarring had been selected as a mediator in the Arab–Israeli conflict as a direct result of Resolution 242 in 1967. However, Rabin had little confidence in him. One reason was the very fact that Jarring was acting under the sponsorship of the UN, an institution for which Rabin had little respect. Another was the ambassador's conviction that only Israel and Egypt — using the good offices of the US — could work out a peace agreement. Furthermore, Jarring wanted Israel to agree to border changes before negotiations. Rabin was careful, however, to be less critical in public about the mediator's efforts, believing, as did most of the Israeli Government, that Israel could not afford to be thought to have a negative attitude to peace initiatives, or to be accused of thwarting the peacemaking process.

Jarring had tried, during endless rounds of negotiations, to implement Resolution 242. He talked to Arabs and Israelis separately, but the two sides never met across the table, and neither side would move from its entrenched position. The Israelis insisted on direct negotiations with the Arabs, although they were willing to consider indirect talks as a prelude to a face-to-face encounter. Until the Arabs committed themselves to direct talks, the Israelis refused to say what kind of border changes they were prepared to accept. The Arabs for their part refused to come to the conference table unless the Israelis promised to return all the occupied lands. During the summer of 1968, Jarring had spent five weeks in New York meeting Israeli, Egyptian, and Jordanian officials, but to no avail. He tried again in 1969, when he was even less successful.

Meanwhile, Nixon's Secretary of State William Rogers had assigned to Joseph Sisco, the Assistant Secretary of State for Near Eastern Affairs, the task of enlisting Russian support for an American peace proposal — the Rogers Plan — which called for the return of virtually all the occupied lands to the Arabs, in return for which the Arabs would recognize the State of Israel and permit it secure borders. Sisco conducted the discussions through the Russian envoy in Washington, Anatoly Dobrynin, and the Soviet delegation at the UN. Rogers had hoped that the US and the Russians could reach prior agreement, and then present the plan to the next meeting of 'Big Four' powers (the US, USSR, Britain and France) in New York for their endorsement. Jarring would then be given the job of persuading the Arabs and Israelis to accept it.

Rabin was more worried about the secret American–Soviet talks than the Big Four meetings. Golda Meir, who had become prime minister after Eshkol's death in February, was alarmed at what might come out of these meetings, but Rabin suggested they were just a holding operation, while the real battle was being waged behind the scenes. The very fact that the Big Four powers were meeting at the UN meant that nothing much would come of them, thought Rabin, who believed the only aspect of the UN of interest to Israel was how the US voted on any given issue. He would have preferred the UN to move out of New York — perhaps to Geneva — so that it would not take up his time or that of other foreign diplomats in the US. He also advocated — privately — cutting down the size of the Israeli mission to the UN.

An attorney and a relative novice in foreign affairs, William Rogers knew little about the Middle East but evinced a strong interest in the region, unlike Nixon's National Security Adivser, Henry Kissinger. Rabin was never able to establish a warm relationship with Rogers, despite the fact that he genuinely liked him: their personalities were in sharp contrast, as were their methods of work. Rabin was serious, straightforward to the point of bluntness, without much humour. Rogers was light-hearted, outgoing, casual, always informal. The ambassador's early difficulties with English gave his presentation a ponderous formality for which Rogers had little patience. To make matters worse, from Rogers' standpoint, in the beginning Rabin spoke from notes. For his part, Rabin regretted that the Secretary had so little knowledge of the Middle East. Rogers saw himself less as a policymaker than as an arbitrator among disputing factions, leaving Rabin feeling helpless after their talks. Discussions between the two men were often lengthy, with Rabin doing most of the talking; Rogers tired quickly of the subjects that passionately interested the ambassador.

The Secretary of State's announcement in December 1969 of his personal plan to solve the Middle East conflict widened the breach, not only between the two men but, more importantly, between their two countries. It brought US–Israeli relations to their lowest point since President Eisenhower had forced the Jewish State to withdraw from Sinai after the 1956 war. Rabin was incensed at the proposal; it seemed to him a major diplomatic affront to Israel. Abba Eban, the Israeli foreign minister, had been in Washington for talks with Administration officials only a few days before the plan was announced; when he, Rabin, Rogers and Sisco had met, it had not been mentioned. In addition, the Israelis had been led to believe that the US would consult them about any new proposals for peace in the Middle East before they were made public. One of the worst aspects of the Rogers Plan, in Rabin's eyes, was the change it reflected in American policy towards the Middle East. Until the plan was announced, the US had never stated publicly what it believed Israel's final boundaries should be. Now, with the Rogers Plan advocating an almost complete return to Israel's pre-1967 frontiers, the Arabs would never agree to anything less; and the US, having taken this public stand, could not bargain for anything more at the peace talks.

New diplomatic procedures were evolving and Rabin found them unacceptable. The Americans were tending more and more to tell Israel what it should do, and to limit Israel's bargaining power. He knew that it was impossible to expect the US to withdraw from its peacemaking role in the region, but he wanted it to concentrate — in public at any rate — on principles, which had been the case under Johnson, and not details. He feared that Rogers was laying the groundwork for an American–Soviet settlement which would be imposed on the parties to the conflict. Israel had long resisted this as ultimately pro-Arab in design.

In addition to his strong reservations, Rabin had to contend with his Government's fears that rejecting the plan might provoke a new postponement of arms deliveries. Rabin argued that Israel had managed to strengthen its relations with the US to the stage where it could afford to turn down peace proposals without fear of the consequences, and he strongly advised the Cabinet to reject the Rogers Plan. When the Cabinet decided to accept his advice, it called upon Rabin to draft the wording of its rejection.

Shortly after the Rogers Plan was announced, Rabin delivered a personal reply to the proposal through the Israeli Embassy. The vehicle was a 'pink sheet' communiqué, an idea conceived by Yehuda Avner of the Embassy staff; it was usually distributed by the Embassy to newsmen and Washington officials to explain Israeli policy. It was couched in forthright terms that were, at least to the mind of the Secretary when he read it, less than diplomatic. 'US policy,' it said, 'as it is now unfolding, comes close to the advocacy and development of an imposed settlement. While this may not be deliberate, the mechanics and dynamics are moving in that direction. Israel will resist this . . . By addressing themselves in detail to matters of substance, the US proposals do more than undermine the principle of negotiation; they pre-empt its very prospect.' Rogers was stung into stating that diplomats on American soil should know better than to make public any criticism of the US Government. From that point on, relations between the two men were beyond repair. In public they remained cordial, but Rabin began to look elsewhere for friends in high places.

His most important achievement in Washington was the intimate dialogue he struck up with some of the key members of the Nixon Administration. Even after his relations with Rogers had soured, he was always allowed access to the Secretary of State. No Israeli ambassador had ever dealt so consistently with the highest echelons of the American Government. One of the most important relationships in this respect developed with Assistant Secretary of State for Near Eastern Affairs, Joseph Sisco, a State Department veteran who had once been considered as pro-Israeli, though by the time Nixon came to power, he had become a strong exponent of the new 'even-handed' American policy towards the Middle East. A deep friendship developed between the two men: where Rogers was often impatient with Rabin, Sisco was not, and Rabin found in Sisco a sympathetic understanding of the Middle East and a skill and optimism in dealing with the region that he felt were lacking in Rogers. Better than others, Rabin thought, Sisco realized that the Middle East had become a focus of Superpower rivalries, and that far more was at stake in the Arab–Israeli conflict than the survival of the Jewish State or the future of Arab nationalism.

Twice a week the two men met for lunch, usually at a favourite French restaurant in Georgetown. They spoke constantly over the telephone; and often watched professional football together. 'I enjoyed a personal relationship with him,' Sisco said, 'as much and probably more than any relationship I've ever had with an ambassador over the years.'[17] Sisco admired Rabin's ability to understand the mechanics of international relations beyond the context of the Middle East. He found that Rabin, with his thorough knowledge of military affairs, could make a very convincing argument that a strong Israel boosted American military potential in the Middle East. In addition, he found the ambassador a man of integrity whose word was his bond.[18]

Though his relationship with Sisco played an essential part in keeping him in touch with the highest levels of the American Government, to effect the change in American policy towards the Middle East which Rabin considered necessary, he had to influence the top policymakers, and one man in particular: Henry Kissinger. The two men had first met in 1966, when Rabin invited Kissinger (then an influential behind-the-scenes figure in Vietnam diplomacy) to lecture at the National Security College in Israel. A second meeting occurred in January 1968, just before Rabin took up his Washington appointment. Kissinger had flown in from Moscow and during his stay in Israel had an extended lunch in Tel Aviv with the ambassador-designate. They talked about the role of the Soviet Union in the Middle East, a subject in which both men were particularly interested. Though Kissinger was impressed with Rabin's grasp of international affairs, the two men had no contact for some time after Rabin arrived in Washington.[19] In late 1968, when Rabin happened to be in Boston, they had made an appointment which Kissinger was subsequently unable to keep: it was the day that Nixon offered him the post of National Security Adviser to the President.

Though Kissinger, in the early stages of the Nixon Administration, showed little interest in the Middle East, Rabin tended to share the sense of mistrust which some American Jews felt about him, which stemmed from the fear that his very Jewishness would make him over-anxious to prove his impartiality in the Middle East. It was not until the time of the Jordanian crisis in September 1970 that the two men got to know one another better, and it became clear that they had much in common: both enjoyed thrashing out the complexities of international affairs, both knew that it was impossible to look at the Middle East without taking into account the larger issues of Superpower politics. They enjoyed the intellectual exercise and found one another stimulating. Each in his own way enjoyed the secret, manipulative aspects of diplomacy. In Rabin, Kissinger found a cool-headed, rational Israeli who didn't stray from the main issues with meanderings into ancient history, as had been his experience with Mrs Meir. Neither man liked to gossip — at least, not to one another. In Kissinger, Rabin found much to admire: 'He is a great manipulator of events and peoople. He has a unique combination of academic knowledge and a pragmatic approach to problems, which is something one doesn't find nowadays.'[20] The American showed a sensitivity to Israel which the ambassador had not met before in Washington. The key, of course, to Kissinger's thinking — and Rabin understood this — was his mistrust of the Russians. 'We have to work together,' he told Rabin early in his ambassadorship, 'to make clear to the Arab countries that there is nothing to be gained through cooperation with the Soviet Union.'[21] It was a goal which Rabin shared. Kissinger pressed the envoy to accept the notion — an alien one to most Israelis that the Jewish State would be better off if the US could develop closer ties with the Arabs. Rabin shrewdly countered that Israel could understand this, but the US would have to offer her some kind of compensation if an American–Arab axis was to be formed. Kissinger accepted Rabin's argument. (After the Yom Kippur War of October 1973, Kissinger would apply something of this notion to the Middle East peacemaking process, trying to reintroduce American influence into the Arab world while at the same time maintaining a close relationship with Israel.)

Rabin was a major influence on Kissinger's thinking about the Middle East, and managed to persuade him to give serious consideration to the need to give the Jewish State military and political support. It was due to Rabin, too, that Kissinger eventually rejected the prevalent view in the State Department about the desirability of the two Superpowers working out a Middle East settlement — the imposed peace which the Israelis feared so much.

Just about every facet of American life fascinated Rabin. He enjoyed travelling around the country, and particularly liked the West Coast for its great natural beauty. An amateur photographer, when he could find the time he would roam the countryside around Washington with his camera. He and his wife had not known such a sense of ease since their days at Camberley in 1952. 'I enjoyed my job, I enjoyed being in America. I enjoyed most the contacts I had, even though there were difficult days and unpleasant meetings, and unpleasant events.'[22] Leah — who was a great social success and made many firm friends in her own right — had charge of their social calendar, a major enterprise since she made a special point of looking after all the arrangements herself, including the setting of the table, arranging the flowers and supervising the meals. The Rabins' cook kept her own diary to make sure that no returning guest was served the same dish twice. The one task Leah forswore was the seating arrangement: 'To decide people's fate, even for two hours at a dinner party,' she once said, 'is cruel.'

In 1970, Rabin's son Yuval celebrated his Bar Mitzvah in a Washington synagogue. A year later, on 5 December, Rabin's father Nehemiah died at the age of 85. He had been taken ill in November, but had refused to allow Rahel to send for Rabin, knowing that his son was busy with a visit that Mrs Meir was making to the US. The funeral was delayed until Rabin arrived in Israel, two days after Nehemiah's death.

The Rabins had a wide circle of friends in Washington. Wherever he went, the ambassador tended to attract a crowd, eager to listen to his military experiences, especially those of the Six-Day War. Talking about such things animated him: 'I used to listen to him with wonderment,' noted Marvin Kalb, who was a frequent guest at Washington cocktail parties. 'When he talked strategy and tactics, he sparkled. The effect was to convey total self-confidence.'[23] A popular lecturer on military subjects at the Pentagon, it was inevitable that Rabin would make friends among the upper echelons of the US army, to whom he was primarily a military man, not a diplomat. While at formal meetings with them, he was addressed as 'Mr Ambassador', though Admiral Thomas Moorer, the Commander-in-Chief of the US Armed Forces, once told him: 'To me, you're General Rabin, and a general is much more to me than any ambassador. So let's be done with this "ambassador" bit.'[24]

When the occasion arose to be present at a ceremony marking the completion of the first training course for Israeli pilots learning to fly Phantom jets, Rabin could not resist asking permission of the US Air Force to sit alongside one of the Israeli pilots as he put a Phantom through its paces that day. The request caused great consternation — who was responsible for a foreign envoy flying in an American Phantom? What if other foreign ambassadors asked for the same privilege? After much to-ing and fro-ing the matter was handed over to the State Department — and Joseph Sisco, who took great pleasure in granting Rabin's request. There were two conditions: an American pilot had to fly the plane, and Rabin had to sign forms accepting responsibility for his own welfare. Rabin agreed and spent a happy 45 minutes seeing the Phantom's capabilities demonstrated.

He made particular friends among the leaders of the Washington Jewish community, mostly men of means who were interested in Israel's cause. His political friends, too, tended to be strong supporters of Israel, like Senators Henry Jackson of Washington, Stuart Symington of Missouri, and Jacob Javits of New York. Jackson liked the ambassador's habit of getting straight to the point ('His greatest asset was his ability to say something in a few words, clearly, concisely, and in a well-organized manner'), and helped Rabin to become acquainted with America's defence establishment.[25] As a member of the Senate Armed Forces Committee, Jackson paved the way for him to visit the Strategic Air Command in Omaha, Nebraska, early in his ambassadorship. Symington felt relaxed enough with Rabin to ask him the most sensitive questions: when the two men were returning from a trip to Sinai soon after Rabin had left Washington permanently in 1973, the Senator asked him point-blank whether or not Israel had the atomic bomb. Without changing his expression, Rabin gently but firmly switched the subject.[26] (Israel has officially denied having nuclear weapons and has said that it would not be the first to introduce them into the Middle East. *Time* Magazine, however, stated in April 1976 that the Jewish State had 13 such weapons, a report vigorously denied by the Israelis.)

At times Rabin was surprised to find how much sympathy for Israel actually existed at the top levels of Government in Washington. At his first meeting (in 1969) with the Labour Secretary, George Shultz, he began explaining Israel's case, but Shultz interrupted him after a few sentences. 'I presume you want to persuade me how right you are, and how much you need help,' he said. 'Well, I'm pretty convinced already.' Shultz told Rabin of an Israeli student who had come to him in May 1967, when he was teaching economics at the University of Chicago. The boy had returned to Israel to fight in the war, and had been killed during the struggle for the Golan Heights. When Shultz visited Israel in 1969, he made a special request to see the Golan Heights, despite the policy of American officials to avoid Israeli-occupied territory.[27]

One unlikely person who became a close friend was the

national newspaper columnist Rowland Evans, a frequent critic of Israel, with whom Rabin was always at odds over American support for the Jewish State. Evans held that the US would be better off paying more attention to the Arabs and less to the Israelis, that the Russians posed no great threat in the Middle East unless the Americans drove the Arabs into their arms by siding with Israel rather than acting even-handedly. He also questioned whether the US needed to invest so much money in Israel. But 'I never persuaded Rabin,' said the columnist, 'and he never persuaded me.' He has described Rabin as 'the hardest-working diplomat I've ever seen in Washington.'[28]

Perhaps the oddest friendship Rabin struck up during his Washington days was with the Russian ambassador, Anatoly Dobrynin. Besides being champions of the Arab cause, the Russians had no diplomatic relations with Israel, having broken them off during the Six-Day War. Yet when Rabin arrived late at the funeral of two American diplomats murdered by Arab terrorists in Khartoum on 2 March 1973, and was unable to find a seat in the VIP section, Dobrynin noticed him, rushed up with a friendly greeting, and ushered him to the VIP stand, where he made room for Rabin next to himself.

Despite its losses in the Six-Day War, Egypt was in a position to renew military pressure on Israel by early 1968, thanks to the rapid infusion of Soviet weaponry into its arsenal. A low-keyed war of attrition began at that time, as Egyptian troops moved up to the western bank of the Suez Canal to begin artillery duels with Israeli soldiers on the other side. The Israelis responded by building a series of fortifications, known as the Bar-Lev Line, along the eastern bank of the canal. By 1969, the fighting had escalated dramatically.

It was clear to Rabin that Israel would have to call upon the US to supply more sophisticated weapons to the embattled Jewish State. But from the very beginning of his ambassadorship, he realized the difficulties that faced him. The United States had opposed supplying arms to Israel for much of the Jewish State's existence. In 1950, the US, Britain and France had signed the Tripartite Declaration, which banned the sale of arms by Western Powers to Middle Eastern countries. This American policy remained in force until the final years of the

Eisenhower Administration. By 1965, an arms supply agreement had been reached between the US and Israel, but both Kennedy and Johnson had refrained from offering fighter planes. Between 1965 and 1967, Israel received about $150 million in arms from the US. With the five-month-long American suspension of arms to the Middle East after the Six-Day War, Israel received only $25 million worth of military supplies from the US in 1968.

Israel's main need, its military advisers said, was a fighter plane that could adequately compete with the growing strength of the Egyptian and Syrian air forces. Their attention focused on the American-made Phantom to such an extent that this — the most modern warplane in the world in 1968 — began to seem essential to Israeli security. The country simply had to have 50 Phantom jets. Some progress had been made during Eshkol's visit in January 1968 to President Johnson's Texas ranch, when Johnson had promised that the Israelis would soon get the planes it had requested. Rabin intended to speed up their delivery when he became ambassador, but his efforts were complicated by the fact that some Israeli leaders — notably Foreign Minister Eban — seemed no longer particularly disturbed by the time the Johnson Administration was taking to reach a final decision. Eban told Rabin that the Israelis were now 'lords of the sea', and there was no other army in the Middle East nearly as strong as the IDF. Rabin found this argument beside the point: holding up the delivery of the Phantoms indicated to the Russians and the Arabs that the US was not fully committed to Israel — which was scarcely the way to induce the Arabs to begin peace talks. In addition, Rabin had a hard time convincing the US Government of Israel's need for the planes. The Americans argued that the Israelis already had strategic superiority in the Middle East and did not need such sophisticated weaponry. More importantly, the US was trying to persuade Israel to adopt a more flexible attitude in order to get peace talks with the Arabs started; arms supplies would no doubt be a useful bait.

The decision to sell the planes finally came in October 1968 — not coincidentally, a few weeks before the American election, when presumably it would most benefit the Democratic Presidential nominee, Hubert H. Humphrey. Johnson made the decision only after the Russians had turned down an American proposal to curtail arms shipments to the Middle East. Johnson was retiring in January, and it would take some time before a new Administration would actually send the arms — perhaps another six months after the inauguration. Even the agreement to sell the Phantoms to Israel wasn't signed until mid-January 1969, just a few days before the Johnson Administration came to an end. Meanwhile the Israelis continued to argue that their current air force was inadequate. Because of the delay in confirming the deal, the delivery of the Phantoms would not now be completed until mid-1970. In August 1969, Israel requested 25 more Phantoms and 80 Skyhawks to supplement an air force of some 260 jets. But the Nixon Administration, talking secretly with the Russians, was reluctant to give its approval, believing that the Israelis would relax their rigid attitude towards peace terms if the planes were withheld long enough. In a dramatic press conference on 23 March, 1970, Secretary of State Rogers announced that the US had decided to turn down the request of 25 more Phantoms and (by then) 100 Skyhawks. To soften the blow, Rogers announced that the US would give Israel a $100 million economic credit. Rogers had met Rabin that morning to deliver the news, which the ambassador received with profound disappointment.

Meanwhile, Israel was facing increasingly violent Egyptian attacks, and some Israeli leaders were advocating air raids deep into Arab territory to strike at airfields and other military installations. However, fears were expressed about what the United States might think and what the Soviet Union would do. American support was seen as crucial, especially since the deep bombing raids might trigger Russian intervention on the Egyptian side. The Israeli Government looked to Rabin for guidance. He told them that the United States understood the argument in favour of the raids — that they might put a stop to the war of attrition — and therefore would not stand in their way. Thus Israel began the raids early in 1970, and during the first three months of the year some twenty such attacks were carried out against Egyptian bases and airfields.

The one Israeli fear about the raids materialized soon after they began. On 20 January President Nasser flew to Moscow and won a Soviet commitment to step up Russian participation in the Arab struggle against Israel. By the end of 1970, 200

Soviet pilots were flying Egyptian aircraft, some 4,000 Soviet instructors were working in various branches of the Egyptian army, and between 12,000 and 15,000 Soviet officers and soldiers were manning 80 SAM missile sites.

Some of the blame for this increased Russian involvement fell on Rabin; but he remained adamant that the raids had been essential, even at the risk of Russian intervention. Israel had been at a distinct disadvantage on the ground, with Egyptian troops far outnumbering Israelis near the Canal; without the raids, Israel might well have faced another full-scale war. In addition, he felt that the raids would serve to bring the US into the region on a much larger scale: as the Soviet presence in the Arab world grew, so too did the American commitment to Israel. By creating a kind of American–Soviet standoff in the region, the raids contributed to bringing the war of attrition to an end. In August 1970, Israel and Egypt agreed to a cease-fire under American sponsorship. Israel accepted it only after US assurances of more military and economic assistance. The cease-fire brought with it fresh hopes that serious negotiations for peace would take place, and both Golda Meir and Nasser made gestures towards improving the atmosphere. The Israeli Prime Minister announced that the Jewish State might give up its demand for direct negotiations with the Arabs in order to help pave the way for peace talks. Nasser replied that he would recognize the State of Israel if the Israelis would agree to withdraw from the occupied territories. However, peacemaking efforts were brought to a temporary halt in September by Nasser's death, while the diplomats watched to find out what new policies would emerge in Cairo with Nasser's successor, Anwar al-Sadat.

Rabin's determination to play a major role in the policy-making of his country inevitably led to a clash with Abba Eban, the foreign minister. His influence grew when Mrs Meir decided early in 1970 that she wanted more personal control over Israeli–American relations. She admired Kissinger's system of receiving direct reports from American ambassadors in such sensitive spots as Moscow and Peking, thus circumventing the State Department, and decided she could do the same with the Israeli Foreign Ministry: Rabin was to report directly to her, and at the same time Eban would get copies of all cables exchanged between the Washington Embassy and the prime minister's office. Eban initially accepted the change, though he was annoyed to find that in fact a number of cables were not sent to him for his information. Rabin's 'direct line' to Mrs Meir prompted reports in the Israeli press of a simmering feud between the ambassador and the foreign minister, though actually Eban showed no animosity towards Rabin for virtually usurping his own advisory role; his quarrel was with Mrs Meir. As for Rabin, the new arrangement gave him greater standing with American Administration officials; it was an obvious measure of Rabin's growing influence on Israeli policy.

Eventually, however, Eban grew increasingly disturbed at the ambassador's assertion of independence. The first of a series of clashes between the two men occurred in 1970 after an article by the Washington correspondent of the Israeli newspaper *Ma'ariv* suggested that the Government was pursuing a futile policy in the war of attrition. The correspondent quoted diplomatic sources in Washington as saying that Israel was not bringing sufficient military pressure to bear on the Egyptians. Eban sensed that Rabin was behind the story, and immediately cabled him. Rabin admitted that he was the source, and added that with so much leaking of information going on in Jerusalem, he saw no reason not to give his opinion in Washington. Eban was furious. He was further incensed by Rabin's practice of granting interviews to Israeli radio and television in which he criticized Israeli policy. At one point, the foreign minister even asked the national radio station to discontinue interviewing Rabin, but met with the response that it was up to Rabin to refuse to be interviewed. There were other occasions when friction was caused — for instance, when Eban announced to the Embassy in Washington that he was coming to New York for the 1970 annual United Nations session. Rabin suggested that, in view of Golda Meir's impending visit to the US, Eban should consider postponing his. Eban immediately suspected that Rabin was trying to keep him from appearing on American television so as not to detract from the publicity that would surround Mrs Meir. However, he was not to be deterred from making his visit.

They clashed over Israeli policy at times: Rabin favoured

reducing the Israeli mission at the UN; Eban did not. Rabin took a jaundiced view of the Jarring mission, while the foreign minister had higher hopes for it. But mostly they sparred on procedural matters. In October 1968, when the Embassy in Washington began distributing the 'pink sheets', Eban was angry. In the past, papers outlining Israeli policy had emanated from Jerusalem, not Washington. However, Rabin felt it was important to set forth the Government's position quickly, without waiting for approval from home on the choice of language; an ambassador needed independence if he was going to function effectively. This was certainly not Eban's opinion, and he bitterly resented not having his approval sought in advance. In time, the Embassy's 'pink sheets' became so popular in Washington that the foreign minister was forced to request Rabin to circulate them to other Israeli Embassies.

In 1972, David Rivlin, the Israeli Consul-General in New York City, aired a view which struck Rabin as inconsistent with the Government's line on a certain issue. He decided to suspend Rivlin, thus incurring the wrath of the foreign minister, who consulted the Civil Service, found the action out of order, and promptly reprimanded Rabin. The feud became public in May 1972 when Rabin implied in an interview that Israel's successful relations with the US were due entirely to him and his Embassy staff — and owed nothing to the Foreign Ministry or the 'shtadlanim' ('hacks') who had previously served in the Embassy. He criticized 'diplomatic schools at the Foreign Ministry', for producing diplomatic staff who were more concerned with the niceties of protocol and etiquette than with the important side of diplomacy. Eban demanded that Rabin explain himself; the Foreign Ministry Workers' Committee found his comments insulting, and protested. Rabin would not retract what he had said, but denied that his remarks had been meant personally. Eban decided to let the incident pass, since the ambassador was due to come home soon anyway.

Though Rabin generally enjoyed a good relationship with Mrs Meir, it occasionally came under some strain. In November 1971, for example, he fell out with the prime minister over the visit to Israel of four African leaders who had come to the Middle East on a peace mission, hoping to break the diplomatic stalemate in the Arab–Israeli conflict. Dispatched by the

Organization of African Unity, they proposed that the conflict could best be resolved by a dialogue between the Israelis and Arabs under UN auspices. Rabin received a memorandum from Jerusalem which struck him as too compromising and yielding in its presentation of Israel's attitude towards the Arabs. The memorandum carried Mrs Meir's signature but Rabin assumed — wrongly as it turned out — that it had been drafted for her by Abba Eban. Cabling the Foreign Ministry, Rabin labelled the memorandum 'absurd'. The cable eventually arrived on Mrs Meir's desk, causing her to explode with anger.

The Government in Jerusalem tended to attach little importance to these personal problems, since the ambassador had so thoroughly proved his worth. That Israeli relations with the US were growing closer was reflected in the increasingly large military aid programmes shepherded by Rabin through the Administration and Congress. 'Rabin,' said a senior Embassy official who worked closely with him, 'managed to change our status from that of a liability to that of an asset. Israel was now a country which took care of itself, kept the Soviet thrust at bay in an area that the US thought essential, and conducted its affairs reasonably well.'[29] The key years in the developing American–Israeli friendship were 1969-71, the first three years of the Nixon Presidency. Rabin's ability to get on well with the senior members of the Administration, including President Nixon, had much to do with this.

It was the Jordanian crisis of September 1970, which, more than any other diplomatic affair, brought Rabin to the attention of the senior members of the Nixon Administration. Rabin had kept an anxious eye on events in Jordan over the previous few years, wondering whether the moderate King Hussein would be able to keep the radical Palestinian guerrillas at bay. These guerrillas claimed to represent the two million Palestinian refugees who had fled when the State of Israel was declared in 1948, and who were now scattered throughout the Middle East. Hussein had long feared that the Palestinians living in Jordan were plotting to overthrow him in order to turn his country into a Palestinian-run State.

The crisis began on 1 September, when Palestinian guerrillas tried to assassinate him. Fighting broke out between the Jordanian army and the Palestinian forces a few days later. On

6 September, Palestinian terrorists, hoping to publicize their cause beyond Jordanian borders, hijacked four commercial jets, flew them to Jordan, and defied the king for days, while the passengers were forced to wait in the hot desert until the incident was resolved. Meanwhile, Syria decided to aid the Palestinians, and by 20 September had sent some 250 tanks across the Jordanian border. Hussein appealed to the US for help. A Syrian advance into Amman, the Jordanian capital, could well trigger Israeli intervention, and if that happened, the entire Middle East would probably flare up in a general Israeli–Arab war, creating the possibility that the Russians might enter the fray.

Israel had mobilized its troops and was poised for war should the Syrians get too close to the Jordanian capital. The US Navy's Sixth Fleet, which normally sailed in Mediterranean waters, moved in closer to the eastern shoreline. The Russians were warned that unless the Syrians withdrew from Jordan the region faced dangerous consequences. The Middle East was on the brink, but unlike the 'Waiting Period' before the Six-Day War, this time the crisis was being played out in secret. Only the diplomats and the generals knew what was going on: the public was kept largely in the dark.

Nixon realized that the US actually needed the State of Israel to keep the crisis from exploding into war. The Russians, like the Syrians, had to be restrained, but the US was scarcely in a position to do this: obviously America was not keen to risk a third World War just to keep Palestinian guerrillas from overrunning a tiny Middle Eastern kingdom. The American deterrent was not much of a weapon in this situation, and the President knew it. Israel, however, could not afford to have the Palestinians in power along its eastern border; hence, the Israeli deterrent was credible.

A shrewd student of geo-politics, Rabin realized the President's dilemma. He agreed that Israel could not allow the Palestinians to take control of Jordan, but he was determined that if the US was going to rely on Israel to such a degree — and in effect, to exploit the Israeli military presence in the region — then it would do so for a price. By coincidence, as the Jordanian crisis deepened, Golda Meir was at the end of a visit to the US. She was a guest at a dinner sponsored by the United Jewish

Appeal, the American Jewish fund-raising organization, at the New York Hilton on the evening of 20 September. Rabin, too, was present. During the evening he received an urgent message from the White House; the President wanted him in Washington immediately for consultations. Within a few hours an official White House plane had brought Rabin to the President. What had prompted the dramatic summons was the American fear that the Syrians might begin to advance towards Amman, and the realization that only the Israeli army could keep them at bay. At a top-secret meeting Rabin and Nixon worked out contingency arrangements for the possible battle. The American leader wanted to know that Israel was willing to move into Jordan on its own. Rabin wanted to make sure that an attack by the Jewish State would not weaken it on other fronts. He pressed Nixon to pledge that if Israel attacked Jordan, the US would protect Israel's rear — at the Suez Canal — with the Sixth Fleet. Never before had Israel won such a promise from the United States, the closest thing to a defence pact the two countries could reach.

The defence arrangement was never put into effect: the significance of the White House meeting between Rabin and the President was not lost on the Russians, and when the IDF began massing on the Jordanian border, they made it clear to the Syrians that it was too dangerous to march on Amman. Syrian tanks began withdrawing on 22 September. Within five days, Hussein was in Cairo, invited there by Nasser to work out a deal with the Palestinians. In late September, Hussein and Yasser Arafat, the Palestinian guerrilla leader, came to terms. The fighting gradually tapered off — and by July 1971, Hussein had eradicated all guerrilla bases in Jordan.

Rabin discovered, in the wake of the Jordanian crisis, that he was being welcomed by top-level Washington officials with more warmth than ever. His shrewd assessment of the situation had made a great impression on American policymakers. Some Israeli newspapers suggested that Rabin, with his coolness under pressure and the quality of his mind, had reminded the President of his hero, General George Patton. During a visit to the home of Arthur Goldberg (a former Supreme Court Justice and UN ambassador) in Virginia, Rabin joked to friends about his new acceptance: 'I know more ways in and out of the White

House than the Secret Service.'

By the autumn of 1970, the United States had reversed its previous policy and decided that only massive arms shipments to Israel would induce the Jewish State to keep the momentum for peace going. This apparent volte face was largely due to Rabin, who had always argued that Israel would be much more willing to enter into peace talks with the Arabs if it was militarily strong. The US announced in October 1970 a $545 million arms package for Israel for the following years, including 18 more Phantoms (by then the Jewish State had 74) and 200 tanks, among them the ultra-modern M-60s. The Administration justified its change of policy on the grounds that it wanted to restore the arms balance which appeared to have shifted in favour of the Arabs. Never before had the US been so forthcoming with arms. In 1969, it had given Israel $85 million worth of arms, and, in 1970, only $30 million. In December 1971, during a visit to Washington, Mrs Meir was able to get American agreement on another major arms deal, this time for $300 million. It was to include 40 more Phantoms and 70 Skyhawks. By the time Israel began negotiating an arms deal for 1973, Rabin was confident that the US had come to look upon the question of supplying arms to Israel as a matter of routine.

The last two years of Rabin's ambassadorship witnessed a flurry of diplomatic activity as efforts were made by the UN and the US to bring the conflicting parties to the conference table, but little progress was made. Egypt made a series of overtures to the Soviet Union in order to prepare itself for the much-vaunted battle with Israel: 1971 was to be President Sadat's 'Year of Decision', but he had to postpone it, and few took his threats against Israel seriously. A year later Sadat fell out with the Russians, and expelled 20,000 advisers from Egypt. It was one of several Arab moves which gave a deceptive impression of tranquillity in the Middle East.

The most controversial incident of Rabin's ambassadorship concerned Richard Nixon, for whom he had made no secret of his warm feelings, and whom he credited with being Israel's greatest benefactor. 1972 was an election year, and Richard Nixon's most likely competitor for the Presidency in the November election was Senator George McGovern of South

Dakota, a Democrat. In Rabin's opinion, the better man for Israel was clearly Nixon. McGovern struck him as the kind of liberal he had come to dislike, one who wanted to cut the American defence budget and to retract American political commitment around the world. Nixon was a known quantity, and could be trusted to keep up arms shipments to Israel.

Most Israelis shared Rabin's view. He privately did his utmost to make sure Israel dissociated itself from the Democratic nominee as much as possible. For instance, in early 1972 he asked the Foreign Ministry to play down McGovern's stopover in Israel on his way back from a visit to the Far East by sending only a low-level official to greet him at the airport. However, the Foreign Ministry overruled him, and sent the deputy director of the North American desk.

There was much embarrassment over a report in the *Washington Post* of an interview with Rabin on Israel national radio in June 1972, in which he remarked: 'While we appreciate the support in the form of words which we are getting from one camp, we must prefer the support in the form of deeds which we are getting from the other.' His intention was unmistakable, and the Israeli Embassy in Washington rushed in to try to repair the damage. It published a text of the interview in its name, but its version was significantly different from the one which had appeared in the newspaper. In the Embassy's text, Rabin simply said, 'It is my view, therefore, that we have to display gratitude to those who acted in support of Israel and not only spoke in Israel's support. We must express thanks for words, too, but more than that, it is important that there be an awareness among American politicians that Israel and the friends of Israel demonstrate gratitude to anyone who stood the test of action, who decided and assisted Israel, who was ready to assume the commitment to help Israel. Israel must thank those who helped her, whether they are of this camp or that camp, whether they are of one viewpoint or the other.'

One sympathetic member of the Embassy contends that the entire incident was due to Rabin's imperfect English. A Washington friend of the ambassador's, however, attributes it to plain bluntness on Rabin's part. The *Washington Post*, headlining its editorial on the subject: 'Israel's Undiplomatic Diplomat', accused him of intervening in American domestic politics, a charge he vehemently denied. 'As a representative of a foreign country, I did not involve [myself in] domestic politics . . . But I think it was my duty. I think I had to express gratitude to those in the Administration, and in the Congress, who showed readiness to help Israel.'[30]

Just over two years after Nixon left office, Rabin took a careful retrospective look at the Nixon Presidency and what it had meant for Israel. The President's personal frailties had led to his downfall, in Rabin's view, but his qualities — especially as regards his readiness to help Israel — far outweighed the disgrace of Watergate: 'I was very much impressed by Nixon's understanding of the nature of the strategic struggle between the US and the Soviet Union, and its interpretations in various parts of the world . . . I had a few talks with him. I don't pretend that I knew him well. I had the impression that he suffered from a little bit of a paranoiac complex and I think this is what brought about his downfall. For example, the fact that he had to create the 'palace guard' who eventually let him down. I feel that he could have been a very good President, a great President. He made two great decisions. One was to start relations with China, to use the Chinese as a balance to the Soviet Union. This was a major strategic decision. I don't remember many as important as that since Truman's resolution to save Europe with the Marshall Plan. The other decision was the airlift during the Yom Kippur War. After Truman's decision in 1948 to declare a total embargo on arms to Israel; after Eisenhower's decision in 1956 to push us back [out of Sinai] without any political settlement; after 1967, when Johnson suspended arms shipments for five months — such active participation as the flying in of arms to Israel by American planes in the middle of a war was a revolution.'[31]

One of the more dramatic examples of Rabin's assertiveness as ambassador occurred when the Israelis shot down a Libyan civilian jet which overflew the Sinai desert — Israeli occupied territory — on 21 February, 1973. It was carrying 113 passengers and crew. In the days preceding the incident, Israel had picked up rumours of an Arab terrorist plan to crash an aircraft into an Israeli target. Thus, news of the approaching Libyan airliner caused great alarm. After signalling the plane to land but getting no response, Israeli jets finally shot it down. Of the 113 aboard, only five survived. The Israelis insisted that they had had no way of knowing whether there were civilians aboard, and that their main concern had been that the aircraft was heading in the direction of the country's nuclear research centre at Dimona. Despite all this, international opinion was very much against the Jewish State. The time of the incident seemed particularly unfortunate for Israel, as Golda Meir was due to visit Washington shortly for talks with President Nixon.

Israeli leaders debated how to handle the incident; some argued that they should try to justify it publicly, others that it was wiser to say as little as possible. Dayan, the defence minister, felt it best to remain silent. Eban said the downing of the plane was senseless, but required some public explanation from Israel. He cabled Rabin for help. 'To ask advice on how to present the incident is nonsense,' was the ambassador's forthright reply. 'It can't be presented well. The best thing is to let it be forgotten. It was the height of stupidity. If Israel had looked for a way to make its position in the world more difficult, it couldn't have found a better one.' He demanded that both the chief of staff, David Elazar, and the head of the air force, Benyamin Peled, be dismissed — otherwise, Rabin threatened, he would resign. The demand seems odd, at least with regard to Elazar, a long-time friend of Rabin's. His ultimatum was ignored in view of the fact that his return was imminent in any case. The effect of his aggressively — almost arrogantly — worded cable on the Government may be imagined.

During her visit to Washington in March, Mrs Meir carefully explained to President Nixon why the plane had been shot down, and her explanation seemed to have been accepted. However, fears were being expressed in Israel that Nixon would take advantage of his new term of office (which had begun on 20 January) to reassess American policies towards the Middle East. Since American–Israeli relations had reached a peak, any reassessment could only be to the detriment of the Jewish State. For his part, Rabin felt that links with the United States were likely to remain strong, and he assured the Government that there was no cause for alarm. When Golda Meir's visit was over, it seemed that the ambassador had been right: the US appeared to have no intention of applying pressure on Israel — at least, in the foreseeable future.

Rabin left Washington in March 1973 with mixed feelings. The prospect of returning to Israel, jobless, after such exciting, productive years was not inviting. He had presided over the best five years in the history of American–Israeli relations. Israel no longer needed to beg for US military and economic aid; it was considered part of the on-going relationship between the two nations. Moreover, Israel had — for the time being — succeeded in convincing the US that a solution to the Middle East conflict could be neither imposed from outside nor found in one bold step; instead, it had to be worked out among the parties concerned and on a gradual basis.

One event during the last weeks of his ambassadorship cheered him. His secretary, Ruhama Hermon, secretly approached many of the American Administration officials and Congressmen with whom Rabin had worked in Washington, and invited them to a farewell party for him. The party was to be televised and shown in Israel in a 'This is Your Life' format on 5 March, 1973. Joseph Sisco was there; so were Senators Jackson and Symington. Kissinger was unable to attend as he was meeting President Sadat's adviser, Hafez Ismail, but he sent a farewell note in which he joked that Rabin should take a staff job on the US National Security Council, so that they could continue working together. In the event, the television programme was not shown in Israel, for reasons that are still unexplained.

Sisco paid Rabin the unusual tribute of an article about him in the *National Jewish Monthly*. 'The over-riding feature of our professional relationship,' he wrote, 'has been frankness. There is a similarity in our approaches to common problems and in our styles of operation. Like myself — and unlike the traditional diplomat — Ambassador Rabin is direct and always to the point — let's face it, at times even blunt. He says what he means and means what he says. This may bother some people — it has never bothered me.'

Rabin's final day as ambassador, 11 March, 1973, was as busy as usual. The night before he had made a speech in Chicago and only arrived back in Washington at 2 am. Six hours later he was at his desk drafting farewell notes to the officials with whom he had worked over the previous five years. Later in the morning he spoke to Israeli consuls who had flown in from different parts of the US to bid him good-bye. Then he rushed off to a final meeting with Secretary of State Rogers and Joseph Sisco. In the late afternoon, back in the Embassy, he cleared the walls of his office, leaving only a panoramic view of Jerusalem and a picture of Mrs Meir during her visit to the US in 1969. He issued no final statement at the airport, but his one brief remark to newsmen as he boarded the plane summed up his feelings well enough: 'I was happy to serve here and at the same time I'm happy to return home.'

He left Washington proud of his achievements, but very aware that he had won himself more friends in Washington than in Jerusalem. Sisco had once told him that when the US turned to Israel now, it did so with the respect shown to a Superpower. No European country could claim as much, he added. Yet the departing ambassador had created a storm of criticism in the wake of this achievement. Notwithstanding *Newsweek*'s praise for him in December 1972 as 'one of the two most effective envoys in Washington' (the other was Soviet Ambassador Anatoly Dobrynin), one journalist wrote: 'It is fair to say that no other diplomat in recent years here has been attacked so often for displaying such a noticeable lack of diplomacy.'[32]

Chapter 7

'But you are my candidate'

Rabin's whole future after he left Washington was a continual source of speculation, giving rise to a stream of rumours; some had even expected him to return to Israel as early as 1969. Israel's domestic politics were volatile and unpredictable, and his possible role in a future Government was constantly being weighed in Jersualem. Rabin enjoyed the speculation; it enhanced his reputation in Washington. In early 1969 he had been mentioned as a possible minister for education, though, ironically, he was not then a member of a political party. Later that year it was rumoured that he might replace Dayan as minister of defence. In 1970, Pinhas Sapir, the minister of finance and leader of the Labour Party (many called him the party's kingmaker), had advised him that he could become prime minister if he returned to Israel quickly and worked hard. But the ambassador had declined, calculating that his chances were slim and his present post was worth too much to yield.[1] In the spring of 1971 press reports were predicting that Rabin would be recalled to Israel by the end of the year. In early 1972, he was being mentioned in Jerusalem as the next minister for development. Sapir had even gone to Washington at that time to offer him the post (which was to be called the Ministry for Commerce and Industry), but it was a particularly delicate period in American–Israeli relations and Rabin had asked for a delay of three months before returning to take up the job. He left the meeting with Sapir with the clear impression that the finance minister had made a commitment; Sapir, however, felt under no obligation because of Rabin's refusal to take up the assignment immediately, and in April 1972, Mrs Meir appointed Haim Bar-Lev, a former chief of staff, to the post. The ambassador was astonished at this turn of events, but there was nothing he could do. Two months later, Rabin's name had again cropped up when Justice Minister Ya'acov Shimshon Shapira resigned unexpectedly. But criticism had been mounting against Mrs Meir for appointing too many generals to the Cabinet — Israelis have reservations about military officers joining the Government immediately after retiring from the services — and Rabin was again passed over for someone else.

In January 1973 Rabin had announced for the first time publicly — at a dinner at the Waldorf-Astoria in New York — that he would be a candidate for the Knesset, when elections were held in the following October. 'I am returning,' he said, 'ready and willing to fit into political life in Israel. But I don't know how it will be done.' In February he had another meeting in Washington with Sapir, but this time the two men had little to talk about. Rabin had hoped Sapir would agree that the previous year's offer of a Cabinet post still stood, but the Labour Party's share of Cabinet portfolios in Mrs Meir's coalition Government had been met with Bar-Lev's recent appointment. Sapir had advised him to act as a spokesman on behalf of the Labour Party during the election campaign; he would not only win votes for the party, but it would be a way of drawing the public's attention to himself. The idea appealed to him, not least since it was the one way he could remain in public life.

For the first time in 32 years Rabin found himself out of public service. Not having the responsibilities attendant upon a senior military officer or a diplomat, he had time to meet people he had never talked with before. The experience convinced him that politics was the right field for him. He hoped for a seat in the Knesset — and a Cabinet post, if only a junior one, in the new Government Mrs Meir would form after her re-election (which was a near certainty) in the autumn of that year: 'I had no illusion in those days that any of the existing ministers was a candidate for replacement, and therefore I knew it would be a long, hard, uphill road to a key post in the Cabinet. But I was ready to travel it. I accepted the fact that I was a newcomer to politics.'[2]

He considered himself a natural candidate for inclusion in the Labour list, though he had not actually joined the party until 1971. 'Whether or not I reach a high position in political life,' he said, 'my place is in this camp. I was raised in a proletarian home and I was educated in the values of the Labour Movement. There can be no cause — and surely no career — which would bring me to change places.'[3] Party leaders assured him that he would be given a safe seat on the Labour list of candidates for the Knesset when it was drawn up in the autumn. He would campaign therefore both as a strong candidate for the Knesset and as a possible Cabinet minister. Party officials in charge of conducting the election were delighted with his decision. 'He was a new man, with a great legend,' said Dov Tzamir, the Labour party's information director and, eventually, Rabin's chief lieutenant during his campaign for the prime ministership. 'We were convinced that a man like Rabin could put some excitement into the campaign. There was no doubt that he would be greeted enthusiastically.'[4]

Tzamir was right. By July, the Labour Party had realized that Rabin was a valuable political property. Yehoshua Rabinowitz (later, Rabin's minister of finance) was facing a tough challenge in his bid for re-election as Mayor of Tel Aviv. He had been an admirer of Rabin for some time and so, when his aides suggested that Rabin might be helpful in his campaign, Rabinowitz approached him. In a short time, the two formed a political partnership which was to have an influence far beyond the confines of Tel Aviv.

There was talk witin the Labour Party that Rabin was an up and coming man who might one day be a suitable replacement for Golda Meir. When the possibility was mentioned to Rabin, he rejected it out-of-hand, addressing himself to the more practical consideration of whether he would win even a junior seat in the next Cabinet. He was cheered in August to read that a public opinion poll on whether he deserved a Cabinet post gave him a 61 per cent rating.

Israel's electoral system is based on the list system of proportional representation, with each party presenting to the voters a list of candidates for the 120 seats in the Knesset. The voter therefore chooses an entire party list, instead of particular candidates; each party is represented in the Knesset according to the proportion of votes its list receives. On 24 September, 1973 the Labour party chose its list of candidates for the Knesset: Rabin was twentieth on the list, a very safe placing. All during August and September, he spoke on election platforms, canvassing votes in factories, assembly halls and homes. He concentrated on the Tel Aviv election, but invitations to speak poured in from around the country; it was a rigorous schedule with as many as nine campaign appearances in a single day. He was usually introduced as a future Cabinet minister; at workers' gatherings he was greeted as the next labour minister.

He talked to audiences about the subjects he knew most about: the Arab–Israeli conflict, American–Israeli relations, and the country's defence. Although the border with Egypt had been quiet since the cease-fire of the previous August, some members of the Government were disturbed that too little was being done diplomatically to preserve the peace. Rabin, however, was confident about Israel's position. Golda Meir, he said, had the best defence line of any King or President in the history of the people of Israel. The chances of war were so slim that Israel should turn its attention to improving long-neglected social conditions in the country. There was no need for nervousness, nor for new diplomatic initiatives.[5]

In this optimistic mood, Rabin was sanguine about the nomination of Henry Kissinger as Secretary of State on 25 August. He knew better than to believe that Kissinger's Jewishness would sway him in Israel's favour. 'All Jews are proud of Kissinger's appointment,' he told Israel's national radio on the day of the nomination, 'but we must remember that every American Jew appointed to a post is first of all an American, and he's going to work for American interests above and beyond any other consideration. We should not entertain illusions that Kissinger is going to behave in any way except according to American interests, as he has in the past under Nixon.' Though he suspected that the new Secretary of State would devote more attention to the Middle East than he had before, this need not create additional problems for Israel. The country could always resist any unfavourable US peace initiatives by keeping to its refusal to accept territorial compromises unless genuine peace would follow. He did not expect any special pressures that had not been withstood before.[6] In any case, he thought, Kissinger had other more pressing problems to deal with than the Middle East: détente with the Russians, Vietnam, and American–European relationships.

*

The Yom Kippur War which began on 6 October took the whole country by surprise. There had been signs of the impending Egyptian and Syrian attacks — the Arabs had moved men and armour into battle position in the days leading up to the war — but Israeli intelligence made a grave error of judgement in assuming that the might of the IDF was sufficient to prevent the Arabs from declaring war.

The war caught Rabin in the midst of a busy campaign schedule. He had completed a week of speech-making around the country on Friday afternoon, 5 October, and planned to spend a day at home with his family. Yom Kippur would begin at sunset on Friday evening. His son Yuval was in the third month of his compulsory service in the navy, and had come home for the holiday, but at 2 pm on Friday he was suddenly summoned back to his base. That was Rabin's first indication that things had taken an abnormal turn. His son-in-law, Avraham Ben Arzi, was also at the Rabins' home that day. An officer in the armoured corps unit directed by Dan Shomron (the commander of the Entebbe rescue mission of July 1976), Ben Arzi was to have had an operation on his knee on Sunday, 7 October, and so was not called up. But when he heard that Yuval had been ordered back to the navy, he contacted his unit in Sinai and shortly afterwards decided to journey south to join his battalion. His sudden return increased Rabin's suspicions, but he could do nothing except wait for news.

At 10 am on Saturday morning he received a telephone call from Israel Galili, the former Hagana commander, and now minister without portfolio. The message was brutally direct: war was imminent. A short while later, the telephone rang again: defence minister Moshe Dayan had summoned all former chiefs of staff to a meeting at 3 pm that afternoon.

It was Yom Kippur, a day so holy that even many non-religious Jews will not drive, and many who keep no other religious holidays go to synagogue and observe the fast. Usually there is no traffic on the streets, and the national radio and television shut down. But that day, army jeeps were rushing to their bases. Young men, many of whom had not eaten since Friday evening, were returning to units preparing for the inevitable battle. At 2 pm sirens sounded throughout the nation. Egyptian soliders had begun crossing the Suez Canal in the south, while Syrian troops in the north had begun moving across the Golan Heights. Rabin turned the radio on instinctively and found that the national radio station had begun broadcasting again. Special announcements told the nation that the war had started. At 2:15 pm Avraham Ben Arzi appeared, explaining that his commander had told him that morning that he doubted there was to be a war, and had sent him back to Tel Aviv for the hospital operation. Rabin was later to recount this story as evidence of how unprepared the army had been for the war.

The meeting with Dayan was not very productive; the former chiefs of staff were given some sketchy information about the first hours of battle, but the meeting had to be hastily adjourned as the situation worsened. Rabin returned home and followed the progress of events on radio and television.

The Yom Kippur War was one of the most difficult periods for Rabin: his country was at war, caught by total surprise: and here was he, with no specific military task to perform, no chance to take part, a one-time chief of staff stranded on the sidelines.

The first few hours of the fighting shattered the myth of the Israelis' invincibility. Thousands of Egyptian troops and hundreds of tanks had successfully crossed over to the eastern bank of the Suez Canal and were establishing bridgeheads to consolidate their gains. Thousands of Syrian troops and hundreds of tanks had overrun much of the Golan Heights and were threatening to advance into Israel proper. The Jewish State had once again to fight for its survival.

In addition to the fears and horror that the sudden outbreak of war had brought, Rabin had to face the fact that all his assurances to the US during the past five years that war would never happen as long as Israel was strong now counted for nothing. He feared for US–Israeli relations in the future: the war would surely bring about a slackening in American confidence and support just when Israel needed it most. Later on, when the American airlift of new military equipment began, those forebodings partially disappeared, only to be replaced by the fear that this aid would increase American pressure on Israel to accept an overall solution to the Middle East conflict, even if the terms were disagreeable.

On Sunday afternoon Mrs Meir summoned Rabin to Tel Aviv, where she briefed him on military developments. Dayan

had just proposed an Israeli withdrawal in Sinai to the Mitla
and Giddi Passes. Rather than accept the defence minister's
plan right away, she had asked Chief of Staff David Elazar to
find out how untenable the situation actually was on the
Southern Front. When he learned that Elazar planned to fly to
Southern Front headquarters later that day, Rabin got
permission to go along 'as an onlooker'. Donning a military
uniform, he joined the chief of staff in the Sinai headquarters,
where Elazar was drawing up plans for a counter-offensive as an
alternative to Dayan's suggested withdrawal. Rabin was very
much in favour of it. The day after the counter-offensive was
launched Rabin met his old friend, General Israel Tal, and the
two men talked about Israeli prospects in the war. 'Unless we
manage to go over to the offensive,' Rabin said, 'and press the
Syrians and Egptians hard, there won't be a cease-fire. Nothing
will force the Arabs to stop as long as they're not being defeated.
There's nothing that can be done on the diplomatic front.'[7]

Other than the visit to southern headquarters and a journey
north to the Syrian Front — both accompanying Elazar —
Rabin remained near military headquarters in Tel Aviv during
the first few days of the war. Instinct rather than a specific job
kept him there, along with a number of other former generals.
The confusion and sense of desperation left little room for
niceties about titles and jobs; hence, Rabin acted as an unofficial
adviser. In theory, he was not in favour of the previous
generation of commanders lingering about at military headquarters and offering advice; it indicated a lack of confidence in
those now in command, and in turn destroyed the confidence of
the soldiers in their commanders. Long after the Yom Kippur
War he was to say: 'I hope that we'll have no repetition of that
bringing in of all the old guard. I believe that in the army there
can be no turning back the wheel. Let the new generation do
what they have to do.'[8] However, at the time, a driving sense of
duty had prevailed over such thoughts, and he was unable to
keep away from the 'war room' at military headquarters.

While scanning the plan of troop deployments Rabin noticed
an obvious weakness along the border with Jordan. Israeli
defences in the Jordan Valley, near the border, were minimal, a
dangerous situation if King Hussein decided to open a third
front. Sensing that Elazar might be more willing to take advice

from former Chief of Staff Yigael Yadin, Rabin asked him to discuss the situation on the Jordanian front with the chief of staff.[9] Though Elazar was under heavy pressure on the Syrian front, he listened to Yadin and ordered the necessary changes in deployment. In the event, Jordan did not enter the battle along its frontier with Israel; though it mobilized its forces during the first week, it refrained from engaging the Israelis directly. On 13 October Jordanian units were sent to fight alongside Syrian units on the Golan Heights.

As the pressure on the army commanders lessened, they began to resent the presence of unofficial advisers like Rabin, and made it plain that they would prefer to conduct the war without outside assistance. Rabin agreed to go, but, though he could understand their attitude he could not help but feel slighted, and his isolation from decision-making was agony to him. Towards the end of the first week of the war, he learned that his brother-in-law, Avraham Yoffe, a former division commander in the Six-Day War, planned to tour the fronts by jeep. Eager for involvement at any level, Rabin joined him and the two men drove around both the Northern and the Southern Fronts. One special task they accepted gladly: taking the messages of soldiers back to their families. Rabin was appalled and depressed by what they found on their tour. The morale of the soldiers was low, and the condition of some of their equipment had fallen far below standard. He was glad, however, to have the opportunity to meet the soldiers.

Pinhas Sapir, the minister of finance, was looking for a public figure — preferably a former military leader who commanded people's respect — to lead a fund-raising drive to secure contributions for the War Loan beyond the sums which would be raised compulsorily. Rabin did not seek the job, but when Sapir approached him during the second week of the war and informed him that Mrs Meir had already approved the idea, he accepted. The Government had previously decided that Israelis would have to donate in loans between seven and twelve per cent of their incomes to help raise $250 million, but the war was costing $10 million an hour. Hence, much more money was needed: Rabin's target was between $100 and $250 million in voluntary loans. He was to head a three-man committee. (Ironically, one of the other two men was Asher Yadlin, then head of the nation's largest medical insurance programme, Kupat Holim. On 5 September, 1976, Rabin, as prime minister, nominated Yadlin Governor of the Bank of Israel, the second most important job in the economy. He was to have taken up office on 1 November, but six weeks after the appointment he was arrested on suspicion of fraud and bribery. In February 1977, he confessed and was given a five-year prison sentence. As will be seen later, the affair was to have important repercussions on the Labour Party, and on Rabin's 1977 re-election campaign.)

Still hankering after a military assignment, Rabin felt little enthusiasm for his new civilian post but was resolved to do his best. Looking over the contributions in the similar voluntary loan drive that had been initiated during the Six-Day War, he saw that the burden had fallen mostly on the wage-earners. He changed this and made sure that the wealthy made their contributions too. He spent a great deal of time, therefore, persuading industrial leaders to give. However, fund-raising, as he had suspected, was not his forte: aides had to coax him to promote the loan drive with the press. He remained in the job for two months, asking to be relieved in early December.

After much bitter fighting, the Israelis managed to keep the Syrians and Egyptians from advancing beyond the territory gained in the early stages of the war. On 8 October, using the full might of its air force and armour, Israel pushed the Syrians back to the highway to Damascus, coming within 35 kilometres of the Syrian capital. After the first week, the Israelis shifted the brunt of their effort to the south. Egypt's main offensive was countered by 14 October, with Israel retaining the initiative for the remaining eleven days of the war. On 16 October an Israeli task force, led by Ariel 'Arik' Sharon, crossed the Suez Canal, moving behind the Egyptian forces; soon an Israeli bridgehead was established on the Canal's west bank and Israeli troops advanced to within 101 kilometres of Cairo. While Israel eventually succeeded in repulsing the Arabs, the disastrous surprise attacks at the outset and the heavy Israeli casualties inflicted throughout the fighting left the nation with little joy at the war's end.

Russia and the United States played major roles in the war:

the Russians provided huge amounts of military aid to the Arabs in the early stages; the Americans countered with an 'air lift' to Israel. Between 14 October and 14 November, the US delivered 22,000 tons of equipment during 566 flights, valued at $825 million. President Nixon asked Congress for a special $2.2 billion appropriation to cover this and subsequent military aid to Israel.

As the tide of the battle turned in favour of Israel in the third week of fighting, the Russians pressed the US to agree to a cease-fire. Kissinger was abruptly summoned by the Russians to Moscow to reach agreement, and the joint Russian–American efforts bore fruit in United Nations Resolution 338, formally adopted by the UN on 22 October. It called for a cease-fire, for the implementation of Resolution 242, and for negotiations towards a just and durable peace in the Middle East to start at once. Neither the Egyptians nor Israelis actually stopped fighting, and fire was exchanged for another 36 hours, leading to Russian threats of direct intervention if the US did not force Israel to abide by the UN cease-fire resolution. In response, Kissinger persuaded President Nixon to place the American military on 'Defcom B' — just below acute alert, a step which caused the Russians to back down. The fighting between Israelis and Arabs finally ended on 25 October after a second cease-fire was called. United Nations military observers and a UN Emergency Force were sent into the region to police the battle zones.

The war had cost Israel some $9–10 billion, leaving its citizens with heavy debts, soaring prices, and runaway inflation. The economy had been hit so hard that every Israeli would have to undertake sacrifices unlike any made before. The human loss and suffering had been devastating. A total of 2,526 Israelis had been killed in battle, with another 7,500 wounded — the country's heaviest losses since the War of Independence. Israeli prisoners of war during the 19 days of fighting numbered 301. A staggering 107 planes and 840 tanks had been lost on the Israeli side (Arab losses were far worse, totalling 421 warplanes and 1,775 tanks). The general gloom was reflected in a public opinion poll published in March 1974, which revealed the shocking fact that 11.6 per cent of the 2.8 million Jews in Israel were considering emigration within two years. It was reflected also in the numerous resignations of army officers after the war. In addition to the despondency and exhaustion felt by the nation, there was a growing mood of indignation that its leaders had been so unprepared for war despite the intelligence reports they had received concerning the enemy's movements.

Following the Yom Kippur War there were almost daily artillery exchanges on both fronts, and there were fears that the Arabs might soon begin another round of full-scale war. In mid-November Rabin travelled to the United States on behalf of Israel Bonds, and while there met Kissinger. He brought back a grim message to Mrs Meir, warning her that the Secretary of State was determined to work out a settlement in the Middle East that would have to satisfy both sides.

Throughout November and December Israel and Egypt fought a war of attrition during which 450 shooting incidents occurred along the Southern Front. Kissinger travelled to the Middle East during December to prepare the way for a peace conference which would bring some stability to the area and implement the goals of Resolution 338; he invited Rabin for a private breakfast and the two men talked like old friends.

The peace conference was convened in Geneva under joint American–Russian auspices on 21 December, 1973. Israel, Egypt and Jordan attended; the Syrians refused to come and the PLO was not invited. As a result of the conference, Kissinger embarked upon his 'shuttle diplomacy', flying back and forth between Egypt and Israel for eight days in January 1974; through his efforts, the two sides signed a separation of forces agreement on 18 January. Israel agreed to withdraw from the west bank of the Suez Canal and from its forward position on the east bank to a distance of fifteen miles from the Canal. Egypt agreed to limit its military presence on the east bank to 7,000 troops, 36 artillery pieces and 30 tanks. UN troops were placed between the two sides in a buffer zone.

Rabin's future seemed less certain than ever. He was still smarting from the army's treatment of him, and though he spoke to audiences in Tel Aviv on behalf of the IDF, he refused to speak to the troops at the front. Ya'acov Halfon, a Labour Party aide, tried to convince him that new men would be needed when the nation passed judgement on Golda Meir's Government.

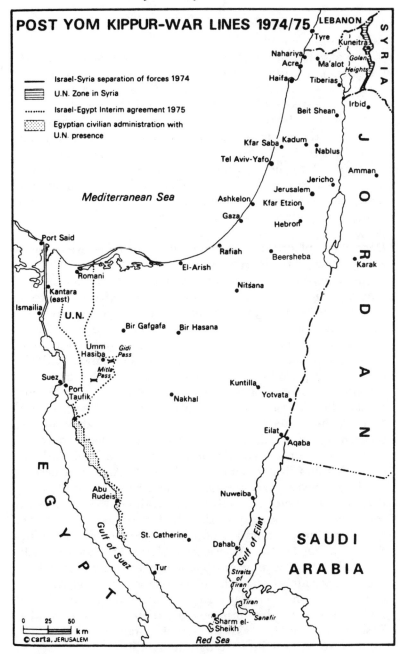

POST YOM KIPPUR-WAR LINES 1974/75

Israel-Syria separation of forces 1974

U.N. Zone in Syria

Israel-Egypt Interim agreement 1975

Egyptian civilian administration with U.N. presence

LEBANON

SYRIA

Tyre

Kuneitra

Nahariya

Acre

Ma'alot

Golan Heights

Haifa

Tiberias

Irbid

Beit Shean

Kfar Saba

Kadum

Nablus

Tel Aviv-Yafo

Jericho

Amman

Jerusalem

Ashkelon

Kfar Etzion

Gaza

Hebron

Mediterranean Sea

Port Said

Rafiah

Beersheba

Karak

El-Arish

Romani

Nitsana

Kantara (east)

Ismailia

U.N.

Bir Gafgafa

Bir Hasana

Umm Hasiba

Gidi Pass

Mitla Pass

Suez

Kuntilla

Yotvata

Port Taufik

Nakhal

Eilat

Aqaba

JORDAN

E G Y P T

Abu Rudeis

Nuweiba

Gulf of Suez

St. Catherine

Dahab

Gulf of Eilat

Tur

SAUDI ARABIA

Straits of Tiran

Tiran

Sanafir

0 25 50

k m

© carta, JERUSALEM

Sharm el-Sheikh

Red Sea

'There were casualties in the war,' he said, 'and there will be casualties in the leadership.'[10]

The national elections had originally been scheduled for 31 October, but within a few days of the outbreak of war, a consensus was reached among all political parties that they should be postponed for two months, until 31 December.

Rabin's morale received a boost when the Labour Party chose him to give the main address at the first Labour Party gathering after the war, held in early November in Bet Berl near Lake Kinneret. With the election campaign now resuming, it was understandable that the party should make its main attraction a man who — unlike the senior members of the Cabinet — was untainted by responsibility for the war. Public opinion polls began to reflect his rising popularity with the voters. One, in late December, placed him second only to Golda Meir in a straightforward popularity contest.

Rabin sensed the country's increasingly angry mood and felt that an official investigation into the state of the country's defences just before the war should be held, but he was careful to say that it should not be a witch hunt. In any case, while an investigation might correct past mistakes, it would not resolve Israel's immediate crisis — its international isolation. 'I don't remember a period when we were witness in such a dramatic way to the collapse of Israel's foreign relations,' Rabin said shortly after the war. 'We had only one friend in the world and that was the United States.'[11] He spoke hopefully about future relations with the US, suggesting that America had proved by its decision to air-lift arms that it would not permit the Arabs to triumph militarily over Israel. Similarly, the American alert in late October was a sign, he said, that the US would not allow the Russians to intervene directly on the Arab side. Yet despite all this, there was no guarantee that the US would see eye to eye with Israel on the question of a peace settlement. In public, Rabin was hopeful that America would sympathize with Israeli claims that the need for secure boundaries was more urgent than ever. But privately he took the more realistic view that Israel was facing one of the most dangerous periods in its history. If the United States decided to impose a settlement on the Middle East at this juncture, with the crippled state of the IDF, the country would have little strength to fight it.

On 31 December, Rabin was elected to the Knesset. The Labour Alignment (composed of the Labour and Mapam parties) had lost five seats, a serious depletion of its electoral strength, but not enough to make it incapable of forming the next Government. It now had 51 Knesset seats, and its percentage of the overall vote had slipped from 46.2 to 39.7. The Likud now had 39 seats (seven more than in the previous election), with 30.2 per cent of the overall vote, a gain of 4.2 per cent. The Labour Party had won by the narrowest margin in its history, but the disgruntled voters were not yet united enough to demand its resignation.

However, the tide of protest was growing, shapeless, leaderless, but angry and persistent. The movement began among the soldiers, who were most aware of the state of unpreparedness in which the IDF had found itself at the outbreak of war. They had been gradually returning from the fronts since November and December 1973. Now most of them were home, full of anguish and horror at what they had seen; a return to normal life seemed impossible to those who had witnessed the heaviest casualties in war for twenty-five years.

The protest movement was initiated by a young captain named Motti Ashkenazi, the commanding officer of 'Budapest', the northern-most stronghold on the Suez Canal, and the only one near the Canal which had not fallen to the Egyptians. He made many accusations, but the main target of his anger was Defence Minister Moshe Dayan. During his one-man demonstrations outside the prime minister's office in Jerusalem, Ashkenazi called for Dayan's resignation. Dayan replied that the minute Mrs Meir asked him to resign, he would do so. Gradually the movement grew, though still retaining its amorphous character. Israel had never witnessed public outrage on such a scale. Rallies attracted hundreds, eventually thousands, whose uncompromising demand was for nothing less than the present leadership's resignation. The protest movement was not a political one, in that it had no policy for reform, no list of candidates; it had simply erupted over a single issue: the removal of the Government.

The new mood of the nation did not bring about immediate political change. The Israeli political system, with its strong tinge of conservatism, was far too well-entrenched to capitulate easily. But the protests made Mrs Meir's task of putting together a coalition Government after the 31 December elections very difficult. With five fewer Knesset seats, she had less room for manoeuvre in dealing with the smaller parties. Beset with defence problems, she took over two months to form a Government. Meanwhile Dayan, increasingly attacked both in public gatherings and within the Labour Party for the mishaps that had led to the war, decided to resign from the Defence Ministry.

Public anger intensified throughout February and rose to a peak in early March as Golda Meir prepared to present her new Cabinet. Party members were disturbed by the lack of change in it. Mrs Meir, who had wanted to retire even before the originally scheduled October elections, announced on 3 March that she intended to resign. In the hours that followed a number of party delegations pleaded with her to withdraw her resignation, and she eventually agreed to continue forming a Government. She was very keen for Dayan to return as Defence Minister, even to the extent of trying the psychological ploy of leaking word to the press that she intended to appoint Rabin. However, Dayan refused, and it appeared that Rabin might become the new minister of defence.

The Labour Party Central Committee met on 5 March at the Ohel Theatre in Tel Aviv to discuss the political crisis. Committee membership was split among the three former parties which had merged to become the Labour Party: Mapai, the largest (60 per cent); Ahdut Avoda (20 per cent) and Rafi (20 per cent). Most of the Labour Party's Government leaders, including Golda Meir, Pinhas Sapir and Abba Eban, have come from the Mapai ranks. Moshe Dayan led the Rafi grouping (with Shimon Peres as his second-in-command) and Yigal Allon headed the Ahdut Avoda faction.

Though Mrs Meir had agreed to continue her efforts to form a Government, in the prevailing uncertain atmosphere it seemed likely that she might once again decide to resign. Throughout the day, Rabin was talked of by party members as the next defence minister. It was against this background that he prepared to make to the Committee one of the most important speeches of his career, one which would establish him as a leader within the party — and a future leader of the nation.

The meeting lasted most of the day. Despite the heat and smoke-filled air of the Ohel Theatre, it was packed. Dayan, Peres, and Eban sat towards the front. Rabin, mid-way back, sat with Aharon Yariv, and Yosef Nevo, the Mayor of Herzlyia. Speaker after speaker mounted the stage to address the by now restless audience, whose conversations were beginning to drown out the speakers. It was late in the afternoon, and the meeting was nearing an end when Rabin's turn to speak came. The members were eager to get home and he was barely noticed as he rose to address the audience, but his commanding voice and the fresh enthusiasm of his delivery soon caught the crowd's attention. Choosing his words carefully, he said enough in support of Mrs Meir to avoid appearing critical, but at the same time left the audience in no doubt about what he really felt. 'The Yom Kippur War was a shock,' he said, 'a shock which has raised questions about the leadership — not about this leader or that, but about the collective leadership of the party.' The country had to find a way out of the crisis which confronted it and which was reflected in the bitterness the public felt towards its leaders. The Labour Party could not resolve it by choosing the path of new elections. This would merely prolong the instability within the nation. A new Government had to be set up by the party, without the participation of the right-wing Likud opposition (some party members had been advocating a Government of National Unity, which would include the Likud). Rabin finished his speech with a plea to the right-wing Rafi faction to preserve party unity: 'Sitting here [he pointed to the front rows] is Moshe Netzer. It seems to me that we began life together at the age of 6. And it's odd to find us not together now — even though we're in the same party. Moshe, I want us to continue together.' Rabin's message was clear: although he was rumoured to be Dayan's replacement in the new Meir Government, he did not want this to be a cause for disharmony between him and the Rafi wing.

Rabin received an ovation at the end of his speech, the only speaker that day to do so, since applause was not customary at party discussions. From that moment, it was clear to everyone in the party — and the country — that Rabin was a new force in Israeli politics.

The committee urged Mrs Meir to continue trying to form a

Government, and asked Dayan to return to office. Their appeal was not necessary: sometime during the day information had arrived in Israel that the Syrians were about to launch an all-out attack along the Northern Front, and the Government met in emergency session. Dayan immediately agreed to return as minister of defence in Golda Meir's new Cabinet. On 6 March Rabin read in the morning newspapers that he was no longer Mrs Meir's candidate for the post. 'All my life,' he told a reporter later that day, 'I have been collecting ex's. I am an ex-chief of staff, an ex-ambassador to the United States, and now an ex-potential minister of defence.' There was some speculation within the Labour Party that Dayan had decided to return to his post, not because of the new threat of war (which in the event did not materialize) but because Rabin had become such a popular rival. With Dayan's return, the National Religious Party, which had left the Meir fold some time before, decided that it too should return, and on 10 March she presented her new Government to the Knesset.

With Dayan's return to the Ministry of Defence, Mrs Meir gave Rabin a choice between three secondary Cabinet posts: the Ministry of Labour, Information, and Transport. He was not attracted by the job of information minister since the main information programmes abroad were in the hands of the Foreign Ministry, and the two finally agreed that he would become her labour minister.

Despite his disappointment at losing the Defence Ministry post, Rabin took up his new Cabinet job with enthusiasm. It gave him the chance to participate in all Government discussions, including those on military and diplomatic affairs, not just those connected with labour. As minister of labour, his priority was to orientate the economy to cope with a situation in which large numbers of men in the labour force had to be mobilized for long periods of time. When he took office there was still a war of attrition with Syria, and it was impossible to know how much longer the troops would be needed at the front.

Meanwhile the national malaise persisted. 2 April saw the publication of the interim report of the Inquiry Commission set up by Mrs Meir in November to investigate the decisions of military and civilian authorities concerning intelligence received before the war, and the IDF's general state of preparedness at

that time. The report exonerated Mrs Meir and Dayan and laid
the blame on Chief of Staff Elazar. Rabin felt it was grossly
unfair to single out one person in this way, since it would make
the position of senior army officers untenable in the future by
implying that they alone bore responsibility for their actions. He
asked for the report to be returned to the Commission, but his
suggestion was turned down. The publication of the interim
report prompted another wave of public fury, and there were
vociferous, almost daily demonstrations outside the Prime
Minister's office in Jerusalem, until on 10 April Mrs Meir
resigned. Her Government would remain in office as a caretaker
regime while a new prime minister was chosen by the Labour
Party. (New elections are not obligatory in Israel after the
resignation of a prime minister. Only if the dominant party
elects a new prime minister who is unable to form a
Government, can the country's President ask another party to
try to form a Government. Of course, the dominant party
always has the option of calling for early elections.)

Throughout the week following Mrs Meir's resignation, the
Labour Party debated whether to try to form a new
Government or hold new elections; while the latter might
provide Labour with a fresh mandate from the people, they
were also risky in view of the country's continuing angry mood.
Finally the Labour Party decided to form a new Government on
the understanding that elections would be held in the near
future.

The choice of the new prime minister was the prerogative of
the 611 members of the Labour Party's Central Committee.
Throughout the years Mapai had always provided the nominee
for the prime ministership. Under normal conditions Mapai
would have found a suitable candidate this time as well, but the
October War had made the faction virtually leaderless: Golda
Meir was resigning, Abba Eban was associated with the wartime Government. Pinhas Sapir, the minister of finance, could
probably have had the nomination for the asking, but had made
it known that he did not want the office. Haim Zadok, the
minister of justice, had some support within the Mapai party,
but he too had no great desire for the job. The left-wing Ahdut
Avoda faction had only one potential candidate, Yigal Allon,
the deputy premier and minister of education. But even before

the Yom Kippur War, the right-wing Rafi faction had found him unacceptable. Rafi's only possible candidate (Shimon Peres, a Rafi man, was never considered one while Dayan was a serious contender), Moshe Dayan, was ruled out by his unpopularity over the war.

The party's titans, though flawed, still had to be courted, however, because they were after all the veteran leaders of Labour. The first question party members asked was whether Mrs Meir really meant to resign this time. No one could afford to offend her, since her support was vital to any future contender. Once it became certain that she had no intention of retracting, attention focused on Pinhas Sapir. He had always been considered the heir apparent despite his expressions of uninterest in the post, and after her resignation he was inundated with appeals from party members to run for the prime ministership. Meanwhile, others were quietly scrambling for the nomination. Rabin made no secret of his ambition, but he held a tight reign on supporters who wanted to canvass for him within the party. As long as Sapir was a possible candidate, he felt he could make no overt move. At first he was convinced that Sapir would be Mrs Meir's most likely replacement, but as time passed, he began increasingly to believe that the minister of finance was adamant and would not yield to party pressure.

One evening Sapir summoned Rabin to see him. Rabin suggested that Sapir was the likely candidate for prime minister.

'Me — no! But you are my candidate!' Sapir caught Rabin by surprise.

Returning home, the astonished candidate-to-be told his wife: 'Strange, but Sapir claims that I'm his candidate for prime minister.'

Rabin still lacked a firm political base in the party and therefore seemed to many at best a long shot. Still, he had received a considerable boost from Mrs Meir the month before when he was tipped to replace Dayan. He had decided in March to join forces with a political circle within the Labour Party which called itself 'Etgar' ('Challenge'), comprised of some 300 ex-senior military officers who were campaigning for electoral reform and other domestic changes. Organized in the summer of 1972 by Yosef Nevo, the circle had no particular policy on foreign affairs or security issues. After the Yom Kippur War it had become decidedly anti-Dayan, and some of its members had called for his resignation. Etgar leaders had first approached Rabin in February and asked him to join them; if the rest of the membership accepted him, which was likely, they wanted him to serve as their leader. Several discussions took place, and on 21 March a crucial meeting was held in the Tel Aviv office of Meir Amit, then the director-general of Koor Industries, the largest industrial enterprise in Israel. A former director of military intelligence, Amit was associated with Etgar. After an hour's discussion Rabin made his decision, and in the week that followed the local press carried reports of his new affiliation. Ironically, he never became an official member of Etgar. The full membership was supposed to sanction his acceptance into the circle, but Mrs Meir's resignation shelved matters: his campaign for the prime ministership following her decision took precedence over his joining Etgar, although to all intents and purposes he had its support and some of its leaders worked with him during the short campaign.

Gradually, a small group of high-level party politicians — among them Aharon Yariv, Rabin's intelligence chief during the Six-Day War, and Haim Bar-Lev, the minister for commerce and industry and formerly Rabin's deputy chief of staff — settled on Rabin as their candidate. But none had the close contact with the Central Committee that certain party officials had. For this reason, Rabin eventually turned to these officials — men like Dov Tzamir, the party's information officer — who were to play a major role in his securing the nomination. The seeds of Rabin's campaign for the prime ministership took root as the meeting of the party's Knesset faction on 11 April broke up. Rabin had listened quietly as the group decided it was futile to try any further to dissuade Mrs Meir from resigning and that the best course of action was to search for a new candidate. Dov Tzamir approached Rabin and asked who his political adviser was. Rabin mentioned Uzi Baram, the young head of the Jerusalem Labour Party and the son of Moshe Baram, a veteran leader. The three men decided to meet later that evening to map out a strategy. Tzamir and Baram had been talking to others in the party and were both now convinced that Rabin had a good chance of becoming the party's new leader. In their opinion he had the major advantage over all the other potential candidates of being likely to win a large segment of votes from Mapai, and of being assured of Ahdut Avoda's vote.

At this stage, Shimon Peres of the Rafi faction decided that he had nothing to lose by making public his candidacy. He had no hope of enlisting Sapir's support: in Sapir's mind, Peres was inextricably linked with Moshe Dayan, and the finance minister was determined to prevent Dayan exerting any influence in the next Government. It was estimated that Sapir controlled between 200–300 (out of 611) votes in the Central Committee. Peres hoped to prove that it was possible to win without his support. He had a flair for campaigning and his strategy of going directly to Committee members began to pay off. In that first week he had spoken to about 250 Committee members by telephone, and people were beginning to feel that he just might win the premiership.

Rabin reported in his *Memoirs* that Peres invited him to lunch 'and treated me to some smooth talk'. According to Rabin, Peres said: 'In the final event, the two of us will find ourselves competing for the premiership. Let us learn from the experience of our older colleagues. Allon and Dayan fought one another, sapped each other's strength, and neither of them became prime minister. Let's conclude a gentleman's agreement to hold a fair contest. Whoever loses will accept the decision in good spirit and be loyal to the winner.' Rabin's response was to be 'wary and my inclination was not to believe a word he said'. Beyond that, Rabin had decided that should Peres win, 'I would not set foot in the Cabinet'. Without finding fault with Peres' suggested terms, Rabin said simply, 'Agreed.'[12]

Mapai, faced with Peres' strong candidacy, intensified its search for an alternative. Its private polls showed Rabin heading the field. Public polls indicated the same. One published on 16 April put Rabin at the top of the list, with Peres sixth. Another poll that same day demonstrated that the majority in the country wanted a new Government right away rather than elections. The search began to focus on Rabin. One important meeting took place on 17 April at the Tel Aviv office of Shikun Ovdim, a housing firm managed by Avraham Ofer, a Mapai leader. He and other Mapai leaders had gathered to assess the political situation. For the first time, Rabin was considered as a serious candidate for the premiership by the

Mapai faction. Significantly, the man who mentioned him at the meeting was Yossi Sarid, Pinhas Sapir's young lieutenant. Sarid, who had realized that Sapir, having served eighteen years in Government, had no desire to become prime minister, and wanted to retire, had worked briefly with Rabin in Rabinowitz's Tel Aviv Mayoralty campaign the year before, and admired him. Rabin had approached Sarid indirectly about obtaining Sapir's support, and his appeal had been received with warmth.

Until that meeting, Rabin had remained unconvinced about his prospects of becoming leader. At one point during the previous week, Tzamir had asked him to hold a strategy session about his campaign, but Rabin declined, saying that his wife had already bought tickets for a concert for that evening. However, now, encouraged by his advisers, Rabin decided to step up his campaign and told them to press ahead in search of votes. Tzamir instructed Yoram Peri, another Labour Party member sympathetic to Rabin, to travel to Jerusalem to activate the campaign there. Rabin was on the brink of declaring his candidacy, but he wanted to secure Pinhas Sapir's support first.

Sapir was the key to Rabin's nomination. He had acted mysteriously throughout the week after Mrs Meir resigned, confiding to his closest associates that he would not run himself; that he no longer believed Eban, his long-standing choice to succeed Mrs Meir, was suitable; that he had another candidate in mind. He leaned at first towards Haim Zadok, the smooth, highly respected minister of justice. But upon reflection and after taking some soundings of his own, Sapir realized that Zadok's reputation as a man of considerable wealth would not sit well with Ahdut Avoda, the most socialistic of the three wings in the Labour Party. Sapir was cool at the outset to the idea of Rabin's candidacy for the premiership, wondering whether he was not too politically unsophisticated to take on such power. But Sarid argued that the country wanted a new man at the top, an untarnished figure who would guide the nation to recovery from the war, and Sapir seemed to concur.

Rabin had another important meeting on 17 April: with Mrs Meir. The meeting — which was at her initiative — was vital because of the influence the retiring prime minister was expected to exert on Sapir. Rabin has said that the question of support for his candidacy was not raised. But whatever was discussed at the session, Rabin emerged smiling and announced to Tzamir, 'Everything's fine.'

One indication that Rabin was coming close to the nomination was the intensification of criticism levelled against him in the Israeli press. One of the key pieces of gossip concerned some $90,000 in lecture fees he had reportedly earned while serving as Ambassador in Washington. Dov Tzamir checked whether previous ambassadors had engaged in similar activity, and found that they had. Rabin had been more successful, that was all. On 5 May, Rabin issued a public statement answering the charges. He acknowledged that he had given a number of paid lectures 'on certain occasions' as was customary before he came, but he declared that civil service regulations permitted the practice and that there was no obligation to pay income tax on the fees thus earned.

He managed to emerge unscathed from the accusations arising from his lecture fees at the time, but in the long term his staunch defence of his actions damaged his reputation with certain sections of the Israeli public, who argued that an Israeli ambassador to Washington, as Israel's key spokesman in the United States, should not allow himself to take advantage of that position to make money from his public appearances, whether before Jewish or non-Jewish audiences. The entire affair would probably have been forgotten had the public not learned in March 1977 that Rabin and his wife had illegally maintained bank accounts in the US. In the eyes of some Israelis, Rabin had committed a worse crime in (apparently) making impressive sums of money from lectures while in the US than in keeping his dollars in a foreign bank acount (thus contravening the law).

Elections for the Labour Party's choice of candidate for the prime ministership were scheduled for Monday, 22 April. The Friday before, Rabin had told a newspaper interviewer that he would decide whether to make a bid for office 'when it becomes clear beyond any doubt that Pinhas Sapir won't accept under any circumstances the office of prime minister.'[13] He was encouraged by the favourable public opinion polls, he admitted, but he was holding back until the proper time. Meanwhile, behind the scenes, he received the most heartening news of the campaign thus far: Yossi Sarid was optimistic about winning Sapir's backing. However, Peres' initiative was giving Sarid cause for alarm. Reports had reached him of over 450 Central Committee members receiving phone calls from Peres in the past few days. Peres seemed likely to win the nomination unless Sapir decided immediately to support Rabin's candidacy. Sarid and Rabin agreed to meet the finance minister at his home in Kfar Saba, outside Tel Aviv, the next morning, 20 April. One of the last obstacles had disappeared that day when Mrs Meir's daughter Sarah had convinced Labour Party leaders who still clung to the hope that her mother would return, that she would not withdraw her resignation. The way was now clear for an approach to Sapir.

Rabin felt nervous driving to the appointment the next day. The meeting would be decisive for his future, and he was unable to share Sarid's confidence. However, he need not have worried: Sapir had already made up his mind to back him two days earlier, when Ezer Weizman had placed in his hands a document he claimed to have written in November 1967 at Moshe Dayan's request. In the document Weizman claimed that Rabin, in effect, had broken down in the despairing belief that he had single-handedly led the nation into war. He also contended that the chief of staff had asked him to take permanent charge of the IDF, and he threatened to release the document to the press unless Sapir withdrew his support for Rabin. Weizman's action backfired; Sapir said much later that his reading of the 'Weizman Document', as the press called it, 'gave me the last push to come to the side of Rabin'.[14]

Sapir greeted Rabin warmly, and assured him from the beginning that he would support his candidacy. Rabin was delighted. With Sapir's blessing the prime ministership was almost certainly his — but, always the cautious realist, he knew that the Labour Party itself was going through a transformation, and that it was too early to say with absolute certainty that Sapir's word was law. The rest of the meeting was devoted to discussing how to gain the greatest number of votes from the Central Committee. Sapir agreed to announce his support for Rabin at a meeting that evening at which a delegation from the Galilee region planned to try to persuade him to run for the premiership. Sarid was to alert Israel's national radio so that it could broadcast the news of Sapir's announcement at 7 pm that evening.

Rabin was now free to campaign openly. During the rest of that day, he and his staff stepped up their efforts. The candidate himself found the art of campaigning a difficult one. He was diffident about asking for people's support, and his staff had a job persuading him to make the necessary telephone calls.

Sapir called a meeting of the Mapai leadership for Saturday evening at the Labour Party's headquarters, at which sixteen of the top figures gathered. Rabin was present, but remained silent throughout. Someone suggested that Sapir would be better off running for the prime ministership himself, rather than supporting Rabin. Rabin winced, but Sapir told the group that Rabin was his candidate, and he expected them to make sure that he was nominated on the 22nd.

Only two men were now in the running for the nomination: Rabin and Peres. On the Sunday morning — the day before the election — Rabin was in a relatively strong position, yet one brutal shock still awaited him. While he was attending the weekly Cabinet meeting of Mrs Meir's caretaker Government, in which he was still labour minister, a member of his campaign staff received word from a correspondent on the morning newspaper *Ha'aretz* that Ezer Weizman had provided the paper with a complete text of his hitherto unpublished document describing Rabin's illness of 1967. *Ha'aretz* planned to run the entire text the next morning, the day of the election. The news sent shock waves through Rabin's campaign headquarters in Tel Aviv, where it had been calculated that he had at least a 100-vote lead over Peres. No one could say with certainty how much damage Rabin would suffer electorally as a result of the disclosure, but his advisers had to take action quickly to lessen the blow, and time was short.

Tzamir telephoned Rabin, calling him out of the Cabinet meeting to break the news, and advised him to go to Tel Aviv as quickly as possible. They had to plan their strategy, and only he could make the final decision. Rabin took the news calmly. Before leaving for Tel Aviv, he telephoned Sarid, who cautioned him against defending himself personally on the matter. Lengthy explanations about what had happened that day in

May 1967 could only hurt him, he said. Perhaps when he became prime minister he could deal with the matter openly, but now was not the time.

Sarid proposed that he should enlist several high-ranking military figures to speak for him in the media at the same time as the Weizman document was printed. Rabin reluctantly agreed, and it was decided that the campaign staff should contact Aharon Yariv, Israel Tal, and Ariel Sharon, a division commander in 1967 and a close friend of Rabin, whose voice would carry special weight since he, like Weizman, was a member of the political opposition. Rabin was diffident about asking support from men with whom he had had a mostly professional relationship, but Tzamir convinced him of the necessity to do so.

In view of the emotional nature of this new crisis, Tzamir asked Leah to join them at campaign headquarters in Tel Aviv to encourage her husband. As soon as he arrived at headquarters in the afternoon, Rabin telephoned Dr Eliahu Gilon, the physician who had ministered to him during his illness in 1967, to ask for his recollections of that day in order to refute Weizman's document. The doctor assured him that all he had been suffering from was a combination of nicotine poisoning and fatigue. 'There was a crisis that day,' he told Rabin, 'but I said there was nothing to worry about; that you needed some help, and that after a few hours' rest, everything would be OK. Everything that Weizman is saying now is nonsense. You have nothing to worry about.'[15] The doctor's words were comforting, but public reaction to Weizman's revelations remained unpredictable.

Rabin's communiqué, drawn up on Sunday afternoon, stated: 'I don't want to enter into a discussion of the motives of those who have seen fit to return to and publish, now of all times, an old story — and one man's version of it, at that. The facts are that I was absent from my post as chief of staff for twenty-four hours, from the evening of 23 May until the morning of 25 May. On the evening of 23 May I called upon General Weizman and asked him to take my place in order to make it possible for me to rest after the draining preparation work for the war. On the morning of the 25th I returned to the command of the army and conducted the action on the eve of the Six-Day War and throughout the war until the victory.' (Although he did not say so at the time, Rabin was convinced that Weizman had not initiated the publication of the document. Two and a half years later, he felt more able to talk about the motives behind Weizman's efforts on the eve of the election: 'I believe it was the beginning of a game that is still going on today — a kind of intrigue against me. I don't know whether Weizman did it on his own or was encouraged to do it by someone else within the Labour Party. I incline to the latter assumption. It's nonsense to believe that he was able to prepare it on the day of the election, if Weizman alone was responsible.[16])

Rabin's aides suggested he should telephone Gershon Shocken, the editor of *Ha'aretz*, and try to persuade him at least to postpone publication of Weizman's document until after Monday's election. Rabin felt that someone else should talk to the editor, but his advisers were agreed that only he could make the call. At 8:30 that evening, he spoke to Shocken, but the editor refused to delay publication, and suggested instead that Rabin produce his own version of what had happened that day in 1967. This was what Rabin's aides had already advised him not to do.

The strategy to deflate the Weizman balloon thus depended on the three generals. Rabin had located Tal at a Tel Aviv restaurant, lunching, ironically, with a *Ha'aretz* editor. He had readily agreed to make a statement of warm support. Sharon was reached in Beersheba and promptly drafted his remarks in defence of Rabin on a napkin in a restaurant. The final draft, which arrived in Tel Aviv that evening, said in part: 'The army which embarked on the Six-Day War was built by Rabin. He built it for the war and he commanded it during the war.' Yariv, then minister of transport, rushed his reply to Tel Aviv: Rabin's illness in May 1967 should not detract from his candidacy for the office of prime minister, Yariv insisted, and called Weizman's charges 'character assassination'. By late Sunday, Rabin had done everything in his power to cushion the forthcoming blow. He had even phoned Hannah Zemer, editor of the morning newspaper *Davar*, to read over his reaction to Weizman's charges, but she had refused to print it since the charges themselves had not yet been published.

Tzamir predicted optimistically that the Weizman accusations would boomerang, since Labour Party committee members were bound to ask themselves why a member of the opposition should enter into what was purely a campaign within the ruling party. (Weizman was then a member of the right-wing Herut Party, the major force in the opposition Likud bloc.) At most, Tzamir assured him, Rabin would lose 25–30 votes because of Weizman, far too few to cost him the election.

The crisis over the Weizman affair had consumed so much time and energy within the Rabin camp that there was little of either left when a strange new development occurred on Sunday evening: in a speech before the Labour Party's Central Committee Sapir pressed the case for new elections — an odd action on the part of someone who was actively backing Rabin in the elections the next day. Sapir warned that whoever became prime minister after Monday's election would face a tough time forming a coalition Government because of the problems of drawing together the embittered parties. Rabin was surprised by these remarks: all sorts of theories were suggested as to Sapir's motives. One was that he wanted to save Mrs Meir's Government since he was certain that it would be impossible to form a new one. Another was that the finance minister genuinely doubted that Rabin would win, and fearing a Peres victory, believed the only alternative to be new elections, with Mrs Meir remaining in charge of a caretaker Government until they were held. Whatever his reason, his speech seemed impulsive, even irrational to Rabin's campaign aides. There would have been more cause for anxiety had the Central Committee not turned down Sapir's proposal of new elections. Rabin, who had his doubts right up to the last moment of the campaign about the efficacy of Sapir's backing, had one more reason to wonder just how much help the finance minister would be. Yet he knew he could not succeed without him.

On Monday, the day of the election, the public read about Weizman's allegations for the first time. Testing the reaction within the party, Rabin's aides discovered, to their delight, that their strategy was working. Peres, Rabin's only rival, said he had seen the charges for the first time only that morning, and regretted their publication. Prime Minister Meir issued a statement in which she praised Rabin's part in the Six-Day War victory, and deplored such personal attacks; she refused,

however, to support either candidate publicly for the prime
ministership. Tzamir had been correct in his prediction: the
allegations were indeed having a boomerang effect. Furthermore,
the comments of the three generals, appearing at the same time,
warded off much of the damage. There were no demands for
Rabin to withdraw from the contest. Professor Amnon
Rubinstein, the head of the new protest group Shinui
('Change'), urged Rabin to request a postponement of the vote
that evening in order to give him time to explain more fully his
crisis of May 1967. Some newspapers, too, called upon the
candidate to present a full version of what happened, and some
editorial writers obviously took the questions raised by
Weizman seriously: 'Unless Mr Rabin can refute the allegations
of the memorandum,' said the *Ha'aretz* leader writer, 'his election
to the premiership must be considered an unwarranted risk.'
Ma'ariv was just as sharp: 'The issue of the prime minister's
ability to stand up to stress is not a personal matter. Whatever
the facts, they should be made public.' Other columnists gave
Rabin the benefit of the doubt, arguing that he could not have
won the support of the nation's key political figures — who had
known of Weizman's charges for a long time — if they had felt he
was prone to mental instability. 'There is no choice but to
conclude,' wrote Yoel Marcus in *Ha'aretz*, taking a different
stance from the paper's editorial leader, 'that either all the
above-mentioned people [i.e., Shimon Peres, Golda Meir, and
Pinhas Sapir] are so crazy that they don't care about the fate of
the country, or that a serious personal injustice has been done to
Yitzhak Rabin.' Marcus reflected the sentiments of most of the
Central Committee members who had originally intended to
vote for Rabin. The harmful effects of the Weizman document
would be marginal, said Rabin's aides. He would still win, they
thought, probably by 50–60 votes.

The Central Committee met on Monday evening in the Ohel
Theatre to choose their new candidate for the prime
ministership. Both Rabin and Peres were allowed three
nominating speeches from their supporters. The vote was
expected to be close. Rabin waited for the ballots to be counted
in a small room at the side of the large hall, where aides kept him
informed of progress. Leah was at home listening to radio
coverage of the balloting. The first reports were ambiguous, but

when the final results were announced, the audience in the theatre broke into loud applause: aides came rushing in to tell Rabin that he had won. A wide grin spread across his face. A second vote was taken, this time in the open, to confirm Rabin as the candidate of the entire party membership. The margin was even narrower than observers had predicted. Rabin had defeated Peres with a majority of 44 (298 to 254). Mapai divided its vote between the two, with Rabin securing a majority. Ahdut Avoda gave its votes to Rabin, Rafit to Peres.

In his victory speech, Rabin praised his rival Shimon Peres, and said that it would be difficult to follow in Golda Meir's footsteps, but 'the sons of the founding generations have come of age . . . We cannot but be sensitive to other countries' views and we must especially take into account our friend the US, but above all, we must safeguard our national needs, even if our friends do not understand all we do. The State of Israel belongs not only to its inhabitants, but to millions of Jews the world over. Its spiritual-traditional boundaries and its influence must extend beyond its physical limits. No one should mistake the fact that there is a crisis of Government in Israel; on the other hand, no one should make the greater mistake of assuming that this signifies a national weakness. In a strong and healthy democracy such as ours, we can shake off political weakness and rise to new heights.' After the speech Rabin rushed to his Tel Aviv apartment to join his wife and some friends in a celebration. Sapir was there, and the two men took the opportunity to confer about the next major task, the formation of the Cabinet.

Rabin's nomination was warmly received by Israeli editorial writers. Most were hopeful that at last the country might throw off the bitterness and frustration it had felt since the war. 'Rabin,' said one, 'will make a good prime minister, symbolizing the change that is sought by the public and that is essential to clear the atmosphere in this country.'[17] The misgivings the Weizman document had given rise to were dispelled at a stroke. 'One day's weakness and doubts,' declared another, 'is as nothing compared to the decades of positive achievement.'[18]

Abroad too, there was optimism about Israel's prospects of stabilizing its Government. Rabin's nomination received front-page coverage in Britain, where the *Financial Times* described him as 'Israel's ideal politician, a good soldier and skilful diplomat, with an impeccable Zionist pedigree'. The *New York Times* termed Rabin's nomination 'a major turning point in the political life of modern Israel'. However, Tass, the Soviet News Agency, wrote that Rabin's nomination would not solve Israel's problems. To do that, he would have to renounce Israel's 'policy of aggression and annexation'. He had been chosen, it continued, only 'after intricate backstage intrigues and struggles' between his supporters and those of Peres. On that point at least, Tass was perfectly right.

Difficult as his nomination had been, it was only half the battle. Rabin had yet to put together a coalition government which would possess a majority of votes in the 120-member Knesset. The task was complicated, and many thought he would be unequal to it. He needed a minimum of 61 votes to govern, but at first he could count on only the 51 seats belonging to the Labour Alignment and 3 more belonging to the Arab lists normally affiliated with Labour. He thus lacked seven votes. The traditional coalition partner, the National Religious Party, was determined to press for a Government of National Unity (to include the opposition Likud bloc): if it failed in this objective it would remain on the sidelines. Determined not to team up with the Likud, Rabin could therefore not count on the NRP's 10 votes. The Independent Liberal Party, with its four seats, was pressing hard for new elections in the near future, and it would be difficult to bring them into the fold. He might be able to persuade some of the other small parties to join the coalition, but at best it seemed likely that he could present only a fragile Government — if he could put one together at all.

In addition to the problems of coalition bargaining, he faced a continuing distraction in the person of Henry Kissinger, who had arrived in the Middle East in early May to begin another round of shuttle diplomacy, this time aimed at a separation of forces agreement between Israel and Syria. The war of attrition between the two had continued off and on throughout the winter and into the spring, with almost daily artillery exchanges in the Golan Heights region. The Israelis had refused to negotiate with Syria until its President, Hafez el-Assad, gave Kissinger a list of Israeli prisoners of war still in Syria after the Yom Kippur War. The list had been handed over to Kissinger in February, and by early May he was confident that peace talks would go ahead. Mrs Meir, still presiding over the caretaker Government, wanted Rabin to be present during the negotiations to give the impression that Israeli policy would continue even after a new Government took over. Rabin was naturally eager to be present, though Kissinger's negotiations with the Israelis, conducted on an almost daily basis, often went on into the late hours and inevitably took up precious time which he needed to fashion the coalition. He grew angry at the distraction, but there was little he could do about it.

He was also upset to find that Mrs Meir was doing nothing to help him form the next Government. She had refused to endorse him publicly after the nomination, and several times during the Kissinger talks, she made comments that seemed designed to embarrass him. During her initial meeting with Kissinger on 2 May, she said she had been impressed with President Sadat for admitting that his chief of staff had broken down during the Yom Kippur War. Rabin, just recovering from the publicity over the publication of the Weizman document, found her remarks distressing. On another occasion, the retiring prime minister, who had never been favourably disposed towards Knesset member Shulamit Aloni, chided Rabin for apparently planning to bring Mrs Aloni's 3-member Civil Rights Movement into the Government. Preoccupied with the coalition bargaining, Rabin said little during the Kissinger talks. Kissinger asked Eban why Rabin was so quiet, seemingly blind to the fact that Rabin could take little interest in diplomatic negotiations while the more immediate problem of forming a new Government was proving so insoluble. (On 31 May, Israel and Syria signed a separation of forces accord, which established a cease-fire, required Israel to withdraw from Syrian land captured in the previous war, and called for a UN peace-keeping force to patrol the battle zone. Israel and Syria agreed as well to limit their forces and arms near the frontier.)

Rabin needed the National Religious Party, and took the unusual step of asking the Chief Rabbi, Shlomo Goren, to intercede on his behalf. Goren did so, but the NRP put forward demands on religious matters which Rabin found unacceptable. He was particularly anxious to have Pinhas Sapir in his Government, and went to great lengths to persuade him. He asked friends of Sapir, both in Israel, and abroad, to urge him to remain as minister of finance. But Sapir refused, choosing instead to become the chairman of the Jewish Agency, the quasi-Governmental organization which deals with the nation's immigration, among other matters. Rabin asked him to choose his successor from among Moshe Zanbar, the Governor of the Bank of Israel; Minister of Justice Haim Zadok; Yehoshua Rabinowitz, the defeated Mayor of Tel Aviv; Asher Yadlin, the head of Kupat Holim, the Histadrut sick fund; and Ya'acov Levinson, the President of Bank Ha'Poalim. Sapir chose Levinson, but he turned it down, and the job eventually went to Rabinowitz.

Another Cabinet position which posed a problem for Rabin was minister of defence. Rabin considered Yigal Allon the most suitable choice for this spot. The two men were close allies and Allon had a strong background in the military: he had been one of the country's leading commanders in its 1948 War of Independence. Rabin had strong views about Shimon Peres becoming defence minister — all negative. 'I did not consider Shimon Peres suitable, since he had never fought in the IDF and his expertise in arms purchasing did not make up for that lack of field experience.'[19] But the choice was not Rabin's to make. He came under strong pressure from both Mrs Meir and Sapir not to choose Peres, but he realized that unless Rafi was represented in one of the top three positions, he would run the risk of not being able to form a Government. He had considered offering Peres the post of minister for foreign affairs at one stage, but Peres had made it known that he was interested only in the Defence Ministry. Peres appeared certain throughout May that he would eventually be given that post, and towards the end of that month, actually told Tzamir so. Tzamir, aware that Rabin was still being urged to keep Peres out of the next Government, told him that it was not at all a certainty. Peres immediately announced that he would go to see Rabin right away to clear matters up. Tzamir advised against this, suggesting that Rabin was bound to regard his intrusion as a threat and would appoint someone else defence minister, probably Yigal Allon. Instead, he proposed that Peres should approach Yitzhak Navon, the highly respected chairman of the Knesset's Foreign Affairs and Defence Committee, who was also a member of the Rafi wing, and a man Rabin admired. Navon and Peres talked together, and afterwards Navon told Rabin that Peres was quite adamant that if he didn't get the defence post, he would not serve in the Government at all. The implication of Navon's remarks was painfully clear: Peres, in not joining the Government, would make sure that his Rafi colleagues did not support Rabin, a loss of seven votes that he was by now counting on, as he had not managed to enlist the NRP or anyone else in his coalition. Fearing that he would thus be unable to form a Government, Rabin appointed Peres as his defence minister. He did so, he wrote in 1979, 'with a heavy heart. It was an error I would regret and whose price I would pay in full.'[20]

He was determined not to have Eban as his minister for foreign affairs. Yigal Allon was an obvious choice, to placate Ahdut Avoda, but to Rabin's surprise, even this choice posed problems. Allon felt that the Defence Ministry should have gone to him rather than to Peres, and turned down the office of foreign minister at first, threatening to return home to Kibbutz Ginossar on Lake Kinneret. Rabin's advisers suggested a compromise: Allon should become minister for foreign affairs and deputy prime minister, which would thus elevate him to the status of second-in-command in the Government, ahead of the defence minister. Allon found the idea attractive, but first asked Eban if he would be willing to step aside for him. Eban said no. In an attempt to placate Eban and keep him in the Government, Rabin offered him the Ministry for Information. He would also be considered a member of the senior staff of ministers who would take part in the expected diplomatic negotiations with the Arabs. Rabin sent Dov Tzamir, David Calderon, a Labour Party leader, and Moshe Baram to talk to Eban, who expressed doubts that Rabin would be able to form a Government, and finally turned down their offer, saying that unless he kept the foreign affairs portfolio, he would not serve.

Few gave Rabin more than a 50–50 chance of succeeding in forming a Government. His prospects fell considerably on 8 May when the NRP dropped out of the bargaining. He had been given until 17 May by President Ephraim Katzir to come up with a new Government, but was granted a further two weeks when this became impossible. Towards the end of May some light appeared on the horizon. Rabin obtained the

agreement of the Independent Liberals (4 votes) and Mrs
Aloni's Civil Rights Movement (3 votes), giving him a razor-
thin 61–59 vote majority in the Knesset. Rabin realized he was
presenting the most fragile Government in the history of the
nation. Indeed, shortly before he took office, he told a close
friend that once his new Government gained power, he planned
to announce immediately that there would be new elections
within a year. He intended to ask the Knesset to adopt
legislation to that effect so that there would be no turning back
from the balloting. (He dropped that pledge after assuming
office, and as his Government gathered strength, the idea of new
elections seemed increasingly irrelevant.)

Rabin was almost prepared to present his Government of 61,
as it was being called, to the Knesset. Kissinger's negotiations,
too — which had been prone to uncertainty during the entire
month — now seemed likely to be successful. There was one final
problem which Rabin had tactfully to overcome. He had
promised Allon jurisdiction over the 'Mossad', the Israeli
equivalent of the CIA, and Yariv, the new minister of
information (who took the post after Eban had refused it) was to
head the new National Security Council. Bar-Lev was still the
minister for commerce and industry, but being a former chief of
staff, Rabin decided he should head the war against terrorism.
Peres was furious, feeling that each of these departments
belonged to the Defence Ministry. A few days before Rabin was
to appear before the Knesset, Peres threatened to resign. Rabin
wrote to him, promising that he would work out the problems to
Peres' satisfaction later. Assuming this meant that the
departments would be placed under his jurisdiction, Peres was
satisfied, and withdrew his threat.

Rabin's precarious Government was announced on 3 June
1974. No one held out much hope that it would survive. Even its
minister of finance, Yehoshua Rabinowitz, predicted privately
that it would last no more than a month.

Chapter 8

Agreement in the Sand

In Rabin, Israel had a new kind of leader. He was the first native-born prime minister; the first to be born in the twentieth century; the first to be educated entirely in the country; the first to emerge from the ranks of the army; the first non-politician. At the age of 52, he was also the youngest prime minister. His freshness on the political scene heightened the expectation that he would strike out in fresh directions both at home and abroad.

Determined to win the confidence of both his party and the country, Rabin decided to set the tone for his Government in his inaugural speech to the Knesset on 3 June. He read it slowly and forcefully, gripping the sides of the lectern with both hands. 'Something has happened to this country since the Yom Kippur War,' he said. 'Even though we scored one of our greatest victories in that war, many of us have deeply troubled hearts.' There was solid enough reason for this, including the 'unwarranted expectations that vanished in the war' and the grief over the loss of life. But there was no justification, he said, for prolonging this feeling of depression. 'We must shake off our despondency. If we look about us, we will see that we are not in the Vale of Tears.'

The task Rabin set himself of lifting the country out of the doldrums was not easy. The separation of forces agreement with Egypt in January, and with Syria in May, eased some of its worries, but the fears of war recurring within the near future persisted, and there was still a state of national emergency. Many were disappointed that a Government of National Unity had not been formed. Rabin had rejected the notion, arguing, as had Mrs Meir before him, that it would be unworkable, since the right-wing Likud opposition would veto most of the Labour Party's proposals for peace agreements with the Arabs.

One of the most immediate tasks facing him in the summer of 1974 was the rebuilding of the Israel Defence Forces. The eight months between 6 October and 1 June had placed the heaviest burden on the IDF since the State was established. Soldiers had been kept at the fronts for periods of active service longer than any since 1948. Planes had been lost and needed to be replaced. Tanks were in need of repair. The weariness that the nation felt permeated the army, too. The wars of attrition on both the Egyptian and Syrian fronts had prevented the army from beginning a serious recovery programme until June, with the cessation of fighting on the Syrian front. Working closely with Defence Minister Shimon Peres, Rabin gave top priority to a three-year rebuilding programme for the IDF. He ordered an immediate study of the country's defence needs — which had increased fivefold as a result of the war — looking ahead to the arms requests Israel would make of the United Sttes in the near future. America had already given $2.2 billion in emergency military aid to cover the costs of the war alone. When he visited the United States in September 1974, Rabin requested $1.5 billion in military aid for each of the next five years, and this was granted. (By the autumn of 1976 the United States had provided Israel with $5 billion in military and economic aid since the Yom Kippur War.)

More immediate steps included improvements in army pay and standards of living to encourage soldiers to prolong their compulsory three-year basic service, and the mobilization on a temporary basis of civilian technicians in order to restore the army's rolling stock to battle readiness. In addition, the army's working day was lengthened. The mobilization system was tested in September, and a re-evaluation began of men previously rated unfit for military service. Trying to plug loopholes in the nation's defence, Rabin initiated plans for a strong civilian armed guard to combat Arab terrorism. He also urged the army to step up its activities against Palestinian guerrilla bases in southern Lebanon.

Besides the rebuilding of the army, the other major task confronting Rabin was to improve the deteriorating economy. Because of the heavy costs of the Yom Kippur War, the nation was going through its worst economic period ever. During the first two years of statehood, Israel could pay only 15 per cent of its way, with the balance coming from financial sources abroad; by 1972 the country was paying two-thirds of the national bill itself. But after the war in 1973, Israel was once again in a situation of major financial dependence on outside sources, able to pay for only 50 per cent of its needs. This was mainly due to the massive increase in defence spending, which now represented 40 per cent of the entire national budget. The trade deficit began to increase dramatically. Inflation in 1974 reached a record 56 per cent. The prices of most goods rocketed, and the impact on the average citizen was overwhelming. The nation had to find a way to reduce the $7 billion import bill confronting it.

Rabin rejected any solution which would lead to high unemployment and be contrary to his socialist ideals, and moved slowly on the economic front at first, waiting until his political hand was strengthened. The time came in October 1974, when the 10-member National Religious Party decided to join the Government coalition. In May, Rabin and the NRP had failed to agree on the party's key demand for new legislation to disallow conversions of new immigrants to Judaism if they had not been undertaken according to orthodox practice. Now, 5 months later, the NRP agreed to Rabin's suggestion that a committee should be appointed to study the matter and report within a year, in return for the party's admission to the coalition. With a firm majority of eleven in the Knesset, Rabin could begin to take necessary, unpopular steps in the economic field without the fear that he would be thrown out of office. On 9 November, 1974 he took the first major action to bring the economy under control, announcing a 43 per cent devaluation of the Israeli pound. It was the start of a prolonged programme of devaluations which by the end of 1976 found the dollar worth nearly nine Israeli pounds. Rabin's economic measures that November also included a six-month ban on the import of cars and luxury items. Though not the first steps he had taken to tame the economy — in July he had imposed a six-month ban on public and luxury building projects — they were the most stringent. Prices rose sharply. In the slum quarter of Hatikva in Tel Aviv, there were riots after the economic programme was announced, but a grim-faced Prime Minister told the nation on television: 'This will not be the last step. We have to face up to all the crises — military, political, economic, and social. I do not claim for a minute that we have solved these problems.'

The public sector, an area of the economy which had slipped out of control gradually over the years, had to be tackled before Israel could pull out of its economic slump. With 300,000 of its 1.1 million labour force employed in public service, Israel had the highest proportion of its working population engaged in this sphere in the world. Rabin campaigned vigorously to bring home to the nation that more people were needed to work in production in order to raise the level of exports. 'I am a socialist,' he declared in October 1975. 'As a socialist, I believe in the paramount importance of the productive worker over the workers engaged in services. The original socialist standards of labour dating from pre-State days still survive in agriculture and in the army and they need to be revived in other branches of the economy.' If they were not, he foresaw grave problems for the security of the nation. Towards the end of 1975, he said: 'There is a direct link between Israel's territorial compromises and the balance of payment deficit. The more Israel depends on foreign aid, the more it will be subject to pressures to give up territory.'

He expected the economic recovery of the nation to take between five and six years, and hoped that by 1978 the trade deficit would be reduced to $2.8 billion. However, it would require major sacrifices on the part of the people, many of whom (principally the middle and lower-class wage-earners) were already paying taxes and loans amounting to 70 per cent of the national income. When Rabin's economic measures began to bite, workers used the one weapon at their disposal: soon the prime minister was faced with wave after wave of strikes. He was in a difficult position; he disliked compulsory arbitration and preferred to avoid such a drastic measure. As a socialist, he sympathized with the workers' complaints and with their right to strike; but he was disappointed at their unwillingness to make the necessary economic sacrifices. 'Our economic future,' he said in October 1975, 'depends upon every individual doing his job as unquestioningly as a soldier does. In this we have not succeeded.' Though the nation could call upon its citizens to be first-rate soldiers, it seemed unable to inspire those same people to make similar sacrifices for the sake of the economy: 'When it comes to fighting, everybody's equal,' Rabin has remarked. 'But in the economic field, people don't feel the same way. They don't seem to feel that they are being treated equally.'[1]

The pace of Middle East diplomacy since the Yom Kippur War had been so frenetic that all sides had seemed to agree that a cooling-off period was in order in the aftermath of the separation of forces accord between Israel and Syria. It was evident in any case that a certain period was necessary to test both this and the Egyptian separation of forces agreement. Besides, Israel was preoccupied with internal problems, and the United States was going through the trauma of deciding whether to unseat a President for the first time in its history, a crisis that would distract its attention from the Middle East for some time.

Yet Rabin had come to power determined not to leave the initiative entirely to the Arabs, as Mrs Meir had done with her insistence that they give up their hostility to the Jewish State in one comprehensive step, symbolized by a formal and final peace treaty. After the Six-Day War, Defence Minister Moshe Dayan had delighted in saying, 'I'm now waiting for the Arabs to ring me up', a statement which was indicative of the Meir Government's attitude.

Rabin took a different, more realistic view. In his inaugural speech he said: 'I see it as the first duty of this Government to explore every reasonable path [to peace], for I believe that even if we cannot achieve peace, the people must be convinced that we have done everything to avoid war. I want to look with a clear conscience into the eyes of fathers and mothers whose sons may fall.' Rather than wait for a comprehensive peace to emerge, he would work towards a series of lesser accords with the Arabs. While territorial concessions would be a part of every agreement, they would form only one side of the equation. The Arabs would have to convince Israel of their peaceful intentions by practical steps that would lead the region away from war.

Rabin was the first Israeli prime minister to talk in specific terms of what compromises Israel was willing to make to attain peace. On his return from a visit to the United States in September 1974, he announced that Israel planned to draft specific political and territorial proposals — which included maps — in anticipation of forthcoming negotiations with the

Arabs. Where Mrs Meir had been absolutist in her policy towards the Arabs, Rabin planned to be flexible and open-minded. In contrast to past attitudes that had seemed passive and rigid, his approach was to be pragmatic and assertive.

He had never been as possessive about the occupied territories as Golda Meir, seeing them as bargaining counters rather than permanent annexations. He had none of the religious attachment for the occupied West Bank of the Jordan felt by orthodox Jews in Israel, who had urged Mrs Meir and were now pressing Rabin to annex the West Bank, since it contained so many Biblical sites which evoked Jewish links with the land. Rabin, however, argued that borders should not be determined by the Bible, but rather by the dictates of sound strategy. Just before he received the nomination for prime minister, he had upset orthodox Jews with a statement that signalled his readiness to yield territory on the West Bank. Referring to one of the religious settlements built there by Jews after the Six-Day War, he had told his audience. 'It's not a tragedy if we have to have a visa to travel to Kfar Etzion.' Shortly after becoming the nominee for the prime ministership, he called the comment 'a slip of the tongue'. It was no coincidence that the apology came as he was courting the National Religious Party, hoping to entice it into his new coalition Government. On the more general question of Jewish civilian settlement in the occupied territories, Rabin felt it would be worth dismantling a settlement here and there, if it brought peace. In 1992, upon becoming prime minister a second time, Rabin had hardened his view on Jewish settlements in one respect: he insisted that he had no plans to uproot any of them.

Although his approach was more flexible, in some ways Rabin's policies were similar to those of Mrs Meir. He opposed the creation of a Palestinian State on the West Bank, and he refused to return to Israel's pre-Six-Day War boundaries. He also ruled out negotiations with Palestinian guerrillas; but he had an idea of what Israel could afford to do to bring the Arabs to a final peace, and he had not hesitated to be specific. In January 1974, six months before he became prime minister, he had outlined in a speech just how far he was prepared to go to attain peace. With regard to the West Bank, he spoke of giving up the areas densely populated with Arabs, but keeping an Israeli military presence in the region for the next 15-30 years, until 'true peace' came. During that period, Arab refugees would be rehabilitated in Jordan and possibly the West Bank. Jerusalem would remain in Israeli hands, with special arrangements for the holy places of the three major religions. Israel would retain the Gaza Strip, too. In Sinai, Israel would yield certain areas but keep a military presence in others, such as Sharm El-Sheikh. In addition, parts of the Peninsula would be demilitarized, but Israeli troops would only vacate it entirely when real peace came. As for the Golan Heights, Israel would not withdraw entirely, but the existing lines would not necessarily have to be the final ones.

When he took up office, Rabin had concluded from the diplomatic activity of the past year that the Arabs had a new interest, however faint, in making peace with Israel, and for that reason alone it was worth pursuing diplomatic efforts as speedily as possible. Since the Yom Kippur War, the Arabs had dropped some of their extreme demands. Perhaps most importantly, they no longer talked of exacting an Israeli commitment to total withdrawal from the occupied territories before negotiations began. Kissinger had persuaded both sides to negotiate, albeit indirectly, although no Israeli pledge had been given on the question of relinquishing all the occupied lands. In addition to these reasons for pursuing a diplomatic initiative, Kissinger had warned the Israelis that he could guarantee only a year of peace after the Egyptian agreement had been signed in January.

Convinced that Egypt was the key to peace with the Arabs, Rabin pursued from the outset a policy of working towards interim pacts with the Egyptians, but he was distracted from this by unexpected pressure from the United States to work out an interim agreement with King Hussein of Jordan. During his visit to Israel on 16-17 June 1974, President Nixon proposed that this would be a way of limiting the increasing power of Arab guerrilla leader Yasser Arafat and his Palestine Liberation Organization. Both Hussein and Arafat claimed the leadership of the West Bank. Jordan's claim rested on the fact that it had held authority over the region from 1948 until 1967; Arafat on the other hand asserted that the PLO was the only proper political authority for the region since it alone could speak for the 670,000 Palestinian Arabs living there.

Palestinian nationalism was a latecomer to the Arab–Israeli conflict. After the Six-Day War had shown that the Arab States were unable to defeat the Israelis in all-out warfare, guerrilla-type operations seemed the only alternative to the thousands of frustrated Palestinian youths who flocked to the PLO's banner. Terriorism became their chief weapon in their aim to create a Palestinian State in place of Israel.

In 1974 there were 2.7 million Palestinian Arabs, of whom 450,000 were living in Israel, and 1.5 million in Israeli-occupied territory (the West Bank and the Gaza Strip). Most of the rest lived in Jordan. One of the main disputes in the Palestinian camp centred on how their purpose should be achieved, with the extremists favouring an out-and-out takeover of the State of Israel, the moderates advocating a gradual takeover, beginning with the West Bank.

Israel and Jordan began negotiating the future of that region — largely through the US, though reports persisted that talks of a more direct nature were going on — during the summer of 1974. Hussein demanded an Israeli withdrawal 10–12 kilometres west of the Jordan River. Rabin offered the king administrative control over both the West Bank and the Gaza Strip, though Israel would keep its troops there until a comprehensive peace agreement could be worked out. Hussein refused, demanding that Israeli troops withdraw immediately without waiting for a final peace. Even if the Jordanians had agreed to Israel's proposal, there was no guarantee that an accord could have been finalized. In his inaugural speech to the Knesset in June 1974, Rabin had announced that he intended to keep the previous Government's promise to hold national elections before authorizing any withdrawal from the West Bank, a policy designed to placate the National Religious Party which was totally opposed to giving up the region. The situation became even more difficult in August when Egypt declared that it no longer supported Hussein's claim to leadership of the West Bank, and would uphold the PLO's right to speak for the inhabitants of the West Bank. Israel wanted to drop the fruitless negotiations with Jordan entirely, and concentrate on Egypt, but the US insisted that some effort be made. There were reports suggesting that Rabin had agreed during his visit to Washington in September to proceed with Egypt in public, but to continue secret negotiations with Jordan. His mind set on Egypt, he could summon little enthusiasm for an early settlement of the West Bank question, over which he was convinced the Arabs would never go to war.

The decision of the Arab States at a summit meeting in Rabat on 26 October, 1974 to give the PLO a mandate to negotiate the future of the West Bank, effectively pulled the rug from under Hussein and made certain that there could be no political discussions over the West Bank in the near future. Some accused Rabin of paving the way for this decision by showing too little interest in a Jordan-Israel interim agreement, but this criticism did not take into account the growing popularity of the PLO and Hussein's uncompromising approach to negotiations with the Israelis. In any case, Rabin's hands had been tied in October, after the NRP entered the Government. Its arrival in the coalition made peace talks with Jordan even more unlikely, since the NRP intended to keep Rabin to his pledge to hold elections before making any decision on withdrawal from the West Bank. On the other hand, the political Left thought Rabin's rigid attitude to the PLO was leaving him no room for manoeuvre where the West Bank was concerned. To counter their criticism, Rabin kept up a dialogue with King Hussein. Ever since the 1960s, Israeli leaders had met secretly with the Jordanian monarch. While prepared to exchange ideas on peacemaking with Israeli officials clandestinely, Hussein was convinced that it was too dangerous for him to meet with Israelis in public. Rabin was one of a number of Israeli leaders who huddled with the king in secret places.

Immediately after the 1973 War, King Hussein proposed that Israel pull its troops back from the Jordan River along a strip 7.5 miles wide. Golda Meir's government did not think much of that idea. After becoming foreign minister in the spring of 1974, Yigal Allon issued a trial balloon: Israel would give back Jericho to Jordan as a first step towards political agreement. King Hussein thought the gesture too modest; his hardline critics would wonder why he was willing to accept so small a 'gift' from Israel when Jordan's position was to regain all of the West Bank.

When President Richard Nixon had visited Israel in June 1974, he urged Rabin and other Israeli leaders to meet with Hussein and try to work out some kind of political accord so that

Israel would not be forced to deal with the PLO later. A separation of forces agreement along the lines of those worked out between Israel and Egypt and Syria seemed appropriate.

With this as the political background, Prime Minister Rabin pursued secret peacemaking with Hussein in a series of meetings. The first such meeting occurred during the evening hours of 29 August, 1974. Accompanying Rabin were Allon and Peres. Though the idea that King Hussein would visit Israel for secret talks with Israeli leaders seemed unlikely, that is precisely what the Jordanian monarch did. He took a Jordanian military helicopter and landed it at Jersualem's Atarot Airport where he switched to an Israeli army helicopter. He was then flown to an Israeli Government guest house outside Tel Aviv. Joining Hussein were his prime minister, Ziyad Rifai, and his military adjutant.

Despite President Nixon's urging, Rabin opposed a separation of forces agreement with Jordan. That would have required Israel to pull back its troops unilaterally, and the prime minister opposed such a step. Still willing to talk with the king, Rabin offered him some kind of federative arrangement for the West Bank. Israel and Jordan would share in security and economic arrangments. Hussein, however, wanted the entire cake, not to share it with Israel. He said no.

While prime minister in the 1970s, Rabin met four times more with the king. Their second meeting took place on 19 October, 1974. The date was important: it was just a week before the Rabat conference where Jordan would lose its right to represent the Palestinian Arabs of the West Bank. At their October meeting, Hussein again raised the separation of forces idea. Rabin sought to persaude the king that Jordan would benefit if Israel started peace negotiations with Egypt. In that way, Jordan would not be burdened with being the first to have to negotiate with Israel. Nothing emerged from this second Rabin–Hussein session, and by 26 October at Rabat, Hussein was forced to turn over his right to represent the West Bank Palestinians to the PLO. This did not prevent Hussein from meeting with Rabin further. Their third encounter occurred on 28 May, 1975 along their desert border in the Arava plain. Hussein had grown annoyed at Rabin and his Israeli colleagues for 'letting him down' on the eve of Rabat. And so when Rabin raised the notion of a territorial compromise over the West Bank, Hussein said sneeringly: 'We are out of the picture. Please talk to the PLO and then we will see.' Rabin and Hussein met twice more during Rabin's first premiership, on 14 January, 1976, and in March 1977. That latter meeting came only a month before Rabin stepped down from office. Though nothing came of that meeting, Rabin presented Hussein with an Israeli Galil rifle encased in an olive-wood box as a gift from the government of Israel. An inscription read: 'To his Royal Highness, King Hussein . . . from Yitzhak Rabin, the prime minister of Israel.' In the 1980s, Rabin, as his country's defence minister, resumed secret meetings with the king.

Despite insistent pressure from the Left, Rabin was determined to do nothing that would encourage international acceptance of the PLO. He believed that the slightest hint that Israel was prepared, after all, to deal with Arafat would have the effect of assuring the establishment of a Palestinian State on the West Bank and in the Gaza Strip. Rabin's own feelings towards Arafat were based on the conviction that he was no more than a common murderer: 'I hate what he stands for, when I see the atrocities that he and his organization carry out. He represents to me all that is evil, and a concept, a philosophy which is contradictory to the very existence of this country.'[2] Early in his premiership Rabin had given the impression that he had more sympathy for the Palestinians than Golda Meir, who had always asked: 'Who are the Palestinians?' Some even claimed that his attitude towards them amounted to 'creeping recognition'. However, Rabin's policy towards the Palestinians and the PLO was as unrelenting as his predecessor's had been. When in July 1974 certain Cabinet ministers tried to swing the Government round to a more dovish policy which would have had Israel negotiate with the Palestinians once they recognized Israel, Rabin recoiled. 'My point of departure,' he said after the Cabinet debate, 'was that the Palestinian issue is not, as others describe it, the very heart of the Arab-Israeli conflict. In my view, the main problem in the Arab-Israeli conflict is the nature of the relations between the Arab States and Israel.'[3] Only the Arab States hold the key to resolving the conflict, he argued, because 'they have the strength, the power and the ability to reach political agreements — and, in the final analysis, a peace agreement. They also have the power to decide on a different direction — that of war.'[4]

The West Bank problem created internal conflicts for Rabin. Orthodox Jews, many of them young people, realizing that the fate of the West Bank was in the balance, had sought to establish permanent civilian settlements near sites of Biblical importance in the hope that these would establish Israeli rights to the territory and make the return of the land to the Arabs impossible. Rabin favoured Jewish civilian settlement in the occupied territories on a limited basis, but in line with past Government policy, he believed that the regions near the major cities on the West Bank, densely populated with Arabs, should not be colonized, and in July 1974 he ordered the army to begin dismantling the settlements and dispersing the youngsters.

The question of Jewish settlement grew into the most explosive issue confronting Rabin. The political Right sided with the settlers, while the Left argued that they were law-breakers who were damaging Israel's efforts to make peace with the Arabs. Matters came to a head in December 1975 when some 100 settlers constructed a settlement at Kadum, near Nablus, the largest city on the West Bank. The matter came before the Government and Rabin decided to permit the settlers to move from their settlement site and set up a temporary camp in a nearby army base. Meanwhile, the Cabinet would deliberate on their future. The Labour Party's dovish wing was incensed; the prime minister threatened to resign if it withheld its support. Deeply divided, the Government put off making a decision for nearly six months. In May 1976, Rabin achieved a compromise: the Kadum settlement was to be abandoned, and the settlers offered a permanent site on the West Bank, somewhere that was not near an Arab-populated area. The compromise, however, did little to bring about a quick solution, since the Government's decision was never implemented. The Kadum affair was significant for the way it reflected Rabin's inability to manoeuvre in the face of coalition politics. Constrained by both the political Left — Mapam and the Independent Liberals, together with doves within his own Labour Party, and the political Right — the National Religious Party together with Labour hawks, Rabin found his choice of action severely curtailed. In November 1976 he said, 'If I had

had the number of Labour seats that Eshkol and Mrs Meir had, believe me, the actions of this Government would have been entirely different. I don't believe that any Prime Minister in the past has had to act with such a narrow margin, or been so dependent on a coalition among parties that are not close to the mainstream of the Labour Government, as I have been.'[5]

There was greater unity in the Government on matters directly affecting Israel's security, such as Arab terrorism. Rabin was determined not to enter into negotiations with terrorists, whatever the circumstances. Mrs Meir's Government had wasted a day in fruitless negotiations when Arab terrorists overran a school building in Ma'alot on 15 May, 1974, and held a hundred children hostage. When the army had finally attacked the building, the ensuing gunfight resulted in the deaths of twenty-two of the young hostages. On 24 June, three weeks after Rabin took office, Arab terrorists raided a block of flats in the seaside resort of Nahariya. Four people were killed, including a child. Arriving on the scene afterwards, Rabin promised to 'do everything in our power to punish those who try in the future to harm us. Terrorism is an on-going activity, and requires constant vigilance.' He had instructed the army to act decisively in the Nahariya incident, and he issued the same orders when Arab terrorists struck at Beit Shean in November 1974 and at the Savoy Hotel in Tel Aviv in March 1975, where, surveying the wreckage, he pledged: 'The only place we will meet the terrorists is on the battlefield.' As he explained during a BBC-TV interview in January 1976, 'We cannot sit down and negotiate with a terrorist organization whose fundamental political position is in direct opposition to the very existence of Israel. The basic philosophy and policy of the so-called PLO is the destruction of Israel.'

However, though the IDF could effectively deal with terrorist attacks on Israeli soil, Israelis abroad were still potentially vulnerable, at the mercy of both terrorists and the host Government, as the events of Entebbe in the summer of 1976, were to show.

While Israel could to a large extent ensure its own security, it could exert very little influence on the foreign policies of members of the international community. The emergence of the

Arab oil threat at the time of the Yom Kippur War had strengthened the Arabs' bargaining position vis à vis Britain, France, and West Germany. In addition to this, Israel was but a pawn in the struggle between the United States and the Soviet Union, as they manoeuvred for a dominant position in the Middle East. In an interview with *Ha'aretz* in December 1974, Rabin described Israel's quandary in view of the current shape of international politics: 'Our power to change international reality is negligible,' he said. 'We must consider how best to emerge from this grim position. The only possibility open to Israel — and this therefore becomes our central objective — is to gain time. By this I mean a period of up to seven years, which I would call the seven lean years.' This was the time it would take the free world to shake off its dependence on Arab oil. It would take Britain and the Scandinavian countries six years, he thought, the US four to five. During the grim period, Israel had to prevent the Arabs achieving a position from which they might force the West to pressurize Israel into an unfavourable peace settlement. Keeping Egypt and Syria apart was important, keeping the pact in force longer than the six-month period of the accomplish both these goals by entering into a new agreement with President Sadat in which territorial concessions would be made. However, the Jewish State would insist on retaining the two strategic Mitla and Giddi Passes in the Sinai; the demilitarization of all territories turned over to Egypt; and keeping the pact in force longer than the six month period of the two disengagement agreements Israel had signed with Egypt and Syria after the Yom Kippur War. Significantly, Rabin talked about dropping Israeli demands for an Egyptian commitment to non-belligerency, but he came under heavy fire from Right-wing critics for this, and for going into such detail on Israel's grand strategy in the interview. The country was not ready to cede territory for anything less than an Egyptian promise of non-belligerency.

The peacekeeping process moved sluggishly in late 1974 and early 1975, though both Israelis and Egyptians agreed that some progress had to be made or the region would slide back into war. The US was eager to contain the Middle East problem — and to halt Soviet penetration into the region. Rabin's main fear, looking ahead with little comfort to the 'seven lean years', was that Israel might come under new international pressure to withdraw from occupied territory under unfavourable terms.

Diplomatic progress was slowed by a disagreement over what the new interim agreement should include. Egypt insisted on the return of both the Mitla and Giddi Passes as well as the economically significant Abu Rudeis oil fields in southern Sinai. These fields, captured in the Six-Day War, produced about 55 per cent of the oil used by Israel, and the Jewish State would only yield them in return for convincing evidence of Egypt's peaceful intentions, and the one proof President Sadat could provide was a promise of non-belligerency. If he could not take that step, Israel was still willing to cede some territory, but not the strategic and economic prizes which the Egyptians had demanded.

Kissinger tended to believe that such hard-line Israeli statements were propaganda rather than a true reflection of the Government's policy, even when Rabin declared on ABC-TV on 5 February — a week before Kissinger was to leave for the Middle East to prepare the way for the new agreement between Egypt and Israel — that Israel would not cede the passes or the oil fields without an Egyptian pledge of non-belligerency. The secretary of state was furious, accusing Rabin of sabotaging negotiations before they had even begun. He was sure the Egyptians would never accept anything less than the passes and the oil fields since Rabin had acknowledged that he was prepared to yield them. Kissinger's visit to Israel left him with the clear impression that Rabin and his Government would eventually give in: however, on 12 February Rabin again assured the Knesset that the Jewish State would not withdraw from the mountain passes and the oil fields until Egypt renounced all intentions of resuming war. He was far from convinced that Kissinger had prepared the ground sufficiently during his visit; the two sides were still far apart, and it would not be as easy as Kissinger thought to bring them to an agreement.

In March, Kissinger undertook his eleventh peace mission to the Middle East since the Yom Kippur War. Three days before it began, Arab terrorists of the PLO attacked the Savoy Hotel in Tel Aviv, killing eight Israelis and wounding eleven more. Peace negotiations began on 9 March in an atmosphere of increasing

Israeli suspicion of Kissinger and scepticism of his step-by-step approach to solving the Middle East conflict. Yet Rabin was convinced that Kissinger represented Israel's best chance of moving towards peace, though he would say very little during the negotiations with Kissinger. The Americans afterwards would complain how difficult it was to find out what the Israeli position was on certain issues. Rabin kept his cards close to his chest for reasons that had to do more with his own negotiating team than with the strategy: he had to reconcile the diverse views of his hawkish defence minister, Shimon Peres, and his dovish foreign minister, Yigal Allon. When sharp divisions arose within the Israeli team, Rabin would ask for a recess. Sometimes he would simply curtail the discussion saying, 'All right, I think they [the US officials sitting across the table] understand our position.'

The talks dragged on for ten days as Kissinger and his entourage shuttled between Jersalem and Aswan each day. But little progress was recorded, and the negotiating gap remained nearly as wide as it had been at the beginning. Sadat told Kissinger early on that he could not promise non-belligerency, but he would promise to solve the Arab–Israeli conflict peacefully, and not by military means. However, this sounded far too vague to Rabin. 'We are supposed to hand back the passes,' he told Kissinger bitterly, 'and all you bring back from Sadat are words, words, words.' If the Egyptians were not prepared to agree to non-belligerency, it might still be possible to arrive at an interim pact, Rabin thought. The very act of reaching an agreement with an Arab State was not something he was willing to give up easily. Working with Kissinger on the formulation, Rabin proposed that Egypt agreed to some of the elements of non-belligerency, rather than non-belligerency itself. Among those elements would be permission for foreign tourists to move freely back and forth across the Israeli–Egyptian frontier, the limiting of the Arab boycott which for twenty-five years had tried to deter firms from doing business with Israel, and the reduction of Arab propaganda against Israel. In return for this, Rabin promised to hand over Abu Rudeis and the western half of the two passes. The accord must have a lengthy duration, he insisted. Sadat, however, turned this new proposal down. He was prepared to extend the mandate of the United Nations peacekeeping force — which had been set up as part of the Israel-Egyptian separation of forces agreement of January 1974 — for one year, instead of the customary six months. Israeli intelligence estimated that Egypt could not afford to go to war for another year anyway, making such an agreement meaningless, unless it was accompanied by concrete proof of peaceful intentions.

By 19 March, Kissinger realized that too little progress was being made to warrant continuing. He made a last appeal to the Israelis to reconsider their stand, but Rabin would not be moved, and instead urged him to try to coax Sadat into a more conciliatory mood. With the peace talks about to break up, Rabin called an extraordinary Cabinet meeing on Friday evening, 22 March. Since the Jewish sabbath begins at sunset on Friday, the Cabinet would only meet in an emergency, and the rupture of the Kissinger talks was considered as such. While the meeting was in progress, Rabin received an angry cable from President Gerald Ford, urging him to moderate his position or face the possibility of an American reappraisal of its relations with the Jewish State. Rabin fully realized the danger Israel was in, but he was determined to avoid an unacceptable peace agreement with Egypt, even if it meant putting at risk Israel's special relationship with the US. He was convinced that in time the United States would come to understand why Israel had to make this decision. The Cabinet agreed there could be no softening of the Israeli position without parallel concessions from the Egyptians.

Kissinger, realizing that he could do little more in the region at the present, announced that he was returning home the next day. Rabin insisted afterwards that the decision to suspend the talks had not been Israel's, but this disclaimer was primarily designed to forestall any blame that might result from the failure of the peace mission, and to prevent the Egyptians from using the breakdown of the talks as a pretext for war. Though the suspension of the peace mission increased the likelihood of war, Rabin was more immediately concerned with the future of Israel's relationship with the US.

In Israel, his popularity increased as a result of the firm stand he had taken. However, anxious about the cost of this brave show of independence, the nation favoured renewing negotiations with Egypt in the near future. President Ford's announcement that the US would 'reassess' its policies towards the Arab–Israeli conflict in the wake of the suspended talks had caused widespread fear that the Arabs would take advantage of Israel's weakened position. Kissinger rushed in with assurances that the reassessment was not meant to be punitive, and would involve no curtailment of arms deliveries. But this was somewhat beside the point: Israel was pressing for a record $2.5 billion in economic and military aid from the US, to begin in July, and it was here that the Administration could easily decide to apply pressure. The new Israeli arms list included F-15 fighter planes and Lance ground-to-ground missiles. Although it was never stated officially, the implication of 'reassessment' was that these specific items would be withheld pending a change in Israeli attitudes towards an interim agreement with Egypt. Rumours began to circulate in Israel that the US was to halve its entire economic aid programme. To make matters worse, President Ford had publicly blamed Israel for Kissinger's failure to reach an accord. In an interview published on 27 March in the Hearst newspapers, Ford had said that more flexibility on Israel's part would have been the best insurance for peace in the long run.

Rabin's continuing hard line was a calculated gamble. From his own experience in Washington, he sensed that Israel could afford to take a tough line with the Ford Administration as long as it retained the backing of the Congress. With Congressional support, Israel would be immune from Administrative pressure, and would survive the reassessment.

The break-up of the Kissinger talks created new opportunities for the Russians who (according to accounts in the Israeli press) had developed a new interest in dealing directly with the Israelis. *Ha'aretz* reported that two Soviet representatives had held secret talks with Rabin and Yigal Allon in Jerusalem during early April in an attempt to make a come-back into the Middle East peacemaking process. They pressed Israel to work towards a comprehensive peace agreement which would be fashioned at Geneva. If Israel would agree to return to the pre-Six-Day War borders, the Russians were prepared to guarantee Israel's security. One of the fruits of such an agreement, they promised, would be the early resumption of diplomatic relations between Israel and the Soviet Union. It was only too clear to Rabin that here was one more pressing reason to restore American involvement in Middle East peacemaking.

In early April, American Defence Secretary James Schlesinger gave a grim warning about the prospect of war in the Middle East in the summer. To ensure that support for Israel in the US Congress remained strong, both in the event of war and in case of new Administrative pressure, Rabin sent spokesmen to Washington for talks with Congressmen. Among those who went — and thus made sure that Israel's case was well-publicized among the American public — were Allon, former Foreign Minister Abba Eban, and former Defence Minister Moshe Dayan. In the meantime, Rabin confronted a new problem that, he feared, might cause acute embarrassment to Kissinger. For six weeks he had been postponing a decision on how to deal with a book written by *Ha'aretz* diplomatic correspondent Matti Golan, which contained classified documents from Kissinger's diplomatic negotiations in the Middle East since the Yom Kippur War, and included a number of the secretary's candid — and negative — comments on world leaders. Golan had submitted the book to military censorship, a normal procedure in Israel. The matter was so sensitive that it was brought to Rabin's attention. In early May, the prime minister called together the Cabinet for an extraordinary meeting, in which he proposed banning the book. He argued that it could, if published, lead to Kissinger's resignation, and worse, to a further deterioration in Israeli–American relations. Rabin gained the Cabinet's agreement, and eventually a rewritten version, without the controversial references, was published. The incident is indicative of Rabin's sensitivity at that time to anything which might prejudice relations with the US.

Meanwhile, Kissinger was coming under intense pressure from the American foreign affairs establishment (outside the State Department) for a reconvening of the Geneva Conference with the aim of attaining a Middle East settlement along the lines of the Rogers Plan. This was the very development which Rabin had feared since the Yom Kippur War: a campaign to force Israel back to its 1967 borders. Indeed, in early May American officials went so far as to suggest 24 June as the date for the Plan's institution, and Joseph Sisco, the Under Secretary of State, spoke about the need for the US to concentrate attention on determining Israel's final borders if the Geneva Conference was reconvened.

Israel's main hope, Rabin still felt, rested with Congress. In mid-May, the Washington-based American–Israel Public Affairs Committee, the key lobbying group for Israel, began to work to counter the Administration's campaign to pressurize the Jewish State. On 21 May, its efforts were rewarded when a group of 76 US Senators sent an open letter to President Ford, supporting Israel's demand for secure and defensible boundaries and urging continued economic and military aid for the Jewish State. The letter received wide publicity and served to warn the Administration that it should not reduce American commitment to Israel. Administrative efforts to put pressure on Israel had been slowed, but the threat persisted of more serious American action against Israel if Rabin's Government remained intransigent.

In June a variety of occurrences helped to ease the atmosphere. Rabin decided, in anticipation of President Sadat's planned reopening of the Suez Canal on 5 June, to withdraw some Israeli troops from positions near the Canal as a goodwill gesture. The decision to reopen the Canal itself was a good sign; it followed a meeting in Salzburg between the Egyptian President and President Ford during which Sadat agreed to resume negotiations towards an interim accord with Israel. In mid-June, Rabin and Ford met in Washington. Ford took a very tough line, warning that Rabin's failure to agree to the renewal of the Kissinger step-by-step approach would inevitably lead to a renewal of the Geneva Conference, where the US would have to press Israel to withdraw to the pre-Six-Day War boundaries. Continued Israeli resistance would mean a drop in American aid, the President grimly reminded him. At home, Rabin was coming under domestic pressure to get back into America's good books; his finance minister, Yehoshua Rabinowitz, had complained bitterly about the effects of reduced American aid on the Israeli economy. The prime minister consequently informed Ford that Israel would henceforth be much more flexible on the final line of withdrawal, and would no longer demand an Egyptian pledge of non-belligerency. Realizing that the agreement which Kissinger would fashion now would be a bitter pill for Israel to swallow, the United States decided to sugarcoat it with substantial sums of economic aid. Kissinger had spoken of $1.8 billion, but Israel now talked of $3.5 billion for the coming year. The US also agreed to provide some extra protection for Israel contained in secret clauses that would oblige the Administration to prevent diplomatic initiatives detrimental to Israel's interests.

In early July, Rabin made a four-day State visit to West Germany, the first Israeli prime minister to undertake such a journey while in office. Upon his arrival, he attended a ceremony at the Bergen-Belsen concentration camp, and later a reception at the Jewish Community Centre in West Berlin, built on the ruins of a synagogue burned by the Nazis on 'Crystal Night' in November 1938. He was greeted there by several hundred members of West Berlin's 6,000-strong Jewish community, the largest in West Germany. Dining with Chancellor Helmut Schmidt, Rabin told him, 'After meeting you, talking to you and talking to other people in this country, I feel much better. I feel there is understanding and friendship here.' Schmidt, replying, said, 'I realize that any Israeli who visits this country has mixed feelings. But that you should talk of friendship after such a short time here has touched me and many other Germans around this table very deeply.'[6] Rabin could not escape the demands of Middle East diplomacy, even in West Germany. Since Kissinger happened to be in Europe, Rabin met him for three hours of talks on 12 July in Schloss Gymnich, outside Bonn. It was there that Rabin reluctantly agreed to Sadat's proposal that American technicians should man electronic surveillance stations in the Sinai passes. The Israelis had previously insisted on using their own men and equipment already in the Giddi Pass, but the Egyptians had refused to agree.

During the summer the final details of the peace agreement were slowly worked out. Kissinger resolved the issue of Israel's yielding the passes by suggesting that Israel put its forward defence line at the foot of the eastern slopes of the hills overlooking the passes, while Egypt advanced its troops to the western slopes of the same hills. The passes would fall within a buffer zone controlled by the United Nations. It was an ingenious solution, allowing both Israel and Egypt to claim that their original demands had been met. Israel could argue that it had not abandoned the passes completely, that in fact it still retained control over the vital entrances on the eastern side, while Egypt could assert that Israeli troops had left the passes entirely. As part of the agreement, the Abu Rudeis oil fields would be returned to Egypt, and some 200 Americans would man early warning sites near the passes. Both sides pledged not to use force during the course of the agreement, which was to last at least three years, with annual renewals of the terms. Israel had tried to insert a secret clause in the agreement which would commit the US to a promise to rescue the Jewish State in case of a Russian military threat, but Kissinger would only agree to 'consult' with the Israelis. The secretary did agree — secretly — to an Israeli request that efforts to obtain an Israeli–Jordanian interim agreement should be dropped. American aid, which had never been higher than $1.2 billion yearly to Israel, would increase to $2.2 billion under agreements between Israel and the US parallel to the Sinai pact.

Virtually all the details of the agreement had been worked out in advance, the final draft being fashioned in Washington by Israeli and American teams in the first few weeks of August. Rabin told Kissinger that, with 90 per cent of the agreement worked out beforehand, he might be able to bring matters to their conclusion within a week in the Middle East. Kissinger, equally confident, said he would like to plan on two weeks.[7] The August shuttle was marked by the noisiest demonstrations the American Secretary of State had ever been faced with as angry Israelis poured into the streets to voice their fury at what they believed to be a sell-out. Rabin had no sympathy with the protestors who, by staging sit-down strikes across main thoroughfares and engaging in violence, were breaking the law. He called them 'a serious blow to the backbone of our life' and said he regarded them as a more serious problem 'than the question of four or five kilometres in the Sinai'.[8] Most Israelis, however, realized that Rabin had had little choice but to accept the agreement. He described the pact in positive terms: 'The main thing,' he told the Knesset in early September, 'is that agreement has been reached that force and fighting will not be the characteristics of Israel–Egyptian relations, tht neither side will resort to the use of force against the other. I attribute great political significance to the very fact that the President of Egypt found it possible for his Government to sign such an agreement with Israel, an agreement that stands on its own, without being conditional upon events on other fronts.' Egypt had gone out on a limb in signing the pact with the Jewish State; only time would tell what the reactions of the other Arab States — particularly Syria — would be. In the clash that would inevitably ensue between Egypt and Syria, overall Arab policy towards Israel would be determined, and if the Egyptians proved the stronger, peace might be that much closer.

Rabin was careful to avoid giving the impression that the agreement meant a final peace was near: the Sinai interim accord could be a catalyst for even more positive developments, but it was impossible to know at that point. However, it had served to buy time; the US had been brought into the Middle East as an official peacekeeper for the first time, with the stationing of the 200 technicians in Sinai, and the Russians had been kept out of the diplomatic process. 'I believe,' he said later, 'that I managed to gain time, during which we improved Israel's political position — compared to what it was immediately after the Yom Kippur War — vis à vis the whole world, particularly the Arab countries and the United States. People tend to forget what the impact of the war was on the Western democracies. They were ready to let us wind up with very unfavourable borders, as we would have done if we had agreed to a political settlement right after the war.'[9]

For the time being, the pressure was off. The United States passed the word quietly that the reassessment had been completed and that Israel could expect a quick renewal of arms deliveries. The vast sums of economic and military aid the US had promised as part of the interim accord were the best indications of American policy towards Israel, at least for the foreseeable future.

Diplomatic movement in the Middle East slowed up once again in the autumn of 1975, partly because the would-be peacemakers wanted to find out if the Sinai pact would hold, and partly because of the growing Lebanese civil war. The war had begun slowly early in 1975 as units of the Christian Falangists fought

Palestinian Arab guerrillas in an apparent battle for supremacy in Lebanon. As long as the fighting continued — pitting Arab against Arab — the prospects for a resumption of the peacemaking process were considered slim both by the US and Israeli leaders, and thus few diplomatic initiatives were tried.

The breathing space in diplomacy gave Israelis an opportunity to turn their attention to domestic politics, in particular to Rabin's political future. In the autumn of 1977, he would face elections and it was always a certainty that he would want to run. His campaign strategy, which materialized gradually during 1975 and 1976, would be to go to the voter on his record in foreign policy. While his achievements on the economics front had been significant, Rabin realized that there was much discontent and unrest; the steps that he had taken had been necessary but inevitably unpopular. The main opposition for the nomination would come from Shimon Peres, his hawkish defence minister. Peres had made little secret of his determination to wrest the Prime Ministership from Rabin and a running feud between the two men had ensued, with almost every national issue becoming a subject of dispute between them. The Labour Party seemed to be divided into two camps, one favouring Rabin, the other Peres. The two men had been rivals from the start of Rabin's term of office. They had clashed over Kadum, they had quarrelled over West Bank policy, with the Defence Minister often taking a more moderate view of how to deal with Arab demonstrators than Rabin; they had differed over peace negotiations, with the prime minister taking a more flexible approach towards territorial withdrawals than Peres. But the feud was also highly personal. Rabin regarded Peres as a novice in military matters, despite the defence minister's long career dealing with defence matters. The feud grew to such proportions that intermediaries had to be brought in during the spring of 1976 to repair the strained relationship between the two men. Peres had been especially stung by a newspaper interview with an unidentified source (whom the defence minister took for Rabin himself) who suggested that Rabin would never fall under Peres' thumb in the way that Golda Meir had come under Moshe Dayan's. In mid May, the two leaders agreed to cooperate, but significantly limited their agreement to 'affairs of state', making it clear that their political struggle would continue. Rabin tried to prevent the contest by declaring that any Cabinet minister who sought the premiership should first resign his post. Peres, eager to remain in the Cabinet, kept a low profile after that, leaving his supporters to criticize and attack the premier.

To undercut Peres and the Right-wing Likud (whom Rabin would face in the general elections if he obtained his party's nomination), Rabin hoped to be able to show even further achievements in Middle East peacemaking. It would be difficult for either the Labour Party or the average voter to toss aside a prime minister who could claim to have made genuine progress with the Arabs. His aim was to show the country that prospects for peace existed, and then ask for a mandate to allow him to continue in office so he could seek further progress. If he could not do that, he wanted at least to be able to tell the country that he had earnestly tried.

Rabin's critics came from both the Left and the Right. Their main complaint was not about his ideology — since the prime minister had more often than not adopted a middle-of-the-road position — but about his tactics. There were charges that he had made errors in judgement about people and issues, that he had been incompetent. His threat to resign over the Kadum affair in December 1975 — which no one believed he would carry out — had marked the start of serious debates within the Labour ranks about his behaviour on a wide range of issues. The first six months of 1976 saw the most intense criticism yet levelled against him. He was attacked for appointing Yom Kippur War hero Ariel Sharon as his special adviser on military affairs, a move that seemed calculated to undermine Peres and Mordechai Gur, the chief of staff. He was criticized for failing to take action quickly enough after a high-level committee had recommended that the Cabinet ministries should be reorganized. Party dissension further increased over a remark he made to Israeli journalists in Washington in January 1976, asserting that Israel's arms requests to the US had lately been exaggerated. He did not say who had been exaggerating them, but the Peres camp was incensed, supposing him to mean the defence minister.

During that Washington visit, an outdoor ceremony on the White House lawn had been scheduled for the visiting Israeli premier. Notwithstanding a heavy downpour, President Ford insisted that it should go ahead, wishing to ensure that Rabin received the same honours as President Sadat had had the previous October. During talks it was agreed that the next diplomatic step should be an Israeli proposal for a series of end-of-war agreements with the Arabs, which could be negotiated individually or simultaneously with more than one Arab state. Rabin addressed a joint meeting of Congress, as Sadat had done, and said he was 'ready to meet any Arab head of Government at any time and in any place'. He quoted Sadat's comment to Congress that 'there is no substitute for direct person-to-person contact', and he was warmly applauded when he said next, 'I wish that he would direct those words to me as well as to you.'

The Lebanese civil war was a pressing concern for Rabin throughout 1976. The fighting was violent, but was concentrated for the most part around the northern part of the country. The danger to Israel at first lay in a possible Palestinian victory, after which thousands of Palestinians would gravitate from Beirut to southern Lebanon, near the Israeli border, from where it was feared they would step up terrorism against Israel. New problems arose when Syria intervened directly in the spring of 1976, eventually introducing 30,000 troops in the fight against the Palestinians. The danger then to the Jewish State was the possibility of a major Syrian military presence in southern Lebanon. Israel issued warnings to the Syrians — through Washington — and the press began to speak of a 'red line' in Lebanon, which the Israelis would not permit the Syrian army to cross. Israeli interest and intervention in Lebanon appeared to grow substantially as it became clear that the Palestinians were the losing side. The most startling suggestion of the scope of Israeli involvement in the war came in a *Time* Magazine report in September 1976, which stated that Shimon Peres had visited the Christian capital of Junieh in northern Lebanon four times since late May. On his third visit, he had been accompanied by Rabin. The main subject discussed at a meeting between them and unidentified Lebanese leaders was the creation of an alliance between Christian and moderate Moslems against the Palestinians and the Moslem leftists, *Time* reported. The magazine went on to document various ways in which the

Israelis were assisting these groups in their fight against the Palestinians. Israel, it said, had also won agreement from Christian leaders and moderate Moslems to permit the Jewish State to destroy Palestinian Arab guerrilla bases in southern Lebanon.

Despite Party dissension, one event in the summer of 1976 sent Rabin's political stock soaring again. On 27 June Israeli passengers aboard an Air France jet were hijacked by Palestinian terrorists to Entebbe, Uganda, a country which was hostile to the Jewish State. The lengthy deliberations over the release of the 105 passengers gave Rabin some of the most anguishing moments of his political career. He had to make the final choice between negotiating with the terrorists, when they made their demands known, or authorizing a military operation. Israel seemed to have little choice: a military operation 2,620 miles from Israeli shores offered faint prospect of success. Rabin decided to proceed cautiously. On Tuesday, 29 June he summoned his Cabinet and for the first time raised the question of sending a task force to free the hostages, an operation which, he said, 'has to provide for a way to bring back the hostages. It won't be good enough if we just kill the terrorists. We must be able to fly our people out of there.'[10]

Rabin rarely left his office throughout the episode except for one special occasion. On that Tuesday, the graduation of Rabin's daughter Dahlia took place at her law school. Long before the events at Entebbe occurred, she had invited her mother to attend but, knowing how busy the prime minister was, said, 'Daddy, you don't have to come.' Rabin replied, 'But Dahlia, I want to be there.' And the prime minister did indeed show up but, as the speeches went on, he kept looking at his watch. 'Remember,' Leah said to him, 'you came here as a volunteer. Find the patience, even if it's hard.'

Mounting such an operation required time and the best possible intelligence. Meanwhile, the terrorists had announced their demands: the release of 53 'freedom fighters' from jails in Israel, France, Switzerland, Kenya, and West Germany. They had also, at President Idi Amin's request, released 47 elderly women, children, and sick from among their victims. One suggestion made by a member of Rabin's Cabinet (as well as some military officers) was that Moshe Dayan should go to Uganda to help negotiate the release of the hostages, in view of his previous close friendship with Amin. Rabin could not agree to this, fearing that Amin might simply humiliate the former defence minister as he had done others in the past, or even hold him prisoner too.

On the evening of the 30th, Yoske and Ahuva Tulipman, parents of one of the Entebbe hostages, their daughter Nili, appeared at the Rabins' door in Tel Aviv. Leah was home alone. They had come to talk with the prime minister. Leah, who knew the couple, told Yoske he could phone Rabin the next morning. Yoske did so. 'Yitzhak,' he told his friend, 'you know that I'm an out and out hawk, but when it comes to my own daughter, my own flesh and blood, you start to see things in a different light. Do everything to release them.'

That evening Rabin asked Chief of Staff Gur if there was the smallest chance of a military operation succeeding the next day, when the terrorists' deadline was due to expire. Gur thought not, so the prime minister obtained the Cabinet's approval for the opening of negotiations with the terrorists. Later he explained why: 'As long as we had no military option, we had no right to tell the hostages that for reasons of principle we could do nothing for them, and that they were at the mercy of the murderers. Life is more precious than a political stand.'[11] However, planning for a military attack continued just in case there was a chance it might be carried out.

Negotiations proceeded; but as the hours passed, hope faded. The terrorists wanted the exchange to be made in Uganda, but Israel insisted on a more neutral location.

On Friday, 2 July Gur presented Rabin with a nearly final plan for the attack, but said it required more ironing out: there was to be a dress rehearsal that evening, after which he would report back. On Saturday morning, Gur walked briskly into Rabin's office and announced that the attack could start that day. Rabin was faced with the toughest of decisions: the failure of the rescue mission could imperil the Government's survival, but 'It's the right thing to do,' he told the Cabinet at 2 pm. He calculated that between 10 and 20 hostages would perhaps be killed, even if the attack went well. Notwithstanding that heavy cost, he was convinced that the operation had to be tried.

The Rabin family in 1927: Yitzhak, 5 and Rahel, 2.

Nehemiah Rabin carrying the flag in the May Day parade.

Yitzhak (kneeling) during his Givat Hashlosha days, about 1936.

Outside Kadoorie Agricultural High School.

Rabin (third from left) at the time of the 1948 War of Independence.

Rabin and Leah in the 1940s.

Rabin with Yigal Allon on the Southern
Front, winter 1949.

Ben-Gurion with senior officers in 1953.
Rabin is standing fifth from left; Dayan
and Peres are seated on either side of
the 'Old Man'.

Rabin gives a speech on Mt. Scopus in Jerusalem soon after the 1967 Six-Day War. (*Werner Braun*)

Rabin with then-Chief of Staff David Elazar (second from right) on the Golan Heights in the early days of the Yom Kippur War, October 9, 1973. (*IDF Spokesman*)

Henry Kissinger and President Nixon with Rabin during Nixon's visit to the Middle East, June, 1974.

Rabin on the tennis court with his wife Leah, January 19, 1976. (*Stern*)

Rabin disguised in wig and glasses. This photo appeared on a special passport which Rabin used during a secret visit to Moroccan King Hassan in 1976.

At a ceremony in the prime minister's office Rabin hands over to Menachem Begin, June 22, 1977.

Rabin with Moshe Dayan at a reception for US Secretary of State Cyrus Vance, August 12, 1977.

Rabin with then-Chief of Staff Moshe Levy (standing centre wearing beret) at the time of Israel's occupation of Lebanon, March 13, 1985. (*Israeli Ministry of Defense*)

Rabin with Shimon Peres in the Knesset, May 19, 1986. (*Zoom 77*)

Rabin speaks to well-wishers on election night, June 23, 1992, in Tel Aviv. To his left (with beard) is Shimon Sheves, his chief campaign aide. (*Israel Government Press Office*)

Rabin meets with President George Bush at Kennebunkport, Maine, August 1992. (*Israel Government Press Office*)

Meanwhile, the negotiations were to continue, he ordered; after all, for any number of reasons the attack might have to be shelved. If the operation failed completely, he would take personal responsibility. The Cabinet gave its assent. The rescue planes had already taken off, fifteen minutes earlier; it would have been easy enough to recall them had the Cabinet turned the proposal down.

At 7 pm that evening Rabin told Leah that the planes were on their way. A half-hour before the prime minister left home, Major General (Reserve) Rehavam Ze'evi phoned from Paris where he had been negotiating with the hijackers through French mediators, completely in the dark about the IDF rescue mission. Though the conversation was of no consequence at this stage, Rabin could not say as much. With no choice, he spoke at length to Ze'evi about his efforts, his voice remaining calm. As he left the house, Rabin told Leah, 'Tomorrow morning — either Israel's shares will be sky-high, or I will be hanged in Kikar Medina.'

At 10:45 pm Rabin and those involved in the special task force operation gathered in the defence minister's office, where they listened to a special receiver which would relay the sounds of the battle being fought at Entebbe Airport. Twenty minutes later the first gunshots came crackling through the set. Near midnight Rabin returned to his office along with the general staff and senior officers. The news came soon after that the hostages had been rescued and were on their way home. One of the first to congratulate Rabin was Menachem Begin, the leader of the Likud opposition bloc in the Knesset.

In the event, four Israelis died of wounds suffered in the rescue mission, three of them hostages and one the ground commander, Lt-Col Yonatan Netanyahu (in memory of whom the Government decided to name the Entebbe resuce 'Operation Yonatan'). One hostage, Mrs Dora Bloch, was missing, later presumed murdered on Amin's orders. Another three hostages and five Israeli soldiers were wounded: all the terrorists were killed.

The rescue gave a much-needed boost to the country's morale, and to its prestige in the eyes of the world. Rabin could not help but be elated: 'I knew the risks, but I also knew that there were good chances that the operation would succeed. And once it succeeded, I believed it would mean a new era in Israel, in the Middle East, and in the world in regard to terrorist activities.'[12]

Supporters of Peres argued that the defence minister had originated the idea of the military operation, and that Rabin had agreed to it only after days of indecisiveness. Rabin dismissed the allegation. 'The story was obviously a fabrication — neither the first nor the last to be disseminated by rivals within my own party in order to undermine my standing and advance their own ambitions.'[13] The prime minister's reputation was at an all-time high, and in September 1976, Rabin was selected as *Ha'aretz*'s 'Man of the Year'. Entebbe had silenced the prime minister's critics — for a while.

The Sinai interim agreement was Henry Kissinger's final act in the Middle East as Secretary of State; in early November 1976, when President Ford was defeated in the election by the Governor of Georgia, Jimmy Carter, Rabin was interviewed over the Israeli armed forces network about his feelings now that Kissinger was departing. Deflecting the question, he said he thought Israelis would look back to Kissinger's era with 'nostalgia'. A reporter asked him, 'Does that mean longing?' And the prime minister quickly replied, 'I said nostalgia.' On another occasion he said: 'I distinguish between the way that Kissinger thinks and operates on the basic issues — which I appreciated, even though I didn't agree all the time — and his personal behaviour, sensitivity, reactions and gossip, which I believe have harmed his dealings. Thus, Kissinger the thinker, the operator, the statesman, the diplomat, the strategist, I appreciate very much. I'm sorry that Kissinger's personal attitudes and behaviour have not matched his professional qualities.'[14] Although he did not say so, Rabin may well have been thinking of a reported comment of Kissinger's on the eve of his mission in March 1975: that he was coming to Israel 'to save Rabin from Peres'. However, Rabin found it possible to praise him for what he had done for the Jewish State: 'Despite our disagreement on many issues, I believe he supported Israel. I believe he did so because he was convinced that a strong Israel would help the kind of foreign policy he wanted in the Middle East. There was a solid, common basis of understanding between him and us.'[15]

After the American Presidential election the Arab States, particularly Egypt, seemed ready to start the wheels of diplomacy turning again. President Sadat spoke of reconvening the Geneva Peace Conference and negotiating an end to the Arab–Israeli conflict within six months. Rabin and other Government leaders pointed out that Sadat had shrewdly cast the peace proposal in terms of an end to the conflict (by pledging non-belligerency) but his real intention was to regain all the territory lost in the Six-Day War without establishing a final peace. To deflect some of the attention the Arabs were getting with their new 'peace offensive', Rabin introduced a new idea of his own. At the annual Socialist Internationalist meeting in Geneva, he proposed on 28 November a Helsinki-type peace conference, dealing with all aspects of the Middle East conflict. He purposely tailored the proposal after the 1975 Helsinki Conference on Security and Cooperation in Europe, in which the US, the Soviet Union, Western and Eastern Europe approved the post-World War Two European borders, and pledged to conduct relationships without resorting to war. 'Coexistence, security, trade, technology, cooperation and human bridges,' Rabin told the Geneva meeting, 'these are the essence of [the] Helsinki [agreements], and I buy them. I buy them as the essence of an agenda for a Geneva Conference on security and cooperation in the Middle East. For lasting peace is a matter of relations and exchange between peoples, not only Governments.' The conference Rabin envisaged would have to be initiated by the Middle East countries themselves — limited to heads of Governments (hence, the PLO could not participate) — leaving the great powers (the US and the Soviet Union) to provide guarantees, but no more. Unlike Helsinki, however, Israel would not insist on ratifying the present borders. 'We do not consider the existing lines as final *de facto* realities,' Rabin declared. 'Unlike the realities of Europe, we do not demand their perpetuation in peace.'

In proposing this Helsinki-style peace conference for the Middle East, Rabin deliberately hoped to force the Arabs to acknowledge that they were not prepared to go as far as he was. He was realistic enough to understand that the Arabs would find such a proposal uncomfortable, since Sadat had already affirmed his conviction that real peace could only be made in the next generation. The proposal was greeted warmly by Europeans at Geneva. The Arabs, as Rabin had calculated, rejected it.

Peace, he knew, was as elusive as ever. Yet he still yearned for it. As he said in the autumn of 1976, in an interview with the American magazine *Parade*: 'I am the father of two children, and not long ago I became a grandfather. I continue to dream that the day will come when they will be able to go freely to Cairo or anywhere else in the Middle East; and Arabs from all over will be able to come here. I continue to dream that we will have peace in the area. But for the moment, we must be not just dreamers. We must go on planning and acting in such a way that life in Israel is still possible, still worth living, even if this dream of ours never comes true.'

In pursuit of that elusive peace, Rabin made a secret journey to Morocco in October 1976. He hoped to encourage King Hassan to persuade Egypt to enter peace negotiations with Israel over a permanent arrangement. Flying to Rabat, via Paris, Rabin wore a wig as a disguise. There was no immediate result from the visit.

As 1976 drew to a close, there were signs that the Lebanese civil war might be coming to an end. Arab States were looking ahead to 1977 with the same curiosity as Israel: a new American President was about to come into office, and undoubtedly he would play a major role in shaping the course of Middle East diplomacy. For now, Israel's borders were quiet, as they had been for the past two years. Rabin was convinced that 1977 would be a year of new pressures on Israel, but he took comfort in the knowledge that it would also be the year in which the Jewish State would reach the peak of its military strength since the Yom Kippur War.

Chapter 9

Leah Rabin's Bank Account

With national elections only a year away, politics had been increasingly occupying the minds of Israelis in 1976. Uppermost was the question of who would be the Labour Party's candidate for the prime ministership in November 1977.

Though he had been prime minister for two years, Rabin had yet to win the mandate of the people in an election. With that mandate, he hoped to be able to exercise stronger Government leadership, perhaps even to demand still greater sacrifices from the nation in order to improve the economy. He hoped that with the backing of the nation he might conclude new peace agreements with the Arab States. Though the popularity of the Labour Party had appeared to drop somewhat in recent months, he looked forward to the party's triumph in the elections. The most serious obstacle to his remaining as prime minister was the minister of defence.

During the early part of 1976, Rabin had given much thought to the possibility that he might have to face Shimon Peres in a fight for the party nomination. The minister of defence had not disclosed his intentions, but the fact that he might enter the contest had to be taken into account, even though their 'agreement to cooperate' in mid May of that year had contributed to Rabin's air of confidence, which was further boosted by the success of the Entebbe rescue mission six weeks later.

In April 1974 Peres had come frighteningly close to defeating Rabin for the Labour Party's nomination for the premiership. It was conceivable that he could, if he chose, mount as strong a campaign again in 1977. The time to prevent the contest was now, before Peres could gather his forces, and while Rabin was riding the crest of his popularity.

Long criticized for displaying too little knowledge of the art of
politics, Rabin prepared a daring political manoeuvre during
August. Acting in almost total secrecy — to protect himself
should he fail — he proposed a long-term pact with Peres that
would guarantee Rabin the party's nomination.[1] He had
apparent reason to believe that the minister of defence would
himself favour such a pact. For some time, Peres had been
hinting that he might be willing to step aside. For instance, on
13 August — Peres' 53rd birthday — the minister of defence had
seemed to shrug off the idea of a party fight: 'Why should I be in
such a hurry?' he told Dov Tzamir, the party's information
chief. 'I'll be prime minister in another four or five years.
There's still plenty of time.' Peres might well have been serious.
After all, he had much to lose by challenging Rabin if the
premier succeeded in defeating him: he would lose not only the
premiership, but also, if Rabin chose to be vengeful, his current
Cabinet post. But shrewdly, Rabin had refused to allow himself
to be lulled into a false sense of security by such utterances.

He spelled out the terms of the pact with Peres and asked Dov
Tzamir to mediate. The key clause would give Rabin the prime
ministership for another four-year term by virtue of Peres'
agreement not to contest the party nomination. The second and
third clauses would go a long way towards satisfying some of
Peres' long-standing complaints. For one thing, Rabin would
agree to allow him to speak out on matters outside his
department; for another, Peres would become privy to all the
Labour Party's decisions and stratagems.

Two subjects were not made part of the proposed agreement,
but were implicit: Peres would be assured of his post as minister
of defence after the election, if Rabin won; and he would have
the option of seeking the prime ministership in 1981.

Tzamir, who was on good terms with both men, arranged a
meeting between them on 26 August in the prime minister's
office in Tel Aviv. It lasted several hours, and when it was over,
Rabin had the clear impression that he and Peres had come to
an agreement. 'We had a good meeting,' he told Tzamir. 'I
think we've concluded the matter.' But Tzamir was sceptical
that such an arrangement could have come about so easily.
Were the two men prepared publicly to announce this
agreement, he asked Rabin. 'No, not yet,' the prime minister

replied. 'Then you haven't agreed on anything yet,' Tzamir told him.

Judging by Peres' impression of the outcome of the meeting, he seemed correct. The minister of defence felt that he and Rabin had improved their relationship, but he could not acknowledge that a long-term agreement had been reached. Talking shortly afterwards to his good friend Yitzhak Navon, the chairman of the Knesset's Foreign Affairs and Defence Committee, Peres said, 'We had a wonderful discussion, but while we agreed on everything, it's only for a limited time.' In short, while Rabin was thinking in terms of an end to their mutual animosity, Peres felt that all they had agreed upon was a cease-fire. Tzamir was angry with himself later for not pursuing the matter with Peres, sensing that had he pressed the minister of defence for an explanation of what had gone wrong at the meeting, he might have been able to bring the two men together.

If Peres was right, and only a cease-fire had been agreed upon, even that did not last very long. The first source of irritation was Rabin's appointment of Asher Yadlin on 5 September as Governor of the Bank of Israel, the second most important post in the Israeli economy. Yadlin's nomination seemed somewhat odd since he had had no previous banking experience. But it proved downright embarrassing when Yadlin, a major figure in the Labour Party and one of its key fund-raisers, came under police investigation for fraud and bribery several weeks after Rabin had placed his name before the Cabinet for approval. Yadlin, the director-general of Kupat Holim, the nation's principal sick fund, was arrested on 19 October. A few days later Rabin felt compelled to withdraw his nomination; Yadlin received a five-year prison term in February 1977.

The Yadlin affair provoked a sharp dispute between Rabin and Peres, as usual conducted in private. The minister of defence, noting that he had not been consulted on the Yadlin appointment, blamed Rabin for neglecting to take counsel which might have avoided such an embarrassing outcome. Rabin accused Peres of maliciously inflating the incident. He suspected that the minister of defence had abandoned any interest he might have had in a political pact and was now intent upon a contest for the leadership. He therefore decided to adopt the offensive. He subtly blamed the minister of defence for the turmoil which had racked the occupied territories for the past year, and promised to take a more active role himself in their handling. The contest was under way.

Had political developments proceeded in the winter of 1976–77 in a straightforward manner, the Labour Party would probably have met to choose its nominee for premier in the spring of 1977. But the political scene was suddenly shaken by events in the early winter which were to force a change in the election schedule.

It all began with the scheduled arrival in Israel of three American F-15 fighter planes late one Friday afternoon in December. The introduction of these, the most advanced warplanes yet developed, into the Israeli air force was sensational military news, but scarcely seemed likely to be the cause of any political upheaval. Acquiring the F-15s was a significant achievement for the country, and Rabin felt some public celebration was in order. He arranged for a welcoming ceremony complete with Government leaders and top military men. The fact that the planes would be landing less than an hour before the onset of the sabbath in Jerusalem (74 minutes before its onset in Tel Aviv) had not seemed important.

However, when orthodox Jews in the Government heard what was being arranged in the name of the State, they were enraged. Under Jewish law, one is forbidden from doing any manner of work on the sabbath — and travel, a form of work, is included in that ban. By holding the ceremony so close to the sabbath, the State in effect was forcing its own leaders to violate a basic Jewish precept.

When he learned of their anger, Rabin first tried to soothe the orthodox Jewish leaders by promising to have helicopters standing by to assure their arrival at home in time for the sabbath, then, when they still balked, he agreed to tone down the official aspect of the ceremony by cancelling invitations already sent to Cabinet ministers and Knesset members. On 10 December, the three planes arrived, performed some spectacular aerobatics, and were praised, filmed, and admired by the spectators. In this atmosphere, speeches seemed mandatory: 'This day,' the prime minister proclaimed joyfully to the crowd at the airport, 'is a holiday that inspires us with faith and trust, which we so need — trust in our might and faith in a better future.' The chief of staff, Lt-Gen Mordechai Gur, announced: 'Today, the State of Israel is a different state and "Zahal" [the IDF] is a different "Zahal".'

With the showing of the ceremony on television the next day, the country saw that the State had sponsored an event which had made it difficult, if not impossible, for the crowd to get home by the sabbath. It hardly mattered that most of those attending the ceremony were not even religious: orthodox Jewish politicians were furious. Even if the prime minister had toned down the official nature of the welcome, the State was still responsible for an event that had led to the desecration of the sabbath. The Government, in their view, had to be reprimanded. The National Religious Party (NRP), a member of Rabin's coalition Government, was in an awkward situation: on grounds of religious principle, it could not but condemn what Rabin had permitted; yet as a coalition partner, it had to display loyalty to the Government. The matter came up at a Cabinet meeting two days after the planes had landed. Rabin endeavoured to convince the three NRP ministers that he had sought to change the time of the event but could not. 'If the sabbath was desecrated,' he said, 'I am truly sorry.'[2]

Reports were circulating that the United Torah Front party planned to introduce a motion of no-confidence in the Knesset. In its anger, the NRP was weighing the possibility of withholding its support of the Government should such a vote take place. An act of rebellion such as that gave Rabin the right, under the law, to dismiss the NRP from his Government, a step with such wide and uncertain political implications that he would only consider it if no other choice existed. He spent hours trying to persuade the NRP to support the Government, but the showdown came on 14 December.

Confronted with the dire prospect of losing a no-confidence motion, Rabin issued frantic pleas to all Alignment Knesset members to be present at the vote. Special arrangements were laid on to ensure that as many came as possible: a helicopter was put at the disposal of Shimon Peres and Avraham Ofer, the minister of housing, to whisk them from Ben-Gurion Airport upon their arrival from New York, to the Knesset building in

Jerusalem. The Alignment's chief whip, Moshe Wertman, was
summoned to vote as well, though his father had died that very
morning. With its narrowest majority ever, Rabin's Government
squeezed by on a vote of 55–48. The NRP had carried out its
threat: nine of its ten Knesset members had abstained.

The NRP had thrown down the gauntlet — and Rabin chose
to pick it up. In his anger over its defiance, he acted more in the
interests of preserving his Government's dignity than out of
political expediency. On 20 December, he dismissed the three
NRP ministers from his Cabinet, thus plunging the nation into a
political crisis. With the loss of the NRP's 10 Knesset seats,
Rabin could count on only 57 votes to support his shaky
Government, four less than the 61 needed for a majority in the
120-member body. He acted, he said, because 'a Government
which cannot adhere to the principle of collective responsibility
has no business functioning as a Government.'[3]

The crisis was only temporary, however, since Rabin was in
no mood to test his chances of surviving motions of no-
confidence while he could command only minority support in
the Knesset. On 21 December he took the one realistic option
open to him — resignation — and pressed the Knesset to
advance the elections so that he might win a mandate to set up a
new, majority-backed Government. Ezer Weizman, who was
shortly to become the chairman of the Likud's election
campaign, remarked: 'It turns out that the F-15 really is an
excellent plane — so excellent that it's even capable of shooting
down a Government!'[4]

Rabin's resignation did not alter his status as head of
Government. With elections now scheduled for 17 May, he
would serve as head of the caretaker administration until a new
Government was formed. The decision did not seem to have
much effect on Middle East diplomacy either. With the Arab
States still so preoccupied with the Lebanese civil war, there had
been little talk of reviving the peacemaking process. Both
Israelis and Arabs were waiting for the new Administration of
President Jimmy Carter to chart its Middle East policies. The
scheduling of the elections in May could mean, however, that a
new Government might be able to begin negotiations with the
Arabs that much earlier.

With his twin strokes of dismissing the NRP ministers and

submitting his resignation, Rabin managed to deflate those critics who had been accusing him of indecisive and lack-lustre leadership, gained himself a breathing space, and prevented a Likud vote of no-confidence. Both steps were greeted sympathetically by large sections of the Labour Party and the nation. Rabin immediately used his newly won support to strike at his most likely opponent in the coming Labour Party struggle for the leadership, Shimon Peres. In a sharply worded message, conveyed through 'friends' to the newspaper *Ha'aretz*, Rabin stated that two members of the Government leadership ought not to be fighting for control of that same Government.[5] Peres himself toyed with the idea of leaving the Labour Party and forming a Government with the Likud Party (a step that would have been possible, if he could have mustered the necessary 61 votes. With Rabin's resignation, President Ephraim Katzir was obliged to canvass other political parties about their prospects of forming a Government before new elections were called). In the end, however, Peres dropped the idea and remained in the Labour fold.

The national elections were bound to be fought on economic issues, with inflation at a rate of 38 per cent annually and the Government's labour policies in a state of collapse. Security and foreign policy, too, would be important issues for the voter, as they always had been. But a new issue was beginning to attract public attention: official corruption. Israelis had begun to look more closely at the qualifications of its leaders after the Yom Kippur War, when the leadership appeared to have made mistakes of such gravity that countless lives had been lost, perhaps unnecessarily. It was only natural that in addition to demanding higher standards of Government the public would keep a close eye on the question of Government corruption.

Rabin's Government had come to office pledged to root out any such manifestations. The very fact that his Government had revealed such misdeeds as those of Asher Yadlin reflected favourably upon the prime minister, although some of his critics took great pleasure in the Yadlin affair, for the discovery of corruption in high places might create the impression that the entire Government was tainted — including Rabin himself. But most were perfectly willing to give the Government the benefit of the doubt. As for the prime minister himself, he continued to enjoy an untarnished reputation. During the winter of 1976–77, however, scandal touched the Government's inner circle when the minister of housing, Avraham Ofer, came under suspicion in the press of embezzlement. Though Rabin was not implicated in any of the disclosures connected with Ofer, a shadow of doubt and suspicion settled over his Government which it was never entirely able to cast off.

The 53-year-old Ofer, a former director-general of Shikun Ovdim, the Histadrut-owned construction firm, had been a strong supporter of Rabin, and in 1973 had been the chairman of the Labour Party's election campaign. When the scandal was rumoured, it was inevitable that Rabin should also be affected. Hence the prime minister worked to clear the air as quickly as possible. He held a secret meeting with police officials and the minister of justice at his Tel Aviv flat on 1 January 1977, after the police had begun inquiries. However, the secret was badly kept and news leaked to the press that the meeting had discussed whether to prosecute Ofer. The next day Ofer, by now distraught over the case building up against him in the public's mind, pressed Rabin to declare his innocence and to put an end to the police probe as quickly as possible. Listening to Ofer protest his innocence, Rabin could offer no comfort.

The following day, 3 January, Ofer drove to a deserted beach in north Tel Aviv, and shot himself. In the note he left by his side, he wrote, 'I have no more strength to bear it. I see no point in continuing even after my innocence is proved.' The suicide of a Cabinet minister is shocking news in any country. In Israel, where suicide is stigmatized (Jewish law forbids a proper Jewish burial in the case of suicides), the tragedy took on immense proportions. Some Israelis tried to condemn Rabin for what had occurred, but the prime minister sought to place the blame on the press. Offering the eulogy at Ofer's funeral two days later (religious authorities found a way within the rabbinic law to enable him to be buried in consecrated ground), Rabin condemned those who had conducted the campaign of rumour, innuendo and prejudice against the dead man. 'These are the sincerest of words,' he said of Ofer's suicide note, 'inscribed at the supreme moment of truth. And they stand as a challenge to all those who maligned him and who spilled his blood . . . Will this tragedy serve to shock people into learning to think twice about what they utter or print, to treat their fellow man's reputation with respect, and not to pass judgement on anyone before he has had his day in court?' He then recalled the conversation he had held with Ofer on Sunday when the minister of housing had insisted he was innocent: 'I replied to you, Avraham,' he said, his eyes fixed on the coffin, 'that I, Yitzhak Rabin, wholly believe in your innocence.'

The accusations against Ofer and his subsequent suicide brought the scent of scandal that much closer to the prime minister himself. There were those who considered the tragic death of the minister as an indictment of the entire Rabin Government. Though no one pointed the finger of suspicion at Rabin himself, and his reputation for integrity remained intact, the corruption issue became an increasingly heavy burden to bear during the coming months.

The contest for the Labour Party's prime ministerial nomination was to take place at a convention of nearly 3,000 members of the Labour Party due to assemble on 22 February in Jerusalem, and the following day in Tel Aviv. Never before had the Party opened the nomination for its top leadership position to this large forum. And never before had an incumbent prime minister been confronted with a challenge from within the ranks of the party. The whole process of choosing the candidate for prime minister was so novel that no one could say whom it favoured.

What was clear was that Shimon Peres would not let go of his hope to unseat his chief rival in the Labour Party, Yitzhak Rabin. Rabin had been increasingly upset with Peres for airing his differences with the prime minister in public. '. . . In order for a government to maintain its authority and credibility, once a decision is reached by majority vote the entire Cabinet is obligated to stand behind it,' Rabin wrote in his *Memoirs*. 'There can be no greater threat to the public's confidence in its government than having Cabinet squabbles splashed across the pages of the daily papers.'[6] Yet that is precisely what Peres did. The two had clashed over the defence budget and over Jewish settlement policy. The Cabinet had supported a policy of excluding new settlements in heavily populated areas on the West Bank; Peres called for 'settlement everywhere'. Wrote

Rabin: 'In his characteristic rhetorical flourish, he proclaimed that "the hills of Samaria are no less lofty than the hills of Golan" — as though politics was a mountaineering contest. Public statements of this kind naturally encouraged the Gush Eminum movement to challenge the Government to a show of strength, though it is difficult to fathom why a Cabinet minister would be interested in encouraging defiance of his own Government's policy.'[7]

Rabin believed that Peres had been the source of one of the most serious leaks: the classified transcripts of talks between Golda Meir's government and Henry Kissinger which were passed on to *Ha'aretz* reporter, Matti Golan. Rabin gleefully noted how Peres had reacted following another sensitive leak, this one concerning the secret visit to Israel by two Soviet representatives in early April 1974. When Foreign Minister Yigal Allon suggested that Rabin, Peres, and he submit to lie detector tests, Peres threatened to resign rather than do so.[8]

Rabin was fighting for the nomination on his past achievements, insisting that he had done a good job and that with four more years and the mandate of the people, he could exercise more decisive leadership. If the Labour Party dismissed a standing prime minister it would be tantamount to expressing a lack of confidence both in the party and in the Government. Peres was insisting — in private, for fear that he would appear to be a source of divisiveness, and hence anger potential voters — that Rabin had to go, that he was a weak leader, and that he would cost the party dearly at the polls in May. Arguing that the country was eager for change, he pointed out the new political parties that were springing up in opposition to Rabin's Government, though in fact these new parties wanted more than just a change of Government: they were after a fundamental change in the entire political system.

The most important of these new protest movements, the Democratic Movement for Change, was led by Professor Yigael Yadin, the 60-year-old archaeologist and former chief of staff, who was now seeking an active role in the political leadership of the country. Yadin was pressing for electoral reform as the key change necessary to put the nation on the correct path. Electoral reform, he said, would make the nation's parties more representative, and the nation would ultimately benefit from the process of democratization.

*

Rabin was, of course, vulnerable on economic issues. Though he could point to progress in reducing the enormous trade deficits after the Yom Kippur War, the inflation-ridden economy had hurt the average wage-earner, who was simply too busy trying to make ends meet to appreciate any long-term benefits of Rabin's economic strategy. The public sector was racked with costly strikes which the prime minister could do little about — the workers' demands were patently too reasonable to ignore. To his Government's credit, it did manage to keep unemployment relatively stable.

Rabin's strong suit was foreign affairs — and here he could claim major achievements and, during the election campaign, play up his role as a statesman and his contribution to Israel's close ties with the US. 'I never regarded Europe as a "shelter for a rainy day",' Rabin told an interviewer during the campaign, quoting a phrase attributed to Peres. 'I attach importance to relations with Europe, but the true shelter if we need one was and is the US.'[9]

The new Administration in Washington could not have helped Rabin's plans along better if they had tried. Cyrus Vance, the new Secretary of State, scheduled a visit to the Middle East just before the Labour Party convention, and planned to arrive in Israel a week before the balloting would take place. He breakfasted with Rabin on the first day of his visit, 16 February, and invited the prime minister to visit the US in the near future, a gesture which enhanced Rabin's prestige during his quest for the nomination. Vance mostly listened to Israeli leaders without outlining American policy, but did suggest that it might be possible to work towards reconvening the Geneva Conference during the second part of 1977. The Israelis indicated that they would prefer the US to help to bring about bilateral agreements between Israel and the Arab States.

Rabin appeared to be moving Israel towards peace in other ways, too. In one of his more spectacular acts of personal diplomacy, he left secretly at 2 am on 4 February, for Geneva, where he held a rendezvous with President Felix Houphouet-Boigny of the Ivory Coast, one of the last African leaders to break off diplomatic relations with Israel at the time of the Yom Kippur War. He was now apparently having second thoughts. Arrangements were made in top secret for the two leaders to

meet at the residence of the Ivory Coast Ambassador to
Switzerland, outside Geneva. They discussed the Middle East
conflict, and Houphouet-Boigny briefed Rabin on recent talks
he had held with the PLO. However, the substance of the
meeting appeared to be less important than the fact that the two
men had met: the meeting seemed to signal a return on the part
of African leaders to the warm relationship they had had with
Israel before 1973. This alone constituted a setback for Arab
diplomacy in Africa, and was a remarkable achievement for
Rabin. Talking to an Israeli TV reporter afterwards Rabin said:
'I believe this way we will be able to return to Africa and
establish greater aid and understanding.'[10] The visit had been
well-timed, but even Rabin's critics — who accused him of
electioneering gimmickry — could say little against the purpose
of the trip. It was, as the *Jerusalem Post* said later, 'a foreign
policy advance which even his foes, however reluctantly, must
recognize.'

The campaign styles of the two candidates remained much
the same as in 1974: Rabin was, as always, the introvert,
unwilling to pick up the telephone to talk to convention
delegates; Peres was just the opposite, the politician par
excellence who could spend hours on the telephone, mixing
small talk with persuasive pleas for support. It was perhaps not
so vital for Rabin to do this; he was after all the incumbent prime
minister whose list of achievements was well known. However,
he could not depend on the support of a powerful figure like
Pinhas Sapir this time; Sapir was dead, and no one had emerged
with equal political sway.

Supposedly the leader of the party himself, Rabin was able to
muster the support of some of the party's stalwarts: Golda Meir,
who had long held a grudge against Shimon Peres, quickly
rallied to Rabin's side; so did most of the Labour Party Cabinet
ministers; he could count on the kibbutz movement as well. But
despite all this, he still could not be certain of triumphing over
Peres. There were too many delegates, and too many undecided
voters among them. The best the pundits could say was that it
would be very close indeed. Peres had announced several weeks
before the balloting that he had enough votes to assure his
victory; Rabin made the same claim, but with less bravado.
Neither could know for sure.

*

On 22 February, nearly 3,000 Labour Party members —
veterans of the kibbutzim, white collar industrial workers from
the cities — gathered in the large Binyenei Ha'ooma Hall for the
opening of the convention. The fact that many were over 50
years old lent an air of conservatism to the proceedings; but this
was a gathering of socialists, and to serve as a reminder of that
Rabin had invited a number of leading socialist statesmen from
Western Europe, including Willy Brandt, the former Chancellor
of West Germany and the President of the Socialist International;
Austrian Chancellor Bruno Kreisky; Dutch Prime Minister
Joop den Uyl; Olaf Palme, the former Prime Minister of
Sweden; Kaleri Sorsa, the former Premier of Finland; and
François Mitterand, the leader of the French Socialist Party.

Their presence, together with the festive mood of the
delegates, tended to blur the harsh realities confronting the
party. Earlier in the day, a Tel Aviv judge had sentenced Asher
Yadlin to a five-year prison term for taking bribes and evading
land taxes. The claim Yadlin had made eight days earlier at his
trial was still reverberating round the country: he had admitted
taking IL 124,000 ($30,000) in bribes, but had contended that of
the sum, IL 80,000 ($20,000) had been transferred to the coffers
of the Labour Party. In addition, he testified that he had raised
'millions more' for the party during and after the 1973 election
campaign at the behest of other Labour Party leaders. The
party which had preached stern socialist morality was now
stigmatized as the party of Asher Yadlin and Avraham Ofer,
and its public image had suffered accordingly.

Rabin, as prime minister, was able to address the delegates
twice — Peres could only speak once. During his keynote
speech, Rabin stressed his achievements in the field of foreign
policy: the American–Israeli partnership, the signs of reconciliation between Africa and Israel, and the improved prospects for
peace in the Middle East. Peres could do little but sit and listen,
realizing that now was not the moment to come out attacking, in
the midst of party acquaintances and in the face of party efforts
to achieve unity.

On the second night of the convention, as the voting neared,
the audience became a massive cheering gallery. Shouting for
both Rabin and Peres, the delegates could scarcely contain their
excitement and enthusiasm. Rabin emerged from his waiting

room, and some noted that luck must be with him that evening:
he was using the orchestra conductor's dressing-room, with the
Hebrew word 'mina'zai'ach' inscribed on the door. When the
TV cameras panned past the door, his image as a winner was
heightened, for the Hebrew word means not only 'orchestra
conductor' but 'victor', too.

Both candidates spoke to the delegates before the vote began.
The prime minister, wisely perhaps, kept his speech short,
sixteen minutes in all. Peres on the other hand, perhaps
misjudging the patience of the audience, spoke for an hour, and
may well have lost himself some votes at the last moment.

The voting took several hours, as the delegates placed their
secret ballots in boxes throughout the large Mann Auditorium
in Tel Aviv. Rabin's aides had sensed that it would be a close
contest, and they were right. The prime minister emerged the
victor by the slim margin of only 41 votes. He had received 1,445
votes to Peres' 1,404. There had been 16 abstentions. When the
result was announced, Rabin, smiling faintly, shook hands with
a glum-faced Peres.

Ironically, he need not have offered to make a deal with Peres
after all — he had won the nomination in his own right. The
victory seemed that much sweeter. He now commanded the
party as never before, and seemed all set to remain in office for
another four years. However, the narrow margin of his victory
reflected a great sense of unrest and dissatisfaction within the
party — and within the country, too, for that matter. The most
likely reason for his victory, it was generally agreed, was his
incumbency; a narrow majority of the party membership had
concluded that he did not deserve dismissal, and should be given
a chance to prove himself for a further term. But he would face a
tough time in the forthcoming election in May.

The Labour Party's main opponent in that election, Rabin
thought, would be the right-wing Likud Party, headed by
Menachem Begin, a former leader of the Irgun and for years the
head of the political opposition. Yadin's new Democratic
Movement for Change appeared to be capturing a sizeable
portion of the votes — some even forecast that it could win as
many as 15 to 20 seats in the Knesset — but the prime minister
was convinced that he and Yadin could team up in a coalition
after the election. Labour and the Likud were not practicable

coalition partners, so he would campaign to persuade people to take their votes away from the Likud. Though Peres had once feared that losing to Rabin in the party leadership contest would cost him the Defence Ministry, Rabin now realized that he must retain Peres in order to run an effective campaign. Thus, shortly after the convention, he let it be known that he would keep Peres in his Government as minister of defence if Labour won in May.

In early March, Rabin went to Washington for talks with President Jimmy Carter. Ironically, this trip, which should have given a much-needed boost to his prestige during the election campaign, was to lead to his political downfall.

The visit began on a hopeful note. At the welcoming ceremony on the White House Lawn on 7 March, Carter surprised Rabin by declaring that Israel should have 'defensible borders' to assure that future peace agreements would not be violated. It had always been Israel's fervent wish to convince the US — and the rest of the world — that the Jewish State required better protection than the borders it had had prior to the 1967 Six-Day War, i.e. that it was necessary to retain a certain part of the territory captured in that war. Rabin could only wonder if Carter had decided to see eye to eye with Israelis on this matter, even before their private talks had begun.

However, once the talks got under way, the prime minister realized that Carter had not intended a major reformulation of American policy towards the Middle East; he was simply using a phrase to which the Israelis attached more significance than he did. At one stage in the talks Carter mentioned that a final Middle East settlement ought to include no more than 'minor adjustments' of Israel's 1967 borders. Rabin interrupted abruptly: 'If the position of the United States is to be formulated and presented publicly in this way, there will be no need for negotiations between the parties.' An American position such as this, he insisted, would become the only basis on which the Arab States would be prepared to negotiate — and negotiations would thus lead nowhere, since Israel differed so strongly on this point.

'What I say here,' Carter assured Rabin in a slow, deliberate voice, 'I am not going to say in public.' Somewhat reassured, Rabin left the White House, believing that Carter at least would do nothing to make negotiations with the Arabs more difficult. He was in for a rude shock.

On Wednesday, 9 March, a day after concluding his talks with Carter, Rabin was at the Kennedy Center in Washington, where an honorary doctorate from the American University was conferred on him for his contributions to peace in the Middle East. During the luncheon, word came that a band of men armed with rifles had attacked the B'nai B'rith headquarters in another part of the city. Hostages had been taken, and it appeared possible that the incident was connected with Rabin's visit. Meanwhile, at a White House news conference, President Carter had been describing the final boundaries in the Middle East in much the same terms as he had used when speaking privately to Rabin. An end to hostilities, he had said, 'would involve substantial withdrawal of Israel's present control over territories. Where the withdrawal might end, I don't know. I would guess it would be some minor adjustments in the 1967 borders. But that still remains to be negotiated.'

From the Kennedy Center, Rabin was to travel to the Shoreham Hotel for a meeting with the presidents of the major American Jewish organizations, but the police asked him to wait in a private lounge at the Center until more was known about the B'nai B'rith attack and it appeared safe for him to leave. Rabin had advised his staff to make no comment when asked by the press for the prime minister's reaction to the attack. There was no need to introduce any fresh elements into a situation that could bring harm to Israel — if indeed this was the object of the attackers. His aides were preoccupied with the B'nai B'rith incident, but Rabin's mind was fixed on the remarks the President had made earlier that day. They seemed to him to have far wider implications than the events inside the B'nai B'rith headquarters. Sooner or later, he told Yehuda Avner, that incident would be over; whereas what the President had said in his press conference could have historic consequences.

The Washington police, however, had to worry about Rabin's immediate safety. To secure a safe exit for him from the city — he was due to leave Washington later in the day for a speaking engagement in Miami — a decoy ceremony was staged on the lawn of the Washington Monument, complete with soldiers, flags and cannons. As Rabin's party approached the

Monument by car, a helicopter hovering overhead descended, paused to give the impression that it had landed to pick up the Rabin party, and then swiftly raced skyward. In the meantime the cars carrying Rabin and his entourage skipped the ceremony and headed straight for the airport.

The prime minister's visit to Washington apparently produced little diplomatic movement, and, thanks to Carter's eagerness to share his views on foreign policy with the American public, served only to introduce some new obstacles into the Middle East peacemaking process. Carter had called for 'defensible borders' for Israel, but then appeared to draw back with the comment that only 'minor adjustments' should be made to the 1967 borders. It is hardly surprising that Rabin returned to Israel uncertain of American thinking on the vital issues of the Middle East. While Israeli aides sought to put a good face on the meeting with Carter, the President revealed that he had found Rabin (in the words of *New York Times* columnist James Reston) 'excessively rigid and stiff-necked.'[11]

However, Rabin was now beset with other — highly personal — problems, and his very political survival was at stake.

The events leading to Rabin's downfall began on Tuesday, 8 March, when, driven by American secret service men in a car provided by the US Government, Leah Rabin visited the Dupont Circle branch of the National Bank in Washington. It was the last morning of the Rabins' visit to Washington, the day the prime minister and President Carter were to meet. On the schedule also: Rabin was to be granted an honorary doctorate by the American University at the Kennedy Center. Leah Rabin went to the bank to close two accounts, one cheque, one savings, both bearing her name and that of her husband. The savings account held $2,000, the cheque account just one penny. The visit might have seemed routine — but it was not. In holding such accounts in a bank outside Israel without the express permission of the Israeli Treasury, the Rabins were breaking the law. At that time Israel had strict foreign currency regulations. When travelling abroad, an Israeli could take only $450 with him or her. Keeping dollars in a bank account abroad without permission was an offence punishable by up to three years' imprisonment and a fine three times the amount of

foreign currency illegally held. The presumed reason for the law
was to prevent Israelis from depositing funds into overseas bank
accounts in order to avoid taxes.

Leah closed the savings account, asking for the $2,000 in
travellers' cheques. In her memoirs, she explains what then
happened: 'At that point it turned out that the branch only had
cheques of $20 each, which would have meant a long time sitting
signing them.

'A limousine, complete with American security men, was
waiting outside, and there were two more bodyguards — one
Israeli and one American — in the bank with me. My
transaction was arousing considerable interest and I was feeling
the pressure from that and from the tight schedule. The
ceremony was to be at 10, and it was already 9:30. After the
ceremony we were leaving town. I was also put off by the idea of
carrying $2,000 in cash, so — under the pressures of the moment
— I decided to leave the arrangement standing until our next
visit.

'Looking back, I now know that I wasn't aware enough of the
gravity of my transgression. I looked on it much like crossing a
traffic light on the amber, in the hope of completing the move
before the light turned red. I knew I had to close the account,
and I had every intention of doing so during that visit, but the
technical obstacles of timetable simply got in the way. And then
— the bomb went off!'[12]

On Thursday, 10 March, three employees of the nearby
Israeli Embassy came to the bank on embassy business. One of
the bank tellers told them: 'A couple of days ago, your prime
minister's wife was here.' They could hardly believe what they
had heard. One of them asked the teller if Mrs Rabin actually
had an account at the bank. 'Yes,' came the matter-of-fact
reply.

Such information was far too explosive for the Embassy staff
to keep to themselves. It took less than a day for the news to
reach Dan Margolit, the Washington-based correspondent for
Ha'aretz. Busy covering Rabin's visit, Margolit had little time to
collect complete information about the incident, so he decided
to keep quiet about it for a while. He and Yehuda Avner agreed
to attend the Fifth Avenue Synagogue in New York together
that Friday evening, but during their unsuccessful search for the

building, the subject of the bank account did not arise. It was only later that evening, after a party given in honour of Rabin by Uri Ben-Ari, the Israeli Consul in New York, that Margolit broached the subject with Rabin's aides. He told Dan Pattir, Rabin's spokesman, that he was sitting on a news story concerning a Washington bank account belonging either to Rabin or to his family, he wasn't sure which. He asked Pattir for a reaction from the prime minister and promised that he would only go ahead and print the story if Rabin refused to give an unambiguous denial of the facts.

Pattir chose to wait until the next day to relate the meeting with Margolit to the prime minister. Saturday, 12 March, was to be mainly a day of rest for Rabin and his party. He had one meeting arranged — with the former American Secretary of State, Henry Kissinger — at 5 pm. Following that, the prime minister was to leave for London for a brief stopover on the way home to Israel. Believing that Rabin would want time to prepare for his meeting with Kissinger, Pattir raised the Margolit matter after the session, two hours before the departure for London.

'What should I do?' asked Pattir, having imparted the substance of the conversation he had had with the journalist.

'Don't react,' was the prime minister's abrupt, terse reply.

Pattir hoped that during the flight back to Israel Rabin would change his mind and authorize some kind of reaction to Margolit's information. But all that the prime minister would permit him to tell the *Ha'aretz* correspondent was that as the prime minister's spokesman, he did not deal with private matters — and the subject raised by Margolit fell into that category.

A few days later, when Rabin's chief political lieutenant, Dov Tzamir, learned of the delay in informing the premier, he exploded. He felt that an opportunity had been missed to keep the matter from coming to public attention, and that Rabin or one of his aides might have been able to intercede personally with Margolit.[13] Meanwhile, on Monday, 14 March, Margolit had been able to prove conclusively that Mrs Rabin had an account at the National Bank in Washington. Realizing that no bank employee would volunteer the account number to him, he went to the bank and announced that he wished to deposit $50 into Mrs Rabin's account, but he did not have the number. Without demur the teller took the money and deposited it into an account bearing the names Yitzhak and Leah Rabin. She gave Margolit a deposit slip bearing the account number and the names of the owners of the account. With that solid proof, the reporter went ahead with his story.

Ha'aretz was due to print it on Tuesday morning, 15 March. The night before, Pattir had finally obtained Rabin's permission to acknowledge the existence of the account. The newspaper featured the story on its front page, revealing that 'Mrs Leah Rabin, wife of the prime minister, is the owner of a dollar account in the National Bank in Washington.' Included in the article was the bank account number, the fact that Mrs Rabin had visited the bank during her recent stay in Washington, and that Rabin had avoided acknowledging the facts for three days. Quoting sources close to Rabin (i.e. Pattir), *Ha'aretz* gave the prime minister's only comment on the matter: the account had been left over from his days as ambassador to pay outstanding bills — and today, only 'a small amount' remained.

Public reaction at first was exceedingly mild. Since there had been no suggestion in Margolit's article that the money in the account had been obtained illegally, it was generally accepted that, at worst, the Rabins had been guilty of a technical error in not closing the account. The *Jerusalem Post* said: 'Mrs Rabin should admit her error, the Treasury should impound the money, and the press and politicians should get back to important matters — and everyone, hopefully, will have learned a good lesson.' Even the opposition Likud Party chose to give the premier and his wife the benefit of the doubt since the violation had appeared merely technical.

Confronted with the public disclosure, Rabin was determined to share full responsibility with his wife for the consequences of their misdemeanour, although he had been a passive partner in the account. 'I will not allow any distinction to be made between you and me,' he told his wife, 'nor will I allow people to call it "Leah Rabin's bank account".'[14] To Leah, her husband's behaviour was exemplary. 'From the first moment that we knew that a journalist was going to publish the story of my bank account in his paper, and up to the moment of his decision to resign, Yitzhak behaved with adamant resolution and chivalry to me. He accepted his joint responsibility for what had happened, though he was totally uninvolved in the whole issue of the bank account. It was only because the account was technically joint that he bore any formal responsibility. But I never once heard him say: "What did you do? Why have you got me in a mess?" Had I insisted on standing trial alone, he would have come with me to the court. [She did stand trial alone. Here she was speculating on what Rabin's behaviour would be were she to stand trial alone.] We travelled this road together and drew strength from each other.'[15] Rabin sought the advice of Israel Galili, the minister without portfolio, whom he respected a great deal. Rabin told him that if his candidacy would now be a problem for the party he would withdraw it at once. Galili consulted other Labour party members, then advised Rabin to wait and see what the results of the Treasury inquiry would be before taking such a step.

Advising the prime minister on the bank account affair was a delicate matter. Dan Pattir tried gently to suggest that his best strategy would be to lay the entire truth before the public in the hope that it would be sympathetic. Rabin thought it better to keep the subject as low-keyed as possible, and to work through his lawyer, Shimon Alexandroni, to try to bring matters to a swift and painless conclusion. Rabin contacted Attorney-General Aharon Barak and notified him what Alexandroni was doing. 'Barak's tone was gentle and conciliatory,' Rabin recalled, 'as he played down the gravity of the whole matter. His attitude went a long way toward reassuring Leah.'[16]

The prime minister and Alexandroni agreed to approach Treasury officials in the hope of arranging a prompt out-of-court settlement in the form of a fine. From Tel Aviv, the lawyer phoned Don Kanterowitz, the director of the Treasury's Foreign Currency Division, at home in Jerusalem where he was recovering from flu. He had learned about the Rabins' bank account from the newspaper. When Alexandroni asked him what the Treasury expected Rabin to do, Kanterowitz suggested that the lawyer should set out the facts of the case as he understood them in a letter. Casually, without pressing the matter at that point, Alexandroni raised the possibility of a fine, and it was agreed that this too should be mentioned in the letter.

Kanterowitz indicated which documents he would need from
the Rabins. From a legal point of view, the matter was in limbo
while the Rabins gathered the relevant documents and filed
them with the Treasury.

Meanwhile, the prime minister had to decide whether to offer
a public explanation of the bank account, even if he did not
reveal the entire truth (as Pattir had proposed). The most
obvious forum would be Israel Television. Its political
correspondent, Ya'acov Achimeir, had telephoned Mrs Rabin
several times on 15 March to try to get some response. She had
continuously held him off, but finally, after a brief consultation
with her husband, she agreed to be interviewed in her Jerusalem
residence that afternoon.

During the interview, she sounded penitent and pointed out
that she had closed the account (in which the Rabins had
indicated about $2,000 remained).[17] 'In the final analysis, a
person who is in the public eye, the wife of a public official, must
be more careful about such things,' she acknowledged. 'We are
all only human and we make mistakes here and there. If one has
the courage to admit one was wrong, it shouldn't cause great
harm.' In this respect, she was obviously expressing a hope
rather than an expectation. Still, the nation's first reaction had
not been censorious, and some of the prime minister's aides
began to feel that he might escape serious legal or political
consequences. 'Things have quietened down,' Dan Pattir told
Yehuda Avner over the telephone to New York, where Rabin's
speechwriter had remained after the Premier's US visit.

Over the next few days, Rabin grew worried that the public
might feel he had thrown the entire problem on his wife's
shoulders. He wanted people to know that he felt equally
responsible for the existence of the bank account. On 20 March,
he told Israel Radio that he shared 'formal as well as moral
responsibility' with his wife for the account. He insisted that,
since it was neither 'secret nor numbered', there had been
nothing sinister about it. The account had remained open only
through neglect.

By mid-March the election campaign was in full swing.
Public opinion polls were indicating that Rabin was still almost
certain to win the prime ministership on 17 May, but the race
was likely to be close, and every campaign appearance

mattered. The prime minister, however, found it difficult to get into the spirit of the campaign while the investigation into the back account continued. Uncertain of its outcome, he chose to reduce his campaign activities in order not to embarrass the Labour Party. He went to Haifa for an election walking tour on 19 March, four days after the *Ha'aretz* story appeared, but he made few campaign appearances after that.

Few realized how seriously the prime minister was taking the matter of the Treasury investigation. Most believed that the affair would end uneventfully, with little harm to the Rabins. But the prime minister was not so certain. 'You've got to understand one thing,' a senior Rabin aide told a journalist towards the end of March. 'There's only one thought in his mind now, how to wind up this business with the bank account. He's haunted by it. It's all he thinks about.'[18]

Returning from New York on 27 March, Yehuda Avner found Rabin far more emotional about the bank account affair than he had expected, having been led to believe that the problem was abating. After seeing a *New York Times* story about Rabin's radio interview on 20 March, Avner tried to comfort the premier at their first meeting by blaming the American press for inflating the issue: 'They take a few sentences from your interview, and make a big headline out of it.'

'Yehuda,' replied the prime minister, 'I wanted that interview to make a statement about the account. I'm not going to hide behind my wife's back.'

His attempt to console Rabin unsuccessful, Avener decided to change the subject.

On 27 March, the last of the bank documents arrived at the Treasury. The next day Dov Kanterowitz called in Mrs Rabin to gather additional testimony. He then decided that enough information was in hand to make a decision on the account without summoning the prime minister for his testimony.

Seeing from the documents that Mrs Rabin had used the bank account actively over the past four years — it had obviously not been mere forgetfulness on her part — he decided to consult first the police and then the attorney-general. The usual procedure for bringing the police into matters of this kind was via a special committee, comprising the Ministry of Finance and police officials, which met regularly to discuss and decide whether to impose a fine or refer the matter to the legal authorities for prosecution. The committee would not examine the case until Tuesday, 5 April.

As Rabin became increasingly aware of the possible consequences to himself and to his wife, he seemed oddly less tense. His associates sensed that he was warmer, more open. On 31 March, he met Avner to discuss some routine matters, and the speechwriter found the prime minister more relaxed than he had been for days. 'His mood was amiable. There was a softness in his eyes, in his voice. He was very forthcoming.'[19] But Mrs Rabin felt the weight of the affair pressing on her: 'We are still going to have a lot of trouble over the bank account,' she told a friend on 3 April.[20]

The special committee recommended on 5 April that a collective fine of IL 150,000 ($16,000) be imposed on the Rabins. Kanterowitz now had to ratify the recommendation. The minister of finance, Yehoshua Rabinowitz, could have interceded at this point and exercised his personal authority. He might have ratified the committee's decision himself and let the matter end there, without consulting the attorney-general. Kanterowitz, too, could have ended the matter there and then by simply ratifying the committee's recommendation. But the Treasury official felt that the attorney-general ought to be asked for his point of view. In cases of this matter involving more than $5,000, the matter often became a question for the courts to decide — though there had been some notable exceptions. With the sum involved here $20,000 (the public would not learn that this was the sum until 7 April), Kanterowitz could find no justification for not involving Aharon Barak, the attorney-general, and immediately began discussions with him.

The following day he went to Barak's Jerusalem office to come to a final decision on the Rabin case. Neither man found the task before them easy or pleasant, but both had a strong conviction that they must be guided by what they felt was proper — and not by the fact that the case involved the prime minister. They searched for a precedent which would allow them simply to impose a fine, but the search proved fruitless. There was no alternative but to refer the case to a court of law. Looking over the material again, they decided that since Rabin had played a passive role in maintaining the account, he should be punished with a fine, whereas Mrs Rabin should stand trial. 'To this day,' Rabin wrote in 1979, 'I cannot understand the legal justification for drawing the distinction, and at the time I sensed a growing resolve to reject the offer with a resounding "no". I would do everything possible to share full responsibility with my wife.'[21]

Since it was late in the day, Kanterowitz and Barak agreed to inform the prime minister and his wife of their decision the next day. That same evening Rabin and Leah were dining at the home of the minister of defence and his wife in Tel Aviv. Rabin seemed depressed and somewhat tense, but did not mention the back account affair.

Thursday, 7 April, was an important day for Israelis, whose basketball team, Maccabi Tel Aviv, was to compete that evening in Belgrade against an Italian team, Mobilgirgi Varese, for the European Basketball Championship. Many Israelis had flown to Belgrade to watch the game; the rest of the nation would watch it live on television in their homes, beginning at 9:30 pm.

As the day began, the nation's leaders were learning of the serious turn events had taken in the Rabins' bank account affair. Stunned, the minister of finance decided to make a special plea to the attorney-general. He confronted Barak, and told him that he thought a fine should suffice. However, the attorney-general was adamant that prosecution was called for; and he would have found difficulty in defending the Ministry of Finance's decision if Rabinowitz insisted upon having his way. The minister therefore let the matter stand.

The Labour Party's Central Committee was due to meet at 10 am at Arlozoroff Hall in Tel Aviv to continue choosing its list of candidates for the Knesset in the May election. Emerging from a meeting in a side room with Haim Zadok, the minister of justice, and Israel Galili, the minister without portfolio, Rabinowitz looked worried. The first person he saw was Dov Tzamir. 'The matter is serious,' the minister told him.

As the committee meeting got under way Rabin took his usual seat in the front row of the hall. His face betrayed nothing of what he must have been feeling. The audience was buzzing with the news that had just appeared in *Ma'ariv*, which had disclosed in a front-page report that the Rabins had had two bank accounts in the US, and that they had contained at one stage $20,000 — not $2,000. Noting that the special committee had recommended a IL 150,000 fine, the report added that the attorney-general would be making up his mind whether to accept this in a few days. In fact, as has been noted, Barak had already come to a decision. Perhaps most significantly, the first rumour that Rabin would submit his resignation in the coming days appeared in the report, though the prime minister's office denied it.

As soon as the *Ma'ariv* article appeared, the telephones began to ring continuously in Dan Pattir's office in Tel Aviv. Was the prime minister going to resign? Were the rumours true? Pattir managed to speak to Rabin back at his office at 11 am and informed him that the press was clamouring for some kind of response. Knowing he must say something, but unwilling to be pressurized without having consulted his associates and his wife, Rabin instructed Pattir to say simply that 'if and when the prime minister has something to say, we will let you know.' But just in case he decided to make a statement to the nation later in the day, it was agreed that Pattir should discreetly alert the political correspondents of both Israel Radio and Television. Meanwhile, though this was anything but a routine day, Rabin tried to maintain a regular schedule. He held a meeting with military men about the latest events in Lebanon, where renewed fighting was taking place; he telephoned Shimon Peres about defence matters.

But around him his associates were gripped with an increasing sense of foreboding. Yehuda Avner, working at the prime minister's Jerusalem office that day, had not even seen the *Ma'ariv* story, but at about 11 am he decided to check with Pattir on the latest developments in the bank accounts crisis. As he was not around he sought out Ephraim Poran. Rabin's military aide was still hoping for a miracle that would rescue Rabin at the last moment. 'It's a mess,' he told him, 'but he's not going to resign.'

The advice Rabin had been getting from those close to him was to stick it out, not to resign over a mere technical offence. 'They insisted,' Leah Rabin wrote in 1988, 'that it would be unconscionable to trample underfoot all those long years of outstanding service to the IDF and the country because of one small mistake.'[22]

At 12 noon, Rabin, grim-faced but polite, greeted Zadok and Barak in his office. The minister of justice slowly, deliberately, related the events that had led up to the attorney-general's decision to prosecute Mrs Rabin. It was a brief meeting. The subject of Rabin's resignation did not arise, but the prime minister did say that he wanted to talk over with others what steps he might take now. Rabin had little doubt what path to take. 'I could no longer remain the party's candidate for prime minister,' he wrote two years later. 'As the experience of the past few days had shown, the gravity of the offence was open to a broad range of interpretation. But I had committed an offence and, although the attorney-general viewed it as a technical infringement, I felt that I had to render my own personal and private account, which demanded consistency and courage. Friends tried to dissuade me from taking any fateful steps, but a man is always truly alone at such times. And alone, my conscience and I came to three interconnected decisions: I would withdraw my nomination as the candidate for prime minister; I would share full responsibility with Leah; and I would try to resign my post as prime minister, so that the Labour Party's nominee could fill the post up to the election (when he would head the party's list of candidates).'[23]

He could not know it at the time, but those decisions, taken during one of the most painful episodes of his life, would serve him well through the years. Leaving office had seemed the wisest, indeed the only course of action open to Rabin, given the circumstances at the time. In later years, his decision to hold himself accountable when others were arguing that he could have somehow evaded responsibility, and his determination to stand by his wife when it might have been possible to make her the sole guilty party, were regarded as acts of valour on Rabin's part. It was of great significance that the scandal was over something relatively minor, a technical violation of a law that many Israelis were themselves violating, and that would eventually be wiped off the books. Had Rabin engaged in some illegal behaviour of a more serious nature — stealing public funds, for example — few would have expressed sympathy, understanding, or forgiveness. Even at the time, Israelis felt a sense of sorrow for Yitzhak Rabin, but not because he had broken the law. They were prepared to overlook that when weighed against his record of public service. They felt that the whole affair was a pity, a pity that Rabin had to give up office, a pity that he had to sacrifice so much over so little. Now that Rabin had decided what to do, he sought out his wife. He was firm about the need to resign and, sensing his resolve, she did not try to dissuade him.

At 1 pm, the prime minister called Dan Pattir into his office. The spokesman had seen Barak and Zadok come and go, and had realized that the matter was grave.

'I'm going to announce my resignation and my withdrawal as the party's candidate for prime minister,' Rabin told him. He spoke so decisively that Pattir found it difficult to urge him to reconsider.

'Are you certain this is your final decision?' he asked.

'Yes,' Rabin said quickly.

The two men decided that the radio and television reporters should be informed that the prime minister might make a statement to the nation at 7 pm. To be prepared for that, they should come from Jerusalem to Tel Aviv immediately. The television reporter Ya'acov Achimeir learned in the course of a telephone conversation with Mrs Rabin that the premier would probably issue a response to the affair later in the day. Rabin wanted to resign from office immediately, sure that the people would not tolerate anything less, but Israeli law does not permit ministers to resign from an interim administration unless unfit to govern. He could not give up the job until the Government was formed, and this might take several months, since elections were not scheduled until 17 May and it could take six weeks or more for a coalition Government to be set up. However, he had come up with an idea that seemed to offer a way of resigning right away. He would give up his Knesset seat, since a prime minister had to be a Knesset member. He discussed this with his aide, Amos Eran.

'I'm against it,' Eran told him. 'You will be punishing yourself more than is necessary, and you will be endangering your chances of making a comeback in the future.' Most importantly, said Eran, yielding his Knesset seat was irrelevant, since the law would still not permit the prime minister to leave office immediately. Reluctantly and after much persuasion, Rabin accepted Eran's point of view.

Close to 6 pm, three of Rabin's chief Cabinet ministers — Zadok, Galili, and Rabinowitz — came to the prime minister's office to find out what the premier had decided to do in the wake of Zadok's earlier news. Rabin seemed in low spirits but was calm. In a strong, resolute voice he informed them that he would announce to the nation that night his intention to resign and not seek re-election as prime minister. Zadok suggested that he might wish to delay his decision to resign until the legal case was disposed of, and he had a chance to gauge the public's reaction. Rabin cut Zadok off.

'I'm not going to agree to come back as long as we are under investigation, as long as my wife may go to jail,' he told the minister of justice emphatically. The one prospect which the prime minister could not face was an angry public crying out for his resignation. By leaving office now, voluntarily, he could avoid that ugly scene and still retain the respect of the nation.

While Rabin and his ministers were conferring, Avner telephoned Pattir. The spokesman conveyed the impression that there would be still more bad news about the bank account crisis, but since he did not know precisely when the prime minister would make his dramatic announcement, he chose to be vague.

'The mood here,' he told Avner, 'is very sombre. I don't know what will happen. My feeling is that it will be bad.' With that, he again went to see Rabin, this time to discuss the final arrangements for the prime minister's announcement to the nation. In the back of Pattir's mind was the hope that, given an extra day, Rabin might review his decision. He asked him to consider letting him issue a statement shortly to the effect that the prime minister 'was considering the situation that had developed and would make an announcement on Friday', but Rabin would not agree. The only concession he made was to put off the announcement until after the basketball match. 'I don't want to disturb the people,' he told his spokesman, 'they've waited so long for this event.'

Rabin asked his wife to join him at the office while he waited for the game to end and prepared to speak to the nation. By 10:30 pm that night, Israelis were in a festive mood. But, unknown to most of the country, a drama was unfolding at the prime minister's office in Tel Aviv.

Asked to stand by for a special announcement from prime minister Yitzhak Rabin, Israel Radio's political reporter, Shalom Kital, had suddenly, a few moments before, been summoned to the drab grey two-storey building sited inconspicuously in the midst of other blocks within the large Ministry of Defence compound. Dan Pattir greeted him at the door. Pattir seemed unusually dispirited.

'He's going to resign,' he said quietly to the amazed reporter. 'Let him talk. He won't keep anything from you.' The two men passed the ground-floor cafeteria on their way to the narrow staircase leading to the prime minister's second-floor office. From inside the cafeteria came the sound of cheering and laughter. Some of the prime minister's bodyguards were seated round a television set, absorbed in the match they were watching.

Indeed, practically the entire nation was watching the same contest, for tiny Israel was competing that evening in the final round of the European Basketball Championship. The game had begun an hour earlier and by now the Israeli team had notched up a 39–30 lead over the rival Italian team, Mobilgirgi Varese.

Basketball, and not the political fate of the prime minister, was all that seemed to matter that evening — except to Yitzhak Rabin, his wife, and the men and women with whom he had worked closely since becoming premier in June 1974. He and his wife Leah sat before a small television set in his office with the game turned on, but neither had much heart for the match. Their minds kept wandering to the events of the past few weeks, and to those of the last twenty-four hours in particular.

Pattir escorted Kital into the prime minister's main conference room on the second floor. Here there was no shouting, no cheering. The atmosphere was sombre and gloomy. Seated around the table were the prime minister, looking sad but alert, his wife, crying softly, and the prime minister's chief aides. One of them, Amos Eran (director-general of the prime minister's office), had an arm and a leg in plaster and walked with the aid of crutches as the result of a car accident a few weeks earlier. It was his first day back at work.

Rabin seemed quieter than usual, but appeared composed and reconciled to the anguishing decision he had just made.

Two pages of handwritten notes lay before him on the table. He had prepared what he wanted to say to the nation carefully, saving the dramatic announcement of his resignation for the end. Kital felt that the listeners should be informed at the outset of the interview that Rabin planned to resign so that the rest of the prime minister's comments would be understood in the context of his leaving office. Rabin looked around the room for opinions and comments. Leah Rabin spoke first. She advocated keeping the news of the resignation until the close of the interview: 'The listeners will just have to be patient,' she said angrily. Pattir and Ephraim Poran, Rabin's military aide, disagreed. A compromise was reached. Kital himself would announce at the beginning that the prime minister had decided to resign. The radio interview would then follow.

The interview took fifteen minutes. The prime minister acknowledged in the interview that there had been some 'misunderstanding' over the precise sum of money involved in the bank accounts. 'I will not overlook or deny that there was some negligence on our part in that we did not close our accounts in time, as required by the law,' he added. Because of this, he had decided to leave office as soon as possible and to renounce his party's nomination for a second term. He had also resolved not to seek parliamentary immunity from prosecution and, because he felt a 'formal and moral responsibility' with his wife for what had occurred, he declared, 'If she must stand trial, so will I. . . .' (Of course, the decision was not up to him, but the gesture was sincere.)

Despite all this, Rabin suggested that he had been forced to take these serious steps which so far outweighed his misdeed. Had the offence not been discovered in the midst of an election campaign, he implied, he might have weathered the storm. Or, he suggested, had he and his wife spent the money or even burned it (neither being a crime), there would have been no fuss. He called what he and his wife had done a 'personal mishap' and at worst a 'minor error', but the circumstances gave him little choice but to do what he was doing. Speaking calmly and with deliberation, Rabin told of his plans to give up the leadership of both the Government and the Labour Party. With a General Election just forty days away, the news was a bombshell. For the premier it was the saddest moment of a career in public life that had spanned thirty years and known many a moment of triumph.

Shortly after 11 pm he learned that Maccabi Tel Aviv had won the European Basketball Championship, 78–77. 'At least,' he told an aide, 'the viewers will be happy when they tune in to what I have to say.' In a few minutes, he was to give an interview on Israel Television on the subject of his resignation.

At the television studio, a thousand yards away from Rabin's office, Ya'acov Achimeir, the political reporter who was to conduct the interview, was frantic. His cameraman was on the other side of Tel Aviv, filming the crowds celebrating the Israeli victory in Belgrade. With the prime minister expected at any moment to make a dramatic announcement to the nation, Achimeir was praying that the cameraman would return in time.

The first of the prime minister's party to arrive was a stenographer, carrying her notebooks, and weeping aloud. It was most out of character for this usually self-composed woman. 'He's going,' she cried to Achimeir at the door of the television studio. Seconds later, Rabin's car pulled up and the prime minister emerged, wearing a blue blazer and a tie. His eyes seemed distant, but otherwise he appeared normal. Inside the studio, he combed his hair while the cameraman, just arrived, asked Achimeir on whom to focus most of the camera shots. 'Keep the camera on the prime minister,' the reporter ordered. As Achimeir chatted with Rabin, he sensed the unusual quietness in the prime minister's demeanour. He seemed, Achimeir thought to himself, like a Buddhist priest reaching a state of nirvana.

In striking contrast, Leah Rabin talked constantly, peppering her remarks with caustic comments about the press. She had regained control of herself and now she appeared strangely detached from the events taking place.

The television interview lasted about fifteen minutes. When it was over, the prime minister gazed in the direction of Poran and asked what he thought of the interview. 'It was fine,' the military aide said helplessly. He could think of nothing to add.

Walking to Rabin's car, Achimeir felt conflicting emotions of sorrow for the prime minister and anger with his wife. He wanted to castigate Mrs Rabin for seeming so cheerful during the interview. Instead he turned to Rabin and whispered:

'Mr Prime Minister, you must remember that you still have friends.' Seemingly moved, Rabin said quietly, 'I know.'

Ironically, the dignity and sincerity of both radio and television interviews won Rabin widespread sympathy. However, this did not alter the facts, which were both dramatic and shocking to the nation, and were to change the political landscape overnight.

The most seriously affected person besides the Rabins was, of course, Shimon Peres. He seemed the natural heir to Rabin as the Labour Party's nominee, and within hours of the resignation announcement was gathering his closest associates to lay plans for securing the nomination. Peres had been dining at the home of Abba Eban, the former minister for foreign affairs, in Herzlyia that evening. Eban had been giving a farewell party for Ephraim Evron, who was about to leave to become Israel's ambassador in London. Peres, who only six weeks before had lost the Labour Party's nomination for prime minister to Rabin, was gleeful. He had heard that Rabin intended to leave office immediately and to renounce the leadership of the party in the coming elections, and he was impatiently awaiting the denouement. The only other possible challenger was Yigal Allon and, in the next few days, the minister of defence laboured unceasingly and eventually successfully to persuade Allon to opt out of the race. Events had to move at a brisk pace for there were only forty days left to the election.

The resignation of the prime minister had implications for Middle East diplomacy too. With Rabin out of the political picture, and the more hawkish Peres his apparent successor, some changes might be expected in Israel's relations with the United States. Indeed, if Peres resisted American overtures for large-scale territorial concessions, the partnership that Rabin had nurtured so carefully might suffer. But it was much too early to predict what might occur as a result of Rabin's departure — and in any case there was little prospect that serious negotiations between the Israelis and the Arabs would take place in the near future, whatever the circumstances.

Yehuda Avner, Rabin's British-born speechwriter, had been entertaining some twenty Jewish tourists at his Jerusalem home. They, too, were watching the basketball game. When it ended, Avner decided to telephone Pattir to see if Rabin would be making a statement soon about the bank accounts. He was worried that the newspaper disclosures earlier in the day would spell political danger for Rabin. Intuitively he suspected the worst.

'Has he resigned?' he asked Pattir's secretary.

'Turn on the radio,' was all she could say, 'and you'll hear the interview he's giving to Kital.'

Surrounded by his guests, all jubilant at the Israeli team's victory in Belgrade, Avner switched on the radio. No one yet sensed that his mind was far from the game. It was an agonizing moment for him. He had been with Rabin longer than anyone on the prime minister's personal staff.

'What is it?' asked Avner's wife after a few moments. Dully, he told her, 'Yitzhak has resigned.'

His first instinct was to speak to Rabin, but there was no answer from the Tel Aviv office. Rabin had already left for home. Unable to sleep, Avner wandered the streets of Jerusalem. He had forgotten that, with the end of the game, people would be thronging the streets, singing and dancing in celebration of Maccabi Tel Aviv's miraculous victory. Many had switched off their TV sets immediately after the game and had therefore missed Rabin's stunning announcement. But there were some who had heard the news.

Avner listened intently to what people were saying about Rabin. He heard one man say, 'I didn't like him, but he's the most honest man in Israel.' I must tell Rabin about that tomorrow morning, Avner thought to himself. Then he heard an elderly woman shouting at her husband over the noise of the crowd, 'Rabin has done one thing at least: he's taught all you men how to behave towards your women.'

Returning home after midnight, Rabin felt strangely relaxed now that the decision had been taken and the nation informed. He prepared himself for sleep, only to be disturbed by guests knocking at the door. Rabin quickly got dressed again.

During the next hour, Yigal Allon, the deputy premier and foreign minister, arrived. So did Shlomo Lahat, the Mayor of Tel Aviv, and several others. They all urged Rabin to reconsider his decision, but the prime minister was adamant.

Around 3 am, Dan Pattir arrived to inform Rabin of first reactions to his announcement. The prime minister tried to pay attention, but his mind was elsewhere.

The next day was Leah Rabin's 49th birthday. It was also the prime minister's first chance to consider his future. Walking into his Tel Aviv office at 9:30 am, he greeted Avner and Pattir warmly. Avner recounted how he had overheard some sympathetic comments. Pattir described a demonstration at Tel Aviv's Dizengoff Square, demanding Rabin's return to power. The prime minister interrupted him.

'That's it,' he said with finality. 'There will be no return. Nothing will make me withdraw my resignation. The issue is not the party, it goes beyond me personally. It is a question of the dignity of the office. It's unthinkable for a prime minister to hold office while legal proceedings are being conducted against him. I have to do what is best for the country.'

Before leaving for an appointment in Jerusalem with President Ephraim Katzir, Rabin visited the Labour Party's Arrangements Committee meeting next door to his office. He emerged with Shimon Peres, and the two men closeted themselves in Rabin's office. Rabin's aides pondered whether the prime minister and the minister of defence might be coming to terms on their respective futures. Each could use the other at this crucial juncture — Rabin could be helpful to Peres in lending his political support to Peres' candidacy, and the minister of defence, for his part, could support Rabin through this difficult time. As the two men came from the meeting, they seemed in a good mood.

'Well,' said one of Rabin's aides, 'did he offer you a deal?'

'No,' replied the prime minister, with a slight smile. 'I invited him to hear about my resignation officially. That's all.'

Rabin appeared to win much public sympathy for sparing the nation and the Labour Party further embarrassment over the bank account issue. When he appeared before certain audiences in the days following, the response was mostly warm, friendly and compassionate. He was helped by the fact that no Government leader or editorial writer had called for his permanent exile from politics. He was given the twentieth place on the Labour Party's list of candidates for the Knesset, the same one he had occupied in 1973. Even his arch-rival, Shimon Peres, who was named the party's nominee for Prime Minister on 10 April, told him, 'With time . . . your abilities and capabilities will surely find expression.'[24]

Rabin decided to say nothing more about his resignation in public, at least in the first few weeks after his announcement. His wife, however, asked the public to believe that the entire affair had been overblown. In two candid interviews given to the Israeli press immediately after her husband's resignation she portrayed herself as saddened, but hardly distraught. 'I . . . tend to think I should have been more cautious,'[25] she acknowledged, but 'I don't have the feeling that I did a bad thing . . . I don't go around with the feeling that I can't look the public in the eye.'[26] Perhaps, 'I might have prevented all this, but what's the use of crying over spilled milk?'[27]

Writing about the affair eight years later, Leah Rabin was convinced that her husband's Labour Party associates had let him down. '. . . On the party level, Yitzhak was fed a constant meal of bitterness. In fact the Party was somewhat less than a broken reed when it came to giving him support in the bank account affair. Had they all stood by him, it would have developed differently. I have no way of proving it, but I am convinced that many agree with me.'[28]

Two matters were still outstanding: the legal cases of the Rabins, and the prime minister's leaving office. In the case of Rabin, the legal authorities acted promptly after his resignation, levying a fine of IL 15,000 ($1,600) on the prime minister, primarily because of his passive role in the holding of the overseas accounts. In Mrs Rabin's case, a decision was made to bring the matter to court as quickly as possible.

Meanwhile, a legal way had to be found for Rabin to leave office. It was finally resolved that Rabin would take leave of absence, and turn his day-to-day responsibilities over to Peres. Rabin, of course, would retain responsibility for the Government's decisions, and hence would be kept informed of the daily proceedings. His leave of absence would begin on 22 April, the day after Israel's 29th Independence Day, thus permitting him to take part in the official celebrations.

Mrs Rabin's trial took place on Sunday, 17 April in the Tel Aviv District Court. The prime minister, who had said ten days earlier that if his wife were to stand trial, so would he, had since changed his mind. He chose not to be present at the trial, suspecting that his presence there might influence the court. So, after he and his wife had driven up to the court building, he escorted her to the door and then left. Crowds of curious onlookers thronged the corridors while the police did their best to hold them back. Only 30 people were allowed in the small courtroom, mostly reporters.

Had the judge wished, he could have sent Mrs Rabin to prison, though this was unlikely since no previous offender in a case of this nature had been jailed. Indeed, the district attorney, Victoria Ostrovsky-Cohen, did not even ask for a prison sentence, though she told the judge: 'The incident has caused considerable public damage, since the accused is the wife of the prime minister, who is in charge of the Government's economic policy. A person in this position should have served as an example to the public.' Shimon Alexandroni, defending Mrs Rabin, asked that the judge treat her leniently since the Rabins had already paid a severe price. Asked if she wished to add anything before a verdict was rendered, Mrs Rabin looked up at the judge, and whispered, 'No, I have nothing to add.'

The court recessed for an hour. When the judge returned with his verdict, he had some harsh words for Mrs Rabin: 'One expects a public figure to observe the law more carefully, and we are all the more disappointed when we find such is not the case.' But he would not send her to prison for she had already suffered enough 'in her downfall from a position of importance to the benches of the courtroom'. Instead, he imposed a fine of IL 250,000 (nearly $27,000), or one year in jail. She had 45 days in which to pay. It was a heavy fine, but the Rabins' one consolation was that the case was now over. Henceforth, they would have to deal with the consequences to Rabin's career and to their personal lives.

Later, Leah Rabin described how she had tried to distance herself mentally from the trial: '. . . I was there yet absent as though, at the press of a button, a partition had slid into place between me and my immediate environment. Nevertheless, when I heard the judge's ruling, I was in shock. He was far more severe than any of the experts had foreseen — and that included our own lawyer.'[29]

The Rabins were uplifted by the public reaction. Two

thousand letters arrived. Hundreds of people phoned, offering support, sympathy, sometimes money. One man suggested to Leah that she did not pay the fine, but he would instead spend the time in jail for her. Likud Knesset member, Elimelech Rimalt, sent a handwritten note: 'This is a transgression that bears with it no stain.' To which Yitzhak Rabin reacted, 'Not one of my Labour Party colleagues but a Likud member found the need to write that.' Leah spent hours answering each letter, writing 30 to 40 a day.

On 6 June 1977, Leah wrote to a friend: '. . . Something extremely severe has happened, and if it happened there had to be a reason [divine intervention, she supposed]. We are planning our removal from Jerusalem and back to Tel Aviv with all our belongings. If there is something I don't regret, it is returning home. You know how much we love our Tel Aviv flat and to what extent Jerusalem was never home. And what now? Yitzhak will be a member of the Knesset and will write his book, and I'll be with Yitzhak and I can be of more help to Dahlia with her small children, and we'll see. . . .'[30]

Rabin had decided soon after his resignation to keep out of the public eye in the hope that the damage he had sustained to his political career might be only temporary. Friends suggested that he might consider becoming the secretary-general of the Labour Party. However, he rejected the idea, and let it be known that while he did not envisage a major public role for himself for the next few years, he would however be open to an invitation to become a member of the Knesset's Foreign Affairs and Defence Committee (though not its chairman).

After 22 April, as Rabin began his leave of absence and Peres took over the reins of the Labour Party's election campaign, the prime minister gradually slipped out of the limelight. He refused all requests from newspapers for interviews about the startling events which had led to his political downfall. He limited his public appearances at first to ceremonial occasions, and only in the week before the 17 May election did he undertake a round of campaign speeches, in which he talked mostly about Israeli–American relations. Only once did he depart from his plan to remain on vacation until after the election: when a military helicopter crashed near Jericho on 10 May, killing all 54 on board, most of whom were soldiers on manoeuvres, he decided to attend the Cabinet meeting called for the next day to mourn the victims.

A public opinion poll on the prime minister's prospects for a future return to national leadership was published in *Ha'aretz* on 4 May, and showed, rather suprisingly, that a large section of the public would eventually be willing to accept his return. 51.1 per cent said they would like to see Rabin in a key state position again; 2.9 per cent favoured his eventual return, though not for several years, and then it would depend on what position he was offered. 35.8 per cent did not want him back in the leadership at all.

Some 1.8 million Israeli voters went to the polls on 17 May, 1977 to choose the ninth Knesset and the men who would govern the nation for the next four years. Most of the professional pollsters had forecast a victory for the Labour Alignment, but the large number of undecided voters near election time made it virtually impossible to say for sure how the balloting would go.

Within minutes of the polls' closing at 11 pm on election day, Israel Television announced that its sample poll of 10,000 voters taken during the day indicated that the right-wing Likud Party, which had been in opposition for the full 29 years of Israeli statehood, would for the first time come out ahead in the voting, and that its leader, Menachem Begin, would finally win the prime ministership after eight unsuccessful attempts. The final results of the election gave the Likud 43 Knesset seats (4 more than in 1973); the Alignment, 32 (19 fewer than in 1973); and the Democratic Movement for Change, 15, a remarkable achievement for a party only six months old. The National Religious Party won 12 seats, two more than in 1973; the rest of the seats were shared between nine other parties.

The election results were, as *Yediot Aharonot* said the next day, nothing short of a 'revolution'.

Gloom had set in instantly at Labour Party headquarters in Tel Aviv as the size of the defeat became evident. For Shimon Peres, the blow was immeasurable. Now he too was on the sidelines, where Rabin had been since 7 April. One of the great ironies of the election was the enhanced status of Ezer Weizman, who until the election campaign had been a plain businessman. He had been minister of transport briefly during the National

Unity Government of 1967–70 under Golda Meir, but he had
never gained admittance to the top circles of leadership. Now
things had changed. He had, as chairman of the Likud's election
campaign, run an unbelievably successful operation. With
Begin in hospital for several weeks in March — at the height of
the campaign — Weizman was, in effect, the key man in the
Likud drive for leadership. Within hours of the election results
he was being spoken of as the likely minister of defence in the
Likud Government.

The formation of Menachem Begin's coalition Government
went quickly, if not always smoothly. Begin himself spent six
days in hospital shortly after the election — this time recovering
from exhaustion — and it was from his hospital bed that he
startled members of both his own party and the Labour Party, as
well as the general public, by announcing his intention to
appoint Moshe Dayan as his foreign minister. By doing so, he
diminished his chances of reaching agreement with Yadin's
more moderate Democratic Movement for Change. But the
prime minister-designate wanted his Government to reflect his
own strongly held views on foreign policy and the West Bank —
and if he had to make concessions he preferred to do so on
religious questions. The choice of Dayan, and Dayan's
willingness to serve in a Begin Government, aroused much
public concern and criticism, and some of Begin's own Likud
membership recoiled at the prospect of finding themselves allied
to the man whom many blamed for the early reverses in the 1973
Yom Kippur War. But Begin was adamant and eventually
overrode the dissenters.

On 24 May, Rabin ended his leave of absence, and decided to
take up his normal duties as prime minister — in order to assure
the smooth transition of Government.

During late May and early June, Begin and his colleagues
were locked in negotiations with Yadin's party but neither side
was willing to give way. The talks finally broke down on
13 June, one week before the prime minister-designate hoped
to present his new Government for Knesset approval. Ironically,
the main issue separating the Likud and the Democratic Party
for Change was the West Bank.

In the meantime, however, Begin had reached accord with

two other parties, the National Religious Party and the Agudat Yisrael Party. Knowing that they would hold the balance of power in the Government, these two orthodox religious parties were able to extract a number of significant concessions on religious issues. Indeed, of the 43 clauses of the coalition agreement, fully 30 dealt with religious matters.

Begin presented his new Government to the Knesset for approval on 21 June, and following a stormy seven and a half hour debate won a 63–53 vote of confidence. As anticipated, Moshe Dayan became his foreign minister, and Ezer Weizman minister of defence.

Rabin was ending a busy day, his last a prime minister. Earlier, he had bade farewell to his office staff, and penned some notes to heads of state, including President Jimmy Carter and former President Gerald Ford. He also wrote to James Callaghan. When the Knesset debate ended late that evening, Rabin rose from his seat and said quietly to Dan Pattir, 'Well, now I'm a free man.' But he still had one final act to perform — to formally hand over the prime minister's office in Jerusalem to Menachem Begin. Rabin and Begin shook hands as they parted from the packed chamber, and the new prime minister called out to Rabin, 'I'll be coming to see you tomorrow morning at 9 am.' Quickly correcting him with a smile, Rabin said, 'No, I'll be coming to see *you*.'

The next morning's ceremony was historic in that it was the first time in Israeli history that a Labour prime minister was turning over power to a member of the right-wing opposition. Begin took care to offer warm praise for the outgoing Rabin. He told the gathering of staff from the prime minister's office: 'Yitzhak Rabin has historic rights in the history of the Jewish people. The people have chosen a new Government, but I'm sure that the citizens of Israel will not forget those rights.' The two men then lifted their glasses and said 'L'Haim' ('To Life').

Rabin worked out of a small office in the government complex in Tel Aviv given to him because he was an ex-prime minister. He began writing his memoirs and took up work in the Knesset though without a great deal of enthusiasm. Power had passed to Begin.

Chapter 10

A Short Political Exile

Had the circumstances been different, had Yitzhak Rabin committed a far more serious violation of the law, he most likely would have been relegated to a minor political role for the rest of his political career. And yet, though his 'crime' had appeared inconsequential to most Israelis, Rabin had every reason to assume that he would remain a Knesset backbencher, climbing no higher. However honest and decent his public image, however much the country felt sorry for the mess in which he had found himself, it seemed preposterous that the nation would forgive or forget. It seemed highly unlikely that a prime minister who had been forced to resign in a financial scandal would be permitted to return to the centres of political power.

And, indeed, Yitzhak Rabin paid a price. He had to pay a fine fixed by the legal authorities. They had been lenient towards him. He did not go to jail, he did not even wind up in court — though his wife did. The political price that Rabin paid was far more severe. He was banished to the Knesset back bench. For someone as active in government as Rabin had been, this was serious punishment. His family and friends gave him conflicting advice about remaining as a Knesset member after the scandal. Some argued that he was better off divesting himself of all political responsibilities — for a while at least — until the public had a chance to decide whether it wanted him back in political life. It might be unseemly to remain in the Knesset, they pointed out. But, Amos Eran, Rabin's director-general, and Leah, thought otherwise. They urged him to remain a Knesset member. To drop out of the Knesset, they argued successfully, would have been Rabin's final acknowledgement that he was abandoning Israeli politics. Why be so hasty? Rabin found such arguments and the many letters of support he received persuasive.

And so he became Yitzhak Rabin, Knesset member. Not surprisingly, he found it boring. As chief of staff he had been the key decision maker on military affairs; as prime minister, he had conducted the nation's business. Now, the kinds of decisions he made were whether to attend a committee meeting; whether to agree to be interviewed by a journalist; whether to show up at the Knesset at all. He planned to write his memoirs, yet even that was hardly the equivalent of past stimulating efforts. He worked with a ghostwriter, laboriously going over his past history, which only served to remind him of how little he was doing at present. Adding to the insult, the nation had become enthralled with its new prime minister, Menachem Begin, and paid little attention to the Labour Party and its key politicians. Leah Rabin recalled, 'He didn't enjoy those years from 1977 to 1984. He was bored to tears. He would call me three or four times a day, sometimes out of frustration and boredom. There was no action. He's basically a doer. He likes the responsibility. But he didn't consider doing anything else outside of politics.'[1]

Politics, after all, had become his profession. If the public allowed him to remain in the political arena, he would not choose some other kind of work. Then too, there was a score to settle with Shimon Peres that would require patience.

After a short withdrawal from public life, Rabin happily discovered that a kind of collective amnesia had befallen the country when it came to the bank-account controversy. Israeli and overseas news representatives sought him out as one of the country's most insightful — and suddenly accessible — political commentators. The United Jewish Appeal and Israel Bonds were all too happy to invite him to speak at their forums in the United States. Later, in 1984, when he became defence minister, he continued to agree to requests from the UJA and Israel Bonds to speak at their engagements in the United States. Rabin's spokesman Nachman Shai once asked him why he was willing to give these groups so much time since they were not that important. Rabin corrected him, 'When I was just a Knesset member, sitting in my empty office in Tel Aviv, they didn't forget me; now as minister of defence, I'm happy to reciprocate.'[2]

Why had Israelis been so forgiving of Rabin? Why had they not cast him into the political wilderness as punishment for the transgression that had brought his prime ministership down? Why had they welcomed him back into the hothouse of Israeli politics, making clear that he would be eligible for any political post, even the prime ministership?

The answer, first and foremost, lies in the conservative nature of Israeli politics where policies changed slowly, but personalities leave the political arena even more slowly. In 1977, a mere 29 years after the State was founded, the country's political leadership still largely comprised the generation of the founding fathers. Unlike American political parties, which have a habit of discarding losing Presidential candidates after only one loss at the polls, Israeli political parties do not feel comfortable, or confident enough, to adopt such a practice. Israelis 'permitted' Yitzhak Rabin to remain in the political arena, because they felt they could not afford to overlook his impeccable credentials in helping to build up and preserve the state. An overseas bank account seemed trivial compared to leading the army to victory in the Six-Day War or rescuing the hostages at Entebbe.

Taking its cue from the rest of the country, Rabin's Labour Party was disinclined to dispense with his political talents. To be sure, Shimon Peres was the undisputed party leader in the wake of Rabin's downfall. Peres, however, would never be permitted to take complete control of the party. He was too mistrusted, too disliked by those party veterans who remembered how he had organized the great defection from Labour in the 1960s that had led to the creation of David Ben-Gurion's Rafi party. Rabin had to carry none of this baggage: he, who had risen through the ranks of the Palmach; he, whose mother Rosa Cohen had campaigned for workers' rights, had no trouble convincing party members that he was 'one of us'. Accordingly, Peres had no power to reduce Rabin to inactivity within the party. Also in Rabin's favour was the undemocratic nature of the Labour Party. Because a handful of politicians, Peres at the helm, controlled party matters, it was unthinkable for a fresh crop of younger leaders to defy Peres, or Rabin, for that matter; no one would step forward to challenge these two men who had been the Number One and Number Two figures in the Labour Party since 1974. Under this closed, oligarchic system, there was a Peres camp, and a Rabin camp, but nothing else. Even though Rabin had been disgraced as a result of the scandal, his erstwhile supporters did not gravitate towards a new face in the party; the natural heir apparent to Rabin's supporters would have been Yigal Allon, foreign minister under Rabin. Allon, however, wavered over whether to seek to replace Rabin as Peres' main challenger. Rabin's supporters were forced temporarily to back Peres for the party leadership. They were not, however, enamoured of him.

Even with the support that he enjoyed within the Labour Party, and the country at large, Rabin felt isolated, lonely, out of the limelight. As much as he wanted to return to national leadership, it would mean working under Prime Minister Peres, and that seemed intolerable.

Following the Sinai accord of September 1975, Rabin, as prime minister, had hoped to work out a further interim agreement between Israel and Egypt. Egyptian President Anwar Sadat, however, eventually abandoned that concept in the belief that a comprehensive peace between Israel and the other Arab states should be pursued. When he became prime minister in June 1977, Menachem Begin too believed that the time for interim agreements was over; he began examining whether it would be possible to reconvene the Geneva conference that had met briefly after the 1973 Yom Kippur War. A comprehensive peace, however, seemed elusive. Given Jordan King Hussein's hard line and the Arab insistence that the PLO was the sole representative of the Palestinians, there seemed little chance of achieving a negotiated settlement on the West Bank and in the Gaza Strip. Signing peace treaties with Jordan and Syria seemed equally remote. Only Egypt appeared to be a possible partner for peace negotiations.

And now, when Menachem Begin was prime minister, the greatest single push in the direction of peace came on 9 November, 1977 when Sadat announced that he was ready to go to the ends of the earth, even Jerusalem, to pursue peace.

Yitzhak Rabin found himself in the United States on that day caught up in a swirl of meetings with American officials. He put a question to Secretary of State Cyrus Vance: 'What were the chances that Sadat would show up in Jerusalem?'

'Fifty-fifty,' Vance replied.

Sadat proved a man of his word, and so when it became clear

that an Egyptian President was in fact going to visit Jerusalem, Rabin raced back home. He arrived the day before Sadat did. In his 1979 memoirs, Rabin described the paradoxical nature of the Sadat visit, calling his journey both courageous and desperate. 'Courageous because until then such a step had been absolutely unthinkable — and still was unthinkable in most of the countries in the Arab world. Desperate because Sadat realized that if the policies of the United States would be allowed to develop along the lines favoured by the Carter Administration, they would bring about the destruction of almost four years of dogged efforts that had been conducted in a very cautious, low-keyed manner but had produced, for the first time after a generation of hostility and stalemate, both negotiations and the signing of an agreement between Egypt and Israel.'[3]

Suddenly, it was a balmy Saturday evening, 19 November, 1977. The Egyptian airliner carrying Anwar Sadat to Israel had just landed at Ben-Gurion International Airport near Tel Aviv. A reception line of Israeli dignitaries had formed on the tarmac to greet the Egyptian President. As he stood in that receiving line, Rabin felt strange, unable to rid himself of the notion that this was an enemy leader about to land in Israel. Neither he, nor any other Israeli, had ever imagined that the President of Egypt would visit the Jewish state so soon after the 1973 war, perhaps in fifty years, certainly only after a peace treaty had been signed between the two countries. Yet, here he was, smiling, as he walked down the ramp and waded into the crowd of Israeli officials. Gazing at Sadat as he walked down the ramp, Rabin felt like he was dreaming. What with all the commotion and excitement, Rabin had only a few seconds to exchange pleasantries with Sadat at that dramatic moment in Israeli history. Sadat appeared terribly poised to Rabin, despite the awkward circumstances.

To Rabin, the highlight of Sadat's visit was the Egyptian President's appearance before the Knesset the next afternoon, 20 November. Until then Sadat had always insisted that he could only make peace with Israel if and when other Arab states did the same. The speech, however, was, in Rabin's mind a veritable 'political coup' for here was Sadat changing his terms for a peace treaty with Israel: he now seemed prepared to make peace with Israel unconditionally. Rabin was particularly moved when Sadat said, 'I understand your need for security, but not for land.' Even though Rabin understood the Israeli need for land, he found the statement extraordinary: '. . . The mere fact that an Arab leader who had waged war against Israel came forth and stated that he understood our need for security and that a way must be found to meet our legitimate concern was absolutely revolutionary.'[4]

Though Rabin himself was caught up in the excitement surrounding the Sadat visit, it annoyed him to hear Israelis suggest that only with the Sadat visit to Jerusalem had serious peacemaking begun. Had he not, as prime minister, signed the Sinai accord with Egypt two years earlier? Had that document not been a necessary prelude to these wonderful events? He found it hard to remain silent. '. . . Whenever I hear talk of "peace breaking out" any moment — as if the history of negotiations began in November 1977 — I feel obliged to set the record straight.'[5]

Still, when he had the chance to address Sadat himself during a meeting the Egyptian President held with Labour Party representatives, Rabin was filled with enthusiasm: 'Your courageous and daring coming over has created, I hope, a new era. I believe that you have removed the barriers that obscured in the past the relations between our two countries. . . . When we talk about defensible boundaries, allow me to say, Mr President, I was the chief of staff of the armed forces of Israel prior to the 1967 war. I don't want any future chief of staff to face what I had to face prior to this war.'

Over the next few months, many discussions were held between Israel and the United States, and between Egypt and the United States, but not much progress was made in peacemaking. Between January and August 1978, Israel and Egypt refrained almost entirely from direct talks until President Jimmy Carter summoned the parties to his mountain retreat at Camp David in September. After twelve days of intensive negotiations, Carter, Sadat and Begin hammered out two agreements known as the Camp David accords. One was a framework for a peace treaty between Israel and Egypt, requiring Israel to relinquish all of the Sinai Peninsula, including its settlements and airfields. The second was a framework agreement for peace in the Middle East. It foresaw peace between Israel and all Arab countries, but focused on the West Bank and Gaza. Israel promised to grant full autonomy to the Palestinian Arab residents there. Employing language that Israel had never agreed to before, the document stated that the political solution must recognize the legitimate rights of the Palestinian people and its just demands. Autonomy was to last for five years; after the first year of autonomy negotiations would begin looking towards a final political settlement.

Begin had made it a condition of his acceptance of the Camp David accords that the Knesset ratify Israel's relinquishment of Jewish settlements in the Sinai. Hence, the parliament was called back from recess for a crucial, stormy session on 25 September to debate and vote on that question. When it was his turn to speak, Knesset member Yitzhak Rabin sounded cautiously optimistic about the new peace accord. Camp David, he declared, contained the promise of peace, but there was considerable uncertainty as to where the process would lead. He reminded the Knesset that, as prime minister, he had favoured yielding territory for peace. Hence, he had no trouble supporting this accord. He praised Prime Minister Begin for seeking to resolve one part of the Arab–Israeli conflict at a time. That, said Rabin, had always been his policy as well. One important advantage of the accords, he added, was in enabling the parties to advance gradually towards a political solution of the thorny issue of the West Bank. The difficulties there could not be overestimated and, said Rabin, constituted a time bomb, one that was so powerful 'that it endangers even the peace agreement we hope will be signed with Egypt.'[6]

Following seventeen hours of debate, the Knesset approved the Camp David accords by an 84–19 vote. Most Labour Party Knesset members, including Yitzhak Rabin, voted for the accords. Only 29 of the Likud's Knesset deputies voted yes.

The Camp David accords were followed by six months of intense negotiations, culminating in Israel and Egypt signing a peace treaty in March 1979. The signing ceremonies were to be held at the White House in Washington DC and Begin had invited Rabin to be on hand. Ron Ben-Yishai was the Washington correspondent for *Yediot Aharonot* at the time. He and Rabin participated in a television broadcast just before the ceremony. Ben-Yishai then drove Rabin to the White House ceremony. During the ride, the former prime minister had been thinking of the irony of a right-wing prime minister like Begin being a partner to Israel's first peace treaty with an Arab state. The conventional wisdom in Israel had always been that the political right had little appetite for peace treaties, only in spoiling them. As the politician and the journalist approached the Treasury Department, driving down Massachusetts Avenue, Rabin blurted out 'If this had happened while I was prime minister of a Labour government, there would have been blood spilled on the streets.'[7]

No political feud had weighed more heavily on the State of Israel than that between Yitzhak Rabin and Shimon Peres. Other Israelis have competed for the prime ministership without displaying the bitterness and hostility these two men have shown each other. More often than not, dating back to 1974, Rabin and Peres have been pitted against one another for the Labour Party leadership and for the prime ministership. They have two very different personalities, though these differences are not necessarily at the core of their constant feuding. Rabin is taciturn, introverted, ill at ease in social situations. Peres is outgoing, able to engage in conversation easily, a friendly sort. A product of the military, Rabin has a special distaste for backroom political manoeuvring. To Peres, however, such behaviour is the very stuff of his existence. He has learned how to manipulate, enjoys it, and finds nothing wrong with it. Both men have achieved much in public life. Because he stayed out of politics until later in his life, Rabin retained the image of someone untainted by the seamier side of political life. Peres, however, has always been identified with wheeling and dealing, knowing the political ropes (inventing a few, too), and has never shaken the image of being just a little bit too slick, too polished, too tricky.

The original seeds of the rift were planted long before the two men had their eyes on national leadership posts. Back in the 1950s and 1960s, when Rabin was a soldier, and Peres a defence ministry official, the two men found themselves on opposite sides of various issues, siding with personalities on different sides of the fence. Although no evidence that the two men were personal enemies in those days exists, Rabin at times has suggested that Peres was operating behind the scenes to undercut him. Certainly, political or ideological differences were never at issue in their dispute. These are two politicians steeped in Labour Party ideology, both advocating territorial compromise over the West Bank, both supportive of Camp David, both seeing the need for strong connections with Washington. What is at the heart of the rift is the simple fact that Rabin and Peres do not like each other — and cannot get out of one another's hair in their common quest for their party and country's top leadership posts.

With Peres the chief beneficiary of the bank account scandal, Rabin needed little encouragement to believe that his political rival had manoeuvred behind the scenes to bring Rabin down. Rabin was never so forthright in public. He did not blame Peres (publicly or privately) for engineering the bank account affair nor was there any evidence linking Peres to the tip-off to Dan Margolit, the *Ha'aretz* reporter, of the existence of the bank accounts. The most Rabin said was that rivals in the Labour Party had been responsible for the disclosure over the bank account. He felt that he had been deprived of the chance to serve out his full term and, leaving aside the question of whether Peres had been behind his downfall, he had a deep desire to wait for the right moment, then try to take away from Peres what had been taken away from him. Dan Pattir, who had served as spokesman to Prime Minister Rabin in the 1970s, noted that Rabin 'believed he was a victim of the tricks of the [political] game. I didn't hear him blame Peres directly but he felt there had been an effort within the Labour Party to push him out. He felt he had been dethroned, that he had not been allowed to complete his mission. There were a lot of things he wanted to accomplish both domestically and internationally. Three years was a very short tenure.'[8]

He hoped some day to complete his mission. Meanwhile, he would wait and try to be patient. Never did Rabin consider opting out of political life. The media played an important role in fortifying his position as a possible contender for the premiership. Reporters sensed that the public had forgiven Rabin; for that reason it was acceptable, even desirable, to seek him out for reaction to major events, interviews that kept him in the public spotlight. The only question now was not whether Rabin would make a political comeback, but if and how he could defeat Peres. In mid-October 1978, when an Israel Radio interviewer asked Rabin if he would seek the Labour Party nomination for prime minister at some future date, Rabin replied, 'I am still very much involved in politics.'

Had Labour Party politicians had their way, they might have preferred both Peres and Rabin to quietly step aside, and allow a younger generation to assume the leadership. For the reality was that the Rabin–Peres infighting had immobilized the party. Rather than devote themselves to rehabilitation after the 1977 election débâcle, party members were instead forced to take sides in the only game in town: the Peres–Rabin feud. For an entire year after the 1977 election, the two men did not meet. They were, however, constantly on each other's mind.

As top dog, it was in Shimon Peres' interest to avoid conflict with Rabin. Party unity was a prerequisite for revitalizing the defeated party. Hence, in early 1979, the Labour Party leader lent a very direct hand to Yitzhak Rabin's political recuperation by declaring that he would consider giving Rabin a senior post in a Peres-led government. At a news conference on 11 February Peres tried to assure that 'Labour will not slide again into its old divisive conflict. We don't all love each other and we are not a band of heavenly angels, but there is party discipline.'

Rabin was not impressed with party discipline, and he certainly agreed with Peres that the two of them did not love each other. It was still too early, however, for Rabin to challenge Peres for the party's leadership. Moreover, Yigal Allon had stopped wavering and had demonstrated some interest in trying to depose Peres as party leader. By the early summer of 1979 Rabin had aligned himself with Allon to that end. That led Rabin to remind him of Peres' behaviour between 1974 and 1977. 'Three years ago,' Rabin told an Israel Television interviewer on 2 July, 1979, 'those who so loudly proclaimed the virtues of competition for the party leadership, although there was a Labour prime minister at the time, are precisely those who say that this process is unacceptable.'

Seething and growing impatient, Rabin was still convinced that someone — perhaps Peres, perhaps one of Peres' supporters — had masterminded his downfall as prime minister.

Meanwhile, it was becoming clear that Israelis were not overly enamoured with the Begin government, even though the prime minister had signed a peace treaty with Egypt the previous March. The public's growing disenchantment with the Likud regime was an open wound for Rabin: his worst fear was that Begin would be forced to step down as prime minister and Shimon Peres would be able to form a government.

Rabin had to find a way to stop Peres from grabbing the top prize. A knock-out blow. Rabin had the ammunition. That much he knew. If he chose to use it, his purpose would be double-edged: to gain revenge for past Peres sins and to force the Labour Party to cast Peres aside, thus denying him the coveted prime ministership. There could be no guarantee that Rabin would succeed. Had he thought carefully, Rabin would have also understood there could be no guarantees that the Labour Party would thank him for slicing up Shimon Peres in public. The farthest thought from Rabin's mind was whether he himself would emerge more sullied than Peres by this gambit. Rabin was too obsessed to give the subject any thought. Still very much the political novice, Rabin was thinking with his heart, not his head. He wanted to 'get' Peres. That was all. The political consequences to himself be damned.

The best means of 'getting' Mr Peres was to use the memoirs that he was writing. Rabin would sprinkle those pages with his true feelings about Shimon Peres, feelings that he had withheld as prime minister on the grounds that it was improper for a national leader to utter such personal remarks about another politician, particularly one in his own party. Now, freed from that constraint, Rabin was eager to act. A number of Labour Party leaders begged Rabin to put off publication — or cancel the book outright. 'Yitzhak, it's going to hurt,' they insisted. They had had enough of the Rabin–Peres 'struggle'. In hurting Peres, they argued, Rabin would be hurting the Party even more. Such 'logic' had no effect on Rabin. Peres had done him an injustice and the effects of Rabin's revenge did not faze him. If it caused a storm, the storm would pass. 'This is what I want to do,' he told those closest to him. Rabin's goal was to keep Peres from the prime ministership. In effect, Rabin would publish and Peres would perish!

The storm erupted in August 1979. The public learned what

Rabin intended when Israel Television broadcast extracts from his about-to-be-published memoirs over the 9 pm news. Peres was fuming. Likud officials quietly cheered: Mr Rabin was doing their work for them. Perhaps there was hope for the troubled Begin government.

What precisely did Rabin write? He described Peres as 'constantly and tirelessly attempting political subversion. He felt that all means were justified in his pursuit of winning the premiership.'

Peres, wrote Rabin, was not above working against him through leaks when Rabin was prime minister and Peres defence minister. 'He not only tried to undermine me but the entire government, trusting in the old Bolshevik maxim that "the worse the situation, the better for Peres". He spread lies and untruths and wrecked the Labour Party, thereby crowning himself as leader of the opposition.'

Once Peres had lost the Labour Party nomination for prime minister in 1974, wrote Rabin, 'Peres decided that he and the office of prime minister were made for each other, and that all he needed to do was kick me out of the way.' Rabin wrote that he knew who had been leaking information to the press, information which was meant to give the impression that Rabin had not been functioning properly and that only Peres was in full control. At one stage, wrote Rabin, the then foreign minister, Yigal Allon, suggested a lie-detector test! 'I saw Peres pale as he objected, and it all became crystal clear to me.'

Noting that Peres had never served in the Israel Defence Forces, Rabin contended that this should have disqualified him from serving as a defence minister. Though Rabin had preferred Yigal Allon as his defence minister, Rabin had been forced to bow to pressures of Peres' Rafi faction in the Labour Party which wanted Peres as defence minister. No longer did he trust a word Peres uttered, Rabin wrote, arguing that Peres was unfit to be prime minister and that he would not serve under him. Rabin also charged that during the days before the 1976 Entebbe hostage rescue operation hours had passed before Peres consulted with the military about a possible rescue operation.[9]

Predictably, Shimon Peres dismissed Rabin's accusations and warned that the only one who would be harmed would be Rabin. In all of the years he had worked with Rabin, Peres said, he had never heard a complaint from him. 'His charges are very general in nature, and reflect more his problems than mine. The book will cause very great harm to its author. He did it all himself. There are standards even in political life, and we will have to take the damage which Rabin did to the party into account.'[10] That was his way of suggesting to Rabin that a political price would have to be paid and Peres intended to make sure that Rabin paid it.

According to Rabin's scenario, Labour Party officials, grateful to him for revealing what a monster Shimon Peres really was, would rise up against their Party leader, toss him out, and beckon Rabin to take over at once. The trouble was that the people whom Rabin had to convince may not have been enraptured with Shimon Peres, but they did not want to rock the boat either. The last thing they wanted to do was act upon Rabin's charges and turn against Peres. In their view, that would have made matters far worse. They wanted Rabin and his nasty little book to go away, to disappear from the daily headlines as quickly as possible. They thought that the only possible beneficiary of the 'struggle' was Menachem Begin, and why do him a favour?

Thus the entire exercise blew up in Rabin's face. Labour politicians turned their venom, not at Peres, but at Rabin himself. They pummelled him with questions: why had he done this? Why had he brought the simmering political feud out into broad daylight? Why was he washing his and the entire party's dirty laundry in public?

Faced with so much rage, the Labour Party Secretariat called a meeting to discuss what to do. One after another, former Labour Party ministers from Rabin's government assailed him with more questions: why, if Peres had been so worthless, had Rabin chosen him to replace him after the 1977 bank-account scandal? (The question was based on an incorrect premise: Rabin had not 'chosen' Peres, the Party had.) Why, if Peres was not worthy of being a leader, had Rabin agreed to run for the Knesset on a Peres-led list right after the scandal? (Again, the question missed the point: Rabin ran for the Knesset for his own reasons, which had nothing to do with being willing to serve under Peres.) Former Justice Minister Haim Zadok argued, 'This book harms Yitzhak Rabin's credibility and his judgement. The author was unbalanced by his personal animosity.'

The politicians wanted to pass a resolution condemning Rabin and the book. Peres said no. He was afraid that the resolution would haunt him later and would only widen the already large gulf within the party. It was clear, said Peres, that the Labour Party had expressed confidence in him — and not in Rabin. He needed no further affirmation. Peres' biographer, Matti Golan, asserted that, in deciding against demanding an official Labour Party response Peres played into Rabin's hands. 'Because of his weak response,' wrote Golan, 'Rabin's version of events was accepted by many, and the accusations against Peres took root. Rabin took on the image of a victim; Peres of an intriguer and saboteur.'[11]

None of the Party turmoil caused Rabin any regret. When asked to comment on the storm his book had created within the party, Rabin could have softened the blow by noting that his comments had been taken out of context or inflated by the newspapers but he did not. He came out punching, just as bitter and angry as when he sat down at his typewriter to write the book: 'I will not take back a single word I wrote about Shimon Peres and I stand by every one of those words.'[12] In Israel Radio and Television interviews, he suggested, 'If someone wants to sue me over what I wrote, let him . . . I never concealed my opinion in the past, but as prime minister I had to mind my public pronouncements. I don't believe in insinuating and leaking. What I did in my book was to put things squarely on the table.'

To show his determination Rabin stated that even had Peres been prime minister, he would still have published his critique of him 'although I'm not sure it would have been permitted to see the light'. Rubbing Peres' nose in the dirt a bit more, Rabin declared at a press conference on 10 August to announce the appearance of the *Memoirs* that he would never serve in a Peres government and that he still had not ruled out running for the prime ministership. 'I have no intention of abandoning political life. I am definitely staying and I will remain a member of Labour and not a conditional member, with all that implies.'

Rabin was incensed at Labour Party politicians for wanting to punish him politically — even to toss him out of the party —

for his harsh remarks about Peres. 'I joined the movement at a
very young age before I ever heard of Shimon Peres. I identified
with concepts and ideals and not with any one man, least of all
the present Labour chairman. Hence my membership in the
party is not contingent on any particular man at its helm. The
party needs a basic examination of itself, without this one time
papering over the cracks, and what I wrote will help it in that
direction. . . . There are things I feel I must impart to others so
that they could learn from my experience. The past must serve
as a guide to the future. I don't think books ought to be just
written about the dead or published 20 years after a person is
buried.'[13]

The Labour Party certainly needed a 'basic examination' of
itself. Rabin was right about that. He was incorrect, however in
suggesting that Peres alone was responsible for the party's woes.
For all of Rabin's insistence that 'the past must serve as a guide
to the future', the last thing these Labour Party politicians
wanted to do was to learn a lesson from the past, with all of its
bitter infighting centred on the Rabin–Peres feud. Maybe
Rabin thought there was some literary or political virtue in
writing books about the living. The Labour Party politicians did
not, at least not when the result was this buffeting of the party.

Even Rabin's supporters were not enthusiastic about the
attack on Peres. Former agriculture minister, Aharon Uzzan,
termed the book 'a cancerous growth, which must be removed
with the utmost urgency'. The most telling anti-Rabin
comment came from David Hacohen, a Rabin relative and a
veteran Labour Party politician. The book had left him with
'sad thoughts about the young generation. I am speaking with
an aching heart. Never in all my years in politics have I seen
such mudslinging. . . . What point does a young fellow like
Rabin see in publishing an autobiography? Let him keep a
diary, or pour his heart out to his wife, but not write himself off
politically.'[14] Rabin had not understood any of this; nor did he
seem to care.

One intriguing footnote regarding Rabin's memoirs, quite
unrelated to his squabbling with Peres, appeared after the book
had been published. On 23 October, 1979 the *New York Times*
published what it contended was a censored part of the

memoirs. In that material, Rabin explained how his Harel Brigade had driven out 50,000 Arabs from their homes in the towns of Lod and Ramle during Israel's 1948 War of Independence. The *Times* said it had obtained a copy of the original manuscript from Peretz Kidron who translated the book into English. According to the newspaper, Rabin attributed the final expulsion order to the then Israeli Prime Minister, David Ben-Gurion. A board of censors of Cabinet ministers, to whom Israeli law requires former government officials submit their memoirs, had deleted the account.

According to the *New York Times*, Rabin's description opened with a meeting attended by Ben-Gurion, Yigal Allon, and Rabin who was then commander of the Harel Brigade. The Brigade had been trying to eliminate Arab Legion bases along the Jerusalem–Tel Aviv road. Rabin, said the *Times*, had written in part:

'While the fighting was still in progress, we had to grapple with the fate of the civilian population of Lod and Ramle, numbering some 50,000 . . . .

'Clearly we could not leave Lod's hostile and armed populace in our rear, where it could endanger the support route to Yiftah [another brigade] which was advancing eastward.

'We walked outside, Ben-Gurion accompanying us. Allon repeated his question: "What is to be done with the population?" Ben-Gurion waved his hand in a gesture which said, "Drive them out."

'"Driving out" is a term with a harsh ring. Psychologically, this was one of the most difficult actions we undertook. The population of Lod did not leave willingly. There was no way of avoiding the use of force and warning shots in order to make the inhabitants march the 10 to 15 miles to the point where they met up with the Legion.

'The inhabitants of Ramle watched and learned the lesson. Their leaders agreed to be evacuated voluntarily. . . . Buses took them to Latrun, and from there they were evacuated by the Legion.'

Yigal Allon denied the whole account. Allon dismissed the notion that 50,000 Arabs were expelled by Rabin's Palmach forces. Allon insisted the Arabs had requested that the IDF help evacuate them to make sure they would escape harm, 'that they wouldn't run into mine fields and get killed'. Allon noted that he had not asked Ben-Gurion, nor had the prime minister given orders to expel the Arabs. The Arabs left, said Allon, because 'they were instructed by the Arab Legion to evacuate in order to enable the latter to recapture [Lod] from us.'[15] What was important, with regard to Rabin, was that in the fall of 1979, further substantiation was supplied, by way of this censored account, that Yitzhak Rabin was one tough fellow.

In the ensuing years, the image makers would increasingly depict Shimon Peres as a political dove — to his detriment. All the while, these same image makers turned Rabin into a political hawk to his great advantage. The *New York Times* story showing Rabin's toughness towards the Arabs during the 1948 war was one of the early steps in the crafting of an image that would serve Yitzhak Rabin exceedingly well all during the 1980s and early 1990s.

As Labour Party leader, Shimon Peres had the temporary advantage over Rabin in the early 1980s. Yitzhak Rabin, however, was carefully, methodically, staking out a claim that would one day allow him to win back political leadership. He continued to make frequent television appearances which went a long way to restoring his tarnished image. Indeed, television interviewers seemed to seek out Rabin more than Peres. The Rabin–Peres 'struggle' still very much existed, but it was played out far from public sight; what the public saw was the statesmanlike Rabin presenting his often astute political analysis on whatever event happened to be in the news. Rabin the pundit was an impressive figure and his public support grew.

Still not ready to make his own move for the Labour Party's leadership, during 1979 and early 1980 Rabin placed his support behind Yigal Allon's bid to unseat Peres as party leader. Then on 29 February, 1980 Allon died suddenly. These new circumstances created a vacuum which Rabin was only too willing to fill.

By the spring of 1980 the polls indicated that Rabin was the country's top choice for prime minister. While Menachem Begin registered the lowest support ever for a prime minister in office (15.8 per cent) in one poll in July 1980, Shimon Peres was even a less popular choice with 13.1 per cent. Rabin led the pack with 26.6 per cent. He was delighted to be back in the public's good graces. 'If I said I was anything less than gratified by the results, I would be dishonest.' Indeed, he seemed to be smiling more, enjoying the nitty-gritty of politics more, less of a political novice. In the meantime, the Begin government plodded through a most mediocre domestic performance, the cabinet torn by internal dissension, the economy disintegrating, creating a most fertile landscape for Yitzhak Rabin to stage his political comeback.

Just what had made Rabin so incredibly popular? To start with, he retained an image of credibility. The people trusted him on the only issue that mattered to them: national security. Writing in the *Jerusalem Post* on 17 October, 1980, David Landau noted: 'It is perhaps the ultimate irony that a prime minister who had to resign because of a legal impropriety followed by some public untruths should now be making his comeback challenge on a credibility ticket. But there it is: another political fact of life, substantiated by all the polls for the past six months. Israelis do appear to regard Yitzhak Rabin as essentially straight, and straightforward, and clearly seem today to disregard his past peccadillo. Peres' contrived rhetoric, full of overstylized metaphors, is contrasted, to Peres' disadvantage, with Rabin's slow, unpolished and simple style. Peres is prone . . . to glibness and sometimes even to gimmickry.'[16]

Much to his chagrin, Shimon Peres could hardly be immune to this rising adulation of Rabin. National elections were to take place the following year and Peres needed Rabin as a part of Labour's leadership. Two days after polls showed Rabin the most popular man in the country, Peres hinted that he was ready to abandon his promise to keep Rabin out of a future Peres-led government. All Rabin would have to do was retract what he had said about him. Peres' pursuit of Rabin was stopped dead with Rabin's own announcement.

In October 1980, two months before the Labour Party was to choose its leader, Rabin announced that he would run for his party's nomination for prime minister. Peres described Rabin's statement as a 'mere ornamentation. The contest has been going on in earnest for a year'. That much was true, for Rabin had acquired more of the skills that a politician needed to survive. He announced that same month that while he was still inclined not to serve in a future Peres government, he did not rule it out. Even if he were far more popular than Peres, that did not guarantee that Rabin would secure his party's nomination. And, if Peres did win the nomination, he might become the next prime minister. Certainly, Begin seemed vulnerable. Part of Rabin's political recovery programme was to attain a senior governing position. If Peres grabbed the top prize, Rabin might still become defence minister, a significant step forward in Rabin's political rehabilitation. Rabin and Peres had not become 'heavenly angels', in Peres' words. It was just that they needed each other.

Once again, Rabin and Peres squared off against one another. Public opinion polls indicated that Labour could win an absolute majority in the Knesset if elections were held at this juncture. The party was, however, still burdened by the 'struggle' between two men who were barely on speaking terms and who had difficulty uttering each other's names. Their only way of communicating with one another was through a sneer.

This time, in December 1980, Peres won the nomination for Labour Party leader decisively, garnering 2,123 out of the 3,028 votes cast by the Labour Party Central Committee. Rabin received only 875 votes. Peres had contended before the balloting that, were he to receive 70 per cent of the votes, Rabin could no longer be considered a viable alternative to his leadership. Peres won 70 per cent of the vote. It seemed unthinkable, however, that Rabin would capitulate so docilely. After the balloting, Peres shook hands with Rabin. For his part, Rabin failed to mention Peres once in his concession speech. Some Labour Party veterans showed up on Israel television that week, their white beards flowing, their voices quivering with old age, to denounce the rivalry. Their octogenarian wisdom had led them to the conclusion that the 'struggle' had hurt Labour and could keep it from returning to power.

Reporters asked Peres and Rabin after the vote what role Rabin would play in a Peres government. Peres was evasive. One option for Rabin was to opt out of Labour and join ranks with former Defence Minister Ezer Weizman's new Knesset list. Weizman wanted Rabin on his ticket. The public opinion surveys suggested that a Weizman–Rabin ticket with Moshe Dayan added to it, could secure as many as 33 Knesset seats,

making it a formidable political force. None the less, Rabin did
not leave the Labour Party.

During the election campaign for the 30 June, 1981 elections,
the Likud, not surprisingly, quoted extensively from the Rabin
Memoirs in its election propaganda. Labour Party officials urged
Rabin to demand that the Likud cease using his book. They
wanted Rabin to declare that, despite what he had written
about Peres, he preferred him above Begin for prime minister.
Rabin made no overture to the Likud, nor would he make any
positive statements about Peres. At election rallies he extolled
the virtues of the Labour Party. He could not bring himself to
mention the name of the party's leader.

Considering how popular Rabin was among voters, it was
ironic that he was so awkward on the campaign trail. A reporter
who accompanied him on one tour of Beersheeba noted that
'. . . Rabin is not a flesh-pumper. He's got a quick-as-a-whip
weak handshake that's as low-key as his baritone.' Wherever he
went, Rabin asked the same monotonous question: 'What do
you do and how long have you been working here?' At one point
during the tour, Rabin actually confessed, 'I don't like having to
walk through the streets.' On occasion supporters of Menachem
Begin tried to disrupt Labour Party election rallies. When a few
hundred such Begin supporters began shouting 'Begin, Begin' at
one of Rabin's rallies in Beersheeba, he grew annoyed.

'Let me finish my speech. Let's act like civilized people.'

'Begin, king of Israel,' the group chanted.

'They're out to provoke,' Rabin said to someone in an aside.

Labour had been leading the public opinion surveys
throughout the election campaign by decisive margins. As the
election date approached, however, Likud began narrowing the
gap. The most important event of the campaign occurred on
7 June, 1981. On that day at 4 pm Prime Minister Begin sent
eight F-16s from the Etzion base in the Sinai, travelling 1,000
miles to their target: the Osiraq nuclear reactor in Iraq. The
attack against Iraq's nuclear reactor proved to be one of the
most spectacular of Israeli military feats, delaying Iraq's
capability to produce nuclear weapons, and making Begin look
very, very good at a crucial period three weeks before the
election.

At first Yitzhak Rabin sounded less than enthusiastic about

the Israeli decision, indicating that the data Israel possessed
indicated that the reactor was no imminent threat. Eventually,
however, he declared himself in favour of the raid, telling Israel
Radio two days after the attack: '. . . Israel is unanimous in
perceiving the threat posed by nuclear weapons in the hands of
an Arab state, certainly of a state headed by Saddam Hussein.
Unarguably, everything should be done to disrupt such an
eventuality, to postpone or prevent it.'

The Iraqi bombing helped Menachem Begin enormously
with voters. Six days after the attack, Eliezer Zurrabin, who was
in charge of the Labour Party's public relations campaign,
visited Shimon Peres at his Tel Aviv party headquarters.
Joining Zurrabin was his researcher, Mina Tzemach. Their
news was grim: a poll they had conducted after the nuclear
reactor attack showed that Begin's Likud was ahead by 20
Knesset seats. The poll indicated even more devastating news
for Peres: if Labour were to replace Peres with Rabin at the head
of its list, the 20-seat gap would be closed. The message was
clear: Peres should step down before it was too late and turn the
party leadership over to Rabin.

Peres wanted more time before making so fateful a decision as
stepping down a few weeks before the election. He asked the
pollsters to check the results again. He prepared himself, if
necessary, to relinquish the role of Labour Party candidate for
prime minister the next day. Happily for Peres, Zurrabin
phoned Peres the next morning with the news that another poll
put the Likud ahead by only six Knesset seats and the gap was
closing. Peres' resignation was no longer crucial.[17]

Concerned enough about the possibility of losing the election,
Peres, on 25 June, five days before the balloting, made a surprise
move. Having announced his shadow cabinet during the
campaign, Peres had named Haim Bar-Lev, a former chief of
staff, as his choice for defence minister. Now Peres decided to
'dump' Bar-Lev in favour of Yitzhak Rabin. At a midnight press
conference Rabin said he was now prepared to serve under
Shimon Peres. He had changed his mind. Peres was jubilant:
'The good of the country comes before our personal feelings.' A
reporter pressed Rabin if he would now urge the Likud to stop
exploiting his memoirs as campaign propaganda. 'The law
won't let me,' Rabin answered ambiguously. No one could be

certain that Peres' last-minute switch would help Labour. Some thought so; some believed Labour had simply panicked. A few Rabin loyalists wondered why their man had to come to Peres' rescue.

It is difficult to assess whether Rabin had helped Peres to secure more votes. However, the move had not helped him defeat Menachem Begin. The Likud had won 48 seats to Labour's 47. Together with the three small political parties (the National Religious, Agudat Yisrael and Tami), Begin put together a coalition of 61 members. Later that summer Rabin described his agreement to join the Labour Party team on election eve as an 'ad hoc' arrangement. In other words, his truce with Shimon Peres was short-lived.

Nearly a year later the Israeli war in Lebanon began. On 6 June, 1982 three Israeli divisions moved into southern Lebanon in order to eradicate PLO bases there, cutting off Palestinian gunmen before they had a chance to escape to the north. The PLO had rained katyusha rockets down on communities and settlements in northern Israel incessantly, leading Israel to take this action. Prime Minister Begin was intent on informing the Labour Party opposition and others that Israel's war aims were limited. Israel's stated objective was to establish a 25-mile security zone in southern Lebanon, not to move into other parts of Lebanon. At a meeting with Begin soon after the outbreak of war, Rabin and Peres heard the prime minister promise that he did not intend to advance the IDF into Beirut or along the Beirut–Damascus road. Meanwhile, the IDF was moving towards Beirut, presumably without the prime minister's knowledge; by the end of the war's first week Israeli soldiers were on the hills outside Beirut.

Rabin's behaviour at the outset of the fighting seemed peculiar in the light of his eventual staunch opposition to the war. For someone who questioned Israel's goals as unobtainable, he sounded very supportive of the war at times. On 4 July, nearly a month after the war had started, the burning issue turned on whether the Israeli army should cut off water and electricity in order to put pressure on the PLO in Beirut. Begin invited Labour Party leaders in for a chat. Peres was against using water and electricity. Rabin favoured the tactic. 'Closing off their water is an extremely effective measure,' he was quoted as saying.[18] Advising Defence Minister Ariel Sharon to 'tighten up' the siege of the Lebanese capital, Rabin said, 'I can live with a twenty-four hour bombardment of Beirut.'

In fact Rabin's behaviour was not so strange after all. He was merely doing what he could to make sure that the IDF did not fail militarily. His affection for Israeli soldiers, for the IDF as an institution was an overriding concern. Even when questioning the overall goals of the war, Rabin, the former chief of staff, wanted to do what he could to save the prestige of the IDF. His concern was not to make Ariel Sharon look good. It was to prevent the Israeli army from looking bad.

And so Rabin visited Beirut a number of times, and his relations with Defence Minister Ariel Sharon grew warm. The two men were often seen together at different war fronts. Both men benefited: Sharon was able to show that one of the two Labour Party leaders supported the siege of Beirut at a time when not everyone agreed the siege was the best tactic. Rabin, for his part, played the part of patriot, a former chief of staff who rallied to the side of Israeli troops during battle.

Something bothered Rabin about the war in Lebanon. He felt that the Begin government's wartime goals were too grandiose and ultimately unattainable: Begin wanted to establish a new political order in Lebanon that would be friendly to Israel, to remove the Syrian army from Lebanon, and to eliminate the PLO's base in that country. The war would not help Israel to realize these objectives, Rabin believed. Had he been prime minister, he would not have gone to war in pursuit of any of these objectives. Instead, he would have sought ways to keep the PLO from attacking Israeli communities — nothing more.

Israel remained in Lebanon until 1985, unable to find a way to extricate itself from what Rabin termed the 'botz ha'Levanoni', loosely translated as the Lebanese quagmire. In January 1983, in a speech at Jerusalem's Hebrew University, he called upon the Begin government to acknowledge that it had been 'a mistake, an illusion', to employ the IDF in order to impose a formal peace agreement on Lebanon. It was a further illusion, he said, for Israeli leaders to believe that their country could launch a war on Lebanese soil, conquer its capital and then force it to make peace.

On 28 August, 1983 Menacxhem Begin rose at a Cabinet meeting and declared that he 'cannot go on'. He was stepping down as prime minister, giving no reason. It was clear, however, that the Lebanon War had taken its psychological toll on him. By that time 500 Israeli soldiers had died in that war. Begin did not say so publicly, but he apparently felt that Ariel Sharon had deceived him by prosecuting the war well beyond the 25 square-kilometre perimeter in southern Lebanon which Begin had described as the IDF's maximum advance.

In a state of shock over Begin's decision and without a clear-cut candidate in mind, the Herut Party, the dominant element of the Likud, convened its Central Committee: it had to choose between Begin's foreign minister, the 68-year-old Yitzhak Shamir who had commanded the ultra right Lehi underground during the British Mandate period, and David Levy, the minister of housing, whose rags to riches rise to political fame made him the pride of the Moroccan community in Israel. Shamir won the contest 435–302, making him automatically the new prime minister. He took office on 15 September.

Shamir's career had been similar to Begin's. He had been born in Tsarist Poland in 1914 and trained in law at the University of Warsaw. Arriving in Palestine in 1935, he joined the Revisionist Irgun Zvai Leumi; serving in the underground, he was imprisoned three times by the British. In 1948, Shamir joined Lehi which had been suspected of assassinating Count Folke-Bernadotte, the United Nations mediator. When Likud was elected in 1977, Shamir was chosen Knesset speaker; three years later he succeeded Moshe Dayan as foreign minister. Shamir was no less hawkish than Menachem Begin, a firm believer in the Jewish right to Greater Israel and a supporter of the Lebanon War. Shamir was only in power four months when his government fell on 25 January, 1984 and early elections were called for 23 July, 1984. It appeared that the Labour Party was headed for a near-certain victory. All signs pointed to a Likud defeat: the IDF remained stranded in Lebanon. Inflation was soaring and would eventually reach 400 per cent a year. The Likud's best vote-getter, Menachem Begin, had sequestered himself in his Jerusalem apartment. Yitzhak Shamir had none of his charisma, none of his ability to stir the masses.

None of this bolstered the spirits of the Likud — or of Yitzhak Rabin.

Chapter 11

Defence Minister and an Intifada

In early 1984 Yitzhak Rabin confronted another difficult decision. Should he compete for his party's nomination for prime minister yet again? The spark of political ambition still burned brightly in him. Labour Party politicians were optimistic about the party's chances of winning the election the following July, but some were still unconvinced that Shimon Peres was their best candidate to head the ticket. Twice he had run as the party's candidate for prime minister, and twice he had lost. The aura of defeat surrounded him. Some Labourites preferred Rabin. The prospect of playing out 'the struggle' once again between Rabin and Peres soured many party members. It was for that reason that, when a fresh face loomed on the political horizon, a certain excitement developed around this alternative to Rabin and Peres. The face was Yitzhak Navon, who had resigned as Israel's fifth President a year earlier than scheduled in order to toss his hat in the ring for the Labour Party's leadership. When some Labour Party figures approached Peres, asking him to step aside in favour of Navon, Peres demurred, and instead offered Navon the Number 2 spot on the ticket under him. Navon said no.

Some of Rabin's supporters urged him to challenge both Peres and Navon. A three-way race, however, seemed risky: Peres and Navon might outpoll Rabin, forcing him to accept Number 3 spot on the ticket. Awkward and ironic as it was, Rabin believed that his best move was to side with Shimon Peres, if only to preserve his chances of retaining the Number 2 spot on the Labour list. And so these unlikely political bedfellows sheathed their swords, ready to do business with one another, not out of a new-found affection, but sheer political expediency. As part of the Peres–Rabin pact, the Labour Party candidate for prime minister would be Peres: Labour's candidate for defence minister, Rabin. Realizing that the deck was stacked against him, Navon bowed out. On 2 April, 1984, Peres was once again chosen Labour Party chairman and candidate for prime minister.

Once again the Labour Party headed the public opinion polls early in 1984. As the summer approached, the Likud trimmed the margin. The Likud turned the contest into a toss-up as the result of a surprise proposal by Prime Minister Yitzhak Shamir aired during his television debate with Peres. The Likud leader called for the establishment of a National Unity Government after the elections, sounding patriotic, ready to share political power in order to solve the country's problems. Even if Shamir were elected prime minister, a unity government would not be assured; Labour would have to agree. Still, the voters seemed to like Shamir's offer. With the country unable to find a way out of Lebanon and troubled by sky-rocketing inflation, a unity government just might prove useful.

On election day, the voters cast their ballots almost evenly for Labour and Likud. Labour captured 44 seats, three more than the Likud, but could not attract enough small parties to form a governing coalition. Likud failed also to win over sufficient parties. Shamir's unity government proposal suddenly looked like the most practical solution. Labour and Likud entered negotiations aimed at sharing political power over the next four years. Peres and Shamir devised a unique 'rotation' scheme, giving Peres the prime ministership for the first two years, and Shamir for the latter two. Shamir would serve as foreign minister for the first two years, Peres for the latter two. Much negotiating occurred over the defence minister post. Shamir at first was prepared to give Labour the prime ministership for two years while Likud would have defence and foreign affairs; after two years there would be a rotation of all three posts. When the Labour Party executive met to discuss this proposal, Rabin, the party's candidate for defence minister, pressed his own case. At one stage he moved towards Peres and whispered in his ear, 'Shimon, you know this is very important to me.' Peres and Rabin had been getting along at that juncture and Peres had every reason to preserve the cordial relationship. Rotating the defence minister post became a dead issue. Labour and Likud agreed that Rabin would serve the full four-year-term as defence minister.

In mid-September 1984 the new National Unity government was sworn in at the Knesset. It was an emotional moment for the new defence minister. 'Seventeen years after removing his uniform,' wrote Leah Rabin in her memoirs, 'Yitzhak had returned to the defence establishment as though coming home after a prolonged absence, full of ups and downs in life. Seventeen years had passed, his hair had turned grey and he was wearing a suit in place of uniform. Yet he strode like a soldier, as in the past, his face not revealing his inner feelings.'[1]

It had taken seven years. Yitzhak Rabin's political recovery was all but complete. He was back in a position of national power. He had risen to become his country's minister of defence. The second most powerful position in government. All that eluded him now was a return to the prime ministership. He harboured no illusions on that score. If it happened at all, it would not be overnight. Still, Rabin had accomplished a great deal since leaving the prime ministership in disgrace in 1977. And, he had had the help of the two men who were his chief rivals for political power — Shimon Peres and Yitzhak Shamir.

As soon as the Peres-led National Unity government took office it set as its main goal ending Israel's 27-month occupation of Lebanon. Shamir, when he was still prime minister, had promised to withdraw IDF troops only after local security arrangements in Lebanon had been worked out. The new prime minister, Shimon Peres, wanted to discard this policy, thinking it likely to delay the IDF withdrawal. Peres, however, needed the agreement of his defence minister, Yitzhak Rabin. The latter believed that the Shamir approach was valid and argued that even a poor agreement was preferable to an IDF withdrawal without an agreement. Eventually, however, even Rabin became convinced that it was not worth waiting for local Lebanese forces to agree to security plans for a unilateral withdrawal; Rabin opted for pulling the troops out gradually —over several stages. None of this pleased Peres who wanted to get the troops home as quickly as possible. But, Rabin got his way, and on 13 January, 1985 he presented the Cabinet with a plan for the withdrawal of IDF troops from Lebanon in three stages; after the withdrawal was completed, only a small number of Israeli soldiers were to stay behind in a 'security zone' on the Lebanese side of the frontier. By June 1985 the pull-out would be over. Two Likud ministers, Shamir and Moshe Arens, objected to the pull-out scheme. Shamir called the plan a 'surrender'. Arens said Rabin and Peres were gambling with the security of Israel's northern communities. A vote was taken in the Cabinet. In favour of the plan were sixteen Labour Party ministers who were joined by two from Likud (David Levy and Gideon Patt) and three religious party ministers. Shamir and the other Likud ministers voted against. The plan was passed overwhelmingly.

And so Rabin and Peres achieved an Israeli withdrawal from Lebanon. It was the first major step Rabin took toward correcting the errors he felt Menachem Begin and his Likud regime had made. Rabin could not wait to get out of the quagmire. 'Israel will withdraw from Lebanon on the date it has determined even if there is no one to whom to hand the territory,' he told the Labour Party Central Committee four days after the Cabinet decision. 'If chaos and perhaps a massacre occur when we vacate our lines in Lebanon, the UN and the Lebanese government will be responsible for it . . .', he told *Time* magazine on 2 February, 1985. Rabin explained why Israel was leaving Lebanon: 'I don't want to be the policeman of Lebanon. It's not the business of Israel. Israel was not created to serve as a policeman of the region. We made it clear we don't link our unilateral decision to anything the Syrians do. They want to stay in Lebanon, let them stay. I know that whoever sets his foot in Lebanon has sunk into the Lebanese [swamp]. They want it, let them enjoy it. We want one thing: that they do not move closer to our borders. That's all.'

For the most part, Rabin's 'security zone' arrangement worked, and Rabin was very satisfied with it in later years. 'Our policy has proven itself,' he said on 27 April, 1988 over Israel Radio. 'Instead of 15,000 Israeli soldiers in Lebanon, only several hundred are permanently posted there. We are achieving our objective of peace in the Galilee. No Israeli civilian has been killed as the result of terrorist attacks originating from Lebanon. Thirty-four IDF soldiers have fallen while carrying out this mission. This is a far lower number than in the three years which preceded these past three years.'

*

In November 1985 an American navy employee, Jonathan Pollard, was arrested outside the Israeli embassy in Washington. Pollard had confessed to selling intelligence material to Israeli officials. The American Administration asked Israel to help it to discover the scope of the 'Pollard affair', as it became known, and to search for those Israelis who had been in touch with the navy man.

Once the news broke, Prime Minister Peres, Defence Minister Rabin and Foreign Minister Shamir met daily at the prime minister's office. They tried to figure out how to handle the devastating news. Their main interest was to convince the public that they had not known who Jonathan Pollard was or what he had been doing. An internal government inquiry was conducted by a three-member committee. The three government leaders hoped the committee would produce no evidence that linked them to Pollard. To their relief, the committee reported on 27 November that Pollard had been part of a 'rogue' intelligence-gathering unit unknown to almost all of the political and intelligence community. Cheering the three leaders, the committee provided Rabin, Peres and Shamir with a clean bill of health.

The next step was to get word of the committee's findings to the public. None of the three leaders could just call a press conference because the committee report was secret. So Rabin's spokesman, Nachman Shai, picked up the phone to the Jerusalem correspondent for the *New York Times*, Thomas Friedman, and asked him to come to the Defence Minister's office. Friedman was treated to a briefing on the results of the report which were being passed on to Thomas Pickering, the American ambassador in Israel.

The *Times* man filed a story the next day quoting an unnamed 'highly placed Israeli source', identified later by others as Rabin himself. According to the source (Rabin), the committee had noted that Pollard had initiated contact with Israeli officials, not the other way around. One motive for the Israelis using Pollard, according to the report, was to discover if the United States had been spying on Israel. Rabin told the *New York Times* reporter that the senior Israeli intelligence man running Pollard's operation had informed no one in the Israeli Government, not him, not the prime minister. That way, the intelligence operative avoided someone above him instructing him to curtail the operation. Yes, acknowledged Rabin to Friedman, this sounded incredible, but it was the truth.

'He [the senior intelligence man] interpreted our basic policy of not carrying out espionage inside the United States as meaning not carrying out espionage against the national security interests of the United States,' Rabin said. 'There was no doubt that it was a mistake on his part to interpret the guidelines in this way. And there is no excuse for obtaining information through non-legal means. But there was no malice on his part. It was a wrong interpretation of guidelines, a sincere mistake.'[2]

Rabin, Peres and Shamir were successful in suppressing any notion that they knew of Pollard in advance or that they had given the green light to his operation. During the winter of 1987 Pollard was sentenced to life for his crime; his wife got five years for assisting him. Though the Israeli government resisted efforts to appoint a commission of inquiry, a subcommittee of the Knesset's Foreign Affairs and Defence Committee that dealt with covert matters began its own inquiry. Abba Eban, the chairman of the overall Knesset Foreign Affairs and Defence Committee, headed the inquiry. In its report, issued on 28 May, 1987, the Eban committee uttered some harsh words about Rabin's behaviour.

'[Rabin] served in the post [of defence minister] for 14 months of the Pollard affair, so that he had ample opportunity to take note of phenomena which should have caused him concern. For during that period, particularly sensitive intelligence material arrived at a growing pace. Had Rabin exercised appropriate supervision over the activity of the [Scientific Liaison Unit] he would of necessity have noted the grave significance of this material.

'Nevertheless, Rabin evinced no effort to maintain procedures of scrutiny or to tighten control, as he was duty-bound to do. During his term of office, the Pollard affair became a protracted phenomenon without Rabin being aware that the source was Pollard. . . . The burden of ministerial responsibility devolving on him is beyond any doubt.'

Here was an Israeli Knesset committee charging, however vaguely, that Rabin, as defence minister, should have known what was going on within the intelligence sphere, should have sensed that a Jonathan Pollard was operating in a way that could embarrass the Israeli Government in its relations with the US. The committee's clout was limited and Rabin was able to dismiss its findings easily. Rabin stressed that the Eban committee had accepted the conclusions of another committee (Rotenstreich-Tsur) which had found that responsibility for the Pollard affair mishaps belonged to the entire Cabinet and absolved Rabin (and Peres) of individual ministerial resonsibility.

In time, the Palestinian issue became the dominant item on Defence Minister Rabin's agenda but not by his personal choice.

Rabin had generally attached little importance to the Palestinian Arabs who inhabited the West Bank and the Gaza Strip. He may have pitied them for their plight; he felt, however, no strong attachment to them. Ephraim Sneh, the head of the Israeli civil administration for the West Bank in the 1980s and currently a Labour Party Knesset member, 'couldn't detect any emotions on Rabin's part toward the Palestinians, not positive, not negative.'[3] Though Palestinian Arabs showed respect for Rabin, they exuded none of the warmth they had felt toward a previous defence minister, Moshe Dayan. For his part, Rabin had trouble getting close to the Palestinians. Conversation did not come easily. And yet, he was in charge of their lives — at least for the time being.

Unbeknownst to him, and to most others, the ground was rumbling under the defence minister's feet.

From the mid-1970s, the Palestinians had succeeded in placing themselves high on the international agenda. Promised full autonomy as part of the Camp David accords in September 1978, the Arab inhabitants of the West Bank and the Gaza Strip felt obliged to resist that 'gift'. They wanted a state of their own. Israel, however, was not prepared to give them one.

For that reason, the Palestinians refused to attend the first round of autonomy negotiations. After the Israel–Egypt Peace Treaty was signed in March 1979, Israelis, Egyptians, and Americans met on a continuing basis in Egypt and in Israel in an effort to establish autonomy for the Palestinians. With the Palestinians boycotting the talks, little progress was made. It hardly mattered. By the summer of 1982 the war in Lebanon put an end to those negotiations. As long as Israel was trying to wipe out the PLO in Lebanon, it was unthinkable for Egypt to remain at the autonomy talks. And so the Palestinian issue festered. By 1987 the Palestinians had grown deeply resentful that the international community had all but forgotten their plight. Their own Arab brethren demonstrated little enthusiasm for their cause as well. Moreover, it bothered the Palestinians enormously that twenty years of Israeli occupation had forced them to adopt Israeli habits, buy Israeli products, wear Israeli clothes, even speak Hebrew. They wanted to be free of Israel so that they could try to forge their own national institutions and character.

Without weapons to foment major acts of violence against the Israelis, the Palestinians sensed correctly that they would have to use their wits, and their numbers — and they would have to catch the Israelis off guard. It would not be easy, for the Israelis had the arms. Though what happened in December 1987 appeared organized and orchestrated, it was not. The anger and violence and mass demonstrations were spontaneous, though they had their roots in the years of impatient waiting. The spark that brought the explosion came one afternoon when an Israeli truck crashed into two carloads of Arab workers, killing four of them. Two days earlier an Israeli had been stabbed to death in the central market in the town of Gaza. The word on the Palestinian street was that this was no car accident, that a relative of the stabbed man had deliberately driven the truck into these Palestinians. Thousands of mourners returned from the funerals of the four men killed early in the evening. Reaching an IDF outpost at the refugee camp, they hurled bottles and stones at the soldiers who fired shots in the air to no avail. The angry crowd moved through the camp. No routine demonstration that fizzled out after an hour or so, it lasted well past 11 pm. The next day schools and shops were closed. In those first two days of rioting Israeli soldiers killed two Arab youths. There was nothing unusual in that. Or so it seemed.

What was extraordinary was the speed with which the Palestinian violence spread. Later that week, 50 miles away in the Balata refugee camp in the West Bank town of Nablus, an enraged crowd of nearly 3,000 Palestinians, mostly women and children, threw stones at Israeli border police. A barrage of rubber bullets failed to stop the mob. Israeli soldiers used tear gas and live bullets. Four protesters were killed, another 30 wounded.

The Palestinian uprising had begun in earnest.

At first the Israelis mistakenly thought the Palestinians were up to their old tricks, a few unruly demonstrations, then back to their routine quiet. The scale and intensity of these riots, however, were different, larger and more ferocious than anything seen in the occupied territories since 1967. In the past, such riots were isolated affairs, with a few hundred people participating. Now, thousands turned out, and it became clear that they had the support of thousands more back home. Those who did not demonstrate, closed their shops and remained at home.

No one seemed more caught off guard by the Palestinian rioting than Defence Minister Yitzhak Rabin. When the first demonstrations occurred, Rabin huddled with his senior aides to decide whether to go ahead with a planned visit to the United States. They could find no good reason. Two Israeli journalists, in their book on the Palestinian uprising, noted: 'The total insouciance in face of the renewed violence in Gaza was striking, almost startling.'[4] Not really. To Rabin and his chief aides, the demonstrations were no different from the kind that had occurred in the occupied territories for the past two decades; they would surely die down in a few days.

And so, the day after the uprising erupted, Yitzhak Rabin went off to the United States. It was an important journey since Rabin was to sign a memorandum of understanding on the sale of Israeli-manufactured equipment to the American government. He was also to agree on the final price for seventy F-16 fighter planes. Visits to American military installations were scheduled as was a speech before an Israel Bonds convention in Florida.

Once in Washington, Rabin was pleased to find that the trouble back home did not monopolize his conversations with American officials. The defence secretary, Frank Carlucci, barely touched on the subject. The new national security adviser to the president, General Colin Powell, said that he had 'seen something' on the news about the disturbances. That evening, however, brought shocking news from the new front.

Television footage on the nightly American news showed Israeli soldiers shooting at rock-throwing Palestinian demonstrators. The following morning American newspapers displayed dramatic pictures of Israeli soldiers kicking Palestinians outside a hospital. The unrest that Palestinians were now calling 'the Intifada' could not be ignored. It became the Number One topic of every American official Rabin encountered.

He began to feel uneasy. Should he return home? Was his presence in America so important that he should leave the control of these riots to others? He could be in telephone contact with the chief of staff, but was that good enough?

Believing that his sudden return would present the Palestinians with an unjustified victory, the defence minister and his entourage seemed to act as if the rioting in the Gaza Strip was taking place on a different planet, not in their back yard. Rabin's advisers thought it safe for him to remain in the US. No one in Israel was pressing him to return. The Americans did not seem overly alarmed. Rabin went ahead and signed the memorandum of understanding with Defence Secretary Carlucci on 14 December. The defence minister then set off for a visit to an F-16 squadron and two combat-helicopter squadrons. Before that excursion, Rabin's spokesman, Eitan Haber, asked the director of Israel Bonds, Yehudah Halevy, how the Bonds audience would react if Rabin had to abruptly cancel his speech.

'If it's due to a military problem, we'll find a satisfactory explanation. Such things have happened before,' said Halevy.[5]

Haber knew all too well this was no 'military problem'. It was just a few youngsters tossing some stones.

Meanwhile, in Israel, Prime Minister Shamir and Chief of Staff Dan Shomron were reacting slowly to events. They too wanted to believe that the disturbances were temporary. To have decided on beefing up forces in the Gaza Strip would have been an admission that something serious was occurring there. Eventually Shomron, after daily telephone consultations with Rabin, decided to increase the number of troops on patrol in Gaza; those patrols were built up to more defensible sizes (15 soldiers each). In order to protect traffic on the main roads from stone-throwing and the tossing of Molotov cocktails, Shomron pulled foot patrols out of the refugee camps and placed them on those main roads. The patrols, now under the command of more senior officers, were equipped with anti-riot gear, including riot helmets, shields, rubber bullets and water cannon.

All of this was designed to minimize the soldiers' use of live ammunition. The mounting number of Palestinian fatalities from such shooting incidents underscored the IDF's inability to cope with events. The seemingly indiscriminate shooting, when screened on American television, brought Israel's image to a new low. Rabin and Shomron kept the refugee camps open and let Palestinian Arabs continue to travel to Israel proper each day to work. Curfews were shunned as well. The two men hoped to isolate the demonstrators from what they perceived to be the silent majority. The theory went that this 'silent majority' despised the rioters and wanted only to lead a normal life. The theory sounded good back at the Tel Aviv military command and among Rabin's entourage in the US. It had little to do with reality.

The new Rabin–Shomron strategy increased the number of IDF soldiers in the Gaza Strip to three times the normal complement. Now elite infantry brigades were patrolling the place. For a few days the approach appeared to work. The number of demonstrations slackened. No Palestinian Arabs were killed. Believing that indeed the week-long protests were no different from past ones, the optimists in Israel argued that order would be restored in a few days. A week later — on 21 December — all hell broke loose again. Now it was the turn of Israeli Arabs. Long a passive partner in the struggle of their Palestinian brethren in the occupied territories, this time the Israeli Arabs insisted on joining the fight. In Nazareth, 4,000 youngsters ran amok in the streets, hurling debris at Israeli soldiers. The violence spread to other Israeli Arab towns and villages. Some 170,000 Israeli Arabs refused to go to work (as did 80,000 Palestinian Arabs from the territories). The Rabin–Shomron strategy was not working.

Months later, when analysts developed some perspective on the early days of the Intifada, it became popular to argue that Israel might have taken steps at the very incipient stages of the rebellion that would have prevented it from worsening. Rabin might have returned from the United States immediately. Shomron might have sent reinforcements into Gaza at once.

The territories might have been closed off to the media. The harsh truth for Israel, however, was that none of this would have changed the seething frustration that existed among Palestinian Arabs. The most such actions might have accomplished would have been to postpone the inevitable.

One strong indication of the disarray among Israeli leaders at the time was the attempt to lay the blame for the unrest on outside elements. For years Israelis had convinced themselves that local Palestinian Arabs did nothing on their own, that only when marching orders came from the PLO or others did the local Palestinians act. To Shamir, the acting minister of defence, the PLO was behind the demonstrations. To Rabin, Syria and Iran were the culprits. No one bothered to ask whether this time the unrest might be self-starting, whether the PLO, Syrians, and Iranians were as out of touch with events on the West Bank and in the Gaza Strip as the Israelis had been. No one bothered to check whether the local Palestinian Arabs had not taken matters into their own hands. The question of whether the local Palestinians had initiated the Intifada was not considered relevant. It should have been.

When he returned to Israel on 21 December, Defence Minister Rabin was asked by a reporter whether he felt he should have returned to Israel sooner. His answer was no, but he sounded defensive: 'I was of the opinion that no one could replace me in the US, while in Israel there is the IDF general staff and the chief of staff, and I have the utmost faith in them and their ability to deal with these issues. And, as is known, the prime minister agreed to my proposal that he take charge of the defence portfolio, and I am sure of his ability.' It was an odd way of justifying his absence. At that moment, however, Rabin was still under the illusion that nothing of great significance had happened in the occupied territories. In the coming days he would learn how wrong he had been. Then, he acknowledged that it would have been wiser to return from the US earlier.

At that airport press conference, Rabin still spoke as if the demonstrations were sporadic outbursts of violence, and not the symbol of a much deeper, more widespread sense of bitterness and outrage. He insisted that Israel would not allow the Palestinians to think they could achieve political gains through violence. 'They won't obtain a single thing via the threat of war, terrorism, or violent disturbances. Therefore, the main problem at present is to enforce order, with all the sorrow and pain over loss of life on the Arab side. Whoever goes to violent demonstrations is placing himself in grave danger.'

It was a theme that Rabin would return to often, but one that missed the point of what was happening in the refugee camps and elsewhere in the territories. It was not that a handful of Palestinians had decided to throw stones. It was that the entire West Bank and Gaza Strip had symbolically joined in the stone-throwing. What Rabin and other Israeli leaders refused to accept in those early days of the Intifada was that the violence was something other than the work of a few extremists. If it had been, the obvious response for Israel would have been to seek to restore order, and not try to deal with the more fundamental problems smouldering in the Palestinian Arab community.

Even if he had wanted to deal with those problems, Rabin had no quick, magic answer. Some Israelis favoured annexing the territories while others thought the IDF should withdraw unilaterally. Rabin opposed both views. The only feasible Israeli option was to continue to occupy the region until a political settlement could be achieved. He was against giving the Palestinian a state; but he was prepared to return as much as two-thirds of the occupied lands to Jordan. Such political solutions seemed remote. The immediate question for Israel in December 1987 was how to quell the Intifada.

All Rabin could offer at the outset was meeting violence with violence, a policy that helped the Palestinian cause. When Rabin threatened the Palestinians with a more intense military response if they continued their disorders, he was inadvertently playing into their hands. What the Palestinians wanted, indeed needed, was to bring their 'case' before the international community. A mob of unruly Palestinians marching through the streets of Ramallah or Gaza was not enough to win time on the US nightly news; but, as long as Israeli soldiers fired live ammunition, or even bullets, into Palestinian crowds, Dan Rather and Peter Jennings were bound to pay attention. For, the truth was that every Palestinian fatality gave the Intifada more impetus, more drama, and made it a bigger, better news story.

So caught by surprise were the Israelis that their soldiers were given little choice but to fire live ammunition indiscriminately into Palestinian crowds. At first there seemed little that Rabin and the IDF could do to stop the killings. For Israeli troops had been placed in the most disadvantageous position. Without the proper anti-riot equipment, Israeli soldiers turned to live ammunition as a first resort when faced with the presence of hundreds of thousands of Palestinian demonstrators, many of whom were throwing rocks their way. Israeli leaders, including Rabin, found themselves defending this practice, and that only reinforced the image of an Israel that had lost control of the situation in the territories. 'Whenever there is clear cut danger to our troops, they have orders to use live ammunition,' Rabin said, never acknowledging that it might be possible to curb rioters without resort to live ammunition. The impression gained abroad, meanwhile, was that Rabin and most other Israeli leaders were unrepentant about the continual killing of Palestinian Arabs. Some 17 Palestinian Arabs died and 100 more were wounded during those first two weeks of unrest.

To Rabin, the Palestinian disorders, while unpleasant, did not challenge the IDF to the same degree as had Israel's past wars. Rabin had fought in two wars — in 1948 and 1967 — that were definite threats to the nation's existence. He had monitored the 1973 Yom Kippur War and knew all too well how close Israel had come to being overrun by Arab armies. He felt no such concern with respect to the Intifada. His wife Leah Rabin said, 'He used to say, "We've had our challenges, the Intifada is not one of them." He was very frustrated but for someone who had gone through the big scare of the Six-Day War or the 1948 war, this experience [the Intifada] didn't present a threat. Only an embarrassment for Israeli soldiers. So he wasn't really that disturbed by it. It wasn't that he didn't sleep at night.'[6]

Throughout the early phases of the Intifada, no television camera caught an Israeli soldier killing a Palestinian rioter. It made no difference. The cameras recorded enough live fire poured on those rock-throwing crowds to bring critics to their feet. At first, Rabin dismissed the critics. When he appeared in the Knesset on 23 December, he asserted that Israel would not shift tactics. Israeli marksmen would continue to try to pick off leaders of the violence. 'They can shoot to hit leaders of disorder, throwers of firebombs, as much as possible at legs, after firing in the air failed to disperse the riot. As Defence Minister, I have responsibility for the lives and safety of the soldiers and Border Police, and it is my duty to give them the means to protect themselves . . . to hurt those out to hurt them.'

To hurt Palestinian Arabs, he meant. This phrase and others he would make gave Yitzhak Rabin a more visible image of Mr Tough Guy. It fell to him to be the Bad Cop.

Though Rabin tried to be consistent in his handling of the Intifada, a whole battery of military steps were tried, none working very effectively. The Intifada would not go away. The situation reached explosive proportions soon after 1 January, 1988 when the Israeli cabinet accepted Rabin's recommendation to expel nine of the main Intifada leaders from Israel, five from the Gaza Strip and four from the West Bank. The Palestinians reacted with even greater violence. In response, Rabin and the IDF's supreme command conceived yet a new strategy for defeating the Intifada, the third in five weeks. This time, there would be no silk gloves. It was decided that as long as there was no law and order in the territories, there would be no normal life for the residents. The main target was the refugee camps in the Gaza Strip and some of the other trouble-spots in the West Bank. Collective punishment and extensive curfews were introduced.

Despite the tough measures, Rabin was growing increasingly frustrated at their ineffectiveness. He was slowly coming to realize that the unrest was no passing phenomenon, that something far more deeply rooted was occurring in the territories. The uprising was not the brainchild of Iran, or Syria, or the PLO, or just a bunch of terrorist troublemakers. Nor was it so isolated that the IDF's iron fist could stamp out the fury with one dramatic blow. No, said Rabin in mid-January, it would require an 'adjustment in our methods of action' to quell the unrest for it was of a 'different magnitude' from past trouble in the occupied areas. This time the unrest reflected genuine Palestinian despair at not being able to end Israeli rule. When the Intifada broke out, the defence minister talked of restoring 'tranquillity'. Now he said: 'It is a complicated and long drawn out affair that cannot be taken care of in a few days. Don't stand there with a stop watch.' Others agreed that the Intifada was complicated. All the more reason, they argued, for Israel not to pump live bullets into Palestinians. Rabin sought a way to reduce the killings — or eliminate them completely. His aim was noble. His thinking, however, was flawed. For the policy that he was about to offer in the place of shooting and killing Palestinians — a policy of using physical force rather than live ammunition — was no more palatable to outside critics.

And so Rabin produced a major public relations disaster for the State of Israel.

Rather than shoot at demonstrators, Rabin decided, the IDF should use physical force to subdue them. On the surface, the new policy seemed to have merit. The number of Palestinians shot dead would subside. With a cutback in the number of those killings, the headlines would lessen as well, and the Western media might get tired of the story. It was a nice thought. Rabin was convinced that the international community would stand up and applaud.

Had Rabin announced the policy publicly, questions undoubtedly would have been asked about his motivation. That he launched the policy in secret clouded the issue all the more. The questions did not stop coming: what had Rabin said precisely? What had he meant? It was taken for granted that the defence minister had advocated 'breaking their bones', a phrase he insisted he had never used. 'I never gave orders to break bones,' the defence minister told the Knesset on 12 July, 1990 when a proposal was made for a commission of inquiry into the responsibility of the political echelon for IDF abuses during the Intifada. 'The decision was mine and I bear full responsibility for it,' Rabin said. 'To the best of my recollection, at no time and in no place did I ever say "break bones".'

Perhaps not. He used strong language. That much is certain. On 12 January he told the IDF officers in Gaza: 'Be more aggressive, but not with rifles. Beat them during a demonstration, but not otherwise.' A week later, facing angry Palestinian residents in the West Bank refugee camp of Jelazoun, Rabin declared that violent demonstrations should be prevented with 'force, power and blows. The first priority is to prevent violence in whatever form it takes, and by force, not by fire.' On 25 January, 1988 he told senior officers: 'Use force during the course of the operation, whether it's coping with a demonstration, or breaking up a roadblock, or dispersing and chasing stone-throwers. But don't beat people in order to get them to open up shops, because business strikes don't constitute violence.' Three days later he told West Bank commanders: 'Where violence erupts, I favour the use of force, but it should not degenerate into sadism and vandalism.'

Whether he used the phrase 'break their bones' in private discussions or not, the fact was that Rabin appeared to be saying as much in public. The effect on local IDF commanders in the West Bank and the Gaza Strip was devastating. They had a hard time understanding precisely what he meant for them to do. But this much they understood: beating up Palestinians was now accepted IDF policy. Rarely did a television camera show an IDF soldier beating a Palestinian Arab to a pulp, but word quickly spread that this was precisely what was happening.

Critics abroad were dismayed. Jacob Stein, a former chairman of the Conference of Presidents of Major American Jewish Organizations, noted sadly: 'While I recognize the need for civil order, I am rather appalled by the reports of random beatings of Palestinians. I can only hope that a more humane and effective way can be devised to deal with these disorders.'[7] The former editor of the *New York Times* and later a *Times* columnist, A. M. Rosenthal, had always been an unstinting supporter of Israel. When he learned of the beatings, he called upon Rabin to resign. 'The Israeli government seems to be edging away from the policy of beating. But more is needed by Israel and for Israel. Mr Rabin can restore his stature and Israel's by resigning. Then Israel can be itself again: a nation with a right to a vision, a right even to be wrong sometimes and to act in self-interest, strong in battle and strong in decency. Jews must not break bones. This is the message that must come from the friends of Israel.'

Such behaviour on the part of IDF soldiers created the impression that Yitzhak Rabin was a brutal, cruel leader who took joy in the pain his army had inflicted on Palestinians. Ephraim Sneh, the former head of the Israeli civil administration for the West Bank, disputed such claims. 'Rabin is not fond of the Arabs but he doesn't despise or hate them. He's not a brutal man. The image was that he enjoyed breaking bones but it's not true.'[8]

One reason Rabin's policy was so misunderstood, by outsiders as well as by Israeli soldiers, was Rabin himself. He may have thought he was being clear in articulating his beatings policy; few others did. He may have wanted to sound compassionate — better to beat someone up than kill them. Yet he wound up sounding more heartless, not less. Take as an example his comments on 27 September, 1988 explaining why the IDF used plastic bullets against Palestinian rioters. Rather than accentuate the non-lethal effects of plastic bullets, he suggested that the move behind using those plastic bullets was to increase injuries. 'Our purpose is to increase the number of [wounded] among those who take part in violent activities, but not to kill them,' he told a press conference at Bet El military headquarters on the West Bank. 'I am not worried by the increased number of people who got wounded, as long as they were wounded as a result of being involved actively, by instigating, organizing and taking part in violent activities. The rioters are suffering more casualties. That is precisely our aim.'[9]

In time, Rabin began to realize that to the international community, beating Palestinians up was just as offensive as shooting them with live ammunition. To an Israel Television reporter on 10 March, he admitted: 'I had believed that shooting would appear much worse in international public opinion than the use of the . . . riot baton. And I was surprised to discover that the sensitivity of world opinion to blows and physical confrontation was greater than to that of shooting.'

Such thoughts were leading Rabin to think much more seriously about what was transpiring in the occupied areas — both to the Palestinians and to the Israeli army. It bothered him that Palestinians were being killed and being beaten up. It bothered him even more that Israel soldiers were the instrument for this bloodshed. He thought it his responsibility as defence minister to find a way out of this mess.

By February 1988, with the Intifada only a few months old, Rabin was moving towards the view that, however much force Israel used against the Palestinians, that would not end the conflict. The Palestinians had got their message across to him and it had not taken long. What was happening in the occupied territories was not, Rabin insisted, a civil war: the Israelis and Palestinians were not one people torn apart (like the American north and south in their Civil War). Rather, Israel was involved in a confrontation between two national entities. On 2 February, Rabin predicted to the Knesset Foreign Affairs and Defence Committee that the unrest would last for 'months to come'. He had no choice but to keep the situation from getting out of hand and plan for the future with a combination of 'perseverance, patience and the conviction that we are in the right'. Being convinced that Israel was in the right, however, did not help bring about a political solution.

Rabin understood this, for on 21 February he acknowledged that the disturbances had taught him important lessons. To a group of Labour Party activists in Tel Aviv, Rabin said: 'I've learned something in the past two and a half months. Among other things that you can't rule by force over one and a half million Palestinians.' He gave an example: earlier in the Intifada he had approved opening the shops of Palestinian merchants by force. 'We learned that it didn't work.' The shops stayed open because, Rabin noted, 'The radicals know that if they close them down, there really won't be any food.' What then should be done about the Palestinian Arabs? Rabin ruled out annexing the occupied territories. 'What would we do with all the Palestinians?' he asked his audience. Why not transfer them elsewhere? some asked. No good, said Rabin: 'Transfer so far has only been done to Jews, we should not forget that. If we make [Palestinian Arabs] citizens, they will have 25 to 30 seats in the Knesset. If we don't, we shall be a racist state, not a Jewish one.'

Such dilemmas cast a shadow over Israel's handling of the Intifada. Perhaps the simple truth was that the IDF had lost control over events in the territories. Rabin was asked whether this was true in a 9 March Israel Television interview.

He replied that Israel had endured the War of Attrition in the late 1960s for 1,000 days, suffering numerous casualties. No immediate solution had cropped up at the start of that war. Israel had been bogged down in Lebanon for three years. Again, no solution emerged at an early stage that would have ended Israel's involvement in that war. As for the Intifada: 'After three months we are facing a problem of a kind with which we haven't previous experience. It is the problem of violence on the part of a large population which is under our control, which is acting not in the framework of terrorism . . . with the possible exception of Molotov cocktails . . . It is far easier to solve classic military problems. It is far more difficult to contend with 1.4 million Palestinians living in the territories who are employing, so it transpires, systematic violence without weapons, and who do not want our rule. Our objective . . . is to bring about a calming, not a solution. Moreover, the matter is continuing because in handling an entire population we cannot use the IDF's principal weapons [the air force, armoured corps, and artillery] . . . at most, IDF soldiers are permitted to use their guns . . . and this takes time.

'The problem would be much simpler if all the territory was Arab territory, void of any Jewish settlements. It would be very simple to close off the area, not to have to handle problems of keeping transportation lines open, to focus on problems with the populace in the large population centres . . . There are 450 villages in Judea and Samaria: the IDF cannot be in every place at once.'

The Intifada had not altered Rabin's thinking about the kind of political solution he preferred. The unrest had, however, given him a greater sensitivity to the depth of feeling that existed among the Palestinian Arab community. On 17 March, 1988, before an audience of high school students in Jerusalem, he outlined his thoughts about the kind of peace he wanted: 'I am opposed to a Palestinian PLO state between Israel and Jordan. Since I am totally opposed to this, I am also totally opposed to negotiations with the PLO. I oppose, under any circumstances, withdrawing to the 1967 borders; [I support] the preservation of Greater Jerusalem, united, under Israeli sovereignty and serving as its capital — its eternal capital; maintaining the Jordan River as the security border. . . . The main thing is [maintaining] the Jerusalem area, Gush Etzion, the Jordan Valley. . . . At the same time, [I support] a readiness to return — within the framework of peace — the densely populated Palestinian areas to a foreign sovereignty, to Jordan. I am against uprooting settlements. I support, under an agreement, allowing Jewish settlements to continue as Israeli settlements even under foreign sovereignty, just as that portion of the territories which will remain under Israeli sovereignty — and in which there will be Palestinians with Jordanian citizenship —

will be offered Israeli citizenship, or will be allowed to maintain their Jordanian citizenship. . . .' While he had been painted as a bully and a monster since the Intifada, Rabin had not hardened his political positions. He could have made that speech in the 1970s or early in the 1980s. He still refused to concede Jerusalem; and he did not favour uprooting Jewish settlements. But, his conclusion after watching the Palestinian Arabs assert themselves over the past few months was still to favour territorial compromise. The Palestinians had not succeeded in softening Rabin's political views: he still opposed a Palestinian state; still refused to deal with the PLO. But, in saying that he would return territory to them, he opened the door to a political solution that could provide the Palestinians with an independent entity. For the Palestinians, this may have been the greatest achievement of the Intifada, given the fact that four years later, Rabin would become prime minister.

One of Rabin's cardinal principles had always been a refusal to negotiate with the PLO. Even on this point he appeared to be softening. In the spring of 1988 Rabin said publicly on US Television that he was prepared to negotiate with PLO officials under certain conditions. Although he was not saying he was now ready to talk with the PLO, by suggesting that he did not rule out talking to the PLO if it altered its character, he at least demonstrated in one important way how he differed from Yitzhak Shamir and the Likud's rigid thinking. Shamir and other hardline Likud leaders had always said they would never deal with the PLO under any circumstances. Appearing on Ted Koppel's 'Nightline', Rabin said he would be prepared to negotiate with any PLO official who renounced the Palestine National Covenant, accepted UN Security Council Resolutions 242 and 338, and stopped acts of terror. 'Allow me to say,' Rabin told Koppel, 'that if you get an announcement by any Palestinian who belongs to the PLO that, first and foremost, he renounces the Palestinian covenant; that he is ready to accept Resolutions 242 and 338, not in the context of the [UN] General Assembly resolutions; and that he is ready to stop violence and terror — with any Palestinian that will come up with this statement, I am ready to negotiate.'[10]

However unpopular Rabin was abroad, he had little to worry about at home. The Intifada had embittered many Israeli families when fathers and sons had been forced into killing and beating up Palestinians. That bitterness, however, was not directed against Rabin. On 6 to 10 March, 1988, the Pori Institute interviewed 1,200 Israelis and found that the defence minister was the most popular Israeli senior government minister. His prestige had increased since the Intifada. A total of 58.1 per cent of Israelis were satisfied with Rabin's performance as defence minister, compared with 50.9 per cent in December 1987, a 7.2 per cent increase. Foreign Minister Shimon Peres' popularity, meanwhile, had dropped 6.5 per cent, from 44.3 per cent in December to 37.8 per cent in March. As for Prime Minister Shamir, he had become only slightly more popular since the Intifada, moving from 29.3 per cent in December to 32 per cent in March. While Israelis did not appreciate the turmoil and suffering, they supported Rabin's tough stance toward the Palestinians. Peres, the dove, was losing popular support, while Rabin, the hawk, was gaining. Among the minority political left, Rabin was called all sorts of nasty names, including war criminal. Clearly, however, the majority backed Rabin.

Israelis responded favourably as well to Rabin's willingness to be held accountable for the Government's policy towards the Intifada. This was in sharp contrast with the attitude of other Israeli defence ministers who, when the going got tough, sought to diffuse and shirk responsibility. At the height of criticism against Israel during the war in Lebanon, the then defence minister, Ariel Sharon, said lamely that he had been acting with the full knowledge of the Israeli prime minister. After Israeli soldiers had been surprised by Arab forces at the start of the 1973 Yom Kippur War, the then defence minister, Moshe Dayan, insisted that he was only supplying 'ministerial advice' to the IDF, nothing more. Rabin behaved differently during the Intifada. With Israel's image abroad slipping disastrously, he did not try to fob off responsibility on Prime Minister Shamir or on the Israeli Cabinet in its entirety. His willingness to take responsibility could easily have boomeranged: Israelis could well have held the whole frustrating affair of the Intifada against him; instead Rabin, who had been a symbol of Israel's hardline policies in the territories, reaped the benefit of those policies. Israelis were saying: we may not like everything Mr Rabin is doing, but he is not trying to hide when things get too hot.

Rabin's behaviour gave him much prestige among tough-minded Israelis who would have a chance to show their appreciation a few years later.

Against whom was the Intifada directed?

Yitzhak Shamir? He was unquestionably the right address. Yet, he was hard-as-nails and gave the clear impression that he had no time for Palestinians. He left no doubt that he had no inclination to grant them autonomy or any political representation. Yet, even when Shamir sounded as though he was prepared to make a deal with the Palestinians, as was the case in the spring of 1989, no one quite believed him. The Palestinians, however, were hungry for a political settlement. They did not want to see their Intifada go to waste. As long as Shamir was prime minister, however, they had little chance of making political gains.

While they were waiting impatiently for the Israelis to see the light, changes were occurring in the mind of one Israeli leader, changes that would have vast significance for peacemaking. Call it the political enlightenment of Yitzhak Rabin.

The Intifada had the most sobering effect on Rabin, convincing him that the Palestinians in the occupied territories should be treated as political equals, should be entitled to a political solution. To a group of correspondents who covered the occupied areas, Rabin acknowledged that 'as defence minister, it took me time until I understood the Intifada as a phenomenon and the willingness of Palestinians to persist with it. Until the Intifada broke out, Israel had not experienced such a comprehensive case of authentic popular uprising.' Rabin added that only after about six months did he realize that it was impossible to bring the Intifada to an end solely through force. A political solution was necessary.

That was no small change of mind. Until the Intifada, Rabin (and other Israeli leaders as well) were against talking to any Palestinians. Prior to the uprising, Rabin and other senior Labour Party politicians advocated the 'Jordanian Option', which called for a return of substantial portions of the West Bank to Jordan in return for a peace treaty. When Peres became prime minister in September 1984, he actively sought such an accord with Jordan's King Hussein. Peres and the king met frequently over the next two years, with Rabin attending a number of the meetings. One official who has worked with Rabin over the years explained: 'Rabin was a partner to the meetings with the king even if he didn't attend all of the meetings. He was involved.' By April 1987 the so-called 'London Agreement' had been carved out, calling for an international peace conference to settle the Arab–Israeli conflict. With Peres and Rabin behind the London Agreement, it seemed only natural that the Jordanian Option would be promoted once again. The trouble with all of Peres' (and Rabin's) efforts, however, was that the Jordanian Option had long been a dead issue. In the early 1970s it seemed reasonable to advocate turning over most of the West Bank to King Hussein. A great deal had happened and, by the late 1980s, the king's position on the West Bank was greatly weakened.

Throughout this pre-Intifada period, Rabin and other Israeli political leaders saw no purpose in holding political talks with Palestinian Arabs on the West Bank or in the Gaza Strip. Israel would not talk with the PLO. And there was just no point in talking to the local inhabitants who, at any rate, claimed to be mere mouthpieces for the PLO or, less so, for the king. 'We have to talk with them,' Rabin would say, 'but they're not partners.' In other words: it was necessary to talk to them about the conduct of their daily lives, but they were not the right people with whom to work out final political arrangements. 'They deposited their authority in Tunis with the PLO or in Amman with the king,' Rabin said. 'They're simply the mailman. If I need to talk with someone, I'll talk with the king.'

Then in December 1987 the local Palestinians rose up, hoodwinking the PLO who could not take credit for an event that surprised them totally; and arrogating to themselves fresh self-confidence. Rabin and the Israelis took notice. 'What changed Rabin's attitude,' recalled Ephraim Sneh, 'was the fact that the Intifada moved the centre of political gravity to the occupied territories. Through their struggle, the Palestinians became partners.'[11] Recognizing that change, Rabin was now prepared to put the local Palestinians to the test.

To accelerate peacemaking with local Palestinians, Rabin had to jettison his conviction that the Intifada must end before political talks could start. He began in May 1988 to hold secret meetings with Palestinians from the West Bank and the Gaza Strip. A way had to be found to build up a local Palestinian Arab leadership that had sufficient political authority to conduct negotiations for the entire Palestinian Arab population on the West Bank and in the Gaza Strip. The means suggested was elections. Those people who were elected would be able to claim that they had the backing of the population to do business with the Israelis. One of the central issues of Rabin's secret talks was what kind of elections should the Palestinians hold. Rabin had favoured municipal elections, fearing that general elections would provide a means for the PLO to gain a greater foothold in the occupied territories. As a result of his secret talks, he changed his mind and now favoured holding general elections. (He may have been influenced by the fact that Peres favoured municipal elections.) 'Rabin thought municipal elections were too little now,' said Ephraim Sneh. 'He would say: "I want elections in order to build a partner for negotiation".'[12]

By early January 1989, Rabin intensified his peacemaking efforts, holding a series of low-key meetings in his Tel Aviv office with key Palestinian Arab figures from the territories. The identity of the Palestinian Arabs was kept secret. Both the Israelis and the Palestinians knew that it was far too early to publicize such talks. Unless and until the local Palestinians could clear the way with the PLO, the most likely result of such publicity would be a bullet for one or more of the Palestinian representatives. Rabin wanted to find out if it would be possible to engage these Palestinians in a dialogue without PLO involvement.

It was in early 1989 that Rabin unveiled his own peace plan focused around Palestinian elections. He spoke of a six-month moratorium on the Intifada as well as elections in the occupied areas to elect local Palestinians who would then negotiate with Israel the terms of an interim agreement. Though his proposals would eventually be swallowed up and co-opted by Yitzhak Shamir, Rabin had shown how far he had come from simply dealing with the Intifada through military means. 'Rabin showed courage,' said Bethlehem Mayor, Elias Friej.[13]

Rabin had the distinction of having his peace plan rejected by both the PLO and Yitzhak Shamir. On 23 January, 1989, Shamir told an Israel Television reporter: 'I do not consider that

I am in any way obliged to comment on this matter . . . I have been informed that all the Arab elements reject this plan. I would, therefore, not advise us — in Israel — to get embroiled in discussions on a notion which has no chance of being implemented.'

Prime Minister Shamir, however, reacting to heavy American pressure in Israel to negotiate an end to the Intifada, adopted the very plan he had rejected: in May 1989, he proposed limited elections in the Palestinian territories as a step toward Middle-East peace. To get the elections off the ground, American Secretary of State James Baker proposed a formula under which Egypt, Israel and the US would select Palestinian delegates for preliminary talks.

The Rabin and Shamir peace plans for the Palestinians differed most importantly over the issue of giving back Israel-held land. Rabin supported the principle of exchanging land for peace; Shamir did not. They disagreed over tactics as well. Shamir was adamantly against PLO involvement in the peace talks. Rabin made it clear that he was prepared for Egypt to draw up a list of Palestinians who would then decide on the election rules. It did not bother Rabin that Egypt planned to consult with the PLO. Mubarak, Rabin said, had the right to consult with whomever he wished. With Shamir in charge, however, the peace process had little chance of moving forward. Meeting with President Bush at the White House in April 1989, Shamir gave the distinct impression that implementing his own peace plan was the last thing in his mind. In June, Shamir's own Likud Central Committee had sought to tie the prime minister's hands by laying down pre-conditions for negotiations with the Palestinians and other Arabs: there could be no Palestinian state; no PLO participation in peace talks; no Palestinian living in East Jerusalem could represent the Palestinians in the peace talks; and negotiations could start only after the Intifada ceased.

In September 1989 Egypt's President Mubarak invited Rabin to Cairo to discuss the peace process. The Egyptian President appeared to believe that Rabin could sway Shamir. To some extent, this appeared true. Certainly, if Rabin disagreed adamantly enough about Shamir's peace proposals, he appeared strong enough to force Labour to leave the National Unity Government. That could have set in motion another Rabin attempt to grab the party leadership from Shimon Peres. Yet Rabin sounded very much as if he preferred to remain defence minister inside a Shamir-led government than risk a process that could result in Peres taking over the prime ministership. In an interview with the author (for *Time* Magazine) in October 1989, Rabin spoke at length about the peace initiative: 'I believe that we are on a course towards a beginning of a dialogue. I can't say that there is more than an opening for moving ahead with the issue that will make or break the whole [Israeli] peace initiative — finding a Palestinian partner with whom we can start the process as described in our peace initiative.'

Did he think Israel was getting ready to talk to the PLO, 'By no means, no.' Israel, he said, regarded the Palestinian inhabitants of the West Bank and Gaza as the proper source for a Palestinian delegation because they 'lead in the struggle of the Palestinian case and suffer for that, not Arafat's gang in the villas of Tunisia'. Rabin exhibited no great appetite for leaving the Government. 'I'll try my best [to keep the Government intact]. The policy of most of my Labour Party colleagues is to do everything to . . . move ahead with the Government's peace initiative.' However he hinted that at some stage he might consider a Labour walkout. 'Policy is not an academic issue alone. Policy has to be measured by the way it succeeded in being implemented. The implementation of a policy is its test.'[14]

Implementation seemed far off. Prime Minister Shamir went through the motions of a meeting with President Bush at the White House again in November 1989 with no real progress in the peace process. It was no wonder. Shamir had permitted the establishment of a Jewish settlement called Dugit in the Gaza Strip. Stunned, the President believed that Shamir had betrayed his trust. For years, the US Government had made clear its opposition to Jewish settlement in the occupied territories, calling these settlements illegal and an obstacle to peace. The Shamir Government, however, exhibited no constraint in its settlement policies, knowing full well that this would antagonize both the Arabs and the Americans.

Expanding Jewish settlements was, in Washington's eyes at least, the most solid evidence possible that the Shamir Government was not interested in advancing the peace process.

Yet matters grew worse in January 1990 when Shamir declared that a 'big aliyah (immigration) needs a big Israel'. That statement and others from within the Shamir Government encouraged the United States to believe that Israel planned to enlarge its Jewish settlement programme, populating the settlements with as many of the newly arrived Russian Jews as possible. In late February, President Bush phoned Shamir and received assurances that Russian immigrants were not being given any material incentives to settle in the territories. Shamir insisted that no more than 1 per cent of the Russian immigrants were reaching the West Bank. (Aides to President Bush meanwhile were putting out a figure closer to 10 per cent, but they were counting Jerusalem suburbs in Israel proper; the US considered those suburbs in occupied territory while Israel did not.) Bush did not seem satisfied and so, in a pique, Shamir rejected American Secretary of State Baker's proposals for peace talks with the Palestinians.

Shamir's growing intransigence would soon provide a new confrontation with the United States. That confrontation would provide an opportunity for Yitzhak Rabin to take centre stage.

Chapter 12

Benefiting from a 'Smelly Exercise'

Yitzhak Rabin had emerged from the political wilderness. He had managed his country's defence policy through one of the most controversial periods of its history. Extricating the troops from Lebanon. Presiding over the Intifada. Rabin acquired from these two acts a reputation that had once belonged to Moshe Dayan: the country felt more comfortable with Yitzhak Rabin as minister of defence than anyone else. The title that Moshe Dayan had once carried — 'Mr Security' — now belonged to Rabin. He possessed a rare combination for an Israeli politician: the ability to convey toughness in dealing with Arab violence and a sincerity to strive for peace. It was that combination which appealed to Israelis.

Rabin grew more popular as Israelis grew less satisfied with the Shamir government, particularly its handling of Middle East peacemaking. Under Shamir the Unity Government had not functioned smoothly. (Many said it had not functioned!) Shamir and Peres had not seen eye to eye on advancing the peace process: Peres had wanted to swap land for peace; Shamir refused to yield territory. Ironically, it was a procedural point, how to choose the Palestinian delegates for the peace conference, that put the National Unity Government to its severest test.

By the spring of 1990, James Baker began a major effort to win agreement for a formula that would have Israel, Egypt and the United States choose those Palestinian delegates. Though it may have seemed mere procedure, how the delegates were chosen and which delegates would be permitted to attend the peace conference became fundamental issues.

Labour Party members were growing increasingly cynical

about Shamir. They doubted that he wanted to advance Middle East peacemaking. They sensed also that, if pushed by the US too hard, the prime minister would let the country decide who was right on this crucial issue — Likud or Labour — by advancing the date of elections scheduled for November 1992.

And indeed, by the spring of 1990, Washington was pressing Jerusalem to agree on the composition of the Palestinian delegation to the proposed peace talks. And Yitzhak Shamir was beginning to find ways to slow down the peace process: he objected to including any Palestinian who resided outside the Middle East or in East Jerusalem. Shamir feared that the presence of non-Middle East Palestinians in the delegation would lead to the Palestinians raising the 'right of return' to Israel proper at the peace conference. Shamir wanted to keep East Jerusalemites off the delegation for fear that their presence would be construed as Israeli acceptance of placing the fate of Jerusalem on the negotiating agenda. Secretary of State James Baker proposed a compromise that would enable a Palestinian who had been deported from the occupied territories and a West Bank resident with a second home in East Jerusalem to participate in a Palestinian delegation in Cairo. Shamir did not want any deportees, arguing that they were PLO-affiliated.

To his Labour Party rivals, Shamir's refusal to accede to Baker's proposals had the broader aim of slowing down the peacemaking. The Labour Party was prepared to accept Baker's proposals. Accusing Shamir of 'murdering the peace process', Shimon Peres asked the prime minister during a Knesset debate, 'Who will believe you again in this country? You have broken every promise.' Shamir lambasted Peres for 'shameful' appeasement of the Arabs, adding, 'We are not afraid of peace, we are afraid of irresponsible concessions.'

Shimon Peres and his closest allies wanted to leave the government over Shamir's intransigence. Together the Likud (40) and Labour (39) had 79 Knesset seats out of the total 120; but without Labour's 39 seats, the National Unity Government would lose its lopsided parliamentary majority. Its collapse would become all but inevitable.

Since Baker was forcing Shamir to choose between his compromise plan and risking the collapse of the National Unity Government, it was an easy choice for Yitzhak Shamir to make.

Shamir assumed that even if his government fell over his rigidity, the electorate would rally to his side. So he stuck to his ideology, rejecting Baker's proposals as too risky for the country. Eventually President Bush got into the act, employing high-profile diplomatic and financial pressure in an attempt to budge Yitzhak Shamir.

The future of the Unity Government depended in large measure on what Yitzhak Rabin chose to do. He, however, was of two minds. Personally, he had prospered under the national Unity Government, becoming its 'strong man'. Rabin had no driving ambition to step down as defence minister or to replace the Unity regime with a new government under Prime Minister Peres. Rabin's stormy relationship with Peres was not the only issue at stake. Rabin cared about the peace process as well. And he was slowly becoming convinced that the Likud had no intention of advancing his plan for elections in the occupied territories. The only way of advancing peacemaking appeared to be to bring an end to Shamir's rule. Rabin was troubled, however, by any step that would advance Shimon Peres' career. On 5 March, 1990, he offered the public observation that there were 'some in Labour who seem to be in a great rush [to bring the Unity Government down], and it isn't the peace process which is their paramount priority, but something quite different'. 'Some in Labour' was Rabin's shorthand for Shimon Peres.

It took Rabin some time to move over to the side of the rebels. While Shimon Peres was trying to manoeuvre a Labour walkout, Rabin on 8 March still insisted that the Unity Government 'constituted Israel's best alternative'. Alternative to a Peres-led government — Rabin was mumbling under his breath, no doubt. For Rabin told Labour Party leaders, 'What ought to guide us above all is the need to carry on with the peace process, preferably in the framework of the existing broad coalition. This should be uppermost in our minds and not the mad rush after one alternative or another . . .' Sure it should, if there had been a peace process, which there was not. And Rabin knew there was not. The simple truth was that Yitzhak Rabin had a hard time swallowing the idea of Shimon Peres becoming prime minister again.

On 11 March, the 'inner' Cabinet, comprising senior

ministers and dealing with the most important issues, planned to
hold a decisive session on whether to accept the latest American
proposals for getting agreement on a peace conference. Before
the meeting even got under way, Peres was certain that Shamir
and his Likud cohorts would veto the proposals. To signal to the
Likud that Labour was getting ready to leave the government,
Peres summoned the Labour Party's 1,400-member Central
Committee into session for the day after, 12 March. Peres had no
doubt that the Committee would agree to end Labour's
participation in the Unity Government.

When the inner Cabinet met on 11 March, Shamir came out
fighting. He would not tolerate Palestinians from East
Jerusalem in the delegation; he would not tolerate Palestinian
negotiators consulting with the PLO.

Rabin tried out a compromise on Shamir: let's tell the
Americans that we will go along with a Palestinian delegation
except on one crucial point: whether East Jerusalem residents
may vote in the proposed Palestinian elections. Let the Knesset
decide that thorny issue. No, said Shamir. No more compromises.
Labour ministers asked for a vote. Again, Shamir said no.
Furious, Peres, Rabin and the other Labour ministers stalked
out of the session. The Unity Government was gasping for
breath. The only point on which Likud and Labour found unity
was — that there no longer was any unity!

Shamir's firmness at the inner Cabinet had a profound effect
on Yitzhak Rabin. He realized that the Prime Minister had
shown how uninterested he was in peacemaking. When the
Labour Party Central Committee convened at Bet Berl on
12 March, it was Rabin's enthusiastic call for the dismantling of
the Unity Government that helped sway the audience. The
Likud, Rabin told the Central Committee, was simply afraid of
where peace talks could lead. Shamir was not interested in a
compromise that would bring about a peace conference. The
Labour Party did not set a date by when it would lead the
Government: no one doubted for a moment, however, that
Labour was counting the hours, not days or weeks.

Events moved swiftly. Yitzhak Shamir seized the moment.
Rather than wait for Labour to take the initiative by walking
out of the government, Shamir fired Shimon Peres as finance
minister. The prime minister's reason: Peres had undermined
the Government.

Responding to Shamir's gambit, all Labour Party ministers, including Defence Minister Rabin, announced their resignations from the Government. The National Unity Government was dead.

Rabin and Peres called a joint news conference: 'We have been discussing these issues for months,' said Rabin, 'the composition of the [Palestinian] delegation and the agenda [of the Cairo talks]. In the inner Cabinet, we held five and a half hours of discussions, but [Shamir] refuses to decide. We have done everything to formulate the issues in such a way that Shamir can give a positive response. The responsibility for the collapse of the government rests on Shamir's shoulders.'

The Labour Party initiated a no-confidence motion against the Government and a vote was set in the Knesset for 15 March. No Israeli prime minister had ever lost a no-confidence vote; rather than risk defeat, the prime minister had always tendered his resignation first, thus bringing down the entire Government. The act of resignation forestalled the no-confidence motion. Shamir, thus, passed word through a highly placed Likud source that he might quit rather than be the first Israeli prime minister to be felled by a no-confidence vote.

Then, oddly, Shamir changed strategy. A full 90 minutes before the vote was to be taken, the prime minister understood that he was going to lose. He could have gone to the President to resign. He chose not to and the vote went ahead. Shamir's coalition, now able to count on only 55 votes, fell 60–55. Helping to defeat the Unity Government was the absence of five of the six members of the ultra-orthodox Sephardi Shas party, a coalition member. Acting on orders from its mentor, former Chief Rabbi Ovadia Yosef, those five Shas Knesset members chose to punish Shamir for refusing to demonstrate flexibility in the negotiating process. Peres assumed that Shas' support was now his for the asking — or at least, for the bargaining. Peres also assumed that, with Shas safely in Labour's camp, he would be able to form a government.

Now that the National Unity Government had fallen, it was up to President Chaim Herzog to examine whether anyone could form a new government. If not, elections would be set. There seemed little question, however, that the Labour Party had a better chance than the Likud of forming a government.

Arguing that their man had a better prospect of establishing a new government, some Rabin supporters insisted that Peres be dumped in favour of Rabin. Peres, however, had no trouble heading off such a move. After consulting with the parties, the President chose Peres to try to form a new government. For a while it seemed that Peres would be successful, though the new Peres-led Government would have a razor-thin majority of only 61 Knesset seats.

What followed was a five-week period during which Labour Party leader Shimon Peres sought to get the small religious parties to join his new governing coalition. He made generous offers of money for the religious parties' educational institutions and of political appointments for the religious parties' leaders. As finance minister, Peres was in an ideal position to make sure that funds streamed into religious institutions. The wheeling and dealing grew messy and complicated. At one stage, Peres struck a bargain with the Agudat Yisrael party only to find out that, if he wished the support of two other small religious parties (Shas and Degel Hatorah), he would have to renege on the Agudat Yisrael deal. These kinds of political deals had been made in the past. This time, however, the public grew incensed, arguing that public funds were being used to 'purchase' a government for Peres. Massive demonstrations and hunger strikes were held at which Israelis pressed for electoral reform as an antidote to the brazen coalition horse-trading. Many wanted a complete overhaul of the political system, making the Knesset more responsive to the wishes of the public. Nearly everyone agreed that the prime minister should be directly elected as a first step in reducing the power that small parties had over the large parties during coalition formation. A half million Israelis, nearly 10 per cent of the population, handed a petition to President Herzog demanding electoral reform. At one rally in Tel Aviv 250,000 Israelis mounted a protest against the political system. Despite the protests, the fear of alienating the ultra-orthodox parties at this crucial and sensitive political juncture kept the major parties silent on the issue of electoral reform.

The basis of all this public dissent was the ability of the small religious parties to hold the big parties in the country to hostage. Never was this demonstrated more clearly than on 12 April, 1990 when Shimon Peres planned to bring his new Government for approval before the Knesset. At the very last minute two Agudat Yisrael Knesset members, Eliezer Mizrachi and Avraham Werdiger, changed their minds and decided to withhold their support for the new Peres-led Government. They had received their orders from the 88-year-old Rabbi Menachem Schneerson, who headed the ultra-orthodox Chabad-Lubavitch movement from his home in Brooklyn, New York. The Lubavitcher Rabbi's long-range intervention in Israeli politics seemed all the more brazen and absurd because Schneerson had never been to Israel. Peres' majority fell from 61 to 59 seats. He was humiliated. He had to announce that he could not after all form a government. The religious parties had held Peres hostage, but ultimately, it was Peres who was condemned. 'The political system has been raped, robbed, bruised and brought to prostitution,' wrote Nahum Barnea, the highly respected political commentator in *Yediot Aharonot* on 26 April.

Yitzhak Rabin was smiling. Peres' misfortune became his good luck. Rabin had genuinely wanted Labour to remain in the National Unity Government. To be on the inside meant power, influence; to be tossed to the back benches of the Knesset was not exciting; he had suffered through seven years as a Knesset member and he had no great desire to return to that status. Still, Rabin had tried to play fair, to give Peres a chance to form a government; Rabin knew that had he tried to torpedo Peres' chances, and Peres had succeeded in setting up an alternative government, Labour would never have forgiven him. So he played the role of Peres' loyal lieutenant, paying a visit to a rabbi or two when a good word from him seemed needed. 'People in Labour asked me to see Rabbi (Eliezer) Shach,' Rabin told intimates at the time, referring to the most powerful ultra-orthodox figure in the country. 'They told me, "He's blind, dumb, deaf, senile. Just go there and say hello." If I hadn't gone, everyone would have said I'd spoiled Labour's chances. He's not deaf, he's not blind. He's very much in possession of his senses. He knows what he wants.'[1] To have gone to a rabbi hat in hand enraged Rabin. All the while he bristled at the back-room tactics Peres was employing, turning the Labour Party into a supplicant.

Peres' ill-fated attempt to form a new government presented Rabin with a golden opportunity to pounce on his long-time rival. Had Peres succeeded in establishing a government, his wheeling and dealing would have been overlooked. Defeat, however, created a stench. In fact, Rabin termed the Peres gambit 'the Targil Ha'masriach' (the Smelly Exercise), a phrase that obviously touched a nerve for it has became part of Israel's political lexicon.

With Peres still in charge of the party, Rabin had to appear loyal. The day after Peres' Knesset fiasco, Rabin issued a statement that was meant to express support for Peres. Rabin said he saw 'national and party importance in preventing this mandate [of Peres'] from being handed over to the Likud, which would form a narrow, right-wing coalition'. So prickly were their relations that analysts scrutinized each word that Rabin penned. Had he indeed been loyal to Peres? Most of the communiqué appeared to suggest that, however grudgingly, Rabin had been. Then came the last sentence. 'When the time comes, Labour's institutions will have to take steps to ensure that such a narrow rightist coalition is not established,' asserted Rabin, using language surely designed to tweak Peres and advance his own political cause.

Rabin had said 'When the time comes.' He could have said 'if', but he deliberately did not. He sounded as if it were a virtual certainly that Shimon Peres would fail to form a government.

Rabin had used the phrase 'take steps'. He appeared to be suggesting that Labour would 'take steps' to remove Peres. The pundits guessed that Rabin hoped to take over the party, then turn to the Likud and re-establish the National Unity Government.

On 26 April, Rabin came out swinging. He appeared before the Labour Party's 150-member Leadership Bureau and coyly noted that he had not exactly been aloof from Peres' manoeuvring, though now he regretted taking part. 'I admit to making the mistake of not checking the stories that we have a narrow government in our pocket, and learned only afterwards what trouble we were in. I admit to a certain degree of responsibility for the mistakes that were made. My main mistake was preferring inner-party peace above other issues.' Rabin's message was clear: he and Labour had paid a heavy price for giving Shimon Peres his way. Now, he planned to be his own man. He announced at that meeting that he planned to challenge Peres for the party leadership.

In the meantime Shamir got busy and over the next few weeks began carving a coalition of the Likud and small right-wing and religious parties. The leadership struggle in Labour was postponed since the party was heading into parliamentary opposition.

Labour was now forced to take up the back benches while Yitzhak Shamir was free to keep the peace process on a low flame and free to expand Jewish settlements in the occupied territories. However uneasy sat the crown, Peres remained Labour Party leader; Rabin seemed no closer to realizing his ambition to wrest power from Peres.

The political landscape was, however, re-arranging itself in Rabin's favour. Advocates of electoral reform had not forgiven Labour and Likud politicians for their high-profile bartering, and for ignoring pleas to change the political system. The man most identified with that bartering was Shimon Peres. Moreover, disenchantment had grown over Shamir's resistance to the peace process. All of this played into Yitzhak Rabin's hands. The country preferred him to Peres or Shamir for prime minister. A public opinion poll conducted by the Smith Research Center appeared in the *Jerusalem Post* on 11 July and indicated that, if direct elections for the prime minister were held that day, Rabin would have been easily elected: he soundly defeated Yitzhak Shamir, 50 to 33 per cent. The poll showed that Shamir could easily defeat Peres, though by a much slimmer margin.

With the Labour Party in agitation, Rabin was itching for a chance to unseat Peres. He wanted a leadership contest as quickly as possible. Rabin told the *Jerusalem Post* on 12 May that Labour had to 'organize itself for life on the other side of the House. Before we can do that, however, we have to vote for "the man" and we have to vote for the "message". In political life, you cannot always draw a clear-cut line between "who" and "what". But there is no doubt that it is "the man" who gives "the message" credibility.'[2]

Peres saw no need to rush. National elections were not for another 16 months, in November 1992. Why rush? There was plenty of time to decide whether Labour needed to change its leader. Sensing the despairing mood among the nation and within Labour, Rabin pressed for a leadership contest urgently: he wanted one by the end of July. On 5 July it was decided that the Labour Party Central Committee would convene on 22 July and decide whether to hold a leadership contest by 1 August (as Rabin wanted) or to postpone it for a year (as Peres sought). Rabin was elated. He called the 5 July compromise 'a significant change, a recognition by Bureau members of the need for change and for preparing properly for serving as an opposition to the Likud. We must remember that the real political and public rivalry is not within the party but with the Likud and today's right-wing government.'

This time it seemed that Rabin would win the day. He appeared to have a powerful argument that, with him at the head of the ticket, Labour had a better chance of defeating Shamir in the next election. Rabin's camp claimed the support of 60 per cent of the Central Committee; Peres' backers thought the race close with a slight advantage to their man. Peres' supporters were nasty. They flayed Rabin, calling him 'Mr Intifada' and an unfit leader. 'He's the leg and arm-breaking man, representing Israel's big moral and political failure,' said Professor Dan Miron at a Tel Aviv press conference. 'The smell of blood has stuck to him.' Dismayed that the party bloodletting might cause Labour irreparable damage in its eventual struggle against the Likud, Peres showed mixed feelings about the contest, and sought to blame Rabin for whatever damage occurred. 'I did not invite Rabin to a duel,' he told supporters a few days before the party contest. 'He has plunged the party into a big whirlpool. But if he asked for a duel, he'll get it.'

22 July arrived. Peres, speaking before the vote, wanted to know what had he done wrong the previous March. 'What trust did I violate? Why do you [Rabin] repeat the Likud's slanders about me? Did I write a book about you? Did I call you names? If there was a failure [in March 1990], Rabin was a full partner to it, step after step. He did not object to anything, not in private conversation and not in the party institutions. And if someone must bear responsibility, he was not number two, he was one of two.' As he sat there listening to Peres, Rabin remained confident that the Central Committee would make Peres pay for his misdeeds.

He was wrong. Confounding everyone, Peres soundly defeated Rabin, garnering 54 per cent of the Central Committee's vote — to only 46 per cent for Rabin. How had Peres achieved this surprise triumph with so much going against him? An indefatigable campaigner, Peres made sure to get in touch with every member of the Central Committee, attending countless meetings around the country. Rabin campaigned less vigorously, less methodically. In fact, while Rabin had captured the hearts of the country, Peres retained an iron grip over the Labour Party. Neither Rabin's popularity nor Peres' faded image after the March 1990 fiasco hurt the Labour Party leader. The lingering memory among Labour Party members that Rabin appeared more sympathetic to Shamir than to Labour aided Peres as well. What drew many in Labour back to Peres in addition was the man's political skills. A key Rabin confidante explained: 'Peres is a party man, Rabin is a statesman. Peres grew out of the party, only the party. Rabin endures the party. Shimon is a battle fox. He knows how to buy people. Peres could talk to all members of the party twice in two weeks. That was something Rabin couldn't do.'

With Labour sliding in the public opinion polls, Peres' July triumph seemed especially hollow. It turned out not only to be hollow, but of no real relevance. While Rabin had appeared the loser that 22 July, he was not. For Peres had won the battle, but lost the war. Grabbing fewer headlines, but far more significant than that day's Peres–Rabin contest was a decision taken by the Central Committee to choose its future leaders by a new system fashioned after the American Presidential primaries. After many years of keeping its leadership contests confined to members of the 1,450-member Central Committee, Labour became the first Israeli political party to turn that decision over to all registered party members. Another crucial decision taken by the Central Committee was the holding of a party census; beginning in November 1990, Labour Knesset member Benyamin Ben-Eliezer directed the effort to register Labour Party members.

Democratizing the Labour Party was as controversial as it was ground-breaking yet Labour understood only too well that this reform was vital if the party were going to stand a chance against the Likud in November 1992. In democratizing itself,

Labour would hopefully carve out a new, positive image. Rabin could only smile quietly. He called the 22 July defeat a mere 'tactical failure' and vowed that his 'strategy remains' ousting Peres from the party leadership. Rabin was counting on the fact that when the next leadership contest would be held, Peres' iron grip over the party would hopefully count for less than the will of the entire membership. Seeking to play down the 22 July vote, Rabin insisted that there had been no showdown with Peres; Labour had not been asked to select its candidate for prime minister. No one should label him the Party's number two figure, said Rabin. 'I don't need any title in the party, such as Number Two. I don't regard myself as second to anyone.'

Dismayed that a right-wing government under Shamir was now capturing the headlines, maintaining a hard line toward peacemaking and expanding Jewish settlements in the occupied territories, the Labour Party lost its aggressiveness. Its Knesset members displayed little zeal for bringing down the Likud government, preferring travel abroad to the nitty-gritty parliamentary efforts that might cause Likud to fall. Some in Labour thought it time to dump Peres as party leader and a number of candidates came forward, among them Mordechai Gur, a former chief of staff; Gad Ya'acobi, a former minister of communications; Moshe Shachal, a former minister of energy; and Ora Namir, a veteran Labour Party member. Peres tried to downplay these challenges. 'Who says I'm not popular,' he asked a reporter in December 1990. 'I have a majority [within Labour].'

Fortunately for Labour, the public began shifting favour away from the Likud. The Intifada had frayed Israeli nerves; it no longer seemed confined to the West Bank or the Gaza Strip. Life seemed all too precarious. On 8 October, 1990 an angry Palestinian mob began throwing rocks at Israelis near the Western Wall. Israeli police came to the rescue, firing into the mob. Nineteen Palestinian Arabs were killed and another 140 were wounded. Such incidents led Israelis to conclude that Palestinian Arabs from the occupied territories should no longer be permitted into Israel proper. As their personal fears grew, Israelis adopted tougher attitudes toward the Arabs. At the same time, they wanted the bloodshed to stop. One public opinion survey indicated that only 9 per cent of the Israeli public was satisfied with the status quo. In that same poll, some (20 per cent) favoured evacuating the Gaza Strip; some (6 per cent) wanted Israel to annex all or part of the West Bank; a surprisingly large number (21 per cent) supported the 'transfer' of some or all of the Palestinian Arabs from the West Bank to Arab countries or farther away.

Cutting into the Likud's popularity, apart from the Intifada, was the way the Shamir Government had been handling the integration of Soviet Jewish immigrants into Israeli society. Russian Jews began arriving in Israel in larger and larger numbers in 1989, an event that Israelis had longed for over the years: 13,000 reached Israel that year; 185,000 came in 1990. At the beginning of this new wave of immigration, the Russian Jews knew housing was in short supply, but came to Israel anyway. They feared growing anti-Semitism; they hated the Russian poverty; they were concerned about the seeming instability of the Soviet regime. With America closing its doors to them, Israel was the most suitable place to go. Not since the early 1950s had the Israelis had to figure out how to handle so many new immigrants all at once. Yet immigration was a *raison d'être* for the Jewish state. No matter how many came, the country would have to cope.

For Yitzhak Shamir's Likud party, the Russian immigrants constituted a marvellous political asset. Though the Likud had not 'caused' the massive immigration (Mikhail Gorbachev had), Shamir was quite happy to claim the immigrants' arrival in Israel as a great political victory. A year later — by January 1991 — however, immigrant dissatisfaction at the lack of housing and jobs caused the number of arrivals to slacken sharply. Discontent began to stir among rank and file Likud members. 'Our leaders,' complained Michael Kleiner, a Likud Knesset member, 'just don't understand the magnitude of the "aliyah" [immigration] problem.'

These two issues — the ever-dangerous Intifada and the failure to handle the Russian immigrants properly — would haunt the Likud in the coming months.

in January 1991, Yitzhak Rabin, now a Knesset back bencher, When the United States began the countdown to the Gulf War in January 1991, Yitzhak Rabin, now a Knesset backbencher, remembered the lessons that Israel had learned from the

Lebanon War. Hence, he was confident that the US would be able to achieve military superiority over Iraq, but less confident that Washington would be able to bring Saddam Hussein to his knees, let alone extricate the Iraqi army from Kuwait. 'As for the military solution, there is no doubt that the US will be able to gain immediate air supremacy and hit any targets it chooses,' said Rabin. 'But that would not necessarily cause the collapse of the regime or the withdrawal of Iraqi forces. The Americans have sent in 400,000 men because they want to be in a position to win quickly. But we have learned by bitter experience just how difficult it is to predict how any war will turn out. As far as Israel is concerned, I take seriously what Saddam has said publicly three times: that if he is attacked, Israel will become a target.'[3] It was an incredibly accurate analysis.

When the war broke out, Rabin, a former chief of staff, once again found himself on the sidelines of an Israeli war. He became embroiled in a minor controversy when he acknowledged on Israel Television that, rather than rush to a 'sealed room' and don a gas mask against the threat of Iraqi chemical warfare, he dashed down the steps of his apartment building and sought safety in his air raid shelter — in effect ignoring army instructions to remain in the 'sealed room'. To be fair, the residents of the Tel Aviv area took the brunt of the Iraqi Scud missile attacks during the six weeks of the Gulf War, and other Tel Aviv area residents also believed it was safer to be in an air raid shelter.

Towards the end of the Gulf War, Likud Knesset member Yehoshua Saguy, a former head of military intelligence, charged that Israeli intelligence, five weeks into the Gulf War, had still not been certain whether Iraq had a chemical capability for its Scuds, or how many missile-launchers the Iraqis had. Such intelligence lapses, said Saguy, stemmed from Israel's 'terrible mistake' during the 1980s when it allegedly neglected Iraq and focused intelligence efforts on Syria.

To Rabin, who had been the defence minister at the time of which Saguy spoke, such accusations were baseless. Israeli intelligence had shifted its focus toward Iraq as early as 1988, Rabin insisted; 'By 1990, we knew all we had to about Iraq's military capabilities,' Rabin asserted, adding that it had been correct to focus on Syria since it was the main threat to Israeli security.[4] Some Likud officials accused the Foreign Ministry of being captive to a 'Concept' that the Iraqis were in the Egyptian orbit and bent on making peace with Israel. Rabin said that as defence minister in the 1980s he had never been taken in by the Concept. From the very outset he saw Saddam as a megalomaniac bent on regional hegemony. But the Concept was still dominant as late as April 1989. When Rabin warned the United States about the Iraqi threat to Israel, journalists in Israel scoffed, claiming that he was trying to divert attention from the Intifada. In September 1989, Rabin talked with Egyptian President Hosni Mubarak in Cairo and tried to warn him of the danger Saddam posed. 'I told him Saddam was a threat to us and would become his most radical opponent in the Arab world. But he just wouldn't hear of it.'

Shamir's policy of 'self-constraint' during the Gulf War, his acceptance of the American request not to reply to Scud missile attacks on Israel, earned the prime minister a temporary political gain. The Americans had argued insistently that any Israeli military response would cause the break-up of the delicately woven coalition of Arab military forces lined up with the US against Iraq. Though damage to Israeli homes from Iraqi Scud missile attacks was severe, few Israeli lives were lost, making Shamir's policy of self-constraint easier to sell to his country. When the war ended with the American-led coalition successfully extricating Iraqi forces from Kuwait, Shamir emerged as a leader who had shown loyalty to the United States, kept Israeli casualties to a minimum, and had not shattered Israel's deterrent power.

Neither Yitzhak Rabin nor Shimon Peres fared well politically from the Gulf War. The Scud attacks against Israel's population centres served to remind Israelis that it had been Peres who had opposed Menachem Begin's decision to destroy the Iraqi nuclear reactor in June 1981.

Rabin's star did not glow either at this juncture. However much he claimed that Israeli intelligence had been on its toes in the 1980s, it was abundantly clear to Israelis that their leaders had done precious little to prepare the country against Iraqi Scud attacks. With Israeli intelligence focusing on Syria, Israel made little effort to beef up its civil defence preparations in the event that Iraq employed chemical weapons on its Scuds.

(Fortunately for Israel, none of the Scuds that landed in Israel during the Gulf War contained chemical warheads.)

One of the main outcomes of the Gulf War was the renewed effort Washington made towards resolving the Israeli–Arab conflict. In the quest for the new 'world order' that President George Bush hoped to fashion, he dispatched his Secretary of State, James Baker, to capitals in the Middle East in the hope that the war had created a new opportunity for peacemaking. The specific aim was to nail down Arab–Israeli agreement on the nature and timing of a Middle East peace conference.

Baker's arrival in the Middle East in mid-March 1991 coincided with the high point of Yitzhak Shamir's personal popularity. Public opinion polls gave Labour no more than 20 Knesset seats if elections had been held at that time. Political observers concluded that the prime minister's optimal strategy was to call for early elections as soon as possible, rather than wait for November 1992. By then, the economy could sour and Russian immigrants might grow even more disenchanted. For the time being, Russian immigrants expressed support for the Likud government. By November 1992, however, those same immigrants might turn away from the Likud.

George Bush sensed that both the Arabs and Israelis were in his debt, and now was the time to capitalize on this favourable conjunction of events. The Arabs were grateful to Bush for forging the coalition and bringing Saddam Hussein down to size; the Israelis too were thankful to the President for bearing down hard on Iraq without requiring Israeli intervention.

Baker visited the region repeatedly, trying to sew together a peace conference that both Israelis and Arabs could abide. By August the American Secretary of State had succeeded, and the parties agreed to convene in Madrid on 30 October. It had not been easy for Baker. The Arabs had wanted a truly international peace conference with UN and European participation. Israel got its way for the most part though the former Soviet Union did become a co-sponsor along with the United States. The Palestinians wanted their own delegation and they wanted to be able to select delegates, even those with PLO affiliations. Baker gave in to the Israelis: the Palestinians would have to be part of a joint Palestinian–Jordanian delegation and there would be no PLO-affiliated delegates among the Palestinians. It seemed that both the Israelis and Arabs were dragged kicking and screaming to the peace table. Yet, the American Secretary of State had won their agreement to attend, a major step forward.

Realizing that Shamir and the Likud were comfortably ahead in the polls, the Labour Party's politicians became convinced that their party needed a shot in the arm. Perhaps it was time to push both Peres and Rabin out and let the younger generation take over. Neither Peres nor Rabin liked that idea. One member of that younger generation, Knesset member Avraham Burg, quipped: 'Fifty per cent in the Labour Party want Peres, fifty per cent want Rabin — and 100 per cent don't want either.' Jokes would not help. Solid political talent among the younger generation would have, but that was sorely missing. No one among the generation of Labour politicians in their mid-40s or early 50s had emerged as a credible successor to Rabin and Peres. It was not for lack of trying. In May 1991, some prospective candidates met secretly and tried to choose from among themselves someone to replace Rabin and Peres. The meeting broke up without a decision. Only Yisrael Kessar, the popular secretary-general of the Histadrut, the large labour federation, exhibited any political strength, but far too little to mount a successful challenge.

By the summer of 1991, Rabin realized that events were working in his favour. No matter how strong a hold Shimon Peres had over the Labour Party, the country was clearly annoyed at the wheeling and dealing that Peres' 'Targil Hamasriach' had come to symbolize. The March 1990 exercise had blemished the Labour Party severely in the electorate's eyes. Labour needed a new identity, and Rabin sensed that he could supply it. Helping Rabin enormously, the Likud made a series of crucial political errors. One was in the area of electoral reform, an issue that had wide resonance in the body politic. To overlook the popularity of this issue was to stick one's head in the sand. Yet, the Likud's Knesset members made sure to torpedo any major electoral reform. To the Likud, electoral reform would have meant leaving the choice of the next prime minister in the hands of the people (in contrast with the existing system in which voters cast their ballots for a political party). Likud politicians believed correctly that exposing Yitzhak Shamir, a most uncharismatic figure, to the whims of the Israeli electorate, could bring about the party's downfall. One Likud politician predicted that the party would lose between 6 and 8 Knesset seats under the proposed electoral reform. What the Likud failed to appreciate was that the voters were growing impatient with efforts to stall electoral reform.

The public opinion polls showed that the Likud's assessment that electoral reform could hurt its political prospects was accurate. The most popular politician in the country was Yitzhak Rabin. Not surprisingly, Rabin was one of the great champions of electoral reform. He argued, 'The present system does not allow a prime minister to take clear-cut decisions. All it does is to make the Haredim (ultra-orthodox) the kingmakers of Israel.' Rabin had learned an unforgettable lesson from the 'Targil Hamasriach': that the Haredim, allowed to play the role of kingmaker, would side with Shamir. 'When they look to heaven and to their voters, they'll never bring us up and bring the Likud down. I am finished with the strategy adopted by the Labour Party over the past three or four years — the running after the Haredi parties trying to woo them with legislation and money. It was a tragic mistake and it failed. Because, if the ultra-orthodox hold the balance of power, they will always go with the Likud.'[5]

Part of the enthusiastic campaign for electoral reform had to do with the sagging Israeli economy. For nearly 20 years the Israeli economy had not been growing. Most of the Government's state-run corporations were in serious economic trouble. The kibbutzim, once the jewel in the crown of Israeli socialism, were in heavy debt. Unemployment had been running at a record high of 10 per cent. Inflation, which had come down from 400 per cent a year in the mid-80s, still hovered at an annual rate of 20 per cent. Naturally, those suffering from the country's economic slowdown blamed the party in power. And, if the existing political system made it more difficult to oust the party in power, electoral reform was needed.

If electoral reform and the troubled economy were to prove valuable cards for Rabin, so too would Shamir's seeming indifference to peacemaking. Rabin believed that Shamir's approach was flawed: by seeking to make peace with the Palestinians, Jordan, Syria, and Lebanon, all at once, he was

only guaranteeing deadlock. 'The basic approach is wrong.
. . . Looking back, we only reached agreements with the Arabs
when we followed two basic principles — starting with Egypt
and leaving Syria to the end. There are no shortcuts to peace,
there are no "Open Sesame" solutions. It has to be done
gradually, step by step. . . .' And, if he were prime minister,
what would he do? 'I would go back to the process that was cut
off in March 1990 — with the United States, Egypt and Israel
focusing on the Palestinians in the territories. I believe the
situation today enables us to pursue it with even better chances
of success. The defeat of Saddam Hussein brought down the
sky-high expectations of the Palestinians.'[6]

Yitzhak Shamir subscribed to none of Rabin's concerns. To
the prime minister, Israel's situation was rosy enough. He began
to think seriously about calling early elections, not out of
desperation, but eager to exploit the excitement generated by
the news that Israel would be sitting at a peace conference with
Arab leaders in a few months. By the end of the summer of 1991,
Shamir's closest aides considered a political strategy that called
for the Likud's election campaign to be launched soon after the
peace conference in late October so that Madrid would be fresh
on the voters' minds. Shamir shelved the idea, worried that the
public would conclude that he was desperate. Perhaps, if
Shamir took no initiative, the small right-wing parties in the
coalition, Tehiya (with three seats) and Moledet (with two)
would do his work for him. All this talk of peacemaking
bothered Tehiya and Moledet. They could be counted on to
leave the government if Shamir became too 'peace-minded'.
That would precipitate the early elections that Shamir so
eagerly wanted. And no one would accuse the prime minister of
seeming rash.

The Likud's political deterioration began in the autumn of
1991. It happened over the loan guarantee issue. Israel had
asked for $10 billion in loan guarantees after the Gulf War to aid
Soviet newcomers in finding jobs and housing; but the US had
asked Shamir to postpone the request until 1 September. When
Israel raised the request at that date, George Bush found it
unthinkable that the US would provide this 'gift' after serving as
the honest broker who had brought about the Madrid peace
conference. The Arabs would be furious. Bush devised a ploy

that would enable him to avoid giving Israel the guarantees. He made them an offer that he knew they would refuse: he told the Israelis they could have the loan guarantees on the condition that they freeze Jewish settlement in the occupied territories. Bush was not surprised when Shamir rejected such 'linkage'. Frequently, Israelis have rallied behind their government when it seeks to 'stand up' to the Americans on an issue of principle such as the attempt at 'linkage'. This time they did not. To Israelis, the loan guarantees and helping Soviet immigrants to settle into Israeli society, were more important than a rift with Washington; more important than expanding Jewish settlements in the occupied areas. The American–Israeli relationship, for over two decades so crucial to Israel's political and economic fate, now loomed more important than ever. With Americans looking inward, and increasingly less interested in pouring huge sums into Israel, Israelis knew that it made little sense to endanger the brittle relationship even further. Shamir would suffer for driving a wedge between Jerusalem and Washington. The dissatisfaction with the prime minister over the loan guarantee issue lay in the future. For the moment, he was enjoying a marvellous moment in the diplomatic sun as the Madrid conference was about to convene.

When the Arabs and Israelis gathered in Madrid at the end of October 1991, despite the fact that it was more a media circus than a diplomatic meeting, despite the fact that the opening speeches were filled with rancour, the simple truth was that for the first time in the history of the conflict, all of the parties were seated around a peace table seemingly ready to do business. Shamir, for his part, devoted half of his 34-minute opening speech to a recitation of the oppression of Jews through the centuries; he demonstrated little willingness to compromise on the issues dividing Israel and the Arab states. Arab representatives were no less conciliatory in their opening remarks. Indeed, the road to peace seemed long and paved with huge obstacles, yet a beginning had been made to resolve the entire conflict once and for all. The spirit of Madrid was tangible, as Israelis and Arabs sensed that, no matter how slow progress might be, there was no turning back.

Shamir confronted a serious dilemma: take the peace process too far, too quickly, and he could lose the support of the political right; drag peacemaking on, and he would lose the support of the political centre. In its immediate aftermath, however, Madrid was a political boon to the prime minister. Public opinion surveys showed that Labour would win no more than 22 Knesset seats to the Likud's 37.

As the year 1991 ended another Rabin–Peres leadership contest loomed, set for February 1992. A combination of factors had arisen that appeared to give Rabin an advantage over Peres. This time, the choice of party leader would be determined, not by the Labour Party Central Committee, but by all Labour party members who had reigstered in Benyamin Ben-Eliezer's membership drive. The total number of registered had reached 150,000, far higher than anyone had projected. Rabin was elated. Surveys had always indicated that he was far more popular among the Labour Party rank-and-file than Peres. Now he would have the chance to prove it. The other factor favouring Rabin was Peres' declining image among Labour Party members.

Other candidates planned to run: Mordechai Gur, Gad Ya'acobi, Moshe Shachal, Ora Namir, and Yisrael Kessar. The first three dropped out, lacking sufficient support to compete. Of the two others, Namir and Kessar, Peres feared Kessar more than Rabin did. The Peres–Kessar relationship had been stormy. If none of the candidates who ran in the leadership contest garnered more than 40 per cent of the vote, a run-off contest would be held between the top two finishers. In a Rabin–Peres run-off, it was assumed that Rabin would attract many of Kessar's votes.

On 24 December Rabin opened his campaign for the party's nomination for prime minister. Aware that the party was tired of the long-time struggle between him and Peres, Rabin sought to take the high road, attacking Shamir and the Likud, steering clear of the chance to denigrate his long-time political rival. Rabin picked Shamir's opposition to electoral reform as his starting point. 'If Shamir is so sure of his ability to win, and that the people are behind him, and the Likud, as he keeps saying,' asked Rabin, 'why is he fighting so hard against electoral reform? He claims it endangers Eretz Yisrael. The truth is, he thinks it endangers his chances to be prime minister.'

Meanwhile, the Shamir government began to unravel. Rafael Eitan, the minister of agriculture and head of the tiny Tsomet party (with two Knesset seats) resigned from the Cabinet, railing against the iniquities of the political system. He protested against Shamir's refusal to allow Likud Knesset members a free vote on revamping the electoral system. Tsomet's defection weakened Shamir's 64-seat parliamentary majority but did not threaten the government's survival. The Eitan departure, however, meant that the withdrawal of only one more party from the coalition would bring down the government. Shamir's government was hanging by a slender thread. If the two small right-wing parties, Tehiya and Moledet, were going to vacate the government over the accelerating peace process, this could be their opportunity. For, in exiting, they would have the satisfaction of being able to bring down the Shamir government.

Shamir remained cool to early elections. He wanted to believe that the US would eventuallly deliver on the loan guarantees, that his firmness would pay dividends: he would be able to preserve Israel's national interests without ruining relations with Washington. Early elections would only play havoc with Shamir's plans to draw out the peace process, and wait for a warmer mood to take hold in Washington. With early elections, Shamir could be thrown out of office sooner rather than later. Yet, he was coming under increasing pressure from his Likud associates to go to the people. Likud Police Minister Ronni Milo let fly a trial balloon on 9 January, advocating early elections. When the prime minister sensed that the public would not warm to advancing the elections, he ordered his bureau chief Yossi Achimeir three days later to prick Milo's balloon.

The Likud should have been pleased at the prospect of an early election; the polls indicated the trend was towards the political right. But some Likud leaders were not enthusiastic. Ariel Sharon, the housing minister, asked his Likud allies, 'How are you going to explain the failure to curb the Intifada and protect the settlers? And how are you going to explain away the terrible unemployment figures?' Sharon's comments reflected a large discontent with the Likud; surveys showed that few (12 per cent) Israelis thought the peace process was advancing quickly enough; and a vast majority (80 per cent) were displeased with the Likud's handling of the economy. Other Likud politicians were worried. Knesset member Reuven Rivlin asserted bitterly, 'People who are hungry won't vote for the Likud.'

On 15 January, 1992 Tehiya announced that it was quitting the government coalition, making early elections a near certainty. Moledet declared that it would follow suit. That decreased Shamir's parliamentary total to 59 Knesset seats, less than a majority. Tehiya leader Yuval Ne'eman explained that Shamir's offer of limited autonomy to the Palestinians had been the final straw: 'We are leaving the government in order to prevent the autonomy, which is, from the beginning, actually a Palestinian state.' Rehavam Ze'evi, the leader of Moledet, had even sharper words: 'This government deserves to die because of two unpardonable sins. Not putting the Intifada down for 49 months and the fact that this government is intent on pursuing the policy of autonomy, which puts the whole State of Israel in grave danger.'

Rabin was thrilled at the turn of events. He wanted early elections, and he wanted them as quickly as possible. It was good for him — and good for the nation. As Rabin put it, 'We can't afford to wait until things get worse. This is the only country we have.'

To Rabin's great chagrin, for a few days it appeared that Peres might try to form an alternative government, an idea that was anathema to Rabin. The last thing Rabin wanted when he ran against Peres in the party's leadership contest was for Peres to be prime minister! Accordingly, Labour Party politicians, spearheaded by Rabin, joined with the Likud in advancing the balloting. No matter what Peres proposed, Rabin seemed to disagree. When Peres suggested that the Middle East peace talks be suspended during the election campaign, Rabin called this 'a most unfortunate utterance. Labour must not be seen at home or abroad as seeking to halt the peace process.' Whenever the two men were in the same room, sparks flew. On 21 January, they appeared together at a meeting of the Labour Party's Knesset faction. Rabin and his allies wanted Labour to introduce a no-confidence motion against the Shamir Government to bring about early elections. Peres denied that he had been trying to trick anyone or that he had hoped to set up an alternative government. Then the debate grew heated.

'I suggest that cultivating the image of a victim is not the way to establish yourself as a national leader,' Rabin contended. 'A victim's image evokes pity.'

Peres retorted: 'Smears are also not the way to leadership. No one here is a victim.'

The no-confidence motion was presented on 27 January. Shamir's Government easily defeated it by a 55–49 vote. The vote meant little. Labour and Likud were well on their way to agreeing to early elections.

Now that Labour and Likud would compete in an election within six months, the next step for Rabin was to defeat Shimon Peres in the 19 February Labour Party primary contest for the nomination of party leader and prime minister candidate. It would not be easy.

Chapter 13

Israel Is Waiting for Rabin

Ever since 1977, Yitzhak Rabin had been waiting for this moment. The moment when he would make a serious bid to compensate for the pain caused by the bank account scandal. The forthcoming primary contest gave him the chance to unseat Shimon Peres.

Rabin's future was on the line in the primary contest. A victory over Peres would place him in command of the party, and give him the chance to become prime minister again. A defeat would put fresh pressure on him to declare that he would no longer challenge anyone for the party's leadership.

Early in the campaign Rabin adopted an odd political tactic out of necessity: he would not attack Peres. Tormenting Labour Party voters with a reprise of 'the struggle' could backfire. Rabin understood all too well that the party was sick and tired of the Rabin-Peres rivalry. Had most members had their way, they would have let younger politicians take over. So Rabin would skip the old animosities, he would avoid mention of The Book, he would concentrate on attacking the Likud and Yitzhak Shamir. Not that Rabin had changed his mind about Shimon Peres. Not that he found him a wonderful fellow. Not at all.

The new primary election system brought massive uncertainty within the Labour Party. Its proponents contended that only by expanding the Labour Party's membership would the Party be able to reinvigorate itself and to create a new, electable identity. Yet, when they proposed that a membership drive be held in the summer of 1990, many Party members were fearful. They had no idea where it would lead. If they feared the membership drive, they were equally worried about the new primary election system. If Labour elected its leaders through a primary, who could tell what the outcome would be? The Labour Party

Central Committee had a certain predictability to it, and even when it was not predictable, its membership was small enough so that one could get a feel for what the consensus was. Now, leaving the election to the 'people', who could tell how they would vote? Benyamin Ben-Eliezer had begun the membership drive in November 1990, registering 150,000 people for the Labour Party, fully 65 per cent of them first-time Labour members. Half of them were under the age of 45. The membership drive was a bit frightening for Yitzhak Rabin at first, though he, of all people, should have welcomed the new system with open arms. As Ben-Eliezer noted: 'The membership drive was the spark that changed Rabin, that made him believe that he had a chance to come back politically.'[1]

Rabin appeared to have the upper hand. With the Likud in growing disfavour, the country was searching for new leadership. It wanted leadership, however, that identified with the political right. This was Rabin's strong card. Both the Lebanon War and the Intifada had helped to turn him into a pseudo-ally of Prime Minister Shamir, an uneasy alliance at best, but one that served to strengthen Rabin's image as an anchor of the political right. He still favoured territorial compromise with Jordan over the West Bank; he still sounded genuine when he said he was prepared to go far to obtain peace with the Arabs. Peres, meanwhile, was being branded as a dove, a pejorative label in a country which sometimes seemed to possess a majority from among the political right. Peres opposed a Palestinian state; he opposed negotiating with the PLO. His hawkish credentials appeared impeccable. Labour Party members knew better, knew that Peres had slipped over to the political left, that, while he mouthed right-wing positions, he was privately telling acquaintances that a Palestinian entity was not out of the question; that Israel might one day have to negotiate with the PLO. Whatever Peres really thought did not matter anymore. He attracted so many members of the political left to his side that he could not escape being labelled their leader. Nothing better could have happened to Rabin on the eve of the primary election campaign.

Shimon Peres had been tainted by the 'smelly exercise', and many in Labour would still not forgive him. Best of all for Rabin, the decision of choosing Labour's new leader had been given to party members among whom he appeared far stronger than Peres. And yet, ever cautious, Rabin worried that once again Peres would triumph. 'He was not sure he'd beat Peres, but he was pretty optimistic,' recalled Leah Rabin. 'He was under control. I was going out of my mind.'[2]

The surveys indicated a decisive Rabin victory. By mid-January, pollster Hanoch Smith's survey of 800 party members had Rabin ahead by a strong 10 per cent. Smith noted, 'If Yitzhak Rabin wins the leadership contest, Labour's policies would appear more credible. Many people would buy the idea that it's a different Labour Party.' Exploiting his popularity, Rabin campaigned heavily on the theme that only he could lead the Labour Party to victory in the forthcoming elections. On 9 January he spoke to 600 supporters in Tel Aviv's Bnei Brith Hall. In an obvious dig at Shimon Peres, Rabin noted that being prime minister for him 'is not an obsession but only an option', since he had already served in this post and had been defence minister, chief of staff, and ambassador to Washington.

Buoyed by those surveys in the midst of the primary race, Rabin's innate pessimism gave way to a new optimism. He sensed that he was getting his message across. Even his erstwhile critics within the political left, critics who had blasted him for his behaviour towards Palestinians in the Intifada, were lining up on his side. 'Our decision to support Rabin,' said one, 'was based purely on electoral considerations. Privately, we all believed that Peres was much more able, more to our taste politically. But Rabin was the only person who could capture the crucial 4-5 Knesset seats which float between Labour and the Likud.' Such changes of heart encouraged Rabin immensely. Ephraim Sneh, who in the 1980s was in charge of the West Bank Civil Administration, was now co-chairman of Rabin's primary contest. Rabin's 'gut feeling was that he had a better chance in the primaries against Peres,' noted Sneh. 'Once he began to feel the warm response from the crowds, once he began to sense that thousands of members liked and wanted him, he began to believe he might win after all.'[3]

Financially, Rabin felt at a disadvantage: Peres appeared to be spending far more money to woo voters. Rabin relied on large numbers of volunteers; on direct mailings. Appearing before small Labour audiences, Rabin discovered that people cared deeply about socio-economic issues even more so than about Rabin's special area of expertise, national security affairs. Hence, Rabin learned a valuable lesson at an early stage of campaigning: that Israeli voters had become preoccupied with improving their economic lot. Still concerned about Arab–Israeli issues, they no longer wanted their prime minister to dismiss economic problems as secondary to the Arab–Israeli conflict. Unemployment was too high, Soviet immigrants were suffering too much, young people just out of the Israeli army were finding it too tough to find jobs.

For someone as popular as Rabin was, he rarely responded by showing much warmth on the campaign trail. It was just not part of his personality. His campaign manager, Ephraim Sneh knew that Rabin was not Mr Warmth. He was not going to wade into a crowd and kiss babies. Talking to voters, Rabin was awkward, giving the impression that he could not wait to escape the premises. Sneh was, therefore, ecstatic when Rabin slowly showed signs of relaxing: 'He started to communicate with people. He began to enjoy the process. Our strategy was to tell everyone that "Only with Rabin can we win". That was our campaign slogan. We said, "OK. Maybe Rabin doesn't hug children. He doesn't smile. Maybe you don't even like him. But only with him will we win. Only with him can we pull away the five Knesset seats from the Likud that we need to win." '[4]

The campaign exacted a physical toll: Rabin eventually lost his voice. Doctors urged him to curtail his speaking engagements temporarily. He could not do that but he did give up smoking, promising himself to return to the habit once his voice was back.

If Rabin used kid gloves on Peres, his supporters did not. They sought to brand Peres a loser, reminding everyone that he had lost four national elections and that he had failed to form a government in March 1990. Rabin, on the other hand, had been a good and honest prime minister during the very critical post-Yom Kippur War; he had started the peace process with Egypt, had lowered inflation and had made important gains in housing and education.

Peres' fans insisted that their man had been one of the best prime ministers Israel had had. Campaigning tirelessly, Peres toured the country, often seeing as many as 1,000 people a day. At night he showed up at five or six campaign rallies. Peres dismissed Rabin's claims that only he could deliver nearly 150,000 undecided but basically right-wing voters. 'It's a myth,' snapped Peres. 'I doubt whether there are even 150 such waverers.' Peres argued that Rabin was popular among Likud voters who would not shift their votes to the Labour Party even if Rabin were to stand at its head.

This time around Rabin was a more polished politician. He had avoided nasty jabs at Peres. He had even surprised political reporters by announcing that he would be 'glad to work with Peres after the primaries'. Should he be elected, Rabin said, 'I will have no problem whatsoever working with him. In fact, every candidate will have a senior position in the Cabinet should I be the one to form the next government.' One incident showed how concerned the party was to avoid giving the impression that the Rabin–Peres feud was still simmering. When an anonymous supporter distributed an anti-Peres sticker which stated: 'How many times have you voted for Peres and nothing happened?', Labour Party officials tried to play the incident down.

All was set for Labour's primary, the first in Israel's history. The members would all vote on one day — 19 February, 1992. Some 718 polling stations throughout the country opened and 150,000 registered party members were expected to vote. The Rabin side tended to regard a high turnout as advantageous, since Rabin was so popular. Peres' people never said it publicly, but they were hoping for a low turnout.

Rabin was up by 7:30 am talking on the phone with regional campaign leaders and workers, urging them to put in a hard day's work. The Rabins showed up at 2:30 pm to vote at the Ramat Aviv's Club Gimmel shopping and recreation centre: part of the complex, with its health club, hairstylist and swimming pool, had been designated as Labour Party polling centre 28.

To win the primary contest outright this evening, a candidate needed over 40 per cent of the vote. If no one attained that percentage, a run-off would be held between the candidates coming in first and second, almost certainly Rabin and Peres. Peres hoped desperately for a second round. It seemed his only chance of winning. In the first round four candidates would be running: Rabin, Peres, Ora Namir, and Yisrael Kessar.

Tension ran high that evening. Rabin closeted himself in his apartment until the results were known. At 9 pm, when the polling booths closed, a member of Peres' staff produced a poll showing that his candidate would get 41 per cent of the vote, Rabin only 32 per cent. Rabin's camp worried that perhaps the poll was right. Rabin's assistant, Shimon Sheves, fumed when someone had put a bottle of champagne in the refrigerator in Rabin's office. 'This is premature,' he shouted. 'It could bring bad luck.' He took the bottle and tossed it out of the window. At 10 pm, just over 5 per cent of the 100,347 ballots had been counted: Rabin had 39 per cent; Peres, 37 per cent, Kessar, 18 per cent and Namir, 6 per cent. For the next few hours, as voting results were announced, Rabin hovered near the crucial 40 per cent mark, always a few percentage points ahead of Peres. At one point Rabin had 39.99 per cent! It was clear that he had done better than Peres; it was not clear whether there would have to be a run-off.

Then the final results were known and Rabin had just squeaked by with 40.59 per cent of the vote; Peres had 34.80 per cent; Kessar, 18.77 per cent and Namir, 5.44 per cent. Pundits said later that Rabin owed his triumph to Kessar. Had Kessar not joined the race, Peres would have won.

Rabin had done it. He had wrested power from Shimon Peres. He became the Labour Party leader after fifteen years of waiting. He became Labour's candidate for prime minister. Rabin, not Peres, would take his party into the forthcoming national elections against Yitzhak Shamir and the Likud.

Once Rabin was clearly the winner, broadcast journalists tried to put Rabin and Peres on the phone to one another — live on the radio. The 'phone call' was hardly a success, what with the hesitant hellos before either man recognized who was on the line. Peres had trouble accepting defeat. Rabin was no more comfortable listening to Peres' grudging congratulations.

The next day, 20 February, Rabin moved into Peres' office at Labour Party headquarters. Soon thereafter, Rabin made his first appearance as Labour Party head at the Knesset Labour Party faction meeting. Peres was absent. Rabin had worked hard. He believed that the primaries would be easier than the general election. Soon he would find out the primaries were just the prelude to an even greater struggle.

The Labour Party would have a fresh look as they went into the national election. For the first time since 1977, Shimon Peres would not be at the head of the Labour ticket. The 'new face' was Yitzhak Rabin, who turned 70 in March.

Labour smelled victory on 23 June. The main reason was Rabin's presence at the head of the ticket. Almost as important, Labour had emerged with a brand-new identity. The leadership primaries had altered Labour's image from a party that engaged in deals, that chose its leaders and Knesset members in backrooms, that kept the selection process from the general membership. Now it appeared democratic, revitalized, eager for its members to participate in its crucial decisions. Later that spring the Labour Party chose its list of candidates for the Knesset using the same primary system. The results gave Labour a younger, more energetic look. Only one Labour Knesset member (Haim Ramon) had been under the age of 50 on the eve of the 1988 election. Labour now had six candidates in their 30s and 18 in their 40s.

Rabin's victory was bad for the Likud. Shamir and his allies had prayed for a Peres victory in the Labour primaries. They had already run against him four times and done very well. He was a known quantity. They knew how to 'sell' him to the electorate. Throughout the 80s, the Likud had painted Shimon Peres as a dangerous dove, ready to sell the country out to the Arabs. Israelis had bought the description. Israelis knew the new Labour Party leader as a hardliner, a tough soldier and commander, a no-nonsense type. Yossi Achimeir, Prime Minister Shamir's spokesman, told the Associated Press that the Likud will 'have to work harder' to defeat a Rabin-led Labour party. The Likud, argued Achimeir, would do its best to paint Rabin as a dove, to hammer home that he favoured territorial compromise no less than Peres did.

Ironically, the Likud was facing an uphill fight. The country had become a modern consumer society during the Likud years and the Likud should have been able to reap political benefit from this growing affluence. Israelis were buying more cars, more video players, travelling abroad more. The Likud could also have taken credit for an immense change in the country's diplomatic standing: the end of the Cold War and the indications that a Middle East peace process might be developing had created new opportunities for the Jewish state. In the second half of the 1980s, Israel's trade had doubled. And 35 countries, including Russia, China and India, had opened diplomatic relations with the Jewish state. And beginning in 1989, 400,000 Russian Jewish immigrants had arrived so that by the spring of 1992 they made up nearly 10 per cent of the Jewish population of Israel. All of these factors should have brought another Likud triumph.

Yet the Likud had come to symbolize a party that rigidly clung to the past, that was against change, that would not change even when it was good for the country, even when a majority wanted it. In fact Israel was growing less comfortable with rigid ideologies, whether political or religious, it was more and more fatigued with its conflict with the Arabs. Israelis wanted the good life, and did not see why they had to postpone that good life for another fifty years. As the *Washington Post*'s Jackson Diehl put it so well: 'There is evidence that Israel in the 1990s is rapidly nearing the final goal of the first Zionists, becoming a "normal" country, driven by the bourgeois material values and secular aspirations common in Western societies, rather than Jewish fears of destruction and another Holocaust, or nationalist dreams of territorial aggrandizement. Israeli politics in the coming years is likely to become less strident and less ideological, and its leaders more open to making compromises of both principle and territory in exchange for peace and prosperity.

'The early heroes of Israel were generals — Moshe Dayan, Ezer Weizman. Today the heroes might be more the heads of Israel's high-tech firms. The generals sought to preserve Israel against its political enemies — and to establish an irreversible presence in the Middle East. High-tech managers are trying to solve Israel's problem of economic viability by creating efficient, technology-intensive new industries that can compete on world markets, making Israel more economically independent.'[5]

While some argued that there were no palpable differences between Rabin and Shamir, most of the country sensed that there were in fact important distinctions in their political outlooks. Were Shamir to win re-election, he would unquestionably feel he had a mandate to keep the peace process on low boil, and to continue to defy President George Bush over Jewish settlements. A Shamir victory, in short, would most likely mean a continuation of the strained relations between Washington and Jerusalem. Rabin, as prime minister, would inevitably draw the United States and Israel together. After all, Rabin and the Labour Party consistently argued that they were ready to trade land for peace with their Arab neighbours.

Contributing much to Labour's new, positive image was the orderly, harmonious manner of the 19 February primary election. The contrast with the Likud was dramatic. The very next day, the Likud chose its leader, not by a primary system, but by a vote of its Central Committee. The three-way race pitted Yitzhak Shamir against Foreign Minister David Levy and Housing Minister Ariel Sharon. Shamir emerged the winner, collecting 46 per cent of the vote to Levy's 31 per cent; and Sharon's 20 per cent. Shamir's failure to win more than 50 per cent was considered a setback and indicative of his faltering stance.

Yitzhak Shamir entered the election campaign a hobbled prime minister. His ideological fervour, his conviction that Eretz Yisrael must be preserved above all else, had served him and the Likud in the past. Israelis had grown uneasy, however, about Shamir's preoccupation with realizing that dream through the expansion of Jewish settlement in the occupied territories. The year 1991 had been a boom year for the settlers: only 20,000 housing units had been built between 1967 and 1990; yet in 1991, 13,000 housing units were built. Moreover, the government had spent over 2.5 billion shekels ($1 billion), fully 15 per cent of its non-military budget, for housing, roads, schools and industrial development for the Jewish settlers. In that year, Shamir had erected 14 new settlements in the occupied lands.

Shamir's tangling with President Bush over the $10 billion in loan guarantees had disheartened Israelis as well. Many applauded his firmness; even Yitzhak Rabin acknowledged that, had he been in Shamir's shoes, he would have refused to cave in to Bush's demand to freeze Jewish settlements as the price for the loans. Israel's embroilment with Washington, however, left Israelis feeling insecure: the man blamed for the deteriorating relations was Shamir. Israelis were turning against Shamir and the Likud, however, for more fundamental reasons.

The country was increasingly eager for a negotiated settlement
of its differences with the Palestinians, Jordan, Syria, and
Lebanon. And yet Shamir and his Likud colleagues seemed to
discredit the Madrid peace process.

Moreover, the Likud's leaders seemed uninspiring, more
prone to bickering among themselves than demonstrating
political leadership. In contrast with Labour, Likud made few
changes in its Knesset list: still dominating its leadership were
Shamir, Defence Minister Moshe Arens, Foreign Minister
David Levy, and Housing Minister Ariel Sharon. None of these
four commanded a large following among the general public.
Rabin defeated all four in popularity polls easily.

Meanwhile, the Likud was busy digging its own political
grave. When David Levy and his supporters did not do as well as
they hoped in the Likud Central Committee's selection of the
party list, Levy sulked and threatened to leave the party. He
demanded increased representation in party institutions, a
guaranteed ministerial appointment and control over an
additional ministerial appointment. Shamir refused, and Levy
announced that he was quitting as foreign minister. Levy
encouraged rumours that he might leave the party, taking his
vote-getting talents and his numerous followers with him.
Shamir caved in to Levy, worried that he might be forced to step
down as prime minister if he allowed the bloodletting to persist.
Shamir's capitulation, however, while soothing Levy, only
angered Moshe Arens, who saw his own political power in the
Likud slipping away. All of this drama was played out nightly
on television. Labour benefited enormously. 'Fighting like that
did the job for us,' acknowledged Benyamin Ben-Eliezer, one of
Rabin's chief political lieutenants.[6] He was right. A survey
published in *Yediot Aharonot* on 10 April showed that 37 per cent
of Likud voters indicated that David Levy's demands had
weakened their loyalty to the Likud. Only 3 per cent said their
tendency to vote Likud had been strengthened by his behaviour.
The rest were indifferent.

The Likud grew desperate. The state comptroller's report
examining the government's behaviour during the previous
year was due out in May, just a month before the balloting.
Fearing that the report would indict the government for
mishandling Russian immigration and the economy, the Likud

chairman of the Knesset House committee, Haim Corfu, tried to pass an amendment to the State Comptroller Act which would have prohibited the publication of the report during the six months before Knesset elections. After a public uproar, Corfu withdrew his proposal. One other sign of the Likud's anxiety was Likud Knesset Speaker Dov Shilansky's sudden decision to send the Knesset out for its recess on 18 March, more than three months before the election so that Likud politicians would have adequate time to campaign. One dividend of that early recess to the Likud was that the bill proposing direct elections of the prime minister would only be completed after the election.

Rabin had the good fortune to run against Yitzhak Shamir. The nation appeared to be tiring of the old Likud veteran. 'I've never seen such consensus,' said one journalist with ties to the Labour Party. 'The foreign press, diplomats, the man in the street, Likud voters, everyone was glad to see Shamir go — because he exuded sterility to such a degree. It was almost like death. He kept saying, "I want nothing. I don't want anything to happen. I am closing down everything. I don't care what the world says." '

A pall of defeat hung over the Likud. Large portions of the party were discontented with Yitzhak Shamir. Many had grown to despise him for being weak, for not being able to take charge. One senior Likud official noted, 'Privately, the Likud ministers mocked Shamir. They didn't think he was a great intellect. He was too extreme. He didn't inspire them, like Begin had. He was their boss, not their leader.'

Twice in the past two years Shamir had encountered 'palace coups' from within the Likud. The first came in March 1990. At that time loyalists to Moshe Arens tried to oust Shamir from the prime ministership. They accused the prime minister of bringing about the fall of the National Unity Government. That 'palace coup' failed. The second attempt came right after the Likud Central Committee meeting of 20 February, 1992. This time allies of Benyamin 'Bibi' Netanyahu sent hints to Shamir to resign. No one ever spoke to Shamir directly about stepping down. They talked instead to Shamir's aides and sympathizers within the Cabinet who passed on these messages to the prime minister. Again, the 'palace coup' failed, but both had illustrated how serious was the Likud's predicament.

Most Likudniks, including Shamir, smelled defeat.

Dr Yossi Olmert, the head of the Government Press Office, went to see Shamir in March 1992 to try to shake the prime minister out of his torpor.

'We're going to lose the election,' Olmert insisted.

'Why do you think that?' Shamir asked, answering before Olmert could: 'The people are tired of us. We don't have a majority of the people. It's an illusion to think we do.' He called that fatigue a 'national weakness', blaming the people, not himself or the Likud.

Questions remained: by what margin would Labour win? Would that margin be sufficient for Labour to form a government? The answers were made more difficult because the nature of the electorate was strikingly different from past elections: a record 3,409,315 voters were eligible to vote; there were a record number of new voters — 536,773. Among those new voters, a large pool of new immigrants (240,000 Russian and 25,000 Ethiopian) would vote for the first time. With 21,000 votes necessary to win a Knesset seat and with 190,000 Russians expected to vote, the Russian immigrants formed a powerful, new political force that could control as many as 9 of the 120 Knesset seats. Their votes would be crucial and for that reason Russian subtitles appeared in much of the television election propaganda. Israeli politicians sprinkled their campaign talks with words or phrases in Russian. Parties geared their electoral strategies towards the Russian immigrants, promising that, if elected, they would improve their lot. Earlier, these Russian immigrants favoured the Likud but by 1992 they were angry at the ruling coalition for failing to deliver proper housing and jobs to them.

Public opinion surveys continued to put Labour out in front. The trouble was that those same surveys had given Labour an advantage early in the election campaigns of the 1980s, and on election day, the voters had produced entirely different results. Labour politicians expressed caution about current polls.

Still, voters did seem to be leaning toward Labour. Rabin's triumph in the primaries had energized the party's rank-and-file and, thanks to Rabin's centrist, hardline image, generated interest among Likud voters. 'People everywhere congratulate me,' said Avraham 'Beiga' Shochat, the head of Rabin's campaign, 'and Likud supporters say: "Now that you've chosen Rabin, we're with you".'

Rabin shrewdly understood that Israelis had become embittered. They were not pleased that Shamir gave preference to Jewish settlements in the occupied lands over all other critical needs. Indeed, between June 1990, when the Shamir Government took power, and March 1992, 3 billion shekels ($1.2 billion) had been poured into the territories. For this reason, and others, Rabin felt that the country was ripe for a change, and he intended to exploit it. In a talk to the Labour Party Central Committee on 1 March, he raised the themes that he would take to the voters.

'Whoever travels around the country and meets the various publics can perceive the beginning of a change, the beginning of a new hope, the beginning of a popular understanding that it is necessary to replace the Likud in order to give the State of Israel a chance.

'I believe that this change stems from two sources. The first is the realization that the Likud misses, is missing and will continue to miss the great opportunities which present themselves to the state, whether in the sphere of advancing peace while preserving security, or in the sphere of the national priorities. In the current erroneous and distorted order of priorities, political settlements in the territories precede everything else: immigration absorption, the future of the younger generation, the war against unemployment, and social and economic progress. There is widespread disappointment with the deficient functioning of this government in almost all spheres of life . . .

'Should I form the next Israeli government I undertake to reach an agreement with the Palestinians in the territories over the establishment of an autonomy within six to nine months. After the agreement with the Palestinians, we shall reach an agreement with Jordan and then with Syria. The second thing which I undertake is to stop the political settlements, whose only purpose is to prevent any possibility of finding a political solution to the conflict.

'If the construction were taking place in Greater Jerusalem, the Jordan Rift and the existing settlements on the Golan

Heights, I would not complain. But the Likud is diverting thousands of millions of shekels to political settlements which have no value in security terms, and in addition to blocking any possibility for peace, prevent the channelling of resources into those spheres where they are really needed.'

In later days, he became more specific on how he differed in his approach towards the peace process from Shamir and the Likud. On 23 April, he told the *Jerusalem Post* that, unlike the Baker–Shamir approach of trying for concurrent peace negotiations with all Arab parties, he planned to give priority to Israeli–Palestinian negotiations. 'Because,' he said in that *Post* interview, 'once you solve the problem between us and the Palestinians in the territories, there is no problem with Jordan. Once you solve the problem between Israel and the Syrians, there is no problem with the Lebanese.' His timetable: first he would try to reach autonomy with the Palestinians, then turn to Jordan, then to Syria to seek peace treaties.

As part of the Madrid peace conference format, the Palestinians had been integrated into a joint delegation with the Jordanians — against the wishes of the Palestinians. Rabin said he would not mind a separate Palestinian delegation. 'Only the Palestinians can speak in their name,' he told Reuters in early March.[7]

In an interview with *Newsweek* on 30 March, he outlined his views on autonomy for the Palestinians. 'They would run all their internal affairs. They would not have a foreign policy, or control of security or defence . . . I am against the uprooting of settlements . . . solving the problem of the Palestinians must come first. After that there is nothing to prevent an agreement with Jordan. Syria is a tougher nut to crack.'

As for Syria, Rabin laid out a novel approach towards a political solution. Israel captured the Golan in the Six-Day War and annexed the territory in 1981. In late April 1992, Rabin told the *Jerusalem Post* that he did not support an Israeli withdrawal from the Golan, but he might support leasing the region from Syria as part of a final peace agreement. 'I believe that Israel should not go down from the Golan Heights, even in the context of a peace treaty. At the same time, there is limited room for a territorial compromise. There might be other compromises which I will not elaborate on, like leasing the land.'[8]

Rabin understood that, in attempting to sound more flexible on peacemaking than Shamir, he could not afford to give the impression that he was 'soft' on national security. If Israelis were growing tired of Shamir, they still wanted their prime minister to protect them. Thus, Rabin wrote in the *Jerusalem Post* on 1 June: 'I am unwilling to give up a single inch of Israel's security, but I am willing to give up many inches of sentiments and territories — as well as 1,700,000 Arab inhabitants — for the sake of peace. That is the whole doctrine in a nutshell. We seek a territorial compromise which will bring peace and security. A lot of security.'[9]

It occurred to Labour Party strategists early on that their greatest electoral asset was Yitzhak Rabin himself. For years, Israelis had been conditioned to vote for parties, not personalities. Never before had a political party in Israel used the personality of its candidate for prime minister as the focus of its vote-getting strategy. Even when such luminaries as David Ben-Gurion, Golda Meir, and Menachem Begin had headed their parties' Knesset lists, campaign strategists had made the political party the centrepiece of their campaigns. This time, however, Labour's strategists wanted to exploit the fact that the public tended to blame the major political parties, Labour and Likud, for all the nation's ailments; and to take advantage of Rabin's great personal popularity. By propelling the hardline Rabin forward, the strategists were confident that they could expunge Labour's long-standing leftist image.

Had Rabin had his way, Israel would have elected its prime minister through a system of direct elections; but the Likud had made sure that the law calling for direct election of the prime minister would take effect only in 1996. 'The Likud was afraid to put Shamir against me — or any other candidates that they could produce,' Rabin told the *New York Times*. So Labour, Rabin explained, adopted a campaign strategy that put unusually strong emphasis on him personally as well as on party policies. 'It is a combination of the who and the what,' Rabin said.[10]

Certain risks existed in following this tactic. The reaction among Labour Party members could have been negative. Nothing worried Benyamin Ben-Eliezer more: 'I was afraid that people would say: "What is this, a one-man show?"'[11] By focusing on Rabin's personality, Labour was virtually inviting the Likud to launch personal attacks against him.

Then too, Rabin lacked charisma. He was certainly no Ben-Gurion, no Begin, no Golda Meir; it could be difficult selling his personality to the electorate. He did not mesmerize. He did not charm. He was almost the last person around whom one would try to form a personality cult. Yet, Israelis were searching for someone who could extricate the country from its deadlocked foreign policy, its atrophied economy. Noted Benyamin Ben-Eliezer: 'They were looking for a leader like Menachem Begin, someone who will lead them, someone who won't let them down.'[12]

To accentuate Rabin, the strategists took a number of unusual steps. The most dramatic being: for the first time Labour used the slogan 'Labour under Rabin' on the ballot rather than just 'Labour'. Not even when David Ben-Gurion, the founding father of the state, ran at the head of the Labour ticket, did Labour use 'Labour under Ben-Gurion'. Shimon Peres was steaming; 'Maybe you want to remove the word Labour also,' he sneered. But there was little he could do about it.

One of the most clever steps was the campaign jingle, 'The People Are Waiting for Rabin', with its not-so-subtle associations with the glorious days of the 1967 Six-Day War. Egypt's Nasser had once said that if Rabin wants to attack me, I'm waiting for him. That led to the classic Six-Day War tune, 'Nasser Is Waiting for Rabin'. Labour's marketing managers shrewdly had parodied that tune, conjuring up images of Rabin, the Six-Day War hero.

A huge banner with a picture of Rabin was draped outside Labour Party headquarters on Hayarkon Street in Tel Aviv. At Labour Party celebrations marking the 25th anniversary of Israel's conquest of Jerusalem (on 31 May) Rabin, the former chief of staff whose army captured East Jerusalem, including the Old City and the Western Wall, was put in the spotlight, re-enacting his famous 'march' into the Old City of 7 June, 1967. In Labour's newspaper advertising, Rabin's photo appeared prominently as it did on the party's television election propaganda; not a day passed in the final three weeks of the campaign without Rabin making a television appearance. 'Labour' was barely mentioned in the election advertising. In that television advertising, it was Yitzhak Rabin, the triumphant chief of staff in 1967, forger of the Sinai interim peace agreement with Egypt in 1975, hero of Entebbe, the man who took Israel out of Lebanon in 1985.

The entire campaign was built around Rabin. Everything was done to get across the image of Rabin as leader. Ordinarily, Labour would have used photographs of its other leading candidates. Not this time.

According to his campaign aides, Rabin did not allow the development of the 'personality cult' to affect him. At first, he was concerned that Labour politicians would be offended. When he saw that the tactic was accepted by most, Rabin relaxed. Gad Ben-Ari, who spent each day of the campaign with the candidate and served as his spokesman, recalled: 'Rabin would be sitting in the car and looking at his photo across the street. He would be listening to the jingle all the time. Such things might have inflated someone's ego. It didn't touch him at all. It wasn't that he didn't believe he should be master of the house. But he saw all of this as sheer technique.'[13] Pretty soon, everyone got the message. Marcus Eliason, the bureau chief of the Associated Press in Jerusalem, called the Labour Party headquarters in Tel Aviv one day during the campaign, and asked, 'Is this the Labour Party?'

'No,' said the female voice on the other end of the line, 'It's Yitzhak Rabin's office.'

As part of the focus on his personality, Rabin's campaign strategists decided to mount an 'American-style' campaign, getting the candidate into the streets as often as possible, placing him before large audiences. Each appearance had to be as colourful as possible. A Rabin campaign appearance had an air of great excitement: the catchy jingle blaring in the background, balloons all around, and the frenzied crowd waiting impatiently for the 'star' of the evening to appear. At the Ha'aretz Museum one Saturday evening, young Labour activists, streaming in from around the country, filled the hall. Gad Ben-Ari recalled: 'It was like a rock show. Lights. Loud pop music. Cheering. The jingle in the background. Then Rabin appeared. Instead of walking slowly to the mike, he ran.'

Rabin's minimal electoral strategy was designed to obtain a
'blocking group' of 60 Knesset seats from among the Labour
Party and left-wing parties. Labour and its left-wing allies had
gained only 55 seats in the 1988 elections. With 60 seats, Labour
would be able to prevent the Likud from forming its own
government. Rabin would be assured of sharing power with the
Likud in some form of National Unity Government. He did not
want to share power, however. So his ultimate aim was to obtain
at least 61 seats. Then he could form his own government.

Rabin's electoral strategy was to fight for the middle ground,
especially the disenchanted Likud voter. He hoped to take as
many as five Knesset seats away from Likud. It did not seem
impossible. The public opinion polls suggested that growing
numbers of Likud voters had become disaffected by Likud
policies that gave preference to Jewish settlements in the
occupied territories at the expense of Israelis in pre-1967 Israel.
What disturbed these Israelis the most was unemployment,
which in the first three months of 1992 had reached a record 11.5
per cent, or 212,000 people out of work. Unemployment was at
its highest levels in the development towns and poor
neighbourhoods, places that had long been Likud bastions. It
was in these locations that Rabin had rising political strength.

Why would Likud voters choose Rabin over Shamir? The
question baffled the Likud's election strategists. They planned
to pound home the twin themes that under Shamir, Israelis had
welcomed 400,000 Russian immigrants, and that under Shamir,
a peace process had begun. Still, this was insufficient to win over
all Likud voters. A growing number of them hoped for a secure
peace, but they were not sure that Yitzhak Shamir was prepared
to deliver. They were willing to give Rabin, whose hawkish
credentials were impeccable, a chance. The one segment of the
population where Rabin was weak was among the nation's
820,000 Israeli Arabs. They remembered Rabin as the hardline
defence minister who had inflicted much pain and sorrow on
their brother Palestinian Arabs in the territories. Yet, in a choice
between Rabin and Shamir, the Israeli Arabs preferred Rabin
because he was the more likely to grant the Palestinians
autonomy.

With Rabin at Labour's helm, the Likud had difficulty

characterizing Labour as a bunch of compromising, give-it-all-away doves. Still, they tried. Labour's Knesset list was replete with left-wing figures (including Shimon Peres); Labour and Meretz, a small left-wing party, had promised to be coalition partners in a Labour-led government. Hence, Likud newspaper ads asserted: 'The Likud is for the people, Rabin is for the Left.' Countering that, Rabin's handlers portrayed him as a centrist.

Trying to appeal to disenchanted Likud voters, as well as Russian immigrants and first-time young voters, many of whom had been inclined towards the political right, Rabin tried to show that he was every bit as tough as Shamir. On 25 March, Rabin told hundreds of supporters at a Jerusalem rally that Labour would also have rejected George Bush's demand to halt building in the occupied areas, rather than meet that condition in order to receive the $10 billion in loan guarantees. Though acknowledging that he would have limited construction to Jerusalem and the border areas, Rabin remained hawkish: 'I will not accept a condition that says we cannot build neighbourhoods in united Jerusalem, or that we cannot strengthen settlements along the Jordan River and the Golan Heights. Based on past experience, I believe that if the Americans understood that we were focusing on building neighbourhoods in Jerusalem and along the border, we could reach an understanding with them.'

By such statements, Rabin convinced the electorate that he was no Yitzhak Shamir, no ideological zealot, yet he was just as tough, just as unwilling to sell the country out to the Arabs, just as prepared to use an iron fist, if and when necessary, against terrorists, against Palestinian troublemakers. The public was given the chance to identify with someone other than Shamir, and feel comfortable with this alternative. For years, Shimon Peres had been that alternative; he had discomforted the political right. Now the voters had a genuine choice.

The thrust of Labour's advertising was to make the voter trust Rabin to provide maximum security. Hence, one Labour Party campaign newspaper advertisement printed on 20 May showed a photo of Rabin with an Israeli flag behind him. Its caption read 'Yes to security and peace from a position of strength. Israel is waiting for Rabin.'

*

Labour had thrust personality into the foreground, not only to exalt Yitzhak Rabin to legendary proportions, but also to pour calumny on the pitiful figure of Yitzhak Shamir. If Rabin could do no wrong, in Labour's eyes, Shamir could do no right. Rather than go into specifics about what he would do as prime minister, Rabin kept to generalities, saying mostly that he planned to correct the distortions and mistakes of the Shamir government, redirect national resources away from Jewish settlement, using those resources for jobs and housing for Russian immigrants, reducing unemployment, helping the economy to grow. Rabin and Labour projected the theme that the Likud had ruined the country. It charged the Likud with the severe decline in Russian immigration. Labour was of course right that fewer Russians were coming. Only 4,142 Russian immigrants reached Israel in May 1992, the month before the election, 1,487 less than in April, and far lower than at the end of 1990, when immigrants were arriving at a monthly rate of 30,000–35,000. Only 28,497 Russians had arrived since the start of 1992.

With Rabin cast as its star, Labour all but invited the Likud to attack the persona of Rabin, and shelve discussion of specific issues. Rabin believed he could handle the personal assaults, if and when they came. Though most of the charges that the Likud brought against Rabin were old, they produced huge headlines, and took on greater significance coming in the midst of the heated political campaign. The most emotional Likud charge was that Rabin, on the eve of the 1967 Six-Day War, suffered a nervous breakdown. As early as 1977, Rabin had discussed the issue publicly. His first public explanation was given to the author at that time. It did not matter to the Likud that the public had not held Rabin's collapse against him in subsequent years. The fact was that Rabin had bounced back from his collapse almost immediately, and gone on to command the IDF in its stunning victory during the Six-Day War; he had functioned as a prime minister for three years, a Knesset member for seven, a defence minister for six more, and again a Knesset member for the last two years. Surely, that record should have told the Likud that the accusation was useless; the Likud, however, was not fazed by such facts. It went after Rabin as if the collapse had taken place a few days earlier. Towards the end of May, Likud strategists released balloons which said, '25th anniversary of the Collapse' into the Tel Aviv skies to 'remind' voters that Rabin was unfit to govern. Also: a special Likud telephone hot-line provided Rabin's own account of the incident to the musical accompaniment of the theme song from *Superman.*

Rabin's strategists were surprised that the Likud brought the charges up so early in the campaign. They anticipated that they would be used, but only in the closing days. Rabin took their early use as a good sign that the Likud was panicking. 'If these are the charges the Likud has against me, it's a sign they have nothing to sell. It brings me political utility. The public sees the full picture. It knows my record and believes me.'[14]

Significantly, the Likud did not play up the bank-account scandal of 1977 in the campaign, sensing that the public had forgiven Rabin, sharply reducing the chance for political gain. Gad Ben-Ari gleefully explained why: 'What people remembered about the bank-account affair is the scene of Rabin, the gentleman, who took personal responsibility for a technical mistake by his wife and was willing to step down and willing to give up so much.'[15] Rabin, however, brought it up, suggesting that his behaviour in the wake of the scandal should become a role model for how politicians who make mistakes should act. 'In the Likud no one resigned because of issues that were far more harsh and serious than this dollar account. I resigned then from the post of prime minister because I made a mistake and when you make mistakes you have to draw conclusions.' A reporter asked him if he was sorry now (fifteen years later) that he had resigned. Rabin replied, 'I was then very satisfied with my decision. That is how a public figure has to behave.'[16]

The Likud charged Rabin with being an alcoholic. Many Israelis, having listened to rumours over the years, had taken for granted that Rabin was a heavy drinker. He was no teetotaller; anyone who had seen him at receptions could attest to that. The fact was, however, that no one could pinpoint any one day when Rabin's drinking had affected his abilities as a public servant. Again, the Likud believed that it could gain some political mileage from the rumours. Party activists passed out paper cups and car stickers on which was written, 'Better to have a sober prime minister than a drunk one'. They chanted to Rabin: 'Go home and have a cognac, and get some sleep.'

Rabin's strategy in dealing with these charges was to offer a candid, immediate response, and hope that the public would side with him. Thus he gave an interview to *Yediot Aharonot* on 25 May in which he said: 'It's correct that an accident befell me 12 days before the Six-Day War. One day I was at home. I slept. I don't conceal this and I have nothing to hide. . . . I felt a terrible isolation. A military man under the orders of the political level. He doesn't accept decisions alone, I have no freedom of manoeuvre, I have to implement, and that was why I felt this isolation. I didn't conceal that this occurred to me. I wrote about this in my *Memoirs*, and when it happened those who needed to know what happened to me, did know. I was in a state of depression. It was after a few days of great tension without food or sleep.'

The period of these personal attacks was anguishing for Rabin. 'It was a tough week,' recalled campaign spokesman Gad Ben-Ari. 'He didn't say a word. He was tense. He took it hard. The collapse charge bothered him more (than the alcoholism) because the collapse took place. The drinking never took place. He said that was nonsense. We considered (but rejected doing) all kinds of things against Shamir. We had things on him. He did the interview in *Yediot Aharonot*. People loved it. He didn't ignore the accusations. He addressed the charges very openly. That made him very human. They forgave him.'[17] Rabin was worried that the voters would punish him, that the good crowds and strong showings in the surveys would disappear. His campaign staff went into the most diehard of Likud political bastions to get a quick read-out of how the headlines were playing. What they found pleased them. Those surveyed pointed to Rabin's integrity and honesty as key factors in their decision to support him. 'After 24 hours,' boasted Benyamin Ben-Eliezer, who took the surveys, 'I realized that the charges would help Rabin. I thought to myself: "Bring on more such charges."'[18]

Still the charges hurt. Angered by the alcoholism charge, Leah Rabin told an interviewer on Israel Radio on 21 May that when her husband 'arrives home, he doesn't drink. The bottle can stand days without his touching it. And if he drinks one glass from time to time, this does not make him an alcoholic.'

Rabin paid less attention to the alcoholism accusation than to the collapse allegations. He felt that the alcoholism charge was 'nonsense', that he was no alcoholic, and the less said about the accusation, the better. When he was asked outright by a reporter, did he drink, he answered, 'Like everyone else, a glass here or there.' If that was the case, the reporter continued, why didn't he speak about this? 'I do speak. Three years ago when the rumours began, I went to the Knesset dining room and seated around a table full of people, I ordered a whiskey with ice and I said that it was forbidden for me to ruin my reputation. I am insulted by all these rumours.'[19] Rabin never showed anger at the alcoholism charge, discomfort yes, but never anger. Once during the campaign he visited the Patt neighbourhood in Jerusalem and was hosted by Rafi Bar Lavi, head of the Georgian community in Jerusalem. Bar Lavi poured half a bottle of white wine into a Georgian drinking horn, and finished it off in one long swig. 'Don't worry,' he told Rabin, who made an expression as if he were aghast at such heavy drinking. 'Only I drink here. That's our custom.' Rabin grinned and then replied in good humour, 'Be careful. You'll get me into trouble.'

By early June, the campaign had moved into high gear. Political analysts had detected some clear signs that voters were less interested in the peace process than in their own quality of life. For that reason, the main question being asked in this campaign was not how much territory Israel should yield to the Arabs, but whether the Likud, which had governed for all but two of the past fifteen years, should be permitted to continue to rule. What some analysts saw in the Likud was a party that had governed for too long, whose leaders had grown too used to power. Bitter evidence of this appeared when the State Comptroller's annual report was issued in late April and strongly criticized the government, singling out Ariel Sharon's Ministry of Housing as having spent government money profligately and wastefully in its effort to absorb Russian immigrants over the past two years. The report charged Sharon's appointees with squandering public funds for personal and political gain. Three Sharon aides were accused of wrongdoings that ranged from paying for vacations with office funds to using ministry vehicles while on Likud party business.

Labour's message appeared to be getting through to the voter. A poll published in *Yediot Aharonot* on 10 April showed Labour getting 44 seats to the Likud's 35. Much closer to the election, on 29 May, *Yediot Aharonot* ran two conflicting polls: the Dahaf polling institute had the Likud bloc getting 60 seats; the Teleskar polling firm had Labour getting 61. Where the two polling institutes agreed was that Labour had a 10-seat advantage over the Likud.

The major parties did not differ radically on their approach to the dominant issues of the day. Labour and Likud both sanctioned autonomy as an interim solution for the Palestinian Arabs of the occupied territories. The main differences were that Rabin made it clear that Israel should try to solve the Palestinian Arab issue first, and leave differences with other Arab states (Jordan, Lebanon and Syria) until the Palestinian issue was resolved. Shamir continued to believe that it was possible to solve all the issues at once. Rabin promised that he would work out an autonomy agreement within nine months to a year after becoming prime minister. Shamir made no such promises on a timetable.

The politicians did not argue how much autonomy to give the Palestinians or, for that matter, how much land must be returned to the Jordanians, Lebanese, and Syrians. When peace and security issues arose, it was always in the context of: who can best protect the country from the Arabs? Who is least likely to 'sell' Israel's security down the drain? In early June Labour and Likud were quarrelling over this issue. In one newspaper advertisement, Likud charged that a Rabin-led government would lead to a Palestinian state accompanied by terrorist action 'in the heart of Israel'. But Labour, in its response, proclaimed simply, 'We are security.' After Rabin chided Shamir for allowing Israel's internal security to deteriorate in recent weeks (symbolized by the fatal stabbing of a fifteen-year-old Israeli girl in Bat Yam on 24 May), the prime minister poured venom on Rabin for permitting three major terrorist attacks (in Kiryat Shemona, 11 April, 1974; Ma'alot, 15 May, 1974 and in Tel Aviv in March 1975). Never mind that Rabin was prime minister only when the Tel Aviv attack occurred!

Rabin's strategists decided to focus its attacks on Shamir personally. They had planned to make Likud corruption the centrepiece of their election strategy in the closing days, but then switched to the prime minister as their main target.

In striking contrast with Labour's focusing on Rabin, the Likud downplayed its own candidate for prime minister. If Rabin's photo was seen everywhere, it was difficult to find Shamir's. The Likud, meanwhile, was shifting away from personal attacks on Rabin and accenting the dovishness of Labour's leadership. It used slogans such as 'The Likud against the entire left wing'. It argued that a Rabin-led government would make the kinds of territorial compromises that would lead to a Palestinian state. Labour responded by building up Rabin as a centrist: 'Neither the extreme of the left nor the right', said one Labour newspaper advertisement.

The public's warm response to Rabin had its effect on him. Reporters sensed that the country was moving into Rabin's corner and faithfully recorded the change. Each low point of the Likud was also duly registered. All of this boosted Rabin's self-confidence. He began to believe that something good was happening out there. He smiled a great deal. He shook hands more. He was more cheerful. It was not easy for him. He was no born campaigner. Rabin disliked physical contact with street crowds. Campaigning at the Ramat Gan shopping centre, Rabin came across a woman with a baby. Spokesman Ben-Ari whispered to Rabin that he should 'do something' with the baby, it would make a good photo for the next day's newspapers. 'Anyone else would have jumped at the opportunity,' recalled Ben-Ari. 'Not Rabin. He simply refused. He didn't like to get beyond the edge, to do gimmicks.'[20] Yet, he was pleased that so many people greeted him around the country. Returning to Tel Aviv Labour headquarters one day, he told Benyamin 'Fouad' Ben-Eliezer, 'Fouad, thousands came. Thousands.' Indeed, they had: 3,100 in Bat Yam. 3,000 in Kiryat Shemona. At some rallies, as many as 5,000 showed up. Often, upon arriving somewhere, a local official would tell Rabin and his entourage, 'Shamir was here last week. He attracted a crowd only half the size.' Leah Rabin was swept up in the enthusiasm too. 'I thought that maybe something great is happening. It was the same feeling that we had after the Six-Day War. That outburst of joy. Relief. Happiness.'[21]

Rabin's campaign strategy was to seek out Likud bastions,

despite the possibility that the candidate would encounter hostile crowds. On 11 May, Rabin went into the Hatikva quarter of Tel Aviv where Labour had received only 7 per cent of the vote last time. He was well received. Gratified, he told his aides: 'They aren't throwing tomatoes at me. That's a good sign.' Once, as Rabin walked to a helicopter after visiting the large Jewish town of Ma'ale Adumim where the Likud believed it would do well, a television reporter asked him if he felt Ma'ale Adumim was with him. 'No,' Rabin answered honestly. 'I don't deceive myself. But our purpose is to go to those places where we didn't have great results in the past.'

Each night Rabin arrived home after midnight. All he had the strength to say to Leah was, 'The feeling is good, excellent. The rallies are great. But how it will be translated at the polls, we'll have to see.' That was Yitzhak Rabin, the born pessimist, speaking.

If things were going well for Labour, they were proving disastrous for the Likud. Shamir, on a helicopter trip to Beersheba for a campaign rally, was confronted by a group of protesters with banners that read: 'Shamir hates Moroccans. We're all Moroccans here.' The group began chanting 'Rabin, King of Israel', and 'liars, liars'. Shamir lost his cool and called the hecklers 'terrorists'. He shouted that they had been hired by Labour. But Shamir knew better. This was, unfortunately, for him, an authentic indication of how the people felt towards him. Shamir had trouble digesting the change. Flying home from Beersheba, he told *Yediot Aharonot*'s Nahum Barnea that he had never been heckled like that in his life. When Barnea pointed out that the protesters had voted Likud last time round, Shamir muttered, 'Impossible, impossible.' More pain was inflicted on the Likud that week when a public opinion poll showed Labour getting 15 more seats than Likud, 46 to 31.

One highlight of the campaign was the television 'debate' between Rabin and Shamir a week before the 23 June election. It was taped on the morning of 16 June, then shown on television that evening. With large numbers of voters apparently still undecided, the performances of the two candidates seemed of critical importance. Though his aides pressed him to run some simulations of the debate, Rabin said no: 'I'm not an actor. I am who I am.' Shamir had been coached carefully, and told to smile as much as possible, apparently to present an image of a leader unburdened by the great problems facing Israel. However dismal Rabin and the Labour Party had been painting life under the Likud, Shamir had his answers: 'This government has achieved great accomplishments in all fields and it would be regretful to stop them. In Gaza — as in other places — they [Palestinian Arabs] are attacking us, but we deal with this and we will prevail. We are interested in peace with Syria, but I will not be prepared to discuss whether the intention is to talk about territorial changes. We have [registered] prominent achievements in the economic sphere. Only yesterday, we were informed of the low [May] cost of living index. The economy has grown by 7 per cent and the GNP doubled itself. This unemployment is the result of the large wave of immigration. Unemployment among veteran residents is decreasing. Every year, we are creating thousands of jobs.'

Rabin stressed the theme of individual security, sensing that Israelis were deeply concerned with the recent spate of stabbings perpetrated by Palestinian Arabs from the Gaza Strip. 'At the end of the process, I do not want to see the 700,000 Gazans participating in [Israeli] elections, carrying Israeli identity cards and walking around in our cities. Our first phase is the establishment of autonomy; we will enlist financial resources from the Arab world, and we will see less Gazans in the streets. I want to see the Gazans in Gaza.' With the Likud trying to portray Rabin and the Labour Party as too left-wing for Israel's comfort, Rabin suggested that no one could pin such labels on him. After promising that he would not bring Arab political parties into his coalition, should he win on 23 June, he added: 'I object to a Palestinian state between us and Jordan. To the same extent, I do not want 1.7 million Palestinians to be citizens of Israel. There are three points upon which I will stand: no Palestinian state; no return to 1967 borders; and a united Jerusalem under Israeli sovereignty.'

Rabin watched the debate that evening at the Jerusalem Gates Hotel in Jerusalem. A group of 'disappointed Likudniks' had gathered there to hear Rabin. A large television screen was put up. The audience was decidedly in Rabin's pocket. When Shamir said during the debate that there was no crisis with America, the audience howled. When Rabin said the Likud was the champion of returning territories, the hall burst into applause. Moments after the debate ended, Rabin phoned Leah to seek out her opinion: 'Nu, what do you say?'

'You were excellent, simply wonderful.' Polls taken afterward suggested that the country was split over who won.

Meanwhile, Rabin concentrated his attention on disappointed Likudniks during the campaign's final days. On a tour in Tel Aviv, he visited Likud country, stopping at the home of Avraham Sharabani, a veteran of the pre-state Irgun underground movement, in Hadar Yosef. Sharabani was once a member of the Likud Central Committee, and still greatly admired Menachem Begin. He and Rabin shared a sofa surrounded by neighbours and photographers. Sharabani then read slowly: 'What broke me as a Likudnik was the constant bickering. They have made Shamir a nonentity. For years I saw what was happening and I warned them, but they took no notice. So I will vote for a man who I think can lead Israel the way I want it to be led.' Worst for Sharabani had been the Likud's personal attacks on Rabin. 'How dare they? You, a former chief of staff, defence minister and prime minister. But take heart, Yitzhak. Filth never won elections. They're only bringing you closer to office.'

It was music to Rabin's ears, and there seemed to be many more Sharabanis out there.

Sometimes Rabin would encounter bitterness. Some Israelis, for instance, still held his behaviour during the Intifada against him. While Rabin was on a campaign visit to the Red Sea resort town of Eilat, a youngster looked into the candidate's eyes and declared, 'I want an answer to only one thing: why didn't you stand behind those soldiers who under your command broke hands and legs? Why did you abandon them?' The crowd grew tense, but Rabin stayed calm, answering firmly: 'I didn't use the expression "break the hands or feet". It is correct. There was an order to beat when there were riots. But there was no order to take citizens from their homes and beat them. Whoever did that was punished. There were all in all four cases like this.'

'You answered me,' the youngster said. 'But I don't accept the answer.' Rabin shook his hand. It transpired that the youngster supported the small right-wing party Moledet.

*

In the final hours before election day, Tuesday, 23 June, an air of excitement crept into the Rabin household. On the Friday afternoon before Rabin attended a performance of the Red Army choir. Speaking engagements had robbed him of his voice. He kept his smoking to a minimum. Exhausted, he slept late Saturday morning, rather than visit the Accadia Hotel in Herzlyia, his usual Saturday haunt, where he and Leah hit tennis balls each week. The Rabin children stayed close. Dahlia was now a prosecutor for the Tel Aviv District. Yuval, who worked for a company that markets Israeli software in the United States, arrived at the last minute from North Carolina, where he had been living.

The campaign wound down to Monday, 22 June. The mood within the Rabin camp was upbeat. When he arrived at the Cinerama theatre in Tel Aviv for a last-minute campaign rally, Rabin was received like a pop star. Labour's election jingle was played and applauding women stood up and screamed. Afterwards, Rabin travelled to a meeting with former Likud supporters in the Hatikva quarter in Tel Aviv.

In marked contrast, Yitzhak Shamir avoided the campaign trail. Trailing in the polls, the prime minister became subject to all sorts of wild proposals from campaign aides to do something dramatic that might attract voters. No one was terribly specific. Mentioned were the areas of capital punishment, the Gaza Strip, Syria, unemployment. Someone suggested that Shamir seek another round of peace talks. To all such ideas, he shrugged his shoulders. He was in no mood for grand gestures. Described by one aide as 'a bit tense', he spent the last day of the campaign in his Jerusalem office making phone calls to campaign staff. Aides advised Shamir to make a spontaneous appearance at an open-air market in a major city — to make one last major bid for votes — before campaigning officially halted at 7 pm Monday. The prime minister grumpily said no. He had told a reporter that day, 'There is no question, I will form the government.' Why campaign further? He went home for lunch at 1 pm, then took his daily two-hour nap. He returned to the office at 4, made calls to party activists, and then went home for the night at 8 pm.

Rabin made a frenetic helicopter tour of the country on his last day. A reporter travelling with Rabin noticed that Rabin no longer seemed embarrassed by hugs and kisses: 'He is quiet, calm, like someone who knows that something good is about to happen to him.'

Labour still led in the polls. Four opinion surveys published the day before the balloting gave the upper hand to Labour, though the margin was too small to be considered decisive. Two surveys published in *Yediot Aharonot* gave Labour and its left-wing allies between 61 to 64 seats, enough to assure victory. But a survey in another newspaper, *Hadashot*, showed the right- and left-wing bloc tied at 55 seats each, with Labour holding only a two-seat advantage over Likud, 40–38.

Finally, it was election eve. In the early evening hours Rabin seemed worried. He told his wife, 'The Likud has put in a lot of effort in the last few days.' Leah tried to comfort him, 'It will be OK.'

At 10 pm, Israelis were glued to their television sets. Here was Haim Yavin, the Israel Television announcer, announcing that the polls had closed and that he was about to announce the results of Israel TV's exit poll. Slightly over 20,000 voters at 54 polling stations had been asked that day to record a duplicate vote for Israel TV. Israelis took the exit polls seriously: they had usually been accurate.

Yavin uttered the next few words, knowing the impact they would have on the entire nation. His voice trembled as he spoke:

'We have the exit poll results and they tell of an upheaval.'

He had used the Hebrew word 'ma'apach' — upheaval. The meaning was clear to everyone.

As soon as Yavin spoke a computer graph popped up on the TV screen and showed Labour winning 47 Knesset seats to only 33 for Likud.

Then Haim Yavin announced that Meretz, the new amalgam of three left-wing parties, had mustered 13 Knesset seats in the television exit poll. This meant that Labour and Meretz commanded 60 seats, an incredibly high figure, more than pollsters had given them during the campaign. Rabin would need only one more Knesset seat to form a government. If the actual balloting confirmed the exit polls, the small religious parties, particularly Shas and the United Torah Judaism Front, would inevitably come running to join Rabin's new government.

Trying to take in the meaning of the upheaval was Yitzhak

Rabin. He and his family were at home in Neve Avavim that tense evening. Rabin wanted as little company as possible before the exit poll was announced. The only ones there were the immediate members of the Rabin family, Leah, their two children Dahlia and Yuval, and the three grandchildren.

Leah burst into tears at the word 'ma'apach'. 'Somehow history has corrected an evil that was done to him,' she said a few weeks later. 'We had always lived with the feeling that what had happened (Rabin's stepping down as prime minister in 1977) then was unjust.'[22]

Neighbours began shouting for joy. Yitzhak Rabin sat quietly. The family walked up to him, hugging and kissing him. He appeared dazed, but still exuding a certain caution. He wanted to hear the actual results before celebrating. Knocks were heard at Rabin's door. Friends streamed in. So did press photographers.

The phone did not stop ringing. Shulamit Aloni, head of Meretz, called. The prime minister-elect did most of the talking. Shulamit congratulated him. She asked him not to make quick decisions on coalition partners (she wanted to make sure Meretz was not put at a disadvantage in the negotiations setting up the new coalition).

Over at the Dan Hotel, the Labour Party's election night headquarters, pandemonium had broken out when Yavin uttered the word 'ma'apach'. Lots of hugs and kisses, and cries of 'Rabin, Rabin, Rabin'. Bottles of champagne were quickly opened. The Labour Party jingle played loudly in the background, and everyone was waiting for the appearance of the new prime minister-elect. Rabin played it cool. He did not want to come to the Dan Hotel too early, before it was definite that Labour was going to win. After all, the cheers and laughter were based on an exit poll.

At 11:20 pm, Shimon Peres walked into the Dan Hotel headquarters. He put on a good face. Though he might wind up foreign minister, he had reason to feel sad. Still, he acted like a team player. 'It's the best thing that could have happened to the State of Israel,' he proclaimed. As he spoke, Labour people shouted, 'Rabin, Rabin.' Peres shouted back: 'We're all united.'

As the hours unfolded, the actual election results showed that the exit poll was on the mark.

Rabin left his apartment for the Dan Hotel. Photographers continued to snap pictures of the prime minister-designate. Over at the Dan Hotel, the place was exploding with joy. 'Israel is waiting for Rabin. Israel is waiting for Rabin.' Over and over the campaign jingle was played, deafening the ears. Everyone was singing. Television recorded the scene, the smiles and the tears live.

The prime minister-designate walked into the hall. It was 1 am. The cheers rose a few more decibels.

One Israeli journalist likened the atmosphere at the Dan Hotel to a sports event. Labour Party politicians wondered whether Rabin might surprise everyone by announcing that he planned to set up a government at once with Meretz and whoever else would like to join. Others thought he would wait and leave his options for coalition partners open. Rabin had informed his close advisers that night that he was in no hurry. He did not want to make mistakes due to haste.

His first words signalled that he intended to take charge, and stay in charge. As leader, he told the party faithful, he had to shoulder all the responsibility and therefore he should have commensurate authority. 'I will lead the coalition negotiations,' he said in his deep voice, 'and I will appoint the Cabinet ministers. The days of political blackmail are over.' On the surface, the statement seemed banal. Of course he would be in charge. Yet, reading between the lines, one sensed that Rabin was really saying, 'No one will sabotage me this time. No one will interfere with my prime ministership. Not Shimon Peres. Not the religious parties. No one. I will run my own show.'

After Rabin spoke, he went upstairs to a hotel room. Shimon Sheves, his aide, worked the phones, arranging meetings with potential coalition partners for the next morning.

Rabin arrived back home by 2 am. The first thing Leah said to the prime minister-designate was, 'You worked very hard and you earned the victory honestly.'

Over at Metzudat Ze'ev, the Likud headquarters in Tel Aviv, Likud leaders sat gloomily. No one moved, no one agreed to be interviewed. Each politician appeared catatonic. They had expected to lose, but not by this much. Meanwhile, seated in front of a television set at his suite in the Tel Aviv Hilton, Yitzhak Shamir looked ill. His face had tightened into a sullen glare. He seemed stunned, utterly depressed, confused. Twelve minutes before 10 pm, Dr Yossi Olmert, the head of the Government Press Office, had informed him that the exit poll would spell disaster for the Likud. He said nothing, though he grimaced, as if someone had tried to strike him. To waiting journalists, he snarled, 'I don't have to confess in front of anyone.'

Shamir never formally conceded to Rabin, nor did he pick up the phone to him. Later in the evening he announced over Israel TV that he planned to resign both from the Likud leadership and from active political life very soon. He gave no date for such steps. His voice a hoarse whisper, Shamir explained, 'I've said this many times — that I'm at the end of my road. Even if we had won, you wouldn't have seen me for a long time.'

Early in the evening some Likudniks hoped that Rabin would consider offering the Likud the chance to join a Rabin-led National Unity Government. They soon realized, however, that they were dreaming. Rabin wanted the Likud in opposition.

The final results were only known three days later (the votes of Israeli soldiers were not counted until the end of the week). Labour had received 906,126 votes (compared with 685,363 in 1988), giving it 44 Knesset seats. That was three less than the exit polls had predicted.

The Likud had garnered 651,219 votes (compared with 709,305 in 1988) for 32 seats, one less than the exit polls had said.

Meretz had won 12 seats; Tsomet, Rafael Eitan's right-wing party, 8; the National Religious Party, 6; Shas, 6; United Torah Judaism, 4; Moledet, 3; the Democratic Front, 3 and the Arab Democratic Party, 2.

Wavering Likudniks had shifted over to Labour, not in the large numbers that had been predicted earlier, but in sufficient numbers to help make a difference. It had been the vote of the Russian immigrants, however, that had been decisive for Labour, adding four Knesset seats to its margin.

All the political analysts agreed that the Rabin triumph signified the beginning of a new era in Israel. What were the elements that had brought about his triumph? The answer seemed to lie in the changing attitudes of the Israeli voter and the unique political persona that was Yitzhak Rabin.

For the past few years, a majority of Israelis, 65 to 70 per cent, had favoured territorial compromise as a means of settling the Arab–Israeli conflict, rejecting Shamir's right-wing strategy of holding on to the occupied lands at any cost. In electing Rabin, they had made clear that they wanted Shamir's firmness, but not his ideology; and they wanted peacemaking that was serious, not a charade.

Rabin fitted the bill. His political credentials matched what most of the voters wanted, not a dove like Peres, not an ideological zealot like Shamir, but a centrist who could stand up to the Arabs, if need be. The country had 'fallen in love' with Rabin, not because of his charisma or charm, not because he was good at wading into crowds, kissing babies, engaging in easy conversation. In fact, he was a social neuter. The country rushed into Rabin's arms for the ironic reason that Rabin had adopted the centrepiece of the Likud platform — autonomy for the Palestinian Arabs; toughness towards the Arab troublemakers; yielding as little land as possible. That had made it more palatable for Likud supporters, disgusted with Shamir, and eager to get on with the peace process, to switch allegiance and vote for Rabin.

Rabin won the election in part because the country had a growing fear that Shamir's tough stance toward the Americans would isolate Israel. And that seemed intolerable to most Israelis. Rabin, on the other hand, with his pro-American stance, was far more likely to tighten the Washington–Jerusalem relationship. Shamir should have won lots of points for telling the Americans 'no deal', when President George Bush linked Israel's receipt of the $10 billion in loan guarantees to a Jewish settlement freeze. Instead, voters appeared to be nervous that weakened ties with the US spelled trouble for Israel. Political analysts concluded from the election results that the big voter shifts had come in Jerusalem, Tel Aviv, Haifa, Ramat Gan, Givatayim and Netanya — communities populated with Israel's large middle-class. Labour majorities in these cities and towns had aided Rabin enormously and those Labourites wanted relations with the US mended.

To Shamir's coterie of aides Rabin's triumph was based on more than the prime minister's 'mishandling' of the relationship with the US. A few weeks after the Likud's débâcle, a Shamir confidante noted that 'Rabin projected to the voter, especially the hesitant person, that he was dependable, solid, that he had a good record in security, and in foreign relations. He succeeded in sweeping under the carpet those elements in the Labour platform that could have antagonized people such as Labour's favouring of territorial compromise or its championing of Socialism. Rabin got good advice. He said he was for continuing autonomy which was Menachem Begin's policy. He reordered the national priorities by focusing on immigrants and unemployment. Shamir did not project an image of leadership. He gave the impression that he was already an older person who had shot his wad. He had not demonstrated leadership in his own party, and he paid a price in the souring relations with the US. Labour put in a major effort to get [the votes] of newcomers from the USSR while the Likud projected an image of infighting.'

As outsiders saw the election, Rabin's triumph was a signal that ideology was no longer in vogue. Writing in the *New York Times*, Jerusalem correspondent Clyde Haberman noted, 'The real winner [in the election] was pragmatism and the big loser uncompromising ideology. While the peace camp may have won, a true debate on peace never really got going in the campaign. And while the hard-core right wing clearly lost ground, the major gains were in the centre and not on the left. In the end, Likud wore out its welcome, through an incremental erosion of public faith that it possesses the vision, cohesion, integrity and competence to keep the country running.

'. . . For [many Israelis], ideology has brought years of rocks and gasoline bombs in the Palestinian uprising; endless fears that the Arab street sweeper in Tel Aviv is not the hard-working man he probably is but rather a terrorist ready to pull out a knife; haunting nightmares that this will be the week that one's son in the army does not come back from the West Bank. These weary people say that if some land must be given up for peace, fine. If it means stopping a new settlement in Gaza to build a drug rehabilitation clinic in Ashdod, also fine.'[23]

Chapter 14

Closing the Circle

The Labour Party election victory was good news around the world. It was an open secret that George Bush and James Baker had earnestly wanted a Labour victory. Indeed, their rough treatment of Yitzhak Shamir on issues ranging from Jewish settlements to the loan guarantees played no small role in Rabin's triumph. The morning after the election, government officials and editorial writers expressed delight that Israel would no longer be governed by the Shamir regime. Some American columnists who had been tough on Shamir were now beaming. Anthony Lewis of the *New York Times* was one: 'In a world of disappointed expectations, the Israeli election had a transforming quality. It was as if the people of Israel had decided to turn a page of history, a page filled with bitterness, and explore the possibility of hope. Yitzhak Rabin . . . is not a man of uplifting eloquence or vision. He is a curt ex-general whose philosophy, if it can be called that, is pragmatism. He has no zest for any ideology. And what a difference that is. For Israel has largely been governed over the last ten years by zealots . . . determined to impose their ideology whatever the cost.'[1]

The euphoria was contagious. Even many Likudniks, those who had defected to Labour, and those who had not, breathed in the new heady atmosphere, and proclaimed that they were glad that Rabin had ascended to power. Perhaps now the days of deadlock would be over. Needing no reminder of why they had turned against Shamir, Israelis still were astonished to read an interview the outgoing prime minister gave to *Ma'ariv* soon after the election. When Yosef Harif, the veteran political reporter, called him for a response to the Likud defeat, Shamir offered this dark prediction had his party won: 'I would have conducted negotiations on autonomy for ten years, and in the meantime we would have reached half a million people in Judea and Samaria.' There it was in black and white. Mr Deadlock was confirming that his strategy had indeed been the slow, steady stall. A day or so later, Shamir vehemently claimed he had been misquoted. It hardly mattered. The quote seemed vintage Shamir, perfectly consistent with his past deeds — no, rather non-deeds.

Few Israelis thought much of the Shamir strategy. His ideology had the staleness of last month's news, and so did he. Most Israelis thought little of a strategy that sought to delude the Arabs so that a half million Jews could settle in the occupied lands. Many, however, thought highly of the ostensible centre of the Likud platform, granting the Palestinians autonomy. For that reason, they were delighted that Rabin might now have a chance of doing what Shamir could not, would not do: implementing the Likud's platform!

Yitzhak Rabin was taking over. He was no longer a candidate running an election campaign. He had a nation to lead. To Gad Ben-Ari, Rabin suggested that the large photograph of the candidate outside Labour Party headquarters in Tel Aviv should be quickly removed.

There would be no more gimmicks.

Given this second chance to run the country, Rabin planned to make the most of it. He had turned 70 a few months earlier. Under any circumstances, he did not have a great deal of time. He could not afford to make mistakes, or to fritter away the new opportunity. No one would be permitted to get in his way, neither Shimon Peres nor the prime minister's coalition partners, neither the opposition Likud nor the small right-wing parties. Rabin planned to rule with a firm hand.

The mandate he had just received from the voters was a clear signal to Rabin to take the country down new paths aimed at accelerating the peace process and revitalizing the economy. Rabin sensed that a window of opportunity had opened, thanks to the ending of the Cold War, the easing of the Soviet threat to the West, and the Iraqi defeat in the Gulf War. Yet, that window would not be open for ever. Arab states were trying to acquire nuclear weapons. Calling this a very grave and negative development, the prime minister-designate believed that this fact alone impelled Israel to try to end the Arab–Israeli conflict as quickly as possible.

The 23 June political upheaval had caused Israeli hopes to soar. 'The public's expectations are sky high,' Rabin told the Labour Party Central Committee on 12 July. 'The change or upheaval has created a new atmosphere among the public, a feeling of hope, a feeling of belief that it can be different, that it can be better.' He was concerned about those expectations, he did not want to disappoint anyone; yet to Rabin, the test of whether he would be able to deliver would come soon: the key lay in persuading President Bush to provide Israel with the $10 billion in loan guarantees. With that would come an improvement in relations with Washington; all the rest would follow.

Rabin was relaxed, but ready to take charge the day after elections when he gave his first news conference at Labour Party headquarters in Tel Aviv. Israel Radio carried the event live. The hall was still festooned with banners and flags from the previous night's celebrations. In an open-necked shirt, Rabin offered an occasional, uncharacteristic smile. Now, it was time to try to implement his political programme. He pledged to push for peace with the Arabs; to reorder Israel's priorities; to curb Shamir's drive to build Jewish settlements. 'National resources will not be diverted to what I call "political settlements",' said the prime minister-designate. He wanted to be clear: he did not plan to 'freeze' settlements entirely; he planned to support them in areas essential to Israel's security — in and around Jerusalem, the Jordan Valley, and the Golan Heights. This news conference was a signal to the Americans that Rabin meant business, that Israel had turned over a new leaf. George Bush should look around for his cheque book.

Rabin talked briefly about the kind of ruling coalition he hoped to establish, one that would be centrist, in keeping with his own personal viewpoint, not dependent upon any of the small parties, whether of the political left or right. He sounded optimistic that he could achieve such a goal. 'I believe I can form a stable government that won't express the policies of the extreme left or those of the extreme right, but of the Israeli mainstream.' (However, to one acquaintance a few days later, he confided that he had been taken aback by Meretz' strong showing. 'I didn't take into account that Meretz would be the second largest party.' That strong showing meant that Rabin might have to establish a left-wing government against his wishes.)

A reporter asked Rabin a personal question: was his election victory the closing of a circle of fifteen years? 'There is something to that,' Rabin allowed. As usual, he had no desire to elaborate on personal aspects of his career.

That evening Rabin went on Israel Television to assure the 'victims' of his new policies — the 115,000 Jewish settlers on the West Bank — that they had no reason to fear him. He had no plans to uproot their homes. 'I don't mean to dry [the settlements] out, but [rather] not to invest in expanding them, not to throw billions of shekels into construction.' How far would the settlers go in trying to sabotage Rabin's plans? Rumours spread that some were stockpiling weapons. The threat of settler violence haunted the early days of the new Rabin regime.

The forging of a ruling coalition was most distasteful to Rabin but had to be done. He would have preferred voters to have given the Labour Party at least 61 Knesset seats, a clear-cut parliamentary majority. Then he could have avoided bargaining with the small parties. That would have been asking a great deal. No Israeli prime minister had ever won a Knesset majority.

Meretz, with 12 Knesset seats, offered Rabin the greatest leap forward in securing a governing coalition. Together, Labour and Meretz had 56 Knesset seats; add to that, the support of the five Israeli Arab Knesset members, and Rabin had 61 seats, a slender majority but one that would allow his Government to function. The one snag was that Rabin had no great desire to have his coalition rest on Israeli Arab support.

So he searched elsewhere for the five remaining Knesset seats. Possible partners were Tsomet, the eight-member right-wing party headed by Rafael Eitan, which had done spectacularly well, raising its Knesset membership from 2 to 8 on 23 June; or Shas, the ultra-orthodox Sephardi party, with 6 Knesset members. Of the two, Rabin seemed to prefer Tsomet, for that would give his Government greater respectability among the country's political right.

Not surprisingly, as Rabin pursued coalition partners, the issue of Jewish settlements in the occupied territories emerged as a key difficulty. Labour's platform had said that no new settlements would be built for one year during peace negotiations. But this potentially controversial clause was omitted from the proposed guidelines so as not to alienate Tsomet. Further placating Tsomet, the wordsmiths mentioned 'strengthening settlements along confrontation lines as part of the new Government's proposed guidelines. It all had seemed so easy during the election campaign. Labour coalition strategists argued that, while the Labour platform had indeed promised no new settlements for a year, that had not meant that existing ones in Jerusalem and the Jordan Valley could not be expanded.

Meretz was adamant on certain issues. One had to do with the high number (20,000) of draft deferments given to Yeshiva students. Labour promised to appoint a committee to develop new criteria for determining which religious students should receive deferments. Meretz was prepared to serve alongside the right-ring Tsomet party. Tsomet's chief Rafael Eitan, a former chief of staff, was prickly, however. He wanted to know what Rabin had in mind for Palestinian autonomy: 'What is autonomy? Where is autonomy? Who is included? Who is not included? As far as I am concerned, a lot is unclear.'

Tsomet did not join the Rabin coalition. Neither did the United Torah Judaism Front nor the National Religious Party.

A major reason for the refusal of Tsomet and the United Torah Judaism Front to join the coalition was Rabin's selection of Shulamit Aloni, head of Meretz, as education minister. Tsomet's Rafael Eitan thought he should have been given the education portfolio. United Torah Judaism's negotiators believed that Aloni would weaken Jewish education. When Eitan learned that the education portfolio had been given to Aloni, he sought the defence minister post; but Rabin decided to keep that for himself. Eitan broke off negotiations at that point.

None of this mattered in the end.

For Meretz joined the coalition. So did Shas. And on 9 July, the prime minister-designate announced that he had a government coalition — comprising Labour, Meretz and Shas, 62 seats in all. Adding the five Israeli Arab Knesset members to those who supported the Government, Rabin could count on 67 votes altogether.

Though he had wanted members of both the political right and left, Rabin had stitched together a coalition with a leftist tinge.

On 12 July, Rabin announced the names of Labour Party ministers in his new cabinet. He chose himself as defence minister, saying that, with the autonomy negotiations looming as a central issue, it made sense for the prime minister (who would handle the negotiations) and the defence minister (who would have responsibility for day to day supervision of the West Bank and the Gaza Strip) to be the same person.

He named Shimon Peres as foreign minister and deputy prime minister. Given a choice, Rabin would have been pleased to have given Peres some minor Cabinet post, or none at all. He had no choice. Peres retained a strong following in the party and could not be wished away. Before Rabin agreed to make Peres his foreign minister, the two men spoke at length. They agreed that Rabin would take charge of the autonomy talks, Peres, the multilateral peacemaking efforts. Rabin had no need to threaten Peres to toe the line this time. Fifteen years after Peres had given him so much trouble, Rabin had no intention to let him get away with such behaviour a second time. As prime minister in the 1970s, Rabin had felt constrained from speaking out against Peres and his efforts to undermine the regime. This time, should Peres act up, Rabin would feel no constraint. He was unquestionably the most powerful political figure in the country, towering above his party and above Peres. It was up to Peres. (On 19 August, 1992, I asked Peres whether he and Rabin had worked out any ground rules to avoid the feuding that occurred in the 1970s. Peres could have dismissed the question with a shrug of the hand. He felt compelled to reply. 'The ground rules are that we both accept the rule of the majority of the party. We try not to forget that we're serving a nation, not an ego. We have to work together. There were struggles but there was a lot of cooperation too.' I could sense the tension in Peres as he struggled with his answer.)

Rabin won quick approval from the 1,500-member Labour Party Central Committee for his Labour Party ministers and the government's guidelines. Those guidelines called for stepping up negotiations with the Arabs and offering the Palestinians self-rule in the occupied areas. They made no direct reference to

a freeze on settlement construction in the occupied lands; but
they did say that during the peace talks, the Government would
'avoid steps and actions that create problems in negotiations'.
The Government would re-evaluate settlement housing started
under the Likud; however, all settlements would be provided
with security and municipal services. The guidelines were
written to please Rabin's voters, and to keep the door open to
Tsomet joining the coalition at a later date.

On Monday, 13 July, Rabin presented his new Government
and its guidelines to the Knesset for its approval. For Rabin, it
was a moment of great personal triumph. Driving from Tel Aviv
to the Knesset, he catnapped while the driver listened to quiet
music on a tape. Leah took one last look at her husband's
Knesset speech.

Once inside, Rabin took his seat in the Knesset plenary on the
Labour side. Shamir remained at the head of the horseshoe-
shaped Cabinet table until the new government was sworn in.
Sitting in the visitors' gallery were Leah and Rabin's sister,
Rahel.

The speech Rabin would make that day was one of the most
important he would ever deliver. He rose to the occasion. Eitan
Haber, Rabin's spokesman during his days as defence minister
in the 1980s, wrote a draft of the speech. Rabin went over it.
Even Leah Rabin had had some input. Rabin wanted to strike
just the right notes. He wanted to convey that his government
was ready to make serious strides for peace and for economic
improvement. He wanted to convey a sense of urgency. He
wanted to let the Americans know that Israel was embarking on
new policies and to let the Palestinian Arabs know that time was
running out for them. Above all, he wanted to communicate
that he was prepared to lead Israel in new directions.

Accelerating the peace talks would be a top priority. Rabin
signalled as much when he invited the Jordanian–Palestinian
delegation to visit him in Jerusalem for informal talks about
implementing autonomy. Rabin also asserted that he was
prepared to visit Arab capitals to reach a breakthrough in the
stalled negotiations: 'I am prepared to travel to Amman,
Damascus, and Beirut today, tomorrow. For there is no greater
victory than the victory of peace.' While not the first Israeli

prime minister to invite the heads of Arab states to come to Jerusalem for direct negotiations, Rabin was sending a strong signal to the Arab side that he wanted to move forward in peacemaking right away. (The Rabin offer was greeted with indifference by the Arabs who believed it was too early for them to see the Israeli prime minister in Jerusalem or to entertain him in their capitals. They made clear, however, that they were eager to keep the peace process alive.)

The key passage in that speech was an appeal to Israelis to cease thinking of themselves as cut off from the world. Once they ceased such thinking, peacemaking could go forward: '. . . In the last decade of the twentieth century, the atlases, history and geography books no longer present an up-to-date picture of the world. Walls of enmity have fallen, borders have disappeared. Powers have crumbled and ideologies collapsed, states have been born, states have died, and the gates of emigration have been flung open. And it is our duty, to ourselves and to our children, to see the new world as it is now — to discern its dangers, explore its prospects, and do everything possible so that the State of Israel will fit into this world whose face is changing. No longer are we necessarily "A people that dwells alone", and no longer is it true that "the whole world is against us". We must overcome the sense of isolation that has held us in its thrall for almost half a century. We must join the international movement toward peace, reconciliation, and cooperation that is spreading over the entire globe these days — lest we be the last to remain, all alone, in the station.'

This passage became Prime Minister Rabin's call to arms. It was the passage that analysts would remember and quote most often.

Rabin also promised, 'We are going to change the national order of priorities. We know very well that obstacles will stand in our path. Crises will erupt; there will be disappointments, tears, and pain. . . . Preference will be given to the war on unemployment and to strengthening the economic and social systems. . . . We intend to increase the rate of economic growth. . . . The new Government has . . . made it a prime goal to promote the making of peace and take vigorous steps that will lead to the conclusion of the Israeli–Arab conflict . . . We do not intend to lose precious time. . . .'

He made a special, impassioned plea to the Palestinian Arabs: 'To you, the Palestinians in the territories, our foes today and partners to peaceful coexistence tomorrow, I wish to say: We have been fated to live together on the same patch of land, in the same country. We lead our lives with you, beside you, and against you. You have failed in the war against us. One hundred years of your bloodshed and terror against us have brought you only suffering, humiliation, bereavement, and pain. You have lost thousands of your sons and daughters, and you are losing ground all the time. For 44 years now, you have been living under a delusion. Your leaders have led you through lies and deceit. They have missed every opportunity, rejected all our proposals for a settlement, and taken you from one tragedy to another.

'You who live in the wretched poverty of Gaza and Khan Yunis, in the refugee camps of Hebron and Shchem: you who have never known a single day of freedom and joy in your lives: listen to us, if only this once. We offer you the fairest and most viable proposal from our standpoint today: autonomy, with all its advantages and limitations. You will not get everything you want. Neither will we. So once and for all, take your destiny in your hands. Don't lose this opportunity that may never return. Take our proposal seriously — to avoid further suffering, humiliation, and grief; to end the shedding of tears and of blood.'

This was not Rabin, the 'break their bones' man, speaking. This was not Yitzhak Shamir, Mr No, speaking.

This was Rabin the peacemaker, exhorting the Palestinians to do business with him.

What came through in Rabin's performance that day, more than anything else, was his sense of ease and comfort at being in charge. As Yosef Goel of the *Jerusalem Post* wrote a few days later: 'The new government's most impressive feature so far is undoubtedly Prime Minister Rabin himself. Without question, he is fully in charge of his own government and party; he has finally mastered the switch from army commander to national and party leader.'[2]

When Yitzhak Shamir spoke, now in the role of head of the opposition, he scolded Rabin for every political sin in the book. 'In return for present, short-term and short-sighted achievements, this government intends to give away the future. It strives for "peace now" at the expense of fundamental national aims. What we have heard today mostly resembles a nihilistic philosophy which will cost us dearly in the long run.' Shamir might as well have been whistling in the dark.

The 16-member Cabinet that Rabin presented for approval to the Knessest included 10 first-time ministers, two women and an ultra-orthodox religious figure. Twelve of the 16 were from Labour, 3 from Meretz, one from Shas. Largely dovish, the Cabinet had a hawk at the helm, Yitzhak Rabin. Some of those doves would, grudgingly or gladly, accept a Palestinian state. All would accept territorial compromise. Whatever they thought, however, it would be Rabin who would call the shots. And right now, he was busy implementing Menachem Begin's and Yitzhak Shamir's plan for autonomy. Rabin, in addition to being prime minister and defence minister, would hold the welfare and labour portfolio and the religious affairs portfolio himself — hoping to turn them over to parties who might join the coalition later.

From the moment he became prime minister on 13 July, Yitzhak Rabin was a man in a hurry. He could not act fast enough. Seemingly ubiquitous, he moved in a hundred directions at once. With good reason. He knew that the same voters who had tired of the Likud could turn sour on Labour if they did not find concrete improvements resulting from the 23 June upheaval. Two days after the election, Rabin warned himself and his party: 'If we don't show tangible socio-economic progress in the first six months, we can expect a public lashing.' He felt the same way towards peacemaking. Hence, he pledged repeatedly that the Palestinians could achieve an autonomy agreement in under a year, if they wished.

Rabin's wish to move forcefully on autonomy appeared to please the Palestinians. They had trouble expressing glee at the political victory of a man they had come to loathe as the architect of Israel's putdown of the Intifada. Yet, happy to have anyone but Shamir, they could not help but exhibit some enthusiasm. Happiest of all was Yasser Arafat, the PLO chieftain. 'Israelis have voted against the terrorism exercised by Yitzhak Shamir against the women and children of the

Palestinian people,' the PLO leader said. 'By making this choice, the Israeli people are pushing their government to act in the direction of peace.' Faisal Husseini, the West Bank Palestinian leader, perhaps as much to prompt Rabin into action as to praise him for expected deeds, likened him to a famous Frenchman. 'Rabin,' he opined, 'could be the Israeli de Gaulle: we feel good that Shamir has left. I can't say that I feel happy that Rabin is in power. With Rabin we will have business, work to do, negotiations that can begin.' Still, Palestinians had great expectations of Rabin, 'too many expectations,' in the words of one Palestinian Arab analyst. Part of the Palestinian optimism was based on the notion that Rabin was an all-powerful figure. As the analyst noted, 'The Palestinian man in the street thinks of Rabin as Colonel Qadaffi because of Rabin's harsh treatment of them in the Intifada. Rabin has a reputation among Palestinians that all he needs to do is press a button and things will get done.'

Ending the Intifada, placating the Palestinian Arabs, giving them a political stature that would satisfy their thirst for independence, would not be easy. Many believed that Rabin had it in him to achieve these goals. No one voiced it better than Henry Kissinger, the former American Secretary of State: 'Israel has no better analytical mind than Yitzhak Rabin. If any of his interlocutors are counting on influencing him by charm or legalistic skill, they are heading for disillusionment. Small talk is not his forte; personal charm not his speciality. Redundancy taxes his patience; the commonplace does not capture his attention. He is as tenacious as he is intelligent. . . . American and Arab leaders are not likely to find Mr Rabin a jolly companion on their journey through the thickets of Middle East diplomacy. But he is relentless in separating the chaff from what is essential. These qualities will now stand him in good stead, for the protagonists need to disenthral themselves from the attitudes that have produced the impasse.'[3]

Rabin's prime ministership got off to a running start. It turned out that someone in Washington was waiting for Rabin — impatiently. No sooner had he been sworn in than a phone call came for the brand-new prime minister from the White House. George Bush was on the line. Rabin grabbed the phone at his desk in his Knesset office a floor below the plenary.

'Congratulations,' said the President, and then declared that he planned to send James Baker to the Middle East, 'to get the ball rolling again.'

This was what Rabin had wanted to hear. He had wanted action. He got it. He was under no illusions. His ascendancy to power was only part of the reason the President was acting so kindly. The other was the tough election fight that Bush faced that autumn against Arkansas Governor Bill Clinton.

Bush had more news. He invited Rabin to visit him at his summer home at Kennebunkport, Maine, in August, quite a coup considering how few foreign leaders received a Presidential invitation to the Maine summer quarters.

Rabin smiled. Kennebunkport in August — the loan guarantees could not be far away.

Rabin's first full day (14 July) as prime minister was a whirlwind of photo opportunities.

In the morning he and Shamir went through the formalities of exchanging offices. In an upbeat mood, Rabin exhibited no apparent grudge against the outgoing prime minister for not phoning his congratulations on election night. 'When the annals of Zionism are written,' he said to Shamir, holding a glass of wine in his hand for a toast, 'you will have an honourable place.' Honourable? Maybe — if the historian was no disappointed Likudnik. Shamir was still reeling from the election loss. He could not avoid a dig at Rabin for holding the prime ministership and the defence minister's job: 'I hope the defence minister will influence the prime minister in ensuring there are not too many unilateral excesses.' Rabin and the 60 staff members of the prime minister's office broke into laughter.

Then it was on to President Chaim Herzog's Jerusalem residence for the traditional photo with the new Cabinet. Then to Tel Aviv for the ceremony marking the exchange of office with outgoing Defence Minister Moshe Arens.

By 4 pm, Rabin was back at his desk in Jerusalem. He ended the long day huddling with his political aides, searching for a way to induce more parties into his coalition.

Rabin had been in office only briefly when Israeli troops sealed off the campus of An-Najah, the largest university on the

West Bank, located in Nablus. Palestinian students had been voting in student council elections inside the school; the IDF contended that six armed Palestinians had entered the school and were trying to influence the elections. Soldiers wanted to seek out the gunmen but the students refused to submit to IDF searches. A standoff ensued as the Israeli soldiers debated whether to storm the building.

The inevitable bloodshed would have had a grave impact on Rabin's early days in office and would have seriously marred the forthcoming visit of American Secretary of State James Baker, scheduled for 19 July. Rabin worked behind the scenes to end the confrontation peacefully. A compromise was reached that sent the six wanted students to exile in Jordan; in exchange, the IDF agreed to pull back its forces from the school. The peaceful resolution seemed to augur good things for the new Rabin administration. Analyst Emanuel Rosen wrote in *Ma'ariv*: 'The episode contains an important lesson: it has been proven that a common denominator can be found . . . that agreements can be reached even with stretched nerves and extremists pushing for conflict.'

Rabin's first week in office was given over to a series of steps designed to show that the election mandate was being implemented. One of the first acts of the new government, as announced by Housing Minister Benyamin Ben-Eliezer, was a freeze on all new building, including construction, in the occupied territories. The timing was not coincidental.

This was what Bush and Baker had wanted to hear from Shamir — and had not. Now — so it seemed — the path was being cleared for the Americans to give Israel those loan guarantees. Jewish settlers reacted angrily to what they termed 'Fouad's Plan'. They called it a declaration of war, and said they would behave as one did in war, an implied threat of violence.

At Rabin's first Cabinet meeting on 19 July the ministers sat around a mahogany table. White place cards with their names were placed in front of them. Some ministers wore open-necked shirts. Rabin had a tie and jacket on. Afterwards, one minister said that everyone had behaved like restrained, disciplined school children. The prime minister had asked each minister not to leak secret information, not to speak to the media upon leaving the Cabinet meeting, and not to speak in fields apart from the minister's area of responsibility. Smiles went around the room. Few expected that Rabin's orders would be obeyed completely. Other prime ministers had tried to run a tight ship without much success.

Word was leaked that Rabin was planning to visit Egyptian President Hosni Mubarak very soon. Again, the new prime minister wanted to distance himself from the lethargy of the Shamir years. Mubarak had refused to meet with Shamir until he took a more conciliatory stance toward peacemaking. The Egyptian leader, however, could not wait for Rabin to take office because he had sounded sincere when he talked of wanting peace.

Politically, the Rabin government seemed stable. Tsomet's Rafael Eitan talked of introducing a vote of no-confidence on the freezing of settlements. Such a vote was doomed to failure. The ultra-orthodox United Torah Judaism Front was still up in arms over the appointment of Shulamit Aloni as minister of education. Its representatives wanted her out of that ministry as the price for its entry into the coalition. Rabin said forget it. The UTJ turned up the pressure. One of its newspapers published a statement comparing the education of Israeli children under Aloni to the destruction of the 1.5 million Jewish children murdered in the Holocaust. Rabin termed the statement offensive; he stood by his appointment of Aloni.

Even before Jim Baker arrived in the Middle East, he was singing the praises of Yitzhak Rabin. Speaking to reporters aboard his US Air Force jet on the way over, Baker lauded the new prime minister for suspending housing contracts in the occupied areas and for creating 'some new possibility to transform the peace negotiations'. Baker added, 'We would like to think that we can begin to hear some new and different signs on the Arab side.'

In their private talks, the prime minister began with an assurance that Jewish settlement activity in the occupied lands would be restricted. To journalists later, Baker said, 'It will make a difference. We now have a government here that is serious about limiting settlement activity.' Baker did not commit the Bush Administration to reversing itself and guaranteeing the loan guarantees. All he would say publicly

was, 'We will continue to have discussions regarding the issue.'
No one had any doubt what Bush and Baker planned to do.
They were thrilled to be dealing with someone other than
Yitzhak Shamir. The contrast between Baker's meetings with
Shamir and these with Rabin struck everyone. Thomas
Friedman of the *New York Times* wrote on 20 July: 'There were
none of the smiles through clenched teeth that appeared in every
meeting of Baker with Shamir. Mr Rabin and Baker clearly
looked comfortable working together.' Later, Palestinians met
with Baker at the American Consulate in West Jerusalem and
told him they too were encouraged by Israeli moves toward
curbing Jewish settlement construction.

Rabin kept moving forward. After only eight days in office he
arrived in Cairo to see Mubarak. He had last been there in 1989
as defence minister. Now he had the chance to ease the long
thaw in relations between Israel and Egypt. With Mubarak
exhibiting little warmth toward Shamir, the former Israeli
prime minister and his aides had replied in kind. That same
contempt flowed through a private memo sent by Yossi Ben-
Aharon, the director-general of Shamir's office, to Rabin on the
eve of the new prime minister's visit, warning him to be careful
of Mubarak. Ben-Aharon suggested that Egypt was not that
important to the peace process, that Mubarak was in effect a
'leader without assets'. The Egyptian leader, the Shamir man
wrote in his memo, was adept at insinuating himself, but that
Egypt was not nearly as important as Mubarak liked to think.
By embarking on his mission, Rabin dismissed the memo. Once
in Cairo, Rabin promoted Mubarak as an Arab leader essential
to peacemaking, contrary to Ben-Aharon's advice.

The Rabin–Mubarak meeting was the first Israeli–Egyptian
summit in six years. Rabin's special Israel Air Force plane flew
two small Egyptian and Israeli flags from its cockpit. And the
Israeli flag was raised at Cairo Airport for Rabin's arrival. The
prime minister planned to lay wreaths at the Tomb of the
Unknown Soldier and the neighbouring tomb of the late
Egyptian president, Anwar Sadat. Rabin also planned to
squeeze in a visit to the Jewish community remaining in Egypt,
about 70 mostly old people.

Stepping off the plane, Rabin was greeted at the foot of the tarmac ramp by Ataf Zidki, the Egyptian prime minister. Rabin took a few strides forward, ready to review the military honour guard. Zidki gently reminded the Israeli leader that the national anthems of the two countries had not yet been played. Rabin gave a large smile. It was another example of Rabin trying to speed things up.

At the ornate Kubbah Palace Rabin mounted the steps to meet Mubarak. The two men met for 90 minutes, then held a joint news conference, sitting next to one another on a large sofa. Mubarak welcomed the Rabin government's decision to review Shamir's settlement programme and its aim of diverting funds to job creation and housing. 'It is a good step on the right track, and we appreciate it, yet we need much more. But we leave it to him now.' It was classic Mubarak, offering a nod to a better past, but a warning that Rabin had not gone nearly far enough. For his part, Rabin asserted that Cairo could be crucial to peacemaking: 'We believe Egypt can play a role. . . . Egypt was in the spearhead of breaking historic walls and bringing a peace treaty between [an] Arab country and Israel.' Reporters sought details from Mubarak of Rabin's plans to curtail Jewish settlements. Mubarak was coy. 'The man is only one week in office. What do you expect him to do? Miracles?' When asked what they talked about, Mubarak again noted that the prime minister had only just taken power, so 'we didn't go through so many details or ask for miracles. I wish Mr Rabin success in his work, and I know that he generally supports peace, and I'm very pleased with that.'

That was the key phrase of the visit — Mubarak's assertion that Rabin generally supports peace. The Egyptian president was signalling to the Arab world that a new man had taken power in Israel, one who was deserving of being given a chance, who seemed sincere in his desire for peace. Mubarak was taking the first small step. Now it was up to the other Arab states to fall in line. Rabin had invited the Egyptian president to Israel and Mubarak had accepted. There was no mention of a date. Should he take up Rabin's invitation, it would be Mubarak's first visit to Israel since becoming president in 1981.

Before flying back to Israel that same day Rabin laid a wreath at the tomb of Anwar Sadat. It was inscribed: 'With respect for the man of peace.' Finally, at the Cairo synagogue, where some of the 70 Jews of Egypt had gathered to greet him, Rabin said, 'We will meet more often, both here and there [in Israel].'

After being in office just two weeks, Rabin gave the impression of being active on scores of different fronts. His name cropped up in headline after headline on the front pages of the newspapers. His face appeared on Israel television routinely as part of the main news item of the day. The media followed his every action, large or small. One day he appeared before the Knesset Labour Committee in his role as Labour and Welfare Minister; another day he travelled to southern Lebanon for a visit to the 'security zone' as his country's defence minister. He presided over crucial Cabinet meetings, but had time to attend ceremonies for wheelchair athletes and the dedication of the re-opened Haifa cable-car. He retained a great deal of good will. Most Israelis continued to think he and his policies were a breath of fresh air, particularly his decision to stop building in the occupied territories. The critics were shocked into silence. Now and again, former Prime Minister Shamir uttered some dissenting words: 'Freezing construction, freezing settlements on lands in Judea and Samaria, the meaning is giving up parts of Greater Israel without negotiations, before negotiations, in exchange for money.' Few, including the prime minister, paid much attention to Shamir. Opposition Knesset members introduced five no-confidence motions to protest against the government's settlement freeze. The outcome was never in doubt. The government survived the no-confidence motions, defeating them 59–48.

A few days after Baker left the region, Housing Minister Benyamin Ben-Eliezer and Finance Minister Avraham Shochat spelled out in more detail the nature of the government's new settlement 'freeze'. It turned out to be more a cooling off, than an outright freeze. The new Rabin government planned to halt the building of 6,500 housing units in the occupied territories but would go ahead with 10,000 already in progress. Rabin had explained this to Baker earlier in the week: the Shamir Government had tied Rabin's hands. For legal reasons, it was not possible to undertake a greater building halt at this juncture. Israeli liberals contended that the Fouad Plan, as it came to be called after Housing Minister Benyamin 'Fouad' Ben-Eliezer, would increase Jewish settlement in the territories by 50 per cent. Rabin's aides grudgingly acknowledged that the number of Jewish settlers would rise, but they hoped it would not be by that amount.

Rabin began preparing for his August visit to the US. The Bush Administration, perhaps hoping to attract a few more Jewish votes, tried to advance the next round of the Middle East peace talks scheduled for Washington to 18 August. Rabin scotched that effort, arguing that he needed more time to get his negotiating team in place.

Before departing, Rabin sought to lower expectations with respect to Israel's obtaining the loan guarantees. The President may not necessarily grant the guarantees during his visit, Rabin said for public consumption. Privately, he knew better. Indeed, the prime minister had every reason to be upbeat. Bush and Shamir had not met for the past two years. Rabin had been invited within minutes of his taking office.

The two leaders, Rabin and Bush, met on 10 and 11 August at Kennebunkport. Arriving at the President's summer home too formally dressed, Rabin ducked into his quarters and took off his coat and tie. He emerged wearing a coat and loose, unbuttoned shirt. At that point he and the President strolled along the beach, then headed for a chat with reporters.

Standing next to Rabin outside his summer home which overlooks the Maine coastline, Bush spoke first. 'The only thing I want to say is that the welcome mat is out for Prime Minister Rabin. He has many friends in the United States including the man he is standing next to. We are looking forward to strengthening a relationship that is strong and will be even stronger.' Rabin offered the hope that the summit would provide a 'better and more intimate relationship between our two countries, our two peoples, and our two governments. Let's hope this visit will give the chance to at least make clear where we stand, what we can do together to achieve these goals.'

The next day, Tuesday, 11 August, was a red-letter one for Rabin and the State of Israel. Bush concluded the two-day summit by announcing that he was ready to grant Israel the $10 billion in loan guarantees.

The President said that he was 'extremely pleased to

announce that we are able to reach an agreement on the basic
principles of the government granting up to $10 billion in loan
guarantees. I am committed to assist Israel with the task of
absorbing immigrants. I am delighted that the prime minister
and I have agreed to an approach which will assist these new
Israelis without frustrating the search for peace. We can pursue
these humanitarian goals at the same time.' Saying that he
supported the loan guarantees 'enthusiastically', the president
urged Rabin to be forthcoming at the peace talks scheduled for
24 August. The prime minister had 'persuaded' him, Bush said,
that Israel was sincere about peacemaking.

Conscious of the controversy swirling about the loan
guarantees and Jewish settlements, reporters asked Bush to
comment on Rabin's approach to Jewish settlements. The
president responded: 'We see a very different approach to
settlements. We salute the prime minister. It was not easy. It
took courage.'

Rabin and Bush had achieved sufficient trust — a trust that
had clearly been lacking between the President and Shamir —
for the two men to agree on the loan guarantees without signing
a document. Details of the unwritten accord were leaked by
Israeli officials: Bush reserved the right of 'discretion' should he
deem that the loan guarantees should be stopped after the first
instalment. Also: the Administration would only deduct funds
from the guarantees for settlement activity after 1 October,
1992, the day the guarantees were to take effect.

Rabin, responding to the President's remarks, said that
getting the loan guarantees meant that Israel needed to push for
economic reform. 'We on our part are determined to improve
our national economy to a more efficient and privatized system.
We should also carry as much as possible the financial burden of
the guarantees, so as to lessen any costs to the American
taxpayer.'

Returning to Israel on 14 August, Rabin declared that his
visit 'bore practical fruit. My visit also brought about a change
in attitudes toward Israel, within public opinion, the
Administration and Congress. I hope we have witnessed the
opening of a new chapter in our ties with the US.'

One incident marred the visit: Rabin's blast at the American
Israel Public Affairs Committee (AIPAC), known as the Jewish

lobby. Appearing before past and present AIPAC leaders at his Washington hotel on 13 August, Rabin sent shockwaves through the American Jewish community. In his remarks, the prime minister raised issues that, while simmering under the surface, had generally been discussed only in private conversation between Israeli and American Jewish leaders. Rabin was determined to put AIPAC in its place. Its sin: failing to coordinate its actions on behalf of Israel with the Israeli Embassy. He was openly critical of AIPAC's efforts on behalf of the loan guarantees. He was quoted as having said: 'You waged battles which were lost in advance, and so you merely caused Israel damage, by generating unnecesary antagonism over such issues as the intelligence-gathering AWACS plane sale to Saudi Arabia, and the loan guarantees request. You did not manage to bring Israel one single cent.' These were some of the harshest comments an Israeli prime minister had ever uttered to an American Jewish group.

By the time Rabin had returned to Israel, he sensed that he had gone too far in his criticism. His spokesman Gad Ben-Ari was instructed to issue a brief statement in support of AIPAC. The prime minister, said that communiqué, 'attaches great value to the importance of AIPAC as an American organization supportive of Israel, and he appreciates what it does. The premier regards AIPAC as an American organization which is independent in its considerations and its activities, and which functions in awareness of the need to maintain close ties between Israel and the US.'

It was all very ironic. No sooner had Bush given Rabin the $10 billion in loan guarantees than some Israelis began to question whether they were worth having. Economists and editorial writers pounced on the guarantees, like a spoiled nephew telling his rich uncle: no thanks! For example: in its editorial on 11 August the Israeli newspaper *Ma'ariv* stated that Bush and Baker were the worst thing to happen to Israel since Eisenhower and Dulles. 'Bush's granting of the guarantees is purely a coldly calculated move to obtain Jewish votes and money. The next time Rabin comes to the US Bush will be the president of a Texan university and Clinton will be in power. Rabin ought to heed this.'

For over two years Israelis had seen the logic behind the request for the loan guarantees. The financial community pressed the need for the guarantees even after the number of Russian immigrants had dropped to only a 70,000 a year.

Accelerating Middle East peacemaking was a major goal of the new prime minister. Though he had long been a proponent of an arrangement that would return territory on the West Bank and in the Gaza Strip to the Jordanians in return for a peace treaty, it was no longer practical to speak in such terms. Jordan did not control the West Bank or the Gaza Strip. The Palestinian Arabs did. The Intifada had given local Palestinian Arabs the self-confidence and the authority to become partners in a political dialogue with Israel that could lead to at least an interim political settlement based on autonomy.

Rabin declared at the outset that he would continue the peace process in conformity with the ground rules established for the Madrid peace conference. Though he had not agreed on every element of those ground rules, the prime minister understood the grave risk posed were he to try to change the procedures. The Arab side might try to improve their lot and that could produce setbacks. Rabin wanted none of that.

Operating within the Madrid framework, Rabin planned to conduct talks with the Palestinians — and with Jordan, Syria, and Lebanon as well — in a different manner from Shamir. Since Madrid, the peace talks had been advancing sluggishly with no perceptible progress. After the meeting in Madrid, a series of meetings had been held between Israeli negotiators and the various Arab delegations in Washington, DC, yet the talks did not last long, often no more than a week or so. The recesses could take a few months. Rabin wanted to step up the pace, to keep the talks going on a continuous basis. The first round of peace talks convened on 24 August in Washington, DC.

Camp David had called for electing Palestinians to negotiate with Israel and also to govern during a five-year period of autonomy. The autonomy plan had been designed to lead to negotiations on the final status of the West Bank and the Gaza Strip. The Palestinians wanted elections for a legislature to operate during autonomy — a step that Israel felt would be a major step toward an independent Palestinian state, and thus not acceptable. Some kind of administrative body, with weak legislative powers, was likely to emerge as a compromise. Rabin set target dates for the implementation of autonomy, hoping this would spur progress. By 1 December, 1992 he hoped for agreement on how the elections were to be conducted, and for what kind of body. By 1 February, 1993 Rabin hoped that the framework of the administrative council could be set up. Elections should occur in April or May 1993.

As optimistic as he was about autonomy, Rabin was sceptical about the chances of reaching an accord with Syria. 'Show me evidence that Syrian President Hafez el-Assad has indeed changed,' Rabin told the Cabinet in early August. When he spoke to the 32nd Zionist Congress in Jerusalem on 30 July, Rabin appeared to have Syria in mind when he said: 'I am willing to believe in the good will of each of our enemies, but above all, I believe in us, only us, and in our strength. Security is paramount for us. We will not concede even one millimetre of security. If we have security, there will also be peace for all the residents of this land as well as its neighbours.'

And yet he was prepared to contemplate returning portions of the Golan Heights to the Syrians — in exchange for a peace treaty. First, Assad had to demonstrate, as Sadat had, that he was truly willing to live in peace with Israel. Rabin's willingness to cede land on the Golan was in striking contrast to Shamir who steadfastly refused to accept that Israel might have to return part or all of the Golan Heights. Rabin, appearing on Israel Television on 15 July, two days after becoming prime minister, told of how he had met with the Golan Heights Communities Committee during the election campaign: 'I told them that, in 1974, we signed [an agreement] on the separation of forces between us and Syria. We gave two kilometres of Kuneitra and reached the separation of forces agreement that the Likud attacked and opposed in the Knesset. For about 17 years, every resident of the Golan has enjoyed personal security from terror and knifings — such as there is not in any other sector . . . I asked them whether those two kilometres were worth that security and not one person answered in the negative. I repeated: we will not retreat from the Golan Heights in peace either. . . . We are not talking about a separation of forces; negotiations with Syria are about peace.'

*

Rabin's first few months in office were remarkable. He had moved swiftly in a host of areas, imposing as much of a freeze on Jewish settlements as was possible; obtaining the $10 billion in loan guarantees; thawing the icy relationship with Egypt by visiting President Mubarak in Cairo; mending the tattered relationship with Washington during a visit to President Bush's summer home in Maine; proceeding with peace talks with Palestinian Arabs, Syria, Lebanon, and Jordan, but this time at a stepped-up pace. One Cabinet minister spoke admiringly of Rabin's achievements in that short space of time. 'He knows what a tough job he has. But he wants to be remembered as a prime minister who made the peace process move. Sometimes, quite honestly, Rabin is hysterical. Fast, fast, fast. He wants to obtain achievements. He knows there are ,expectations out there. I've never seen him so aggressive about the peace process. Some asked why he kept Eli Rubinstein [Shamir's chief negotiator in the talks with Palestinian Arabs]. He kept him because he doesn't want to lose a moment. This is a wonderful time for Rabin. He once said that if he lost the election, he would step aside as party leader. Then he told everyone that if he won the election he would step aside after four years. Now he doesn't say that.'

Rabin's rush to get things done seemed contradictory to his cautious nature. More in line was a cautious streak that led him to calm Israel down. When an Israel TV reporter caught him as he entered an Egyptian embassy reception during the summer of 1992, Rabin said tersely, 'Don't expect miracles.' He was constantly trying to deflate the bubble of euphoria that had been blown up after the elections. He told the Labour Party's Knesset faction on 27 July that changing national priorities had proven more difficult than he expected. When he went to impose the housing freeze, Rabin learned that Shamir had set so much investment in motion that it was difficult to turn the entire operation off. 'We are faced with a situation in which the previous government spent billions on projects in the territories which are of no benefit to security or the needs of the nation. We cannot simply put the film projector into reverse, and recoup the money which was poured into settlements. . . . We cannot fulfil the great expectations of those who yearn for change right away. Even to bring about change in the course of time, we shall require immense resolve and unpleasant compromises. We shall have no choice but to reach agreement with coalition partners, and so I shall not paint a rosy picture when the situation does not warrant it.'[4]

Rabin is far more tough-minded as prime minsiter this time around. He invokes strict discipline within his Cabinet and within the Labour Party in order to make sure that his own agenda is pursued unremittingly. Few gave him trouble in the early days. Peres behaved loyally, if not lovingly. When anyone seemed to get out of line, Rabin reacted quickly and decisively. When opposition arose to the appointment of former Labour Party secretary-general Micha Harish's close aide, Yuval Frenkel, as acting secretary-general, Rabin quashed it unmercifully. Appearing at the Labour Party political bureau meeting at Kibbutz Ramat Rahel on 23 July, where the appointment was debated, Rabin called the party leaders to order reproachfully. 'When I hear the discussion, I realize that we need not only a revision of national priorities, but of party priorities as well. What does it matter who is appointed to what position? What's important is that the Government stands behind its platform. The confrontation is superfluous and belongs to another era of the party. The party's support of its ministers' decisions in matters of roads, settlements and security and foreign affairs — that's what's important.'

Rabin especially singled out Labour Party Knesset member Avraham Burg for criticism after Burg had lashed into leaders of the United Torah Judaism Front for their attacks on Shulamit Aloni. What incensed the prime minister was the timing of Burg's comments, coming as they did as Labour was trying to bring the United Torah Front into the coalition. 'Not every opinion must be expressed every day,' chided Rabin. 'There is no reason to say these things, unless one wants to sabotage the government.'

Lest anyone had any doubts, the new prime minister has made it clear who is in charge.

The peace talks, which had been in limbo until after the Israeli election, resumed in Washington in late August. Before the Israeli delegation set out for Washington, Rabin laid down a proposed timetable: by December Israel would draft an autonomy agreement with the Palestinians. By February or March 1993, agreement on the precise powers of the new Palestinian administrative council. By April or May, elections to select Palestinian members of the administrative council. None of these dates seemed wishful thinking to Rabin nor did he doubt that an autonomy accord could be wrapped up by the spring of 1993.

To demonstrate goodwill towards the Palestinians, Rabin on 23 August, 1992 announced steps designed to ease the atmosphere in the occupied territories. Some 800 Palestinians were released from jail that day; streets and alleyways, blocked off to curb riots, were opened; houses, sealed as punishment for anti-Israeli actions at least five years earlier, were opened. A day later, Rabin's government cancelled deportation orders issued eight months earlier against 11 Palestinians.

If Rabin appeared to place greater hopes on the Israeli–Palestinian negotiations than the Syrian ones, it was in no small measure due to his conviction that the Syrians had little interest in peacemaking. Still, the prime minister wanted to demonstrate a readiness to treat the Syrian talks seriously. Aware that the Syrians would not settle for anything less than a complete return of the Golan Heights to Syrian sovereignty, Rabin sought to delay talk of withdrawal until after the Syrians committed themselves to live in peace with Israel and to sign a peace treaty with the Jewish state.

Rabin planned to show new flexibility aimed at testing Syria's readiness to live in peace with Israel. He would back off from his predecessor Yitzhak Shamir's intransigent stance of not countenancing even one inch of Israeli withdrawal from the Golan. In return for a promise of partial withdrawal, Rabin wanted the Syrians to agree to a peace treaty with Israel.

When the Israeli and Syrian negotiators renewed discussions in Washington in late August, Rabin ordered his chief negotiator for Syria, Itamar Rabinovich, to articulate a new Israeli flexibility. Rabinovich acknowledged to the Syrians that United Nations Security Council Resolution 242 should be the basis for their bilateral talks. Whether the Israel Defence Forces would withdraw only partly (as Israel wished to do) or entirely (as the Syrians wanted) was left unspoken — for the time being.

The size of the withdrawal would have to be negotiated.

Then, on 25 August, in an appearance before the Knesset Foreign Affairs and Defence Committee, the prime minister sounded a similar flexible note: 'We will not give up the Golan Heights, but that does not mean we have to cling to every single centimetre of land there.'[5]

Still, the prime minister expressed his firm opposition to a complete Israeli withdrawal. 'This government,' he told a UJA Prime Minister's Mission at the Knesset on 30 August, 'is resolved not to repeat with Syria, the precedent of the Likud government in its 1978 agreement with Egypt, whereby it returned every square inch of Egyptian soil occupied in the Six-Day War of 1967.'[6]

Rabin had public opinion on his side. Fully half the country was adamantly opposed to any withdrawal in the Golan Heights and only 5 per cent said they would hand it all back to the Syrians. Only 34 per cent were prepared to give back a small part of the Golan.[7] Israeli public opinion is not unalterably etched in stone. The public's hardline attitude toward the Golan was based, in part at least, on the parallel hardline attitude coming out of Damascus. A softening of the Syrian position would likely trigger a softening of Israeli public opinion toward returning part or all of the Golan.

Rabin believed that the best way to soften up the Syrians was the personal approach. Understanding the value of personal summitry, Rabin was eager to meet Assad face to face. He could not offer the Syrian all he wanted, but their conversation might induce Assad to enter into a partial accord with Israel. It was certainly worth a try. Even meeting the Syrian leader secretly would be an incredible accomplishment, and could pave the way for a major breakthrough in the talks, and perhaps even lead to a public meeting between the two leaders. Rabin worked aggressively, trying every possible avenue. He made clear that Israel was prepared to enter into serious negotiations with the Syrians over the Golan and other related issues. A whole host of emissaries paraded before Rabin, then Assad, the Americans, Germans, Austrians, and Egyptians, all trying to coax the two men to a private summit. Rabin, however, was unable to convince the Syrian leader that the time was ripe, that Syria could get what it wanted from serious peace talks at this juncture. Assad, perhaps with a sense of disappointment, relayed back the message: 'Not now. Not at this stage. It's too early.'

Knowing that Assad had replied negatively, Rabin still hoped to score some points with international opinion. He constantly conveyed a willingness to meet Assad anywhere, anytime. The prime minister, however, was banging on a closed door.

Assad sought to keep alive the possibility of serious peace talks with Israel. During the fall, the Syrian leader issued a series of statements, however indirect and ambiguous, that Israel interpreted as fresh Syrian willingness to talk peace. The media focused on this new flurry of diplomatic activity as if peace were at hand, yet nothing was further from the truth. Israel was still offering only a partial withdrawal from the Golan Heights which was unacceptable to the Syrians. Rabin, however, remained upbeat. At least the Syrians and Israelis, he said, had moved beyond the previous year's stalemate and the prospect of true negotiations seemed in the offing.

Early October brought fresh, hopeful news. In a message from Syrian Foreign Minister Farouk a-Shara to Israel's Foreign Minister Peres, the Syrians appeared to consider an Israeli–Syrian summit. The foreign minister of a western European country was the middleman who conveyed the message. Syria had one condition for the summit, however: Israel had to declare its intention to withdraw totally from the Golan Heights. The actual withdrawal did not have to be immediate. As a bonus for such an Israeli declaration, the Syrians, a-Shara said, were ready to announce their willingness to establish full peace with Israel.

It sounded positive, and the media attention paid to the new Syrian gambit gave the impression that the diplomatic front was bubbling. Indeed, the good news was that the Syrians were finally talking about an Assad–Rabin summit. The hitch was that Rabin could not bring himself to meet the condition for the summit. If he had any plans to give up all of the Golan in order to reach peace with Syria — and it was not clear he had such plans — he would not yield that most valuable bargaining card before the negotiations began. He would save it for the end.

*

Even with the hope of progress with the Syrians, Rabin still remained convinced that the best bet for a peace accord was one with the Palestinians. Even into the fall of 1992, Rabin thought his prediction of autonomy by the spring of 1993 was realistic. Events, however, soon turned him into a disappointed pessimist. The Palestinians, he noted in early September, 'are unable to come to grips with real-life problems. Their tactics are to talk about human rights, detentions, demolitions of houses. They are dealing with the symptoms of the disease and not the disease itself.'[8]

What seemed to irk the Palestinians the most, however, was not so much their lack of human rights as the fear that Israel and Syria were about to make peace. An Israeli–Syrian peace negotiation would divert Israel's attention from the autonomy talks, and essentially leave the Palestinians out in the diplomatic cold for a long period. The Palestinians needed to grab some headlines. PLO chief Yasser Arafat found the way.

He urged the Palestinian delegation to adopt a new hardline approach toward the autonomy talks and they listened attentively. If the Israelis could promise to apply Security Council Resolution 242 to the Golan Heights, why not force them to apply 242 to the West Bank and the Gaza Strip as well? The Palestinian delegation now demanded not only mere autonomy, but also an Israeli withdrawal from the West Bank and the Gaza Strip. A useful public relations device that won the Palestinians some headlines, the ploy was a non-starter: members of the Palestinian delegation had little interest in forcing Rabin away from the negotiating table. By late September they had softened their tone, saying only it was their opinion that their talks were based on Resolution 242.

If peacemaking was ploddingly and disappointingly slow, at least Rabin had the opportunity to make important strides on the economic front. The prime minister had gotten off to a good start in trying to straighten out the economy. He had reordered national priorities so that large subsidies no longer flowed into the hands of Jewish settlers in the occupied lands. And, he had secured the $10 billion in loan guarantees during his summer 1992 visit to President Bush's summer resort in Maine. This was only the beginning and much more needed to be done. The

main questions were: how to stimulate economic growth and
how to put a dent in the country's massive unemployment.

Given the mandate Rabin had received from voters in June, it
seemed likely that the prime minister would exploit the goodwill
he had built up and take some dramatic, quick steps. Thousands
of Israelis, many new immigrants, many young men just out of
the army, were out of work. Ways had to be found — at once —
to get these people to work. Rabin had neither the great interest
nor deep understanding of economic issues. The economy
needed major surgery, not the application of Band Aids. Only
by stimulating the economy to grow would unemployment
taper off. By the time Rabin had taken office, the economy had
started to show signs of recovery. The economy was growing at a
strong 6.5 per cent rate. Inflation remained below 10 per cent,
the lowest level in 20 years.

Trouble, however, loomed on the horizon. Yitzhak Shamir
had, however unintentionally, seriously crippled Rabin's efforts
to improve the economy. To aid new Russian immigrants, the
Shamir government had promised contractors who built
apartments for these immigrants that, in the unlikely event that
these apartments could not be sold, the government would
purchase them. No one had foreseen, however, that, with little
chance of finding work in areas where the apartments were
going up, the new immigrants would not buy the newly-
constructed apartments. At first, government statisticians led
Rabin to believe that 3,000 apartments remained empty. By
September, however, that figure had mushroomed to 42,000 at
a total cost to the Rabin government of 4.5 billion shekels ($1.7
billion). Although Rabin felt betrayed, he did not blame Shamir
personally, or even the Likud's Housing Minister Ariel Sharon.
He did blame the faceless bureaucrats who should have known
better and who had not provided accurate information.

Unable to reduce unemployment overnight, Rabin had to
build into the 1993 budget projections an 11 per cent level of
unemployment, roughly the same level of unemployment as
before his election. That led Dov Lautman, president of the
Israel Manufacturers Association, to complain: 'It wasn't for
this that we elected the government. It's impossible to agree to
an economic plan and a budget based on 11 per cent
unemployment. This is unthinkable.'[9]

Rabin was pinning his hopes on 1993, the year when he would be able to earmark millions of shekels for beefing up the nation's infrastructure — its roads and railroads and mass transit facilities — all in an effort to spur economic growth. The $2 billion first instalment of the loan guarantees would go a long way to encouraging foreign investors to pour investment capital into these projects. By early 1993 hopes were high that the Rabin approach of stimulating long-range economic growth would work.

Before he could engage in peace seriously or tackle the economy aggressively, Rabin had to decide what kind of government coalition he wanted. By September, 50 days in office, Rabin had all but abandoned the quest to balance his left-leaning coalition government by bringing into the fold the eight-member Tsomet Party headed by Rafael 'Raful' Eitan. His original fears that a government dominated by Labour and Meretz would not be able make peace with the Arabs had dissolved, and by now the prime minister sensed that, on the contrary, it might be easier to enter into peace accords without the hardline Eitan at the cabinet table. If the goal was to secure the support of the political right for peace accords with the Arabs, it made little sense to Rabin to draw the tiny Tsomet party into the government, rather than the Likud, 'because with Raful I would have to make compromises on security. So why should I do it with eight? It is better for me with 32.'[10]

Rabin's decision not to cave into Tsomet's demands, chief among which was to scale back peacemaking and increase Jewish settlement in the occupied lands, gave increased strength to Meretz. Education Minister Shulamit Aloni, experienced a new sense of self-confidence that manifested itself in public statements that left the orthodox Jewish community and Yitzhak Rabin wondering how to tame her.

By the fall, Rabin became preoccupied with the 'Shulamit Aloni' question. His two key coalition partners, Meretz and Shas, were squabbling over Aloni's right to remain as Education Minister. Never one to mince words, Aloni fired verbal bullets at the orthodox Jewish community repeatedly, and Rabin seemed unable to get her to button her lip. She had suggested that at state ceremonies a text of the 'Yizkor' memorial prayer be used that omitted the name of God. She had also been quoted in a magazine as disparaging the belief that the world was created in six days. Then, on 23 September, Aloni remarked that the Golan Heights belonged to Syria under international law. For a member of Rabin's cabinet to make such an indelicate utterance could only have a negative effect on Israel's ability to bargain with the Syrians.

Rabin had had enough. On 24 September, the prime minister acknowledged that he had a loose cannon on his hands. The orthodox Jewish parties were up in arms. Shas was threatening to bolt the cabinet unless Aloni was given a portfolio other than the high-profile education ministry. Rabin sought to distance himself from Aloni's more caustic outbursts. Without referring to her by name, he told Labour party activists in Tel Aviv that 'I am now serving as a fireman every day, due to certain declarations from the left.' One of Rabin's cabinet ministers said forlornly: 'Because of the six days of creation, she'll end up destroying our government.' Even Aloni realized she had gone too far. She sent a letter to Shas spiritual mentor Rabbi Ovadia Yosef, expressing regret that her statements had been taken out of context. She could not, however, refrain from declaring that she was within her rights to express views that were different from those of orthodox Jewry. 'One must recall there are "70 faces to the Tora",' she wrote to Yosef. She promised, however, to try to lower her profile.

While on an official visit to Germany and France in early October, however, Aloni managed to discomfort the opposition's ultra-orthodox National Religious Party. The NRP charged her with desecrating the Sabbath and eating 'all kinds of abominations' at non-kosher restaurants during that visit.

Faced with the Shas ultimatum, Rabin did not intervene directly in trying to resolve the crisis. He preferred to let his lieutenants try to patch up the quarrels. He was unquestionably disturbed at Aloni's statements and acknowledged to aides privately that he had made a mistake in appointing her as education minister. He would not, however, cave in to Shas by dismissing her from that cabinet post. That would have been a sign of weakness. A compromise was worked out: Aloni kept her job but agreed to moderate her tongue.

The crisis was a reminder to Rabin and everyone else of how

much power lay in the hands of the small (six-member) Shas religious party. It was always in a position to threaten the government's future.

From the moment he became prime minister in July, Rabin plunged into the job with great zeal. He began his day at 6 am, reading the newspapers, drinking coffee and eating a grapefruit or apple. By 7:30 or 8 am he was at his office, ready to start what often amounted to 16-hour workdays. Saturday, the Jewish sabbath, was nearly a full workday for him except for the hour on Saturday morning when he squeezed in some tennis. Aides compared Rabin's busy schedule with Shamir's, noting that the former prime minister often napped in the afternoons while the most Rabin did was catch a nap in the car.

Rabin had good reason to stay awake day and night. The June election euphoria created huge expectations. Many Israelis believed that the new Rabin government would advance peacemaking and curb unemployment — within a matter of months. Dramatic, sudden shifts in policy were not consistent with Rabin's style of government. He took his time deliberating before making a decision when the issues were as complicated as peacemaking and the economy. This deliberation seemed like hesitation to the Israeli media and segments of the Israeli public. The country had hoped for breakthroughs, and all it seemed to be getting from Rabin was one meeting after the other, followed by laconic and confusing announcements that things would undoubtedly get worse before they got better. That was not what the voters who had sought revolutionary change and thought they had obtained it, wanted to hear.

Reinforcing the public's disappointment was the prime minister's style of government. The public wanted drama and excitement in those first few months of Rabin's rule, yet their prime minister appeared closed off, unenthusiastic, unable to make bold decisions. Rather than move forward on the economy, he blamed Shamir — and of course he was partly right. Rather than advance in peacemaking, he blamed the Palestinians and the Syrians — and again he was partly right. Rabin's style of governing was called 'Presidential', a derogatory term in Israel, largely because he appeared to trust just a few people, mostly those on his office staff. Critics called him 'Napoleon' behind his back. It was not that he was power hungry. He had tasted power for much of his life. But he arrived in office in July 1992 as a man of 70, with far more experience in public life than those around him, a man who had learned all throughout his career to trust very few people.

At the 100-day mark in his administration, Rabin encountered a batch of unfriendly articles in the Israeli press. Then the opposition Likud, dormant for a few months after the shocking loss of the elections, began to stir. Likud Knesset member Benyamin Netanyahu, competing for his party's leadership, charged that Israel had experienced '100 days of retreat. In every aspect of our national life, the government has failed to deliver.'[11]

Such criticism from the Likud was expected. Yet, even political allies wondered when the Rabin government would deliver some good news. Rabin's government seemed overwhelmed by events. Peacemaking was at a standstill. Plans to tackle the economy were moving through the bureaucracy slowly. And, to his chagrin, Rabin found that the smaller political parties, some within his coalition, some outside, were presenting new challenges and burdens to his government coalition.

Though Rabin sensed that it would take much work to reach agreement on Palestinian autonomy, by late October he was growing increasingly frustrated. On 25 October, he told the Knesset that the Palestinians had exhibited no 'responsiveness' to Israeli proposals thus far. 'I fear that the Palestinians are again deluding themselves. Again, they may be hallucinating. Instead of learning from their mistakes over generations, instead of accepting what has been offered to them — or to at least discuss it seriously — the Palestinians are still adhering to "everything — or nothing". If it will be this way, if they are not willing to change their positions, they will ultimately remain with nothing.'

In mid-November *Time* magazine sought interviews with both Rabin and Syrian President Hafez el-Assad. The interviews were to run in the same edition. Assad granted the interview on 13 November. Two days later, Rabin sat down with three reporters from *Time*, one of them this author. *Time* had hoped that Assad and Rabin would make dramatic news in the interviews that would propel the peace process forward. Perhaps Assad would make a turnabout and indicate his readiness to meet Rabin at a summit. Or, perhaps Rabin would acknowledge that, under certain circumstances, Israel would be prepared to leave the Golan Heights completely.

Neither Assad nor Rabin offered such statements. Indeed, Assad told *Time*: 'A meeting of heads of state to discuss the Arab–Israeli conflict might lead to war instead of peace because when there are differences at the [top] leadership level, there is nobody to mend things.' As for Rabin, one might have tried to read between the lines and suggest that he would ultimately countenance a total Israeli departure from the Golan. But he did not say so outright. Asked whether there were any circumstances under which he would consider full withdrawal from the Golan, he answered: 'I will not even go so far as addressing the question of withdrawal from the Golan without first knowing that Syria is ready for full-fledged peace, a peace that stands by itself.'

When I asked him, 'If Assad came to Jerusalem prepared to sign a peace treaty, would that change your position on the Golan?' Rabin grew tense and with some annoyance in his voice, said: 'You are not Assad. You don't represent Assad, and you are not prime minister of Israel. Unfortunately, the Syrian position as it was expressed by Foreign Minister Farouk Shara — "total withdrawal for total peace" — is not very clear. I don't know what total peace is. I do know what total withdrawal is. It is not limited to Syria. It also concerns the West Bank and the Gaza Strip.'

By December 1992, despite the parlays in Washington, Israel and Syria appeared to be no closer to a peace agreement. Rabin was busy trying to assure the Jewish settlers on the Golan that their settlements were not about to be dismantled. 'In any peace agreement with the Syrians which includes withdrawal from the Golan Heights,' he told the Labour Party's Young Guard on 30 December, 'only the [Israeli] army will withdraw.' Rabin remained adamant that he was not going to announce the scale of an Israeli withdrawal until he heard from the Syrians that they were ready to talk genuine peace. 'Syria must first respond regarding the content of the peace it is talking about,' he told the Young Guard, 'which will include normalization, exchanging ambassadors, freedom of movement, tourism, etc. Until then, I will not begin any negotiations regarding the scope of the withdrawal.'[12]

Rabin had campaigned on the promise that he would make Israel safer. He did not mean that his election would prevent war. He was referring to the question of what Israelis call 'internal security', making sure that Israeli civilians and soldiers are not attacked and injured by Arabs within Israel's borders. Keeping that promise would prove difficult since Israel's internal security was closely linked with the peace process. Any progress in peacemaking was likely to increase Arab violence against Israelis in an attempt to sabotage the peacemaking. The dissenters would try to use violence to create tensions between Arabs and Israelis. Rabin was determined not to let the dissenters have their way. It was not easy. Each Israeli death gave Israelis less incentive to sit and talk peace with the Arabs.

Violence occurred. On 25 October five Israeli soldiers were killed when a roadside bomb planted by the Lebanese Shi'ite group, Hizbollah, blew up near the soldiers' convoy in south Lebanon. That same day another Israeli soldier was shot to death when gunmen fired at his army post in the West Bank town of Hebron.

Hoping to terrorize Israel into abandoning the peace process, the Hizbollah increased tensions in late October by firing Katyusha rockets into the northern communities of Israel. On 27 October, 14 year-old Vadim Schuchman, a Russian immigrant who had come to Israel two years earlier, was killed when a Katyusha fired from south Lebanon landed on his house in Kiryat Shemona. Israelis in the north went into air shelters. Rabin ordered a show of force and the IDF beefed up its units along the northern border. Israeli military sources leaked threats that the IDF might move troops into Lebanon. Given Rabin's displeasure with the 1982 War in Lebanon and the subsequent three year IDF occupation in Lebanon, it seemed unlikely that he would take such a step. As it turned out, the Israeli show of force was enough. Hizbollah's activities dissipated after a few weeks.

Trouble was brewing for Israel from another Arab quarter angry with the peace process. Hamas, the Islamic Resistance

Movement which was fast becoming the dominant rejectionist group in the occupied territories, sought to undermine peacemaking through stepped-up violence. Hamas got its start as the outgrowth of a segment of the Egyptian-based Muslim Brotherhood. It was formed in the Gaza Strip in February 1988 by quadriplegic cleric Sheikh Ahmed Yassin. Its platform called for a holy war to liberate the entire pre-1948 Palestine from Israel's grip.

Throughout the fall of 1992 Hamas attacked Israeli forces. It staged attacks on Israeli soldiers on 21 and 25 September in Hebron, killing one soldier; it killed three Israeli soldiers in the Gaza Strip on 7 December and a fourth soldier in Hebron two days later.

Then on 13 December came the worst incident of this period, creating the most serious crisis of Rabin's five month old government. Hamas activists kidnapped a 29 year-old Israeli Border Policeman named Nissim Toledano as he was leaving his home in Lod for work at 4:40 am. Six hours later two masked men entered the Red Crescent office in Al-Bira, near Ramallah on the West Bank and identified themselves as Hamas members. They left a photocopy of Toledano's ID card and a letter demanding the release of Hamas's spiritual founder Sheikh Yassin from an Israeli jail in return for Toledano. The kidnappers threatened to kill Toledano if Yassin was not released by 9 pm Sunday. Rabin responded, suggesting that negotiations were possible, but only after Hamas gave a sign that Toledano was alive. Israeli authorities permitted Yassin to be interviewed on Israel Television shortly after 9 pm, hoping his appeal to the kidnappers to spare Toledano's life would work. 'I say that I am not for killing this person,' the Sheikh said in his high-pitched, whining voice. 'The authorities must be given the chance to respond to the demands.' Meanwhile, Israeli security agents began arresting 2,000 Hamas activists in the occupied territories. The 9 pm deadline came without the kidnappers offering a sign that Toledano was alive. Two days later Toledano's body was found by a Bedouin woman on the road between Jerusalem and Jericho. He had been knifed and strangled. His murder had occurred soon after the deadline.

Rabin would not allow the violence to force Israel away from the peace table. He told Israel Television on 15 December:

'Why has there been an increase in shooting incidents in recent months? I have no doubt that those who propose this action are, first and foremost, the ones who want to kill Israelis, and also the peace and the chance to achieve peace.'

Speaking in the Knesset that same day, hours after Nissim Toledano's body was discovered, Rabin said: 'The heart bleeds and feels pain today, but this is what I want to tell those who seek to harm us. We will hurt, we will pay the price, we will grit our teeth and go on — and we will win. Terrorism does not stand a chance against us. Nothing will move us from here — not stones, fire bombs, or knives; not Hamas, the Popular Front, or the Fatah; not Ahmed Yassin, Ahmed Jibril or Yasser Arafat. We are here — and we will live here forever.'

After the murder of Nissim Toledano, Prime Minister Rabin sensed that some dramatic Israeli action was essential. Otherwise, Hamas, and all others who were in the rejectionist camp, would take heart that it was possible to jab away at the Israelis and go unpunished. More of this, thought Rabin, and Israelis would begin to wonder why their leaders were sitting at the peace table with the Arabs. By its deeds during the fall, Hamas had begun to capture the imagination of Palestinians in the occupied territories. The Palestinian peace delegation seemed to be dithering, getting nowhere in the autonomy talks. Hamas, meanwhile, was capturing the headlines, keeping the Intifada alive, keeping the Israelis on the defensive.

So Rabin decided to act. Later, critics would wonder whether he had taken sufficient account of potential international criticism, of damaging the peace process, of risking an early Arab departure from the peace table. He seemed unfazed by such worries. He knew that what he had in mind would ignite controversy abroad. He knew that Israel would be condemned by the United Nations, by Washington, by the European Community.

He decided, however, the condemnations would be the price Israel could pay to show muscle.

Rabin ordered the deportation of 415 Hamas activists. As a form of punishment against Palestinians, deportation had been used sparingly by Israel over the years. Since the start of the Intifada in December 1987, Israel had deported 66 Palestinians from the occupied territories; only eight in the past two years; 45 had been deported between 1985 and 1987; and one between 1981 and 1985. The act of expelling someone from his or her homeland, no matter what that person's crime, seemed exceptionally unjust in a world that placed such a premium on the notion of national identity. Moreover, it was questionable whether deporting large numbers of Hamas activists would temper the anti-Israeli violence; surely others within Hamas would rise to the surface and maintain the violence. None of these arguments prevented Rabin from this dramatic step.

On 16 December, the day after Nissim Toledano's body was found, Israel's cabinet met and voted 14-0 that the Government would temporarily expel 415 Hamas activists who had been part of the 2,000 Hamas members picked up by Israeli authorities a few days earlier. Only Justice Minister David Libai abstained, concerned that the cabinet's action was not legal. This expulsion was by far the single largest group of Palestinians to be sent into exile since soon after the 1967 war. In an attempt to alleviate international criticism, Rabin's government avoided using the word deportation which implied permanent expulsion and which was forbidden by international law. The 415 were being temporarily banished and given the right to appeal within 60 days of their removal.

Put on buses that night, the 415 Hamas deportees headed for the north but before they reached the Lebanese border, Israeli human rights groups and lawyers representing the activists approached the Israel Supreme Court and obtained a temporary rescinding order. One indication of how urgent was the case in the eyes of the Supreme Court justices was their decision to schedule a hearing for 5 am, the next morning (17 December). Only a month earlier the court had moved into magnificent, new premises situated between the Prime Minister's office and the Jerusalem Hilton. The deportation case was by far the most important they had heard in their new building. Lasting all day and into the early evening, the hearing focused on the defendants' claim that they had been denied due process. The court, however, decided by a vote of 5-2 that the government could deport the activists immediately, if only on a temporary basis. Scheduling another hearing within 30 days, the court ordered the government to explain why it was proper to carry out these deportations. Soon afterwards that evening, the 22 buses carrying the Hamas activists rolled into Lebanon. The deportees were taken to a point five kilometres north of the Israeli security zone in Lebanon and left there. Then events took an odd turn.

The Lebanese government refused to permit the 415 to enter into what it called Lebanese territory. The deportees were forced to remain out in the cold. They were denied food and water but not media attention. The international media managed to reach the deportees and televised pictures of their plight around the world, stranded in the winter cold, living in tents provided by relief agencies, passing the time by praying and talking, waiting for someone to rescue them. On 18 December the Security Council voted to condemn Israel for the deportations and demanded that Israel allow the activists back into Israel. Two days later the Supreme Court was asked to rule on whether Israel should not permit the Hamas activists back on the grounds that they had not been deported in a manner that guaranteed their safety. Attorneys for the deportees insisted that they be returned, if not to their homes, then at least to a place in Israel where they would be safe. The court ruled on 22 December that the deportees had not been prevented from entering Lebanon, they were in Lebanon, and therefore the court had no reason to intervene on their behalf. Essentially, the court said that Israel had deported the 415 to Lebanon and it was now Lebanon's responsibility to take care of these people.

Rabin was bitter toward the human rights groups who had rushed to defend the Hamas deportees. Appearing before the Labour Party Central Committee on 18 December, he criticized these groups. 'Nissim Toledano was not granted the right to appeal the brutal, bloody sentence passed on him. The Hamas deportees do get that right . . . Of all the options at our disposal this deportation for a limited time is the most human move we could make. This means the least damage in life or property to the Hamas figures involved. Let's not forget the mood out there and the demands for the imposition of the death sentence, for more curfews, or for less strictures for security personnel to open fire.' Rabin argued that for this measure to be effective it had to be done quickly. 'It will lose its value if, as was the case all too often in the past, we have to wait for months and even years in order to implement punitive decisions.'

In the immediate aftermath of the deportations, Rabin described the act as a daring blow to the Hamas cause. The deportations, he said, were 'one of the most audacious moves taken by any government in the struggle against terror'.[13]

The political right in Israel was won over — at least temporarily. Rabin had acted more decisively than Shamir had in meting out punishment to the Palestinians and the Likud and others on the political right applauded him for it. 'I don't believe any other defense minister, including Ariel Sharon, would have carried out the deportations better than you,' observed Likud Knesset member Eliahu Ben-Elissar at a meeting of the Knesset Foreign Affairs and Defense Committee on 22 December.

Over the next few weeks, the deportees remained in their tents, as the international community wrestled with the question of what to do with them. Lawyers for the deportees swamped the Israel Supreme Court with petitions to win the Hamas people's immediate return to Israel. The United Nations Security Council threatened sanctions against the Jewish state. Rabin remained firm, insisting that the deportees would not be permitted back into the country. When an Israeli security agent, Haim Nachmani, was murdered in Jerusalem in early January, Hamas boasted that this deed had proven that the deportations had not prevented further violence against Israeli targets. Rabin, however, stood firm.

Just prior to the deportations, the political left had begun to flex its muscles. While the doves in the Labour party and the Meretz party had little reason to believe that Rabin would veer from his centrist views, they were convinced that in time he would be won over to a more leftist stance. Their opening shot came on 2 December when legislation began moving through the Knesset to drop the 1986 ban on unauthorized contacts with the PLO or any other terrorist group. The 1986 law had been adopted to keep Israelis from meeting informally with PLO figures, meetings that were likely to increase the pressure on the Israeli Government to hold formal negotiations with the PLO. Violators could be jailed for three years and indeed peace activist Abie Nathan did go to jail, drawing the ire of left-wing groups. Once the Shamir government sat down in Madrid and later in Washington with Palestinians who were 'guided' by the PLO in Tunis, the ban on PLO contacts lost all meaning. For, even the Shamir government seemed to be negotiating, however indirectly, with the PLO. The legislation to drop the ban was adopted on 19 January 1993.

Meanwhile, on 13 December came another gambit from the political left. Four cabinet ministers (Health Minister Haim Ramon, Tourism Minister Uzi Baram, both of Labour; Energy Minister Amnon Rubinstein of Meretz, and Interior Minister Aryeh Deri of Shas) responded to the deteriorating security situation in the Gaza Strip with a far-reaching proposal. They urged Rabin that he put Israel's immediate withdrawal from the Gaza Strip on the cabinet's agenda. Rabin rejected the request, arguing that a unilateral Israeli departure from the Gaza Strip was not consistent with the Madrid format that called for negotiations over the political future of that very piece of turf.

The deportations provided one more setback for the political left. The three Meretz ministers and the Labour doves in the cabinet voiced no objection to the deportations, and in fact voted in favour of them. Later, when the scope of the deportations became known, the Meretz ministers acted as if they had been somehow duped by the prime minister who had misled them about the actual number of deportees.

When grass-roots Meretz supporters took their ministers to task for supporting the deportations, it was clear that the political left had to move to alleviate the damage it had caused its own movement.

The Israeli media became an unexpected ally. On 20 December, Israel Radio provided a great boost to the left's cause by carrying out a poll of Labour party Knesset members. The poll showed that fully two-thirds of the Labour Knesset deputies favoured direct negotiations with the PLO: 30 were for direct talks; 14 against. The survey was significant if only because Rabin's coalition guidelines as well as the Labour party's platform ruled out negotiations with the PLO.[14]

Three days later came yet a new achievement for the leftists. The Rabin cabinet held its first debate ever on the possibility of integrating the PLO into the peace talks. The proposal came from three Meretz ministers. It was significant that the trio did not propose holding negotiations immediately with the PLO. Instead, they asked merely that the cabinet agree to 'declare that the government will re-examine its attitude to the PLO if it gives constructive backing during the current state of negotiations'. Rabin turned them down again. The Meretz ministers did not push for a vote. Though the outcome appeared to be close, Rabin might have brought down the government rather than take the risk of the cabinet adopting the proposal. The Meretz ministers did not want to take that risk.

The new aggressiveness on the part of the political left came up against the indomitable figure of Yitzhak Rabin. He may have seemed increasingly isolated. Even if he did, he remained far stronger than any of his opponents, within or outside of his cabinet.

Rabin faced the most serious crisis of his prime ministership — the deportations and the attendant international criticism — with no sign of self-doubt whatsoever. After all, according to public opinion polls taken soon after the deportations, he had an overwhelming majority of the country behind him. A poll published in *Yediot Aharonot* on 19 December, for instance, indicated that no less than 91 per cent of the nation supported the deportations.

Over the coming weeks, however, matters grew complicated. International criticism, however much Rabin had hoped that it would abate, only grew. The outgoing American Secretary of State, Lawrence Eagleburger, called the deporations 'a terrible mistake'. Members of the United Nations Security Council began to grumble. Perhaps most importantly, the international media provided non-stop coverage of the deportees' plight.

The deportees, meanwhile, had quickly realized that, by dumping them collectively into one place beyond Israel's borders, instead of scattering them in a number of Arab countries in smaller groups, the Israelis had provided them with a golden opportunity to score points with the international community. With both Israel and Lebanon refusing to take responsibility for their welfare, the deportees seemed indeed, as the title of a CNN 30-minute special on their plight in early

February 1993 suggested, 'Trapped in No Man's Land'. Stuck
out in the harsh winter cold, with little food or water, their fate
uncertain, these Palestinians had become a metaphor for the
entire Palestinian people.

The media, allowed to mingle freely with the deportees,
understood the drama of the deportees' plight. Day after day,
throughout January and into early February, television footage
of the deportees was beamed back into millions of American and
European homes, increasing the pressure on Rabin and Israel to
alter the 16 December deportation decree. Repeatedly, Israel
refused to allow humanitarian aid to reach the deportees,
strengthening their claim that they were being mistreated.
Searching for a quick solution, the prime minister raised ideas
that were non-starters. Without any real hope that it would
happen, Rabin, on 30 December, appealed to any 'third
country' (other than Israel and Lebanon) to take in the
deportees. None responded to the appeal. Then, on 2 January,
Rabin offered to shorten the deportations to nine months (down
from two years) if the Palestinians stopped the Intifada. He
added that he knew it was a 'pipe dream'. The Intifada
continued.

In early January, Rabin made a series of minor concessions.
He allowed Red Cross convoys to visit the deportees; he agreed
to have a small number of deportees who had been mistakenly
deported return home. He also permitted some who were ill to
return home. The deportees clung to the principle that either
they would all return home, or none would. Nonetheless,
mistakenly-deported and ill deportees began coming home.

Gradually, the television pictures had their effect on the
United Nations Security Council. Enthusiasm built up among
its members for action against Israel that was more biting than a
mere verbal condemnation. Before deciding on what action to
take, the UN sent a few emissaries to Israel who tried to convince
Rabin to back down on the deportee issue. The prime minister
would not bend. UN Secretary-General Boutrus Ghali grew
furious at Rabin. For his part, the prime minister was enraged
at what he considered Ghali's one-sided treatment of the
deportation issue, ignoring in his report to the UN that Hamas
engaged in terrorist acts against Israel. Did the Ghali position
surprise him, Rabin was asked? 'I am not at all surprised by the

United Nations — nor by Ghali, he is an Egyptian.' Israeli relations with the UN, never great, were once again plummeting. By mid-January members of the Security Council believed that Israel's behaviour toward the deportees warranted unprecedented United Nations action: the imposition of sanctions against the Jewish state. Never before had the UN imposed such measures against Israel.

The threat of those sanctions added more pressure on the Prime Minister of Israel. For his part, Rabin was convinced that he had to withstand such pressure — to demonstrate his toughness toward those who wanted to destroy the peace process; to avoid having to acknowledge that perhaps he had erred in deciding on the deportations. And yet, the more time that passed, the more the peace process appeared to be in danger.

As long as the deportee issue lingered, as long as American television showed Palestinians 'trapped' in a no man's land in southern Lebanon, the Israeli–Arab peace talks would not resume. That became the new reality in mid-January.

The next round of talks had been scheduled for sometime in February. In the immediate aftermath of the deportations, it appeared that the Arabs would not let the issue stand in the way of their attending the February round of peace talks. Arab foreign ministers, holding emergency talks in Damascus soon after the deportations, concluded their discussions on 24 December without calling for a boycott of the peace talks. They did hint, however, that the talks could be in trouble if the US and Russia did not pressure Israel to return the deportees home. Yet, over the next few weeks, Syria, Lebanon and Jordan, refrained from declaring publicly that they would not return to the peace table unless the deportees were allowed home. The Palestinians spoke more harshly: On 2 January, PLO chief Yasser Arafat said that the Palestinians would return to the peace table only if Israel reversed its expulsion of the 415 Palestinians.

Even if some Arab states seemed less inclined than the Palestinians to boycott the peace talks, Rabin understood all too well that it was increasingly unlikely that the February round would come off if the deportees were still out in the winter cold in southern Lebanon. Moreover, if, as now appeared possible, the Security Council imposed sanctions on Israel, there was no way that Rabin could permit the Israelis to sit down at the peace talks. Still unwilling to compromise, Rabin laboured feverishly in mid-January to head off United Nations sanctions.

It would not be easy. On 20 January Bill Clinton would become the new American President. Though Clinton was determined to focus his attention and energy at first on the American economy, by allowing the deportees issue to fester without resolution, Rabin and the Israelis were inadvertently forcing him to divert himself from what he had set as his main task upon taking office. This was bound to get Israel off on the wrong foot with the new administration, something Rabin, who had always prided himself on getting along with the Americans, did not want. Beyond that, if the Security Council appeared likely to impose sanctions on Israel, Rabin could further complicate Clinton's early days in office by giving the new President no choice but to order the American representative to the Security Council to veto the resolution on sanctions. For Clinton to use that veto would reduce his credibility with the Arabs at a time when he wanted to show impartiality in the Arab–Israeli peace process.

Adding to the complicated picture that had emerged as Clinton took office on 20 January was the fact that very soon Israel's Supreme Court would give a final ruling on the question of whether the deportations were or were not valid. In effect, a Supreme Court ruling that the deportations were not valid would mean that Rabin would have to allow them home immediately, a resolution of the affair that would have not pleased the prime minister, but would have at least ended the crisis, and gotten Clinton off the hook — for now.

On 23 January, three days after Clinton had become President, he held a ten-minute phone talk with the Israeli Prime Minister. Significantly, Clinton refrained from pressing Rabin to return the deportees at once. He did inform the prime minister that the United States had persuaded the UN Security Council to hold off a vote on sanctions until after the Supreme Court ruled. That ruling was expected in a few days.

Ever since 16 December, Rabin had been able to point to the support he had received both from the country and his own cabinet as reason not to compromise. The country remained overwhelmingly behind him. But, as he would learn over the weekend of 23-24 January, support in his cabinet was dwindling. Israel Television's diplomatic correspondent Gadi Sukeinik had polled 18 of the 19 cabinet ministers and found that ten now supported an early return of a large number of the deportees.

Bending a little, Rabin declared that family members and lawyers would be permitted to meet with the deportees to help them determine whether they wanted to appeal the expulsion order. The deportees turned down the offer.

Now, everyone waited for the Supreme Court. The night before the decision Rabin was interviewed on Israel TV. He was still deeply worried that the Americans might side with the Arabs and vote for sanctions. 'For 35 years, all American presidents have made it clear, at every opportunity, including during the Lebanon war and all other [junctures], that not only would they not support sanctions against Israel — but they would oppose them.' Accordingly, he said it was hard for him to believe that Clinton would take such a serious step against Israel.

The Supreme Court's decision came on 28 January. Shrouded in legalese, ambiguous to many, the ruling of the seven-justice panel was to uphold the Rabin government's decision to deport the 415 Hamas activists. Nonetheless, the Court issued so many caveats and heaped so much criticism on the manner in which the deportations were carried out that it appeared extremely unlikely that any Israeli government would be able to act in the same way a second time.

Among the caveats the Court issued: Israel would not be able to deport so many people in the future in a similar fashion. Unquestionably annoyed that the deportees had not been given the full measure of due process, the justices cautioned that only 'concrete, exceptional circumstances' could justify setting aside that right. The court found that such circumstances were not spelled out in the deportation order. It ruled that the legal instrument chosen to carry out the mass deportation — a general Temporary Deportation Order — was not valid.

None of this, however, kept the Court from ruling in favour of the Government.

In the past, the Court had ruled that, under the Fourth Geneva Convention, mass deportations were not legal.

Individual expulsions, on the other hand, were legitimate. Describing these deportations as individual ones, the justices, citing an emergency British Mandatory regulation that provided for individual deportations, ruled in favour of the December expulsions. In effect, the justices treated the event as if it were 415 individual deportations with each deportee being ejected on the basis of evidence against him individually.

However dissatisfied the justices were with how the Rabin Government had handled the matter, the bottom line was this: the deportees would have to stay put. Clinton was not off the hook. Sanctions might still be imposed. Rabin still needed the American administration to keep the situation from deteriorating further — and to get the peace process back on track.

Pleased with the Supreme Court's decision, Rabin turned his attention to halting UN sanctions. 'Should the UN Security Council opt for any operative steps against Israel,' he said right after the decision, 'it would wipe out the chances for peace in the Middle East. If the message the Arabs get is that they can use the Security Council to coerce Israel to do as they wish, then I tell you that there is absolutely no chance for peace with them.' Earlier that day, at a conference of hoteliers in Tel Aviv, Rabin argued that 'it is inconceivable that the Arabs should make the continuation of the Middle East negotiations conditional on Israel halting legal measures against terror.'

If Rabin was cheered by the court's ruling, the deportees were not. They continued to demand that the UN Security Council force Israel to allow them home. Retaliating for the ruling, Hamas gunmen on 30 January shot and killed two Israeli soldiers in the Gaza Strip. The ambush further demonstrated that the expulsions had not brought Hamas terrorism to a complete halt. That same day, 1,000 Jews and Arabs marched in Jerusalem to protest the deportations.

That kind of pressure had little effect on Rabin. The phone call from the new Secretary of State Warren Christopher on 29 January, however, did. The Secretary suggested to the Prime Minister that the new Clinton administration did not want to be forced into imposing a veto on UN Security Council sanctions. It was up to Rabin, Christopher argued, to find a way that would avoid the need for the American veto. Around the same time, Egyptian President Hosni Mubarak phoned the Prime

Minister and asked whether Israel would allow the deportees into the Israeli-controlled security zone in southern Lebanon where they could remain in a newly-built detention camp. Dismissing the idea as impractical, Rabin retorted that the deportees were supposed to be located in a place beyond Israel's control.

To Rabin, what mattered more than anything else at this stage was winning the support of the new Clinton administration. Were President Clinton to adopt a negative view of Israel in his first few days of office, it would be virtually impossible for Rabin to make progress in the peace process. And the continuation of the peace process was what was most important to him. He knew that he would be judged almost exclusively on whether he had been able to achieve results on the peace front. Though he had repeatedly declared that he would not compromise on the deportation issue, it seemed either he must compromise or run the risk of losing the needed support of the American administration. He had also reluctantly begun to acknowledge in private that the original decision to deport the Hamas people was flawed. To cabinet ministers, he admitted that 'We have gotten ourselves into a "plonter" (Hebrew for mess).' The 'plonter' had developed, Rabin admitted, because he had failed to take into account the possibility that Lebanon would refuse to take in the deportees. He had sensed that the international community would not be thrilled with the deportations; but he had hoped that the United Nations and the international media would lose interest in the deportees' cause after a while. They had not.

Frantically, the Prime Minister engaged in secret discussions with senior American officials, trying to find out what it would take to satisfy Washington without being forced to return all the deportees at once. In a matter of days, Rabin was able to reach what he later called a 'written understanding' with the Clinton team.

And so on 1 February, he convened the cabinet in a special session in the Knesset. In his pocket was an agreement he had worked out with the United States over the previous few days, an agreement that required Israel to compromise on the deportees and obligated the United States, in turn, to make sure that sanctions were not adopted against Israel; and to seek the renewal of the peace talks. The ministers needed little convincing that a compromise was in order.

When the vote came it was unanimously in favour of the package deal Rabin had worked out with the US. The elements of that deal were: that some 100 deportees could return home at once; that the remaining deportees' terms of expulsion would be cut in half. For its part, the Clinton administration had promised to try to find 'host countries' for any deportees who preferred not to return, but no deportee would be forced to move. Of critical importance, administration officials had agreed that its understanding with Israel was not temporary (in other words, it would make no further effort to get more deportees returned home) nor was the accord dependent upon whether the 100 deportees were willing to accept the offer to come home at once. Soon after the cabinet compromise, Christopher said he was now 'quite optimistic' that no sanctions would be brought against Israel. The White House called Israel's partial turnabout 'a step in the right direction'.

At a news conference after the cabinet meeting, Rabin declared that 'We needed to reach an understanding with the US for the four years ahead and buttress our position in the international arena'. He had no regrets over the original decision. 'On the contrary, I am proud of it. No previous government ever delivered such a massive blow against terror. The right-wing government [of Shamir] did not have the courage.'

The deportees, who had been slamming the door to any compromise until now, remained consistent. They would not take the half a loaf that the Israeli Government was offering them. Only when all deportees could go home, would they move from their tent encampment. Meanwhile, the Israeli army began compiling a list of the 100 deportees who could return. Israel was not bothered if any or all of the 100 refused its offer. The written understanding with the US would not fall.

Had Rabin gone too far in compromising? Did he have the support of his own countrymen? A public opinion poll, taken within 24 hours of the cabinet decision, showed that the Prime Minister did not have the nation in his corner. The question was asked: 'Is the decision of the government to return 100 deportees and to cut the period of deportation of the others justified?'

Some 61 per cent said no, it was not justified; only 36 per cent said it was justified (three per cent had no response). A second question was asked: 'In retrospect, and in light of developments, was the decision to deport [in December] correct?' Agreeing that the deportation was still correct were 77 per cent of those surveyed; 22 per cent disagreed (one per cent had no response). The poll gave ample evidence that Rabin had the overwhelming backing of the country for the decision to deport the 415 Hamas activists. Many of those same people were disturbed by the 1 February compromise; but then again, no doubt so was Rabin.

Though Rabin had little support around the country for the compromise, the politicans were unable to create a major crisis over the 1 February cabinet decision. Predictably, the right wing parties condemned Rabin for backing down on the deportations, and noted that here was proof that Rabin would not be able to withstand pressure from the Americans during the peace talks. Nonetheless, the prime minister's support among the political left was solid. Increasingly anguished by the deportations and the international criticism which followed, the left had become deeply troubled that the peace process would fall victim to the deportations. Now, at last, it seemed that there might be a way out of the impasse.

By 8 February, the number of deportees had slightly decreased — from 415 at the outset to 396, some returning home because they had been mistakenly deported, some because they were ill. The remaining 396 were still hoping that international pressure would force the Israelis into further compromise. Yet, in the wake of the cabinet decision a week earlier, the Arabs began sounding as if they were unwilling to keep the peace process hostage to the deportees. In December and January, it had seemed unthinkable to reconvene the peace talks as long as the deportees were left out in the cold in southern Lebanon. Now, with the US making it clear that it would no longer lend support to the Arab side on the deportation issue, Arab states grew increasing discomforted by their original stance. They now appeared ready for a return to the peace table. A face-saving way still had to be found. For that reason, President Clinton announced that he was sending his Secretary of State, Warren Christopher, to the Middle East later in February for talks with the parties. The main topic: getting the peace process reactivated. Christopher made clear that his goal was resuming those talks no later than April.

The overriding question regarding Yitzhak Rabin and the rest of his tenure as prime minister was this: can he bring peace? He has already given the impression that he, more than Yitzhak Shamir, is resolved to bring peace. Israelis believe that; so do the Arabs. Can he, however, take the decisions that are needed to make peace possible?

Complicating matters is the fact that the peace process Rabin inherited from Shamir is not the kind the prime minister prefers. The Madrid peace conference embraced the notion of a comprehensive peace, one that included Israeli peace treaties with Jordan, Lebanon, and Syria, and autonomy for the Palestinians. Rabin had learned his Middle East diplomacy at the side of Henry Kissinger, and Kissinger's technique focused on the step-by-step approach, one peace treaty at a time. Rabin seemed uncomfortable with the comprehensive approach: he seemed frustrated to have to shift his attention and his energy back and forth between the Palestinians and the Syrians.

Rabin's ability to make peace was caught up in the separate, but equally important question of whether the Arabs were capable of making peace. Few could fathom what was in Hafez el-Assad's mind. He appeared as staunch as ever in his insistence on getting back all of the Golan Heights for Syria. Rabin appeared as staunch as ever in resisting that demand. To whet the appetite of the Syrians, Rabin had gone farther than Shamir, moving away from the Likud leader's rigid opposition to yielding even one inch of the Golan. Rabin had left deliberately obscure the question of whether he might one day be convinced to give all of the Golan back to the Syrians.

Rabin has been open about his eagerness to grant the Palestinians political autonomy. The Palestinians, however, have wanted an autonomy that would be a way-station to their ultimate goal, a state. Rabin has been no different from Begin or Shamir in not wanting to grant statehood to the Palestinians. He has been different, however, in being willing to give the Palestinians far greater political authority than either of his two predecessors envisaged. Rabin, however, has a far more complex problem with the Palestinians than with the Syrians. The Syrians are united behind Assad. If Assad decided to make peace with Israel, it could be presumed he would figure out how to get his countrymen behind him. Not so with the Palestinians. It has become difficult to imagine Rabin and the Palestinians reaching an agreement that would be acceptable to the majority of Palestinians on the West Bank and in the Gaza Strip. So riven with divisions have the Palestinians been that the Palestinian delegation has had only the shakiest authority to make peace with Israel.

In some important ways, Yitzhak Rabin was in a far better position to make peace with the Palestinians and other Arabs than previous Israeli leaders. It fell to Menachem Begin to make peace with Egypt, the most important state and the first Arab state prepared to sign a peace treaty with Israel. That accomplishment cannot be minimized. Yet it fell short of a comprehensive peace. And, no Israeli prime minister was more adamant than Begin in resisting a peace agreement with the Palestinians and the Syrians. The most significant result of the June election was the signal Israelis were sending to the Arabs. That signal was: now we are ready to make peace with you.

When Rabin came to power the Palestinians and Syrians finally faced the possibility of making peace with Israel. In fact, the Arabs seemed more eager than ever. That gave Rabin a certain latitude. He could behave in ways that were inimicable to the Arabs. The Arabs knew deep in their hearts that, if they wanted to move toward their goals, they could only do so with Yitzhak Rabin at the helm. To undermine Rabin, to force him to step down from office, was to risk the return of someone as intransigent as Yitzhak Shamir, and the Arabs had had their share of such Israeli leaders.

Peacemaking, for Rabin, required not only a margin of flexibility on the Arab side. It required that he possess the correct constellation of political forces in his government coalition. He had thought — back on the night of 23 June when it was clear he would be Israel's next prime minister — that the best way to make peace was to have a government that was balanced by members of both the political left (Meretz) and the political right (Tsomet). To his sorrow, he wound up with a left-leaning government that included Meretz, but not Tsomet.

For months, Rabin agonized that such a government would keep him from serious peacemaking. He changed his mind. He began to sense that bringing in any members of the political right (whether Tsomet, the National Religious Party, or even the Likud) would only jeopardize his peace efforts. Relying on the political left, however, could have its bitter side-effects for Rabin as well. The longer the peace process remained stalled (as it had been through January 1993), the more reason for Meretz to seek to force Rabin to take even more far-reaching steps, chief among which is recognizing and negotiating with the PLO.

How fast was Rabin moving toward negotiating with Yasser Arafat's PLO?

Officially, not at all. He still insisted that he would not talk to the PLO. Rabin argued that he wanted to preserve the Madrid peace conference peacemaking format, fearful that were he to seek any change in that framework, Arab demands for other changes would arise. That Madrid format was organized in part around the notion of a two-stage solution for the Palestinian question (first autonomy, then a permanent solution). Because Arafat favoured negotiating only on a permanent solution, Rabin contended that negotiating with the PLO would require that Israel change the Madrid format. Rabin was not totally comfortable with the Madrid framework. For one thing, it seemed to run counter to the step-by-step approach where Israel would negotiate with one group of Arabs at a time. In the case of the PLO, however, the Arabs' agreement to follow the Madrid framework played into Rabin's hands. He had a good excuse for not dealing with Yasser Arafat. Begin and Shamir made no distinction between Arafat and the rest of the PLO, Rabin did. He aimed his worst barbs at Arafat, not, interestingly enough, at the PLO. Rabin appeared to imply that he could never do business with Arafat, but one day might sit down with moderate elements of the PLO. It seemed logical that if Rabin could find moderate elements in the PLO, i.e., elements who favoured a two-stage solution, not just a one-stage solution, for the sake of peacemaking Rabin might one day take this bold step. Were that to happen, it seemed likely that it would come only after autonomy had been functioning for three years.

*

Here then is Yitzhak Rabin at the threshold of a possibly brighter future for his country. Here then is Yitzhak Rabin, leading the State of Israel at a time of great opportunity and challenge. For years — indeed ever since Menachem Begin took power in 1977 — many in Israel and abroad waited for the moment when Israel would be ruled by someone like Rabin, when it would be ruled by someone who was both toughminded and diplomatically skilful. When Israel would have a leader who had the support of most of Israel's wildly emotional political spectrum. When a leader would come to power who had the ability to reach out both to the political right and to the political left, to command their respect, to represent a consensus that would enable Israel to make the compromises that were necessary for the forging of peace agreements with the Arabs. How ironic that it was Yitzhak Rabin to whom the Israeli people had given a mandate to make peace with the Arabs by negotiating the ultimate political fate of the occupied lands. How ironic that the former Chief of Staff, Yitzhak Rabin, whose army had captured the West Bank, the Gaza Strip, and the Golan Heights, had now returned to power as Prime Minister Yitzhak Rabin to settle the question of these lands once and for all.

The moment of truth for Rabin had indeed arrived. It came as the world was changing radically. Would Israel change as well? The Cold War was over, the Soviet Union no longer existed, Eastern Europe's Communist regimes had given way to new-old ethnic orientations. Once a part of that Cold War struggle, the Middle East was no longer a potential battlefield for East-West rivalries. It was no longer a focus of so much media attention. Other international problems seemed more pressing, more dangerous. That presented Yitzhak Rabin and the State of Israel with an opportunity to undertake their own shift away from the imprisonments of the past.

Was Yitzhak Rabin up to the challenge? One could always find Israelis to note that Rabin lacked the qualities of other Israeli leaders: that he was no match for the towering presence of David Ben-Gurion; not as impressive as such past Israeli icons as Golda Meir or Moshe Dayan; that he could never compete with the fiery oratory of Menachem Begin; that he would never reach the heights of eloquence of Abba Eban.

The State of Israel once had had need for towering figures, for icons, for oratory and eloquence. No more. Its needs had changed. It no longer had to charm the world with its heroes and heroines, nor rally its countrymen to acts of great bravery. Israel in the early 1990s had to figure out how to end the state of belligerency with the rest of its Arab neighbours. It had to come to grips with the fact that peace had a price, perhaps a heavy one, a price that entailed the sacrifice of land, land that had once defined and delineated Israel's security. It had to turn away from sacred cows, and do so without the frenzy and emotional bloodletting that had characterized the Israeli withdrawal from Sinai at the time of the Israel–Egypt peace treaty a decade earlier. To accomplish all that, it had to put its trust in someone whom it could respect.

Rabin fit that bill precisely. For, he had a reputation for toughmindedness that did not compete with or get in the way of his strivings for peace. If Rabin lacked the qualities that other Israeli leaders possessed, it hardly mattered. For he possessed the qualities that the country needed at this juncture. And if he turned the country away from war, if relations with the Arab world became anchored in peace agreements that endured, Rabin would have his own special place in Israeli and Jewish history.

It has not been easy, but Rabin has figured out how to exhibit this rare combination of toughness and flexibility. During the 1992 election campaign he portrayed himself as a moderate opposed to Yitzhak Shamir's extremism — and Rabin prevailed in the voting booth. He has replaced Moshe Dayan in Israeli eyes as 'Mr Security', as the person best able to defend Israel against Arab military might. That image was reinforced when, as Minister of Defense, he presided over Israel's handling of the Intifada.

All along, he took positions that were no different from those of Likud leaders, refusing to negotiate with the PLO, refusing to allow a Palestinian state to rise on the West Bank and in the Gaza Strip, refusing to return all of the Golan Heights to Syria. And yet, Rabin was able to present himself to the public as a man of compromise, as a man peace. Shamir tried, and even though he was the prime minister who took Israel to the Madrid peace conference, it was Rabin the voters favoured to take them farther down the road, into the more complicated, more difficult aspects of serious peacemaking. Rabin the peacemaker. As the 23 June election proved, he had a majority of the country behind him, urging him to take the steps necessary to make peace. By early 1993, he was beginning to mould a consensus within the country that could allow him to take those steps.

Just as the country had been united in the conviction that Israel had every right to defend itself against Arab aggression over the years, there was a new consensus growing in the wake of the Intifada: that Israel had to find a way out of the mess; that it should no longer have to send its fathers and sons to act like policemen in the West Bank; or force it mothers and daughters to worry about kidnappings and stabbings in pre-1967 Israel. The country was fed up with the violence that Arabs were perpetrating on the Jewish state.

The country put its trust in Yitzhak Rabin. It seemed something of a miracle that he was back in power, reason enough for him to do everything to achieve peace. Brought back from the political wilderness, returned to political power, given a mandate to act aggressively to reach peace, Yitzhak Rabin, the Prime Minister of Israel, was now the key Israeli figure, the focus of world attention, the basis for a variety of questions all adding up to the same thing: was he capable of leading the State of Israel to peace? As the year 1993 unfolded, it seemed clear that he was prepared to shoulder that responsibility, indeed he seemed eager to get on with the task of peacemaking.

Notes

Chapter 1

1 Rabin in conversation with author, 2 August 1976.
2 Yitzhak Rabin, *Bet Avi (My Father's House)*. Tel Aviv: Kibbutz Hameuchad, 1974, p. 57; and ABC News Documentary, 'Rabin: Action Biography', 15 April 1975.
3 Rahel Rabin in conversation with author, 14 August 1976.
4 Yitzhak Rabin, *The Rabin Memoirs* (English version), Weidenfeld and Nicolson, 1979, p. 3.
5 Yitzhak Rabin, *My Father's House*, p. 25.
6 Rahel Rabin in conversation with author, 14 August 1976.
7 Yitzhak Rabin, *The Rabin Memoirs* (English version), p. 4.
8 Yitzhak Rabin, 'I Was One of the "Sons of Yoreh"', *Ha'aretz*, 19 November 1965.
9 *Ibid.*
10 *Ibid.*
11 Rabin, *My Father's House*, p. 39.
12 *Ibid.*, p. 57.
13 *Ibid.*, p. 48.
14 Rabin in conversation with author, 2 August 1976.

Chapter 2

1 Rabin in conversation with author, 2 August, 1976.
2 Rabin, *My Father's House*, p. 58.
3 ABC News documentary, 'Rabin: Action Biography', 15 April 1975.
4 *Ibid.*
5 Rabin in conversation with author, 2 August 1976.
6 *Ibid.*
7 Leah Rabin, *All the Time His Wife (Cal Ha'zmon Ishto)*, Idanim, 1988, p. 41.
8 Leah Rabin in conversation with author, 8 August 1976.
9 Rabin in conversation with author, 2 August 1976.
10 Leah Rabin in conversation with author, 8 August 1976.
11 Rabin, *My Father's House*, p. 55.
12 Yitzhak Rabin, *The Rabin Memoirs* (English version), p. 13.

Chapter 3

1   Rabin in a speech in Tel Aviv, 1 June 1973.
2   Yigael Yadin in conversation with author, 17 June 1976.
3   Yitzhak Rabin, 'Harel in the Jerusalem Campaign'. Zarubavel Gilad and Matti Megged, eds., *Sefer Ha-Palmach*. Tel Aviv: Kibbutz Hameuchad, 1953, p. 908.
4   Uzi Narkiss in conversation with author, 21 October 1974.
5   Yigal Allon in conversation with author, 18 May 1976.
6   ABC news documentary, 15 April 1975.
7   Rabin in conversation with author, 31 August 1976.
8   Yigael Yadin in conversation with author, 17 June 1976.
9   Rabin in conversation with author, 31 August 1976.
10 *Ibid.*
11 Dan Kurzman, *Genesis 1948: The First Arab-Israeli War*. New York: Doubleday; London: Vallentine Mitchell; 1970.
12 Rabin in conversation with author, 31 August 1976.
13 Yeroham Cohen in conversation with author, 7 October 1974.
14 Kurzman, *op. cit.*
15 Yigal Allon in conversation with author, 18 May 1976.
16 Yeroham Cohen in conversation with author, 7 October 1974. Walter Eytan, the head of the Israeli delegation at Rhodes, tells the story slightly differently. When the Governor-General of the Dodecanese (of which Rhodes is the capital) invited the Israeli delegation to dinner, Rabin balked at having to wear a tie for the first time in his life. 'I've never worn one before, and I'm not going to start now,' he told Eytan. In the end he consented to borrow one from Eytan, though he complained throughout the dinner that the tie was choking him.
17 Rabin in conversation with author, 31 August 1976.
18 Yeroham Cohen, *By Light and Darkness*. Tel Aviv: Amikam Publishers, 1969, pp. 253-56. The exchange of letters between Rabin and Allon during the Rhodes negotiations is cited here.
19 Kurzman, *op cit.*, p. 756.
20 Yigal Allon in conversation with author, 18 May 1976.
21 Cohen, *op. cit.*, p. 256.

Chapter 4

1   Raphael Bashan, *Ma'ariv*, 13 June 1967. Rabin is quoted in the article.
2   Rabin in conversation with author, 31 August 1976.
3   Interview with Rabin, *Yediot Aharonot*, 1 February 1974.
4   Rabin in conversation with author, 31 August 1976.
5   The exchanges between Rabin and Ben-Gurion in 1960 and 1965 were recounted to me by Leah Rabin, who was present on both occasions.
6   The source — someone who worked intimately with both Rabin and Dayan at the time — asked not to be identified during our conversation on 28 April 1976.

7   Rabin in conversation with author, 31 August 1976.
8   *Ibid.*
9   Quoted in Edward Luttwak and Dan Horowitz, *The Israeli Army*. London: Allen Lane, 1975, p. 142.
10 Aharon Doron in conversation with author, 2 May 1976.
11 Oded Messer in conversation with author, 19 May 1976.
12 *Ibid.*
13 Leah Rabin, *All the Time His Wife*, p. 101.
14 *Ibid.*, p. 108.
15 Oded Messer in conversation with author, 19 May 1976.
16 *Ibid.*
17 Ruhama Hermon in conversation with author, 24 June 1976.
18 *Ma'ariv*, 24 January 1961.
19 Rabin's remarks during a speech at a Soldier's House in Netanya are quoted in *Ma'ariv*, 18 December 1962.
20 *Ibid.*
21 Hezzi Carmel, who travelled with Rabin in the Far East, in conversation with author, 1 June 1976.

Chapter 5

1   Quoted in Robert J. Donovan (and the staff of the *Los Angeles Times*), *Six Days in June: Israel's Fight for Survival*. New York and Toronto: New American Library, also a Signet Book, 1967, pp. 48–49.
2   Dr Benjamin Geist, *The Six-Day War*. Jerusalem: doctoral dissertation, Hebrew University, October 1974.
3   Quoted in Michael Bar-Zohar, *Embassies in Crisis*. Englewood Cliffs, New Jersey: Prentice Hall Inc., 1970, p. 29.
4. *Ibid*, pp. 27–29.
5   *Ibid*, p. 46.
6   Rabin in conversation with author, 31 August 1976.
7   Leah Rabin in conversation with author, 8 August 1976.
8   Rabin in conversation with author, 31 August 1976.
9   *Ibid.*
10 Ruhama Hermon in conversation with author, 24 June 1976.
11 The official, who worked closely with key Government figures during this period, asked not to be identified.
12 I have relied heavily on the account of the Rabin–Ben-Gurion meeting furnished by Arye Disencheck in *Ma'ariv*, 14 April 1976. Bar-Zohar, *op. cit.*, also discusses the meeting.
13 Leah Rabin, *All the Time His Wife*, p. 112.
14 Leah Rabin in conversation with author, 14 August 1976.
15 Yitzhak Rabin, *The Rabin Memoirs* (English version), p. 63.
16 Ya'acov Hefetz in conversation with author, 26 August 1976.
17 The document appeared for the first time publicly in *Ha'aretz*, 22 April 1974.
18 Ezer Weizman, *On Eagles' Wings*. Jerusalem–Tel Aviv: Steimatzky's Agency with Weidenfeld and Nicolson, 1976, p. 211.

19 For Weizman's version of the events of 23-24 May, I have relied on a conversation I held with him on 16 May 1976, as well as on the Weizman document and *On Eagles' Wings*.

20 Leah Rabin in conversation with author, 14 August 1976.

21 Yitzhak Rabin, *The Rabin Memoirs* (English version), p. 64.

22 *Ibid.*

23 Ya'acov Hefetz in conversation with author, 26 August 1976.

24 Avraham Yoffe in conversation with author, 14 June 1976.

25 *Ma'ariv*, 2 June 1972.

26 Rabin in conversation with author, 31 August 1976.

27 Quoted in Abraham Rabinovich, *The Battle of Jerusalem*. Philadelphia: Jewish Publication Society of America, 1972, pp. 66-67.

28 Quoted in Randolph S. and Winston S. Churchill, *The Six-Day War*. London: Heinemann, 1967, pp. 104-05.

29 Quoted in the *Jerusalem Post*, 9 October 1967, from a speech by Rabin in Tel Aviv on 21 September 1967.

30 Quoted in Moshe Ben Shaul, ed., *Generals of Israel*. Tel Aviv: Hadar Publishing House Ltd., 1968, p. 24.

31 Interview with Rabin, *Ma'ariv*, 4 October 1967.

32 Quoted in *Ma'ariv*, 9 June 1967.

33 ABC News documentary, 15 April 1975.

34 *Ibid.*

35 Quoted in Shabtai Teveth, *Moshe Dayan*. Jerusalem: Steimatzky's Agency with Weidenfeld & Nicolson, 1972, p. 340.

36 Rabin in conversation with author, 31 August 1976.

37 *Ibid.*

38 Leah Rabin, *All the Time His Wife*, p. 117.

39 Quoted in *Yediot Aharonot*, 14 November 1976.

Chapter 6

1   Interview with Rabin, *Ma'ariv*, 5 June 1968.

2   Rabin in conversation with author, 7 October 1976.

3   Associated Press story in the *Jerusalem Post*, 21 February 1968.

4   Letter dated 22 February 1968.

5   Interview with Rabin, *Ma'ariv*, 13 April 1973.

6   Rabin in conversation with author, 7 October 1976.

7   *Ibid.*

8   *Ibid.*

9   *Ibid.*

10 Senator Henry Jackson in conversation with author, 15 September 1976.

11 Maurice Amitai in conversation with author, 15 September 1976.

12 Rabin in conversation with author, 7 October 1976.

13 Norman Bernstein in conversation with author, 17 September 1976.

14 Rabin in conversation with author, 18 November 1976.

15 Interview with Rabin, *Ma'ariv*, 13 April 1973.

16 Dan Pattir in conversation with author, 24 August 1976.

17 Joseph Sisco in conversation with author, 9 September 1976.
18 *Ibid.*
19 Kissinger's attitude towards Rabin was described in several off-the-record conversations I had with Rabin's aides from his days as ambassador.
20 Rabin in conversation with author, 7 October 1976.
21 *Ibid.*
22 Rabin in conversation with author, 7 October 1976.
23 Marvin Kalb in conversation with author, 15 September 1976.
24 Interview with Rabin, *Ma'ariv*, 13 April 1973.
25 Senator Henry Jackson in conversation with author, 15 September 1976.
26 Senator Stuart Symington in conversation with author, 8 September 1976.
27 A report of Rabin's meeting with Shultz, recounted by Rabin in a Tel Aviv speech, appeared in the *Jersualem Post* on 5 April 1973.
28 Rowland Evans in conversation with author, 15 September 1976.
29 The official asked not to be identified.
30 ABC documentary.
31 Rabin in conversation with author, 18 November 1976.
32 'A Very Unusual Ambassador', *Jerusalem Post*, 16 March 1973.

Chapter 7

1 Arye Avneri, *Sapir*. Tel Aviv: Peleg Publishers, 1976, pp. 316–18.
2 Rabin in conversation with author, 7 October 1976.
3 Interview with Rabin, *Ma'ariv*, 10 August 1973.
4 Dov Tzamir in conversation with author, 20 June 1976.
5 From a speech to the Haifa Rotary Club, quoted in *Ma'ariv*, 18 September 1973.
6 Interview with Rabin, Israel Radio, 25 August 1973.
7 The source asked not to be identified.
8 Rabin in conversation with author, 18 November 1976.
9 The relationship between Rabin and the men of the senior command at military headquarters was recounted to me during several off-the-record conversations with men who were present at headquarters while Rabin was there.
10 Ya'acov Halfon in conversation with author, 30 June 1976.
11 Interview with Rabin, *Al Hamishmar*, 16 November 1973.
12 Yitzhak Rabin, *The Rabin Memoirs* (English version), p. 188.
13 Interview with Rabin, *Yediot Aharonot*, 19 April 1974.
14 Avneri, *op. cit.*, pp. 316–18.
15 One of Rabin's campaign aides related the Rabin–Gilon conversation to me during an off-the-record conversation.
16 Rabin in conversation with author, 18 November 1976.
17 *Davar*, 23 April 1974.
18 *Hamodia*, 23 April 1974.
19 Yitzhak Rabin, *The Rabin Memoirs* (English version), p. 189.
20 *Ibid.*

Chapter 8

1 Rabin in conversation with author, 18 November 1976.
2 *Ibid.*
3 Interview with Rabin, *Yediot Aharonot*, 26 July 1974.
4 *Ibid.*
5 Rabin in conversation with author, 18 November 1976.
6 Quoted in the *New York Times*, 10 July 1975.
7 The source asked not to be identified.
8 Interview with Rabin, Israel Television, 22 August 1975.
9 Rabin in conversation with author, 18 November 1976.
10 Dan Pattir in conversation with author, 24 August 1976.
11 Rabin in a speech to the Jewish Agency Assembly, 15 July 1976.
12 Interview with Rabin, 'Face the Nation', American Television programme, 11 July 1976.
13 Yitzhak Rabin, *The Rabin Memoirs* (English version), p. 226.
14 Rabin in conversation with author, 18 November 1976.
15 *Ibid.*

Chapter 9

1 Details of the Rabin–Peres proposed pact were recounted to me by a source who asked not to be identified.
2 Dr Yitzhak Rafael, the then minister for religious affairs, in conversation with author, 21 December 1976.
3 Quoted in the *Jerusalem Post*. Rabin was speaking to a meeting of the Labour Party's Leadership Bureau.
4 Ezer Weizman in conversation with author, 24 December 1976.
5 *Ha'aretz*, 26 December 1976.
6 Yitzhak Rabin, *The Rabin Memoirs* (English version), p. 241.
7 *Ibid.*
8 *Ibid.*
9 Interview with Rabin in *Davar*, 22 February 1977.
10 Quoted in the *International Herald Tribune*, 5 February 1977.
11 *International Herald Tribune*, 13 March 1977.
12 Leah Rabin, *All the Time His Wife*, p. 212.
13 Dov Tzamir in conversation with author, 10 April 1977.
14 Interview with Leah Rabin, *Ma'ariv*, 10 April 1977.
15 Leah Rabin, *All the Time His Wife*, p. 213.
16 Yitzhak Rabin, *The Rabin Memoirs* (English version), p. 244.
17 The *Jerusalem Post*, 16 March 1977 quotes Mrs Rabin as telling a reporter that there had been some $2,000 in the account.
18 The source asked not be identified.
19 Yehuda Avner in conversation with author, 13 April 1977.
20 Quoted in *Yediot Aharonot*, 10 April 1977.
21 Yitzhak Rabin, *op. cit.*, p. 244.
22 Leah Rabin, *op. cit.*, p. 213.

23 Yitzhak Rabin, *op. cit.*, pp. 244-45.
24 At Labour Party Central Committee meeting, Tel Aviv.
25 Interview with Leah Rabin in *Ma'ariv*, 10 April 1977.
26 Interview with Leah Rabin in *Yediot Aharonot*, 10 April 1977.
27 *Ibid.*
28 Leah Rabin, *All the Time His Wife*, p. 185.
29 *Ibid.*, p. 214.
30 *Ibid.*, p. 216.

Chapter 10

1 Leah Rabin, interview with author, 28 July 1992.
2 Nachman Shai, interview with author, 12 August 1992.
3 Yitzhak Rabin, *The Rabin Memoirs* (English version), p. 252.
4 *Ibid.*, pp. 253-54.
5 *Ibid.*, p. 215.
6 'Rabin: Promise of Peace', *Jerusalem Post*, 28 September 1978.
7 Ron Ben-Yishai, interview with author, 19 July 1992.
8 Dan Pattir, interview with author, 25 July 1992.
9 Yitzhak Rabin, *The Rabin Memoirs* (Hebrew; *Pinhas Sherut*). Tel Aviv: Ma'ariv Books, pp. 534-35.
10 'Peres Subverted Government for His Own Aims', *Jerusalem Post*, 9 August 1979.
11 Matti Golan, *The Road to Peace: A Biography of Shimon Peres*. New York: Warner Books, 1989, p. 193.
12 'Labour to Discuss Rabin's Attack on Peres Today', *Jerusalem Post*, 12 August 1979.
13 *Ibid.*
14 'Labour Veteran Decries Party Feud', *Jerusalem Post*, 10 August 1979.
15 'Allon Counters Rabin on "Expulsion" of Arabs in 1948', *Jerusalem Post*, 26 October 1979.
16 'The Credibility Stakes', *Jerusalem Post*, 17 October 1980.
17 Matti Golan, *The Road to Peace*, pp. 207-208.
18 *Ibid.*, pp. 222-23.

Chapter 11

1 Leah Rabin, *All the Time His Wife*, p. 240.
2 Wolf Blitzer, *Territory of Lies*. New York: Harper & Row Publishers, 1989, p. 199.
3 Ephraim Sneh, interview with author, 11 August 1992.
4 *Intifada*, Ze'v Shiff, Ehud Ya'ari. New York: Simon & Schuster, 1989, p. 23.
5 *Ibid.*, p. 24.
6 Leah Rabin, interview with author, 29 July 1992.
7 'Sharp Condemnation of Rabin Policy from American Jewish Leaders', *Jerusalem Post*, 25 January 1988.

8   Ephraim Sneh, interview with author, 11 August 1992.
9   'Rabin: More Injuries Is Precisely Our Aim,' *Jerusalem Post*, 28 September 1988.
10 'Rabin Would Talk to PLO,' *Jerusalem Post*, 27 April 1988.
11 Ephraim Sneh, interview with author, 11 August 1992.
12 *Ibid.*
13 Elias Friej, interview with author, 29 July 1992.
14 Yitzhak Rabin, interview with author, 4 October 1989.

Chapter 12

1   Rabin's comments were related to the author by Dan Pattir, interview with author, 25 July 1992.
2   'We Must Invariably Negotiate from Strength', *Jerusalem Post*, 12 May 1990.
3   Interview with Yitzhak Rabin, *Jerusalem Report*, 3 January 1991, p. 15.
4   'Was Israel Looking the Wrong Way?' *Jerusalem Report*, 28 February 1991, pp. 16–17.
5   'Leave Syria to the End', interview with Yitzhak Rabin, *Jerusalem Report*, 4 July 1991, p. 17.
6   *Ibid.*

Chapter 13

1   Benyamin Ben-Eliezer, interview with author, 9 August 1992.
2   Leah Rabin, interview with author, 28 July 1992.
3   Ephraim Sneh, interview with author, 11 August 1992.
4   *Ibid.*
5   'The Hunt for Clues to Israel's Future Starts at the Mall', *Washington Post*, 9 June 1992.
6   Benyamin Ben-Eliezer, interview with author, 9 August 1992.
7   Interview with Yitzhak Rabin, *Jerusalem Post*, 3–5 March 1992.
8   Interview with Yitzhak Rabin, *Jerusalem Post*, 25–26 April 1992.
9   'Pragmatism and Compromise', *Jerusalem Post*, 1 June 1992.
10 'Rabin Invokes Old Victory to Seek a New One in Israeli Election Campaign,' *New York Times*, 21 May 1992.
11 Benyamin Ben-Eliezer, interview with author, 9 August 1992.
12 *Ibid.*
13 Gad Ben-Ari, interview with author, 24 July 1992.
14 'They Call Me an Alcoholic and This Only Strengthens Me,' *Yediot Aharonot*, 25 May 1992.
15 Gad Ben-Ari, interview with author, 24 July 1992.
16 'They Call Me an Alcoholic and This Only Strengthens Me,' *Yediot Aharonot*, 25 May 1992.
17 Gad Ben-Ari, interview with author, 24 July 1992.
18 Benyamin Ben-Eliezer, interview with author, 9 August 1992.
19 'They Call me an Alcoholic and This Only Strengthens Me,' *Yediot Aharonot*, 25 May 1992.

20   Gad Ben-Ari, interview with author, 24 July 1992.
21   Leah Rabin, interview with author, 28 July 1992.
22   *Ibid.*
23   'Israel's Vote Shows It's Tired of Ideology,' *New York Times*, 28 June 1992.

Chapter 14

1   'A New Life,' *New York Times*, Anthony Lewis, 28 June 1992.
2   'Enter the New, Street-wise Rabin.' *Jerusalem Post*, 17 July 1992.
3   'With Rabin, Talks Can Get Moving,' *International Herald Tribune*, Los
     Angeles Times Syndicate, Henry Kissinger, 3 August 1992.
4   'Rabin Having Unexpected Trouble Changing Priorities,' *Jerusalem Post*,
     28 July 1992.
5   'PM: We don't need every inch of Golan', *Jerusalem Post*, 26 August 1992.
6   'Rabin not convinced Syria ready for peace with Israel', *Jerusalem Post*, 31
     August 1992.
7   The poll was published in *Yediot Aharonot*, 18 September 1992.
8   'Rabin: It is Safer in the Golan than in Tel Aviv and Bat Yam', *Yediot
     Aharonot*, 4 September 1992.
9   'Rabin Government's Top Priority is Dealing With Unemployment,'
     Jerusalem Post, 3 September 1992.
10   'Rabin: It is Safer in the Golan than in Tel Aviv and Bat Yam', *Yediot
     Aharonot*, 4 September 1992.
11   'Hail to the Chief', *Jerusalem Report*, 19 November 1992.
12   'Only Army Would Leave Golan — Rabin', *Jerusalem Post*, 31 December
     1992.
13   'Deportation Most Audacious Move vs Terrorism', *Jerusalem Post*, 23
     December 1992.
14   'Poll: Most Labour MKS Back Talks with PLO – Party in "Confusion"',
     Jerusalem Post, 20 December 1992.

Index